# Managing Wetlands

One of our colleagues and a contributor to this volume, Dr. Ian Langford, died suddenly in 2002. His loss will be sorely felt by all of us, his friends and colleagues. Ian was a constant source of academic support and inspiration for all of his co-workers in CSERGE and wider afield. We dedicate this book to his memory.

*Kerry Turner, Jeroen van den Bergh and Roy Brouwer*

# Managing Wetlands

## An Ecological Economics Approach

*Edited by*

## R. Kerry Turner

*Director, Centre for Social and Economic Research on the Global Environment (CSERGE) and Professor of Environmental Sciences, School of Environmental Sciences, University of East Anglia, UK*

## Jeroen C.J.M. van den Bergh

*Professor of Environmental Economics, Department of Spatial Economics and Professor of Water, Nature and Space, Institute for Environmental Studies, Free University, Amsterdam, The Netherlands*

## Roy Brouwer

*Environmental Economist, RIZA, National Water Policy Division, The Netherlands and Associate Research Fellow, Centre for Social and Economic Research on the Global Environment (CSERGE), University of East Anglia, UK*

**Edward Elgar**
Cheltenham, UK • Northampton, MA, USA

Published by
Edward Elgar Publishing Limited
Glensanda House
Montpellier Parade
Cheltenham
Glos GL50 1UA
UK

Edward Elgar Publishing, Inc.
136 West Street
Suite 202
Northampton
Massachusetts 01060
USA

A catalogue record for this book
is available from the British Library

**Library of Congress Cataloguing in Publication Data**

Managing wetlands : an ecological economics approach / edited by R. Kerry Turner,
    Jeroen C.J.M. van den Bergh, Roy Brouwer.
        p. cm.
    1. Wetland management—Economic aspects. I. Turner, R. Kerry. II. Bergh, Jeroen
    C.J.M. van den, 1965– III. Brouwer, Roy.

    QH75.M356 2003
    333.91'8—dc 21

2003044892

ISBN 1 84376 130 0 (cased)

Typeset by Cambrian Typesetters, Frimley, Surrey
Printed and bound in Great Britain by MPG Books Ltd, Bodmin, Cornwall

# Contents

# Figures

# Tables and boxes

# Box

# Contributors

**Aat Barendregt** is Senior Research Fellow and Lecturer at the Department of Environmental Sciences, Utrecht University, The Netherlands.

**Ian Bateman** is Professor of Environmental Economics in the School of Environmental Sciences, University of East Anglia, UK and a Senior Research Fellow at CSERGE.

**Jeroen van den Bergh** is Professor of Environmental Economics at the Department of Spatial Economics, Free University, Amsterdam, and Professor of Water, Nature and Space at the Institute for Environmental Studies, Free University, Amsterdam, The Netherlands.

**Martin Blackwell** is Senior Research Fellow at the Royal Holloway Institute for Environmental Research, University of London, UK.

**Roy Brouwer** works as Environmental Economist at the National Water Policy Division of the National Institute for Integrated Freshwater Management and Waste Water Treatment (RIZA) in The Netherlands; and is Associate Research Fellow at CSERGE, University of East Anglia, UK.

**Steve Crooks** is joint Research Fellow at the Department of Marine Science and Coastal Management, University of Newcastle and the Jackson Environment Institute, University of East Anglia, UK.

**Tom Crowards** is Associate Research Fellow at CSERGE, University of East Anglia, UK.

**Stavros Georgiou** is Senior Research Fellow at CSERGE, University of East Anglia, UK.

**Alison Gilbert** is Senior Research Fellow at the Institute of Environmental Studies, Free University, Amsterdam, The Netherlands.

**Michael Green** is Director of Research and Strategy, Broads Authority, Norwich, UK.

**Marjan van Herwijnen** is Senior Research Fellow at the Institute of Environmental Studies, Free University, Amsterdam, The Netherlands.

**Peter van Horssen** is Senior Research Fellow at the Department of Environmental Sciences, Utrecht University, The Netherlands.

**Patricia Kandelaars** is presently working as a consultant for KPMG, The Netherlands.

**Areti Kontogianni** is Senior Research Fellow and Lecturer at the Department of Environmental Studies, University of the Aegean, Greece; and Associate Research Fellow at CSERGE, University of East Anglia.

**Ian Langford** was Senior Research Fellow at CSERGE, University of East Anglia, UK.

**Therese Lindahl** is a Ph.D. student at the Department of Economics, Stockholm School of Economics, Sweden.

**Caroline Lorenz** is presently working as a consultant for Witteveen en Bos, The Netherlands.

**Ed Maltby** is Director of the Royal Holloway Institute for Environmental Research, University of London, UK.

**Neil Powe** is Lecturer in the School of Architecture, Planning and Landscape, University of Newcastle, UK.

**Michalis Skourtos** is Professor of Environmental Economics at the Department of Environmental Studies, University of the Aegean, Greece; and Associate Professorial Fellow at CSERGE, University of East Anglia, UK.

**Tore Söderqvist** is a Research Associate at the Beijer International Institute of Ecological Economics, Royal Swedish Academy of Sciences, Stockholm, Sweden.

**Andreas Troumbis** is with the Environmental Studies Department, University of the Aegean, Greece.

**Kerry Turner** is Professor of Environmental Economics at the School of Environmental Sciences, University of East Anglia, UK and Director of CSERGE and the Zuckerman Institute.

**Heather Voisey** is presently working as an urban development consultant for a local government in Aberdeen.

# Acknowledgements

This volume describes work originally carried out in the research project, Ecological Economic Analysis of Wetlands: Functions, Values and Dynamics (ECOWET). Funding from the EU/DG XII Environment and Climate Programme (Contract No. ENV4-CT96-0273), the Swedish Council for Planning and Co-ordination of Research (FRN) and the Broads Authority, UK is gratefully acknowledged.

We are indebted to Merryl Turner and Ann Dixon for their patient and expert proof reading and word processing respectively.

# 1.  Introduction

## R.K. Turner, J.C.J.M. van den Bergh and R. Brouwer

## 1  WETLAND DEFINITIONS

Wetlands provide many important services to human society, but are at the same time ecologically sensitive and adaptive systems. This explains why in recent years much attention has been directed towards the formulation and operation of sustainable management strategies for wetlands. Both natural and social sciences can contribute to an increased understanding of relevant processes and problems associated with such strategies. This volume examines the potential for systematic and formalized interdisciplinary rese
arch on wetlands. Such potential lies in the integration of insights, methods and data drawn from natural and social sciences, as highlighted in previous integrated modelling and assessment surveys (Bingham *et al.*, 1995).

There is some disagreement among scientists on what constitutes a wetland, partly because of their highly dynamic character, and partly because of difficulties in defining their boundaries with any precision (Mitsch and Gosselink, 1993). For example, Dugan (1990) notes that there are more than 50 definitions in current use. Likewise, there is no universally agreed classification of wetland types. Classifications vary greatly in both form and nomenclature between regions; see Cowardin *et al.*, (1979) for one influential classification system. Some features of wetlands, nonetheless, are clear. It is the predominance of water for some significant period of time and the qualitative and quantitative influence of the hydrological regime that characterizes and underlies the development of wetlands. The Ramsar Convention definition, widely accepted by governments and NGOs world-wide, is as follows: 'areas of marsh, fen peatland or water, whether natural or artificial, permanent or temporary, with water that is static or flowing, fresh, brackish or salt including areas of marine water, the depth of which at low tide does not exceed 6m'.

While lacking scientific exactness, this definition conveys much of the essential character of wetlands, as well as implying the complexity involved. What it does not provide, however, is any guidance on the generic characteristics of wetlands that influence how wetlands actually function. Any integrated wetland research approach has somehow to make compatible the very different perceptions of what exactly a wetland system is, as seen from a range of disciplinary viewpoints (Maltby *et al.*, 1994, 1996b). In this volume the main characteristics of wetland processes and systems are reviewed in a cross-disciplinary way.

## 2   WETLAND LOSSES

Globally wetlands have been lost or are under threat, despite the existence of various international agreements (such as the Ramsar Convention which lists over 1000 sites of international importance covering almost 800 000 km$^2$) and national conservation policies. This situation has been caused by: (1) the public nature of many wetlands products and services; (2) user externalities imposed on other stakeholders; and (3) policy intervention failures that are due to a lack of consistency among policies being enacted across different sectors of the economy. All three causes are related to information failures, which in turn can be linked to the complexity and 'invisibility' of spatial relationships between ground and surface waters and wetland vegetation (Turner *et al.*, 2000).

Integrated wetland research combining natural and social sciences can play a significant part in a strategy to reduce information failure and increase consistency and co-ordination across various government policies relevant to wetlands. An integrated wetland research framework suggests that a 'mixed' methodology based on a combination of integrated modelling, stakeholder analysis, economic valuation and multi-criteria evaluation can provide complementary insights into sustainable and welfare-optimizing wetland management and policy. Just such an approach is presented in this volume, with Part I covering methodological issues and Part II a series of applications across a spectrum of spatial scales.

According to the European Environment Agency, wetlands continue to be under particular pressure because of the extensive drainage of lowland areas for agriculture, forestry, peat exploitation and urban development, together with the impacts of river system regulation for power generation, water storage and flood control and the maintenance of navigation channels (European Environment Agency, 1999). The key to a better understanding of the wetland problem and its mitigation through more sustainable management lies in the recognition of the importance of the landscape ecology scale. A better scientific understanding of wetland structure and processes together with socio-economic and cultural values and significance is predicated on an appreciation of at least catchment-wide systems. Thus wetlands have been and are being degraded or destroyed by eutrophication and acidification, the causes of which lie 'off-site' and even beyond drainage basin boundaries. These pressures can be exacerbated by more local pressures such as over-consumption of surface and groundwater resources, or by the more ubiquitous effects of climate change, including sea level rise.

A more holistic approach to catchments and floodplain management requires administrative structures and appropriately refined scientific support that match the spatial and temporal scale of catchment and floodplain processes. These requirements are currently lacking in most European countries (Crooks *et al.*, 2001). In the past, management of such systems has been sectoral, dominated by land-use pressures, local flood perception and management and to a lesser extent by environmental concerns. All too often the scale of flood interventions has been constrained by political and institutional considerations and has devolved down to the lowest common denominator, for example, local pressures focused upon short lengths of a river. The proprietorial interests shown by local people in 'their' section of the floodplain is an extremely powerful force and one which democratic systems find difficult to accommodate. Yet natural floodplain systems are driven by processes that transcend the local 'space' and the short run timescale.

The precise configuration of wetland pressures and consequent damage varies across Europe. Generalizing, industrial development combined with agricultural intensification in North-western Europe has historically been responsible for the majority of wetland loss (around a 60 per cent loss of total wetland area). In Southern Europe, the long term occupation and exploitation of wetland goods and services has served to build up stress in these systems, lowering their resilience. This capacity to cope with stress and shock has been further diminished by low winter rainfall during the last decade. In Central and Eastern Europe and parts of Scandinavia, the less extensive spread of industrial, urban and high intensity agricultural activities has served to protect relatively large reserves of natural and semi-natural wetlands. Future development plans in these regions pose a potential threat to these remaining wild wetlands (European Environment Agency, 1999).

The contemporary plight of Europe's wetlands is a classic example of what has become known as a 'scaling mismatch problem' (Boesch, 1999). This is that the juxtaposition of different spatial, ecosystem functioning and temporal scales is often inherent in any given environmental management problem. The scaling mismatch poses difficult challenges for both science and resource management/governance. In Spain, for example, over the last 30 years or so, 'the la Mancha Occidental aquifer' (encompassing some 5500 km$^2$) has been heavily utilized to service irrigated agricultural regimes. This private extraction process has led to the establishment of more than 100 000 ha of new irrigated farmland, but is not in itself sustainable. The rate of abstraction often achieved (> 600 Mm$^3$/year) was more than the recharge rate in a typical year

(200–500 Mm$^3$/year). The falling water levels in the aquifer damaged the ecological integrity of some important wetlands, including those in the National Park 'Las Tablas de Daimiel'. The policy response was a controlled abstraction programme with compensatory payments to local farmers, but also a consequent negative economic multiplier effect in the regional economy.

But why should society be concerned about wetland loss? The simple answer is that wetland ecosystems are a component of our natural capital and wealth creation potential (Costanza *et al.*, 1997). The many functions that wetlands provide – flood control, groundwater replenishment, coastal protection, sediment and nutrient retention, climate change mitigation, water purification, biodiversity storehouses, products such as fish, reeds etc., recreation and tourism and cultural and historical/symbolic services – are of significant economic and social value. While this is undoubtedly the case, aggregate (global scale) estimates of ecosystems' value are problematic. Such macroeconomic extrapolations are inconsistent with microeconomic theory and many policy decisions are made at the margin and so are more appropriately informed by marginal rather than total valuations (Balmford *et al.*, 2002).

Economic valuation research can help in this context. Such research will provide findings that can help inform societal decision mechanisms trying to cope with the allocation of scarce resources (for example to conserve remaining wetlands more effectively) among competing demands (new schools, hospitals infrastructure and so on). Economic valuation is based on preference-related approaches (consumer and/or citizen preferences) and is compatible with a common monetary metric deployed across competing uses. The fundamental aim is not to put a '$ price tag' on the environment, but to express the effect of a marginal change in ecosystem services provision in terms of a rate of trade-off against other things people value (van den Bergh, 1999). Economic, monetary valuation therefore is not applicable to ecosystems as a whole, but rather to relatively small changes in their structure and functions. They can be represented by realistic change scenarios that are readily and generally understandable. While we believe that there is a strong case in favour of environmental economic valuation as a decision aid, we also recognize that there are limits to its meaningful use (Turner, 2000).

Nevertheless, studies valuing multiple ecosystem functions and uses and studies that seek to capture the 'before and after' states as environmental changes (for example wetland degradation or conversion) take place, are relatively rare. More research of this type would aid rational decision-taking in wetland conservation versus development situations involving different stakeholders (local, national and global). The marginal valuation data that does exist suggests that net ecosystem service value diminishes with biodiversity and ecosystem loss (Balmford *et al.*, 2002; Turner *et al.*, 2002). New institutional processes and arrangements are also required in order to best realize benefits from multiple ecosystem use and non-use provision, across different (often competing) stakeholders.

Now is the time in Europe for the further strengthening of integrated water and wetlands policy, bringing together land-use planning, flood management and environmental pollution control and nature conservation. This policy should include the strengthening of planning controls to prevent unnecessary/inappropriate development on floodplains, creation of financial schemes to encourage reactivation of floodplains and component wetlands and management based on long-term rather than short-term perspectives. Positive action is required to remove public uncertainty and increase awareness of floodplain functioning. Mechanisms such as direct purchase of suitable land, mitigation banking and agri-environmental schemes designed to deliver multiple (including environmental) benefits to society, will serve to increase floodplain functionality and reduce social vulnerability. The implementation of a more holistic water management approach will of course be conditioned by prevailing and prospective economic, social and political networks and contexts, together with the regulatory system and underlying culture. The new EC Water Framework Directive provides a more or less positive regulatory context for greater holism, while at the same time allowing adaptation (subsidiarity principle) to be tailored to national/regional conditions and cultures (Crooks *et al.*, 2001). Both the methodological and institutional issues surrounding the formulation and implementation of a more integrated water and wetlands policy in Europe are covered in this volume.

## 3   A FRAMEWORK FOR ECOLOGICAL–ECONOMIC ANALYSIS AND EVALUATION OF WETLANDS

The origins of the analysis presented in succeeding chapters lie in a research project funded by the European Commission (contract no. ENV4-CT96-0273) called ECOWET (Ecological–Economic Analysis of Wetlands: Functions, Values and Dynamics). This interdisciplinary project brought together teams of social and natural scientists from the UK, Netherlands, Sweden and Greece. The basic aims of the project were to provide an integrated methodology for wetland and water management policy, and to test the various elements of the overall methodology in national case studies (Turner, van den Bergh *et al.*, 1999).

In order to scope the many issues, problems and arguments surrounding the scientific analysis, valuation and management of temperate wetlands in Europe, a simplified organizational and auditing framework was adopted which was an augmented version of a schema originally formulated by the OECD. This is the Driving forces–Pressures–State–Impact–Response

(DPSIR) approach, which although simple, is flexible enough to be conceptually valid across a range of spatial scales. It also serves to highlight the dynamic characteristics of ecosystem and socio-economic system changes, involving multiple feedbacks within a possible co-evolutionary process – see Figure 1.1.

Wetlands have traditionally been regarded by societies as having very little, or even negative, value, often being described as wastelands or sources of disease. As a result, wetlands have been actively drained and converted to other uses, while the essentially 'open' nature of wetland systems has made them susceptible to indirect damage from other human activities. This has led to the stock of wetlands, particularly in Europe, being substantially diminished.

Environmental pressure builds up via socio-economic driving forces – demographic, economic, institutional and technological – which cause changes in environmental systems 'states'. These changes include increased nutrient fluxes, wetland habitat loss due to conversion, fragmentation and quality degradation; pollution of soil and water; and climate alteration. The processing and functioning capabilities of wetlands will be affected and this results in impacts on human welfare via productivity, health, amenity and other value changes. The impacts impose social welfare gains and losses across a spectrum of different stakeholders, depending on the spatial, socio-economic, political and cultural setting. Policy response mechanisms will then be triggered within this continuous feedback process.

It is now apparent that wetlands, far from being valueless, perform a wide array of functions that can be of considerable value of society. The physical assessment of the functions performed by a wetland is an essential prerequisite to any evaluation of a wetland's worth to society, but simply identifying these functions is insufficient. Where a wetland is under pressure from human activity that provides measurable economic benefits to society, it will be necessary to illustrate the economic value of the functions performed by the wetland. The provision of such economic information is essential if an efficient level of wetland resource conservation, restoration or re-creation is to be determined.

Maintaining a wetland will almost always involve costs. There will be costs associated with forgoing other uses of the land or with limiting activities that might impinge upon the ability of the wetland to continue functioning. Hence the importance of making explicit the value of the multiple functions that wetlands perform to society, and of assessing this value within a framework which allows comparison with the gains to be made from activities that might threaten wetlands. This should serve not only to better protect these threatened ecosystems but also to improve decision making for the benefit of society. A framework for the ecological–economic analysis and evaluation of the functions and values of wetlands is presented in Figure 1.2.

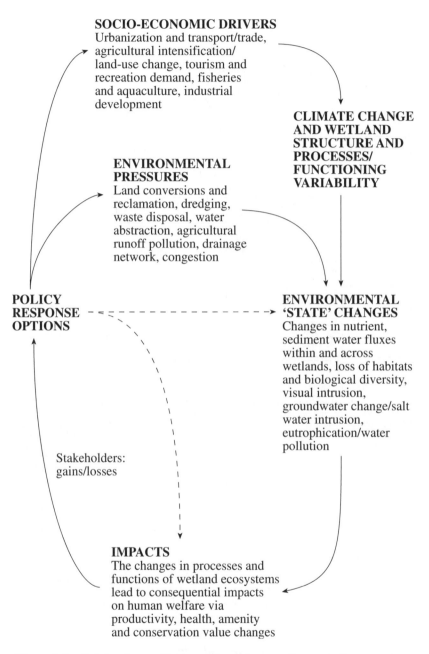

**SOCIO-ECONOMIC DRIVERS**
Urbanization and transport/trade,
agricultural intensification/
land-use change, tourism and
recreation demand, fisheries
and aquaculture, industrial
development

**CLIMATE CHANGE
AND WETLAND
STRUCTURE AND
PROCESSES/
FUNCTIONING
VARIABILITY**

**ENVIRONMENTAL
PRESSURES**
Land conversions and
reclamation, dredging,
waste disposal, water
abstraction, agricultural
runoff pollution, drainage
network, congestion

**POLICY
RESPONSE
OPTIONS**

**ENVIRONMENTAL
'STATE' CHANGES**
Changes in nutrient,
sediment water fluxes
within and across
wetlands, loss of habitats
and biological diversity,
visual intrusion,
groundwater change/salt
water intrusion,
eutrophication/water
pollution

Stakeholders:
gains/losses

**IMPACTS**
The changes in processes and
functions of wetland ecosystems
lead to consequential impacts
on human welfare via
productivity, health, amenity
and conservation value changes

*Figure 1.1    Driving forces–Pressure–State–Impact–Response framework
applied to wetlands*

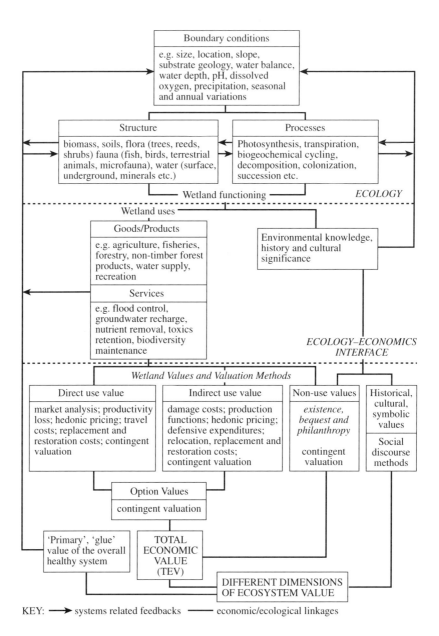

*Figure 1.2    Wetland functions, uses and values*

At the core of the interdisciplinary analytical framework is a conceptual model, based on the concept of functional diversity, which links ecosystem processes and functions with outputs of goods and services, and which can then be assigned monetary economic and/or other values (see Figure 1.2). Functional diversity can be defined as the variety of different responses to environmental change, in particular the variety of spatial and temporal scales with which organisms react to each other and to the environment (Steele, 1991). This diversity concept encourages analysts to take a wider perspective and to examine change in large-scale ecological processes, together with the relevant socio-economic driving forces causing wetland loss. The focus is then on the ability of interdependent ecological–economic systems to maintain functionality under a range of stress and shock conditions. Another important facet of this approach is the derivation of scientifically valid and practical indicators of environmental change and sustainability. This approach also requires the coupling of economic, hydrological and ecological models (see Chapters 2 to 6 in this volume).

Wetland *characteristics* are those properties that describe a wetland area in the simplest and most objective possible terms. They are a combination of generic and site-specific features. A general list would include the biological, chemical and physical features that describe a wetland, such as species present, substrate properties, hydrology, size and shape. Adamus and Stockwell (1983) give 75 wetland characteristics (Table 1.1). However, in principle this list is endless and site-specific.

Wetland *structure* may be defined as the biotic and abiotic webs of which characteristics are elements, such as vegetation type and soil type. By contrast, wetland *processes* refer to the dynamics of transformation of matter or energy. The interactions among wetland hydrology and geomorphology, saturated soil and vegetation more or less determine the general characteristics and the significance of the processes that occur in any given wetland. These processes also enable the development and maintenance of the wetland structure which in turn is key to the continuing provision of goods and services. These ecological concepts constitute the upper part of Figure 1.2.

Ecosystem *functions* are the result of interactions among characteristics, structure and processes. They include such actions as floodwater control, nutrient retention and food web support. The concept of ecosystem functions and ecosystem functioning is essential in linking ecology and economy (that is, the step between *wetland functioning* and *wetland values* which is labelled 'wetland uses' in Figure 1.2). Although multiple definitions of (environmental) functions exist in the literature, they have in common that they all reflect an anthropocentric perspective on ecosystem functioning, where ecosystem characteristics, structure and processes contribute to human welfare and well-being.

*Table 1.1    Examples of wetland characteristics*

- Size
- Shape
- Species present
- Abundance of species
- Vegetation structure
- Extent of vegetation
- Patterns of vegetation distribution
- Soils
- Geology
- Geomorphology
- Processes (biological, chemical and physical)
- Nature and location of water entry and water exit
- Climate
- Location in respect of human settlement and activities
- Location in respect of other elements in the environment
- Water flow/turnover rates
- Water depth
- Water quality
- Altitude
- Slope
- Fertility
- Nutrient cycles
- Biomass production/export
- Habitat type
- Area of habitat
- Drainage pattern
- Area of open water
- Recent evidence of human usage
- Historic or prehistoric evidence of human usage
- pH
- Dissolved oxygen
- Suspended solids
- Evaporation/precipitation balance
- Tidal range/regime
- Characteristics of the catchment

*Source*:    Claridge (1991).

*Table 1.2    Classification of wetland benefits (goods and services)*

| Services | Goods |
|---|---|
| • Flood control | • forest resources |
| • prevention saline intrusion | • agriculture resources |
| • storm protection/windbreak | • wildlife resources |
| • sediment removal | • forage resources |
| • toxicant removal | • fisheries |
| • nutrient removal | • mineral resources |
| • groundwater recharge | • water transport |
| • groundwater discharge | • water supply |
| • erosion control | • recreation/tourism |
| • wildlife habitat | • aquaculture |
| • fish habitat | • research site |
| • toxicant export | • education site |
| • shoreline stabilization | • fertilizer production |
| • micro-climate stabilization | • energy production |
| • macro-climate stabilization | |
| • biological diversity provision | |
| • cultural value provision | |
| • historic value provision | |
| • aesthetic value provision | |
| • wilderness value provision | |

Wetland ecosystem functions provide goods and services to society that are deemed valuable. These goods and services are the benefits derived from wetlands and they can be valued through various qualitative and quantitative valuation methods and techniques. An assessment of the complete range of benefits at a wetland site using a standard classification of benefits, as listed in Table 1.2, is an essential step before the overall value of the wetland can be derived. Table 1.2 also makes it clear that there are strong linkages between the various types of benefits.

While the adoption of a functional perspective is advocated in this volume as the correct way to identify wetland goods and services, if each of them is identified separately, and then attributed to underlying functions, there is a likelihood that benefits will be double counted. Benefits might therefore have to be allocated explicitly between functions. For instance, Barbier (1994) noted that if the nutrient retention function is integral to the maintenance of biodiversity, then if both functions are valued separately and aggregated, this would double count the nutrient retention which is already 'captured' in the biodiversity value. Some functions might also be incompatible, such as water extraction and groundwater recharge, so that combining these values would overestimate the feasible benefits to be derived from the wetland. Studies that attempt to value the wetland as a whole based on an aggregation of separate values tend to include a certain number of functions although these studies do not usually claim to encompass all possible benefits associated with the wetland (see Appendix 4.1).

The conceptual model we advocate is *not* reductionist in the sense that it neglects the overall systems perspective that is key to the understanding of the environmental change process. Rather it is narrowly drawn in foundational terms (at the level of individual ecosystem-functions) in order to provide analytical rigour, as well as practical regulatory/policy relevance. At no time is the overall value of a healthy evolving set of environmental systems lost sight of. The term 'total economic value' is meant to describe, when appropriate, an aggregation of use values and other non-use (option and existence value) values, in cases where it is feasible and meaningful to quantify such values in monetary terms. Total economic value is therefore less than total system value which incorporates the life support function and maybe other dimensions of environmental value such as intrinsic value, that is the value of a wetland that resides in itself, rather than of itself.

However, if wetlands perform many functions and are potentially so valuable, a reasonable question would be, why have these values been ignored and wetland losses and/or degradation allowed to continue? To some degree, the desirability of the flat, fertile and easily accessible land upon which wetlands are often found, has inevitably put some of them under pressure from other uses such as agriculture, industry and urbanization. Some conversion might well have been in society's best interests, where the returns from the competing land use are high, but wetlands have frequently been lost to activities resulting in only limited benefits or, on occasion, even costs to society. This is the result of what Turner and Jones (1991) refer to as interrelated market and intervention failures, which derive from a fundamental failure of information, or lack of understanding of the multitude of values that may be associated with wetlands.

The multifunctional characteristic of wetland ecosystems makes comprehensive estimation and valuation of every function and linkages between them a formidable task. Hence the need for a useful typology of the associated social, economic and cultural values. In this book, we will mainly focus on socio-economic values. These values depend on human preferences, that is what people perceive as the impact wetlands have on their welfare. In general, the economic value of an increased (or a preserved) amount of a good or service is defined as what individuals are willing to forego of some other resources in order to obtain the increase (or maintain the status quo). Economic values are thus relative in the sense that they are expressed in terms of something else that is given up (the opportunity cost), and they are associated with the type of incremental changes to the status quo that public policy decisions are often about in practice.

Economic values will always be contingent upon the wetland performing functions that are somehow perceived as valuable by society. Functions in themselves are therefore not necessarily of economic value. Such value derives from the existence of a demand by society for wetland *goods* and *services*. While the total amount of resources society would be willing to forego for an increased (or preserved) amount of a wetland service reveals the total economic value (TEV) of this increase (or preservation), different components of TEV can be identified (see Figure 1.2). *Use value* arises from humans' direct or indirect utilization of wetlands through wetland goods and wetland services, respectively. A value category usually associated with use value is that of option value, in which an individual derives benefit from ensuring that a resource will be available for use in the future. Another type of value often mentioned in the valuation literature is quasi-option value, which is associated with the potential benefits of awaiting improved information before giving up the option to preserve a resource for future use. Quasi-option value cannot be added into the TEV calculation without some double counting; it is best regarded as another dimension of ecosystem value. *Non-use* value is associated with benefits derived simply from the knowledge that a resource, such as an individual species or an entire wetland, is maintained. Non-use value is thus independent of use, although it is dependent upon the essential structure of the wetland and functions it performs, such as biodiversity maintenance.

Various components of non-use value have been suggested in the literature, including the most debated component, existence value, which can be derived simply from the satisfaction of knowing that some feature of the environment continues to exist, whether or not this might also benefit others. This value notion has been interpreted in a number of ways and seems to straddle the instrumental: intrinsic value divide (see Chapter 4 in this volume). Some environmentalists support a pure intrinsic value of nature concept, which is totally divorced from anthropocentric values. Acceptance of this leads to rights and interests-based arguments on behalf of non-human nature. The existence of such philosophical views is one reason why the concept of TEV should not be confused with the 'total value' of a wetland. Moreover, the social value of an ecosystem may not be equivalent to the aggregate private TEV of that same system's components. The system is likely to be more than just the aggregation of its individual parts (Gren *et al.*, 1994).

Finally, an important aspect of the economics–science interface is the existence of thresholds and the potential for irreversible change. Where the additional change in a parameter has a disproportionate effect, this might be associated with relatively high economic values. And if the change is irreversible, account needs to be taken of the uncertain future losses that might be associated with this change, and the possible imposition of Safe Minimum Standards. While it may not be possible to identify exact thresholds or the precise effects of crossing those thresholds, it will be important to acknowledge the possibility of approaching limits of tolerance within the ecosystem.

## 4   THE ECOWET RESEARCH PROJECT

The valuation approach adopted in ECOWET encompassed a mixed methodology. Wherever feasible and meaningful, monetary valuation methods and techniques were deployed to assess wetland functional value and change. At this level, interdisciplinary insights can be derived and exploited, as economic theory is combined with geographic information systems and focus group work buttressed by psychosocial and cultural theory, in order to enrich the valuation process. In the context of ECOWET, spatial modelling was undertaken by the Dutch team to integrate descriptions of hydrological, ecological and economic systems and their interactions. Integration involved formulation of scenarios at the level of polders and grids, heuristic linking of models, and aggregation of spatial data in various performance indicators. The programme MODFLOW (a regional groundwater flow model) linked to ICHORS (a probability-based vegetation model) translates environmental change into impacts in terms of the likely spatial distribution of wetland plant/fauna species. The economic model was used to assess the efficiency and distributional equity implications of the environmental impacts. This was complemented by both multi-criteria and spatial equity assessment approaches (van den Bergh *et al.*, 2001 and 2002). The resulting integrated modelling tool allows for an explicit matching of spatial characteristics of a region dominated by wetlands with policies – mainly focused on water management and land use – that aim to realize a particular trade-off between economic benefits, nature conservation and spatial equity.

ECOWET also identified and explored some of the systemic and intangible elements of local wetland value, which are less susceptible to economic valuation. A participatory appraisal method, that is, a structured process of learning with, and from people in a locality about their own situation, conditions of life, perceptions, aspirations and preferences, has been deployed in the UK case study (Burgess, Clark and Harrison, 2000). The Swedish team and the Greek team have also conducted focus group sessions with local stakeholders in order to analyse the effectiveness of Swedish wetland creation policy and links between tourism development pressure and pristine wetland areas respectively (see Chapters 7 to 10 in this volume).

Scenarios of environmental change and consequent wetland impacts were constructed and evaluated in order to derive policy-relevant findings for management. In the UK case different management strategies were assumed, in the Swedish case different nitrogen reduction policy scenarios were examined, and in the Dutch study land-use change scenarios were utilized (see Chapter 11 in this volume).

The case study work programme addressed a number of different problems across different temporal and spatial scales – from individual wetland function valuation, through whole area management in the context of a single (or small number) of environmental pressure(s), to catchment/landscape scale problems as highlighted in the Dutch polder study. A common policy analysis structure was adopted for all the case studies. It encompassed an examination of all the relevant environmental pressure trends, actual and potential stakeholder conflicts and the prevailing institutional and property right regimes, or lack of regimes, relevant for wetland management.

## REFERENCES

Adamus, P.R. and L.T. Stockwell (1983), 'A method for wetland functional assessment: Volume 1', *Critical Review and Evaluation Concepts*, Washington, DC: US Department of Transportation, Federal Highway Administration, Office of Research and Management.

Balmford, A. *et al.* (2002), 'Economic reasons for conserving wild nature', *Science*, **297**, 950–53.

Barbier, E.B. (1994), 'Valuing environmental functions: tropical wetlands', *Land Economics*, **70**, 155–73.

Bergh, J.C.J.M. van den (1999), *Handbook of Environmental and Resource Economics*, Cheltenham, UK and Northampton, MA, USA: Edward Elgar.

Bergh, J.C.J.M. van den, A. Barendregt and A. Gilbert (2002), *Spatial Ecological–Economic Analysis for Wetland Management: Modelling and Scenario Evaluation of Land Use in the Netherlands*, book manuscript, under review.

Bergh, J.C.J.M. van den, A. Barendregt, A. Gilbert, M. van Herwijnen, P. van Horssen, P. Kandelaars and C. Lorenz (2001), 'Spatial economic–hydroecological modelling and evaluation of land use impacts in the Vecht Wetlands area', *Environmental Modelling and Assessment*, **6**(2), 87–100.

Bingham, G., R. Bishop, M. Brody, D. Bromley, E. Clark, W. Cooper, R. Costanza, T. Hale, G. Haydon, S. Kelhert, R. Norgarrd, B. Norton, J. Payne, C. Russell and G. Suter (1995), 'Issues in ecosystem valuation: improving information for decision-making', *Ecological Economics*, **14**, 73–90.

Boesch, D.F. (1999), 'The role of science in ocean governance', *Ecological Economics*, **31**, 189–98.

Burgess, J., J. Clark and C.M. Harrison (2000), 'Knowledges in action: an actor network analysis of a wetland agri-environment scheme', *Ecological Economics*, **35**, 119–32.

Claridge, G.F. (1991), 'An overview of wetland values: a necessary preliminary to wise use', *PHPA/AWB Sumatra Wetland Project Report No. 7*, AWB, Bogor.

Costanza, R., R. d'Arge, R.S. de Groot, S. Farber, M. Grasso and B. Hamon (1997), 'The value of the world's ecosystem services and natural capital', *Nature*, **387**, 253–60.

Cowardin, L.M., V. Carter, F.C. Gollet and E.T. LaRoe (1979), 'Classification of wetlands and deep water habitats of the United States', *US Fish and Wildlife Service Publication*, FWS/OBS-79/31,Washington, DC.

Crooks, S., R.K. Turner, J.S. Pethig and M.L. Parry (2001), 'Managing catchment–coastal floodplains: the need for a UK water and wetlands policy', Centre for Social and Economic Research on the Global Environment (CSERGE) Working Paper PA 01-01, University of East Anglia, Norwich.

Dugan, P.J. (1990), *Wetland Conservation: A Review of Current Issues and Required Action*, IUCN, Gland, Switzerland.

European Environment Agency (1999), *Environment in the European Union at the Turn of the Century: Environmental Assessment Report, No. 2*, European Environment Agency, Copenhagen, Denmark.

Gren, I-M. and T. Soderqvist (1994), 'Economic valuation of wetlands: a survey,' *Beijer Discussion Paper Series No. 54*, Beijer Institute, Stockholm.

Maltby, E., D.V. Hogan and R.J. McInnes (eds) (1996a), 'The functioning of river marginal wetlands: Improving the science-base for the development of procedures of functional analysis', *Environmental and Waste Recycling, Water Pollution Research Report Series*, Commission of the European Communities, DG11 (Sci. Res and Develop).

Maltby, E., D.V. Hogan and R.J. McInnes (eds) (1996b), *Functional Analysis of European Wetland Ecosystems*, final report – Phase one EC DG11 Step Project, CT90-0084, Wetland Ecosystems Report Group, University of London.

Maltby, E., D.V. Hogan, C.P. Immirzi, J.H. Tellam and M.J. van der Peijl (1994), 'Building a new approach to the investigation and assessment of wetland ecosystem functioning', in W.J. Mitsch (ed.), *Global Wetlands: Old and New*, Amsterdam: Elsevier, pp. 637–58.

Mitsch, W.J. and J.G. Gosselink (1993), *Wetlands*, New York: van Nostrand Reinhold.

Steele, J.H. (1991), 'Marine functional diversity', *Bioscience*, **41**, 470–74.

Turner, R.K. (2000), 'Integrating natural and socio-economic science in coastal management', *Journal of Marine Systems*, **25**, 447–60.

Turner, R.K. and T. Jones (eds) (1991), *Wetlands, Market and Intervention Failures*, London: Earthscan.

Turner, R.K., J.C.J.M. van den Bergh, *et al.* (1999), *Ecological–Economic Analysis of Wetlands: Functions, Values and Dynamics*, ECOWET, Contract No. ENV4-CT96-0273, Vols. 1–3, European Commission, Brussels.

Turner, R.K., J. Paavola, P. Cooper, S. Farber, V. Jessamy and S. Georgiou (2002), 'Valuing nature: lessons learned and future research directions', Centre for Social and Economic Research on the Global Environment (CSERGE), Working Paper EDM 02-05, University of East Anglia, Norwich.

Turner, R.K., J.C.J.M. van den Bergh, T. Söderqvist, A. Barendregt, J. van der Straaten, E. Maltby and E.C. van Ierland (2000), 'Ecological–economic analysis of wetlands: scientific integration for management and policy', *Ecological Economics*, **35**, 7–23.

PART I


Methodological issues and wetland ecosystem
management

# 2. Integrated assessment as a decision support tool

## R. Brouwer, R.K. Turner, S. Georgiou and J.C.J.M. van den Bergh

## 1 INTRODUCTION

In the light of an increasingly emancipated society, decision-makers are held responsible and are made accountable for their decisions, sometimes even years after decisions were taken. Decisions have to be explained, especially to those who are affected by them. In complex decision-making situations, various, often competing, interests may be at stake. Demand for information which reflects this plurality and diversity of interests and the way these interests are affected by decisions is increasing. Ideally information has to encompass the various relevant aspects related to the problem a decision-maker tries to solve, that is information has to be comprehensive and complete, even though in practice decision-making takes place in contexts in which uncertainties and incomplete information are present to different degrees.

At the same time information has to be communicated in a meaningful and persuasive way to both decision-maker and those affected by decisions. As societal–environmental change becomes more complex and decisions, interests and value systems more inextricably connected, there is growing interest in integrated approaches to inform policy and decision-making. Integrated assessment procedures have been developed in order to avoid as many unforeseen consequences of policy decisions as possible (de Vries, 1999).

In the context of water resources management, Mitchell (1990) has argued that effort directed towards more integrated management has three related dimensions. In the case of the management of wetlands, integration can be interpreted as follows:

1. In systems ecology terms, that is to gain a better understanding of how each component of the wetland system at catchment level influences other components.

2.  In wider biogeochemical and physical systems terms, that is where water interacts with other biophysical elements (one of the most characteristic features of a wetland).
3.  In socio-economic and socio-cultural terms, that is where wetland management is linked to relevant policy networks and economic and social systems with attendant culture and history, so that the chances of a co-operative solution or mitigation strategy are maximized.

Socially and politically sensitized forms of integrated assessment are an important step towards:

i)   increasing awareness about the complex nature of the interdependency between our physical and socially constructed environment; (that is co-evolutionary processes of change);
ii)  greater recognition that uncertainties and risk of irreversible change require careful consideration (precautionary principles) in decision-making, which may be facilitated by prior agreement on a sensible, preferably social learning based, evaluation process;
iii) recognition that change and corresponding costs and benefits in complex decision-making circumstances are characterized by dynamics, as knowledge and experiences progress;
iv)  increasing public support for and trust in decisions because of greater transparency in the *ex ante* evaluation phase.

The main objective of this chapter is to analyse the means by which more procedural rationality (Simon, 1964) can be introduced into decision support systems for integrated water resources policy and management. Procedural rationality refers in this context to the manner in which complex decisions can or should be better informed based on integrated assessment. The concept of integrated assessment is first defined in a preliminary way and is then reviewed from a range of methodological and policy analysis viewpoints. This overview addresses issues such as:

*   the need for vertical and horizontal integration when linking information demand and supply;
*   procedural steps in integrated assessment;
*   useful frameworks to structure and handle complexity and uncertainty;
*   the distinction and correlation between ecological and social values of aquatic ecosystems;
*   available evaluation methods and techniques.

## 2   TUNING INFORMATION SUPPLY AND DEMAND

In our co-evolving society and environment, public scrutiny, accountability and trust have become of paramount importance. Both the provision of information and access to it have been profoundly affected by revolutions and progress in information technology. Information provided to support decisions is determined to a large extent by the political characteristics of the decision-making system and the phase in the decision-making cycle (Figure 2.1).

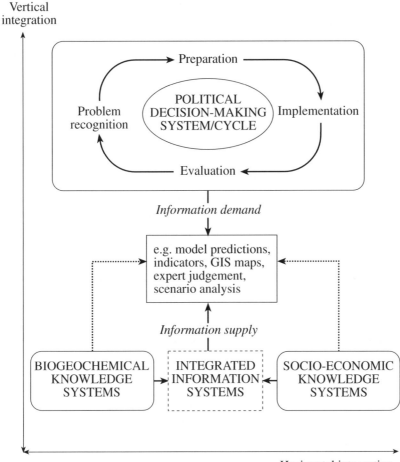

*Figure 2.1   General framework linking information supplied by multi-disciplinary science and decision-maker demand for information*

Figure 2.1 provides a very general characterization of a three stage decision-making cycle:

1.  Identification of opportunities, problems and crises, activating the decision process (*recognition and diagnosis*).
2.  Development of solutions (*search and design*).
3.  Selection from available solutions (*screening, judging, bargaining*) and obtaining approval for the selected solution (*authorization*).

In Figure 2.1, two axes are included, depicting the demand and need for horizontal integration across scientific disciplines and the demand and need for vertical integration of information as decision-making contexts become ever more complex. An important issue linking knowledge and information across different sciences and between sciences and decision-making processes is the temporal and spatial relevancy. The same problem may, for instance, be seen in significantly different geographical areas and on different timescales, from a natural scientific perspective, a social scientific perspective and a political perspective (Boesch, 1999). In the literature, frameworks (such as the Driving forces–Pressures–State–Impact–Responses (DPSIR) scoping system depicted in Figure 1.1), and models have been developed, which try to link scientific knowledge and information systems (for example OECD, 1994; and Turner *et al.*, 1998). These information systems provide an important interface between natural and human systems. Perceptions of interactions between natural and social systems are reflected in the way research is carried out and information systems are constructed (information supply).

Models and indicators are examples of information system types. By definition, models try to simplify in order to describe and predict (parts of) complex reality. Indicators help to reduce the complexity of real problems and hence also qualify as an analytical component. They may describe a state or condition which is considered relevant in terms of a more general phenomenon of interest, but which cannot be measured directly because of a lack of sufficient scientific understanding, or on feasibility grounds.

Two main approaches to integrated modelling can be distinguished (van den Bergh, 1996). One aims for a single model, while the other employs a system of heuristically connected sub-models. Linking natural and social scientific models within one integrated model inevitably involves compromises and simplifications. In general, in systems analysis based on models, a trade-off exists between generality, precision and realism (Costanza *et al.*, 1993). Connected scenarios can provide an integrating context for models and indicators, and help to achieve consistency among units, spatial demarcations, and spatial aggregation of information in various sub-models (for example Lorenzoni *et al.*, 2000a, b).

# 3   INTEGRATED ASSESSMENT

Recently, there has been growing interest in integrated approaches to inform policy and decision-making, for instance in the climate change discussion (Janssen, 1996; Rotmans and van Asselt, 1996). Various forms of integrated assessment exist, including technical, health, environmental, economic and social appraisals. In general, the need for these appraisals results from problems of choice, where decision-makers (for example policy makers, producers, consumers) face one or more options (for example policies, projects, measures, products) in a given policy context.

The literature contains various definitions of integrated assessment. According to Weyant *et al.* (1996), an assessment is integrated when it draws on a broader set of knowledge domains than are represented in the research product of a single discipline. Parson (1995) argues that integrated assessment is a policy-relevant whole, which is greater than the sum of the disciplinary parts. An appealing definition is given by Rotmans and Dowlatabadi (1998, p. 292), who define integrated assessment as

> an interdisciplinary *process* of combining, interpreting and *communicating* knowledge from diverse scientific disciplines in such a way that the whole cause-effect chain of a problem can be evaluated from a synoptic perspective with two characteristics:
> 1) integrated assessment should have value added compared to single disciplinary oriented assessment;
> 2) integrated assessment should provide *useful* information *to decision makers*. (emphasis added)

This definition contains three important components, which are considered essential in such an approach. First of all, integrated assessment not only provides a conceptual framework, it is an interdisciplinary learning process, for experts and decision-makers, and in its most inclusionary form other types of stakeholders. Setting up a collaborative framework between experts with different scientific backgrounds and experiences is often a time-consuming procedure. Participants have to get used to and acquainted with each other, overcoming different uses of language, and their often fundamentally different ways of thinking, before their work can actually be put together in a meaningful and coherent way (Turner, 2000).

Secondly, in order for this collaborative process to be successful, communication is essential, that is communication between experts (scientists) and communication between experts and (lay) policy- or decision-makers, especially in the case of complex decision-making contexts. One could argue that policy- or decision-makers should be involved in this process right from the start for a number of reasons.

The inclusion of their policy or decision objectives determines the scope of the assessment. Although assessments may be set up in such a way as to minimize subjectivity, judgements are inevitable in any evaluation. If these judgements influence outcomes in a major way, they should be made explicitly clear to the users of the evaluation. Discussing this sooner rather than later with the users of the information generated by the assessment will minimize the risk of producing overly controversial results.

Given the inevitability of scientific uncertainties and risks, the involvement of lay decision-makers in discussions about these uncertainties and risks may (a) improve the decision-maker's understanding of the complexity of the problem, (b) modify accordingly expectations regarding 'the deterministic truth' behind the outcome of the integrated assessment should these uncertainties persist throughout the research, and (c) encourage the adoption of policy principles such as the Precautionary Principle or use of Safe Minimum Standards.

Involving policy- or decision-makers in the integrated assessment is more likely to ensure that the assessment will deliver useful information to decision-makers (the third component emphasized). According to Rotmans *et al.* (1996), integrated assessment is policy-motivated research to develop an understanding of the issue, not based on disciplinary boundaries, but on boundaries defined by the problem. It offers insight to the research community for prioritization of their efforts and to the decision-making community on the design of their policies. Also Janssen (1996) argues that integrated assessment is an iterative process where, on the one hand, integrated insights from the scientific community are communicated to the decision-making community and, on the other hand, experiences and learning effects from decision-makers form the input for scientific assessment. This complex and value-loaded process cannot be captured by one single approach. Depending on the problem it tries to address, it usually consists of a variety of approaches and methods, including formal, explorative, experimental and expert judgement methods.

An interactive, participatory and more inclusionary bottom-up approach right from the start, involving decision-makers, experts and other stakeholders, may be beneficial for a number of reasons:

1.  It will help to elicit public perception of problems and possible solutions besides expert judgement and therefore ensure that decisions focus on the right problems (as perceived by all parties involved). In the field of risk assessment, Cvetkovich and Earle (1992) argue, for instance, that effective management of environmental hazards requires knowledge of both physical environmental systems and the social–psychological processes affecting human responses to environmental conditions. Integrated assessment can also be seen as a (communication) process bringing together the knowledge and experiences of policy- or decision-makers, experts and lay public.

2.  Early involvement of stakeholders can be expected to increase broader social support for decisions, whatever the outcome.
3.  Early involvement of other stakeholders will facilitate the identification of the distribution of costs and benefits to different groups of people.
4.  It may also help decision-makers and experts to identify relevant criteria to evaluate policy outcomes, planning and implementation procedures.
5.  The exchange of information between (representatives of) various stakeholder groups and communication of different perspectives on perceived problems will inevitably result in some sort of social learning process, which may change perceptions, attitudes and behavioural patterns underlying these initially perceived problems.[1]

# 4   PROCEDURAL STEPS IN A DECISION SUPPORT SYSTEM

In Figure 2.2, an attempt is made to represent the various steps underlying decision support systems in general, including integrated assessment. The stepwise approach is closely related to ideas, which have been referred to in the literature as procedural rationality (Simon, 1964; 1972 and 1982), that is the manner in which decisions are made.

The stepwise procedure encompasses an iterative communication and learning process, including various feedbacks to previous levels of analysis and evaluation. In Figure 2.2, six steps are distinguished, which will be discussed in more detail below. The first step involves problem recognition, the identification of objectives and of potential solutions. Any assessment procedure starts with an analysis which scopes the present situation, resulting in the diagnosis of (potential) problems, their nature and scale, the definition of objectives and the identification of possible solutions to perceived problems. Although not necessarily yet commonly understood, a (shared) belief in and a sense of (shared) responsibility about the problem is essential in this first stage to mandate an integrated assessment.

A number of conceptual frameworks have been developed, which help to map cause–effect relationships underlying environmental problems, including problems related to wetland management. These frameworks are especially helpful when facing complex problems surrounded by uncertainties.

The DPSIR framework, for example, provides a conceptual and organizing backdrop for the contributions of different disciplines to the description and analysis of environmental problems.[2] The socio-economic aspects of environmental problems are an integral part of the framework. Environmental problems can be described, analysed and evaluated *vis-à-vis* the economic, social and cultural context in which they arise (Figure 2.3). The framework may

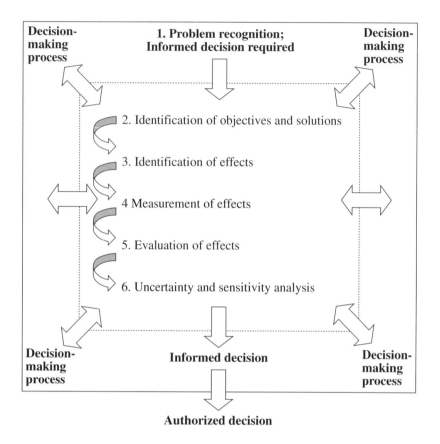

*Figure 2.2    Procedural steps underlying a decision support system*

provide an important tool for achieving a common level of understanding and consensus between researchers, natural resource managers, policy makers and other stakeholders. It provides the link between the various driving forces (endogeneous and exogeneous such as climate change or sea level rise), which pose threats to ecosystems (Turner *et al.*, 1998; Turner, 2000).

These pressures include, for instance, land conversion, agricultural development, hydrological perturbation and pollution, and their consequent impact on the various interest or stakeholder groups, who utilize the goods and services provided by wetland ecosystems or contribute to the pressures exerted on them. The observed or perceived impacts usually stimulate some kind of social and political response, involving the identification of policy scenarios, options and measures which may be deployed throughout the cause–effect

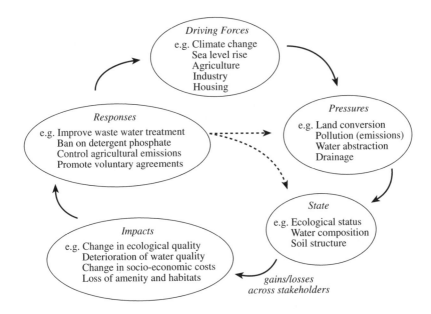

*Source*: Adapted from Weber and Crouzet (1999).

*Figure 2.3    The DPSIR-framework in the context of general wetland policy and management*

chain and focusing on driving forces, pressures, state and impacts again, (Turner, Subak and Adger, 1996).

The DPSIR framework is a framework, not a model, but it does allow for dynamic, non-linear relationships between social and ecological systems. Its main aim is to enable decision-makers to scope complex problems surrounded by uncertainties, by structuring them in a comprehensive, yet understandable way. For instance, the framework can indicate at which point in the cause–effect chain decision-makers are actually authorized to intervene in the first place (locus of control), or where they can realistically do something about a specific problem (for example prevention) and not merely treat symptoms. In the latter case, the framework is still helpful, as it may show that the real problem exists at a different level or scale, outside the scope of the policy- or decision-maker's remit of control.

Solutions are usually worked out in more or less detail progressively, usually stepwise, sometimes even over several years, from wetland policy scenarios to concrete wetland management measures and instruments to implement solutions. This process occurs in a given institutional setting in which several decision-makers may play a role, at different institutional and

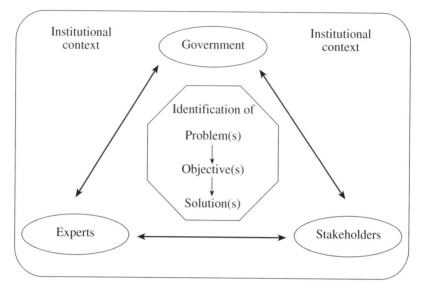

*Figure 2.4    Decision-making environment*

administrative levels. Through interactions with their decision-making environment, including stakeholder groups and other groups of experts, deliberation occurs within existing or, perhaps as a result of the decision-making
process, shifting formal and informal power structures (Figure 2.4).

Although the Government is depicted at the top of Figure 2.4, it is not
meant to imply a top-down decision-making structure. It only shows the main
players in general in a certain institutionally constrained decision-making
setting concerning the management of wetlands. Government includes here
both policy makers and/or wetland managers.

In the second step a preliminary assessment based on individual experience, expert knowledge and judgement, is usually made of the nature of fore-
seen impacts related to different policy options, even though quantitative data
and information about the exact magnitude and extent of the impacts may not
(yet) be available. It is usually at this stage when potential effects are
discussed that previously implicit criteria become explicit and the grounds are
laid on which policy options or management actions ultimately will be evaluated. Ideally, evaluation criteria should first be made explicit based on the
objectives set out in the previous stage. Subsequently the relevant effects associated with these criteria would be identified. However, in practice the identification of evaluation criteria often follows after discussion of the relevant
effects. Including (other) stakeholders at this stage in the process may help to
identify the distribution of positive and negative effects (costs and benefits in

physical and monetary terms), across environmental assets and different institutionally categorized groups of people.

The third step involves the measurement of effects. As mentioned in section 2, models and indicators are two important ways to assess the effects of alternative policy options or management actions. However, effects can be measured in a large variety of ways, quantitative and/or qualitative, based on highly advanced models in which dose-effect relationships are formalized in mathematical terms, or simply by means of expert judgement. The choice of any method obviously depends upon the specific nature and scale of the problem and decision-maker demand for specific types of information. Natural and social scientists have developed their own tools, methods and procedures to measure the impacts of human intervention on wetland ecosystems (environmental, social and economic impact assessment methods and procedures).

However, wetland policy and management will directly or indirectly affect both the environment and society (depending *inter alia* on the scale of implementation). Environment and society are usually inextricably linked. For example, groundwater management affects the economic activities, such as agriculture in an area, but it also affects the biological diversity present. Waste water treatment and water purification are essential for good-quality drinking water. However, it does not only affect public health, but also the ecological quality of water and wetland systems. The presence of water in a landscape often gives it its characteristic feature(s), and may play an important role in people's perception of its beauty, or be an important determinant in people's motivation to live in or visit a particular location.

Understanding the interactions between wetland ecosystems and society, including the economy, cannot be achieved by observational studies alone. Modelling of key environmental processes is a vital tool that must be used if wetland management is to achieve its overall sustainability goals and objectives, including a further quantification of the uncertainties in existing ecological process based models. For any group of researchers wishing to investigate and model a particular local wetland system, or aspects of that system to provide upscaling data for larger models, there are initially two types of information required (Turner, 2000):

1. Estimations of biogeochemical fluxes in the system as it is now and dynamic simulations of processes in wetland ecosystems which can be used to explore the consequences of environmental change and produce forecasts of future fluxes.
2. Understanding of the forces of socio-economic changes (for example population growth, urbanization) on fluxes of toxics, nutrients and sediment (pressures), and assessment of the human welfare impacts of these flux changes. Such assessments of the socio-economic costs and benefits

involved will provide essential wetland management information about possible resource and value trade-offs.

The assessment of the impact of changes in wetlands on human use of resources (wealth creation) and habitation (quality of life aspects) requires the application of socio-economic research methods and techniques.

Key issues related to the functioning of wetland ecosystems and the assignment of values to ecosystem structures and functions at a catchment level, which must be considered, include:

- The spatial and temporal scales of ecological processes and socio-economic resource use.
- The structure, complexity and diversity which underlies ecosystem functions and their value to society.
- The dynamic (in space and time) nature of interactions between society and wetland ecosystems.
- The uncertainties associated with these dynamics.

The essence of integrated assessment is to determine how society is affected by the functions the wetland ecosystem performs and changes in ecosystem functioning (possibly as a result of human use or exploitation of these functions). The key to valuing a change in a wetland ecosystem function is establishing the link between that function and some service flow valued by people. If that link can be established, then the social value of a change in an ecosystem function can be derived from the change in the ecological value of the ecosystem service flow it supports (see Figure 1.2). However, the multifunctional characteristic of wetland ecosystems at the catchment level makes comprehensive estimation of every function and linkages between them difficult. It will for example be necessary to assess features of socio-economic activities and behaviour and how these respond to changes in ecosystem functioning. Research efforts aimed at overcoming these difficulties are presented in the subsequent chapters in this volume.

In complex decision-making situations, where a range of management options are available, each having a different impact on human and natural systems across different spatial and timescales, impacts can be measured with the help of indicators. Environmental indicators are generally understood as quantifiable variables, which provide information about changes in environmental conditions. The variable itself may describe an environmental state at a certain point in time and an analysis of these variables over time will provide information about the relevant changes and the rate of change (OECD, 1994)[3]. However, indicators can also be descriptive (qualitative) in nature. For example, it may be difficult or even impossible to reduce a complex situation into one or more uni-dimensional variables. The variables may be highly interrelated, making the compilation of one or more presumably independent indicators meaningless. Capturing the whole range of relevant impacts on natural and social systems within different management scenarios, given the overall goal of sustainable development, will require a combination of environmental, social and economic indicators.

In practice, three main approaches can be distinguished when using indicators for integrated assessment purposes:

1. A phenomenon in one area is indicated with the help of a phenomenon in another area. For instance, the use of biological or organic indicators for evaluating inorganic environmental pollution, or vice versa inorganic environmental indicators to evaluate biological disruption.
2. Sets of different types of indicators are linked in a multi-criteria type of framework. For instance, the Gross Domestic Product (GDP) measure together with unemployment rate and one or more environmental indicators are presented together to highlight overall societal well-being and welfare.
3. Integration interpreted as aggregation, where various types of concerns are summed into one single indicator. For instance, the economic, social and environmental performance measures mentioned above (GDP, unemployment and so on) are expressed in one overall societal welfare indicator.

One of the main problems when using indicators is the scientific uncertainty over whether they actually measure features of the environment that are of interest; and whether they change in some meaningful way with respect to environmental change (Norris and Norris, 1995). Ideally, one indicator can be constructed that captures the whole spectrum of relevant ecosystem attributes at different levels of organization for sustainable management of that specific ecosystem, but this will rarely be the case. In fact, Landres *et al.* (1988) point out the danger of, for example, wildlife habitat management policy which relies on a single indicator such as a species indicator. Given the complexity of natural systems, the probability is small that a single indicator (abiotic, biotic, or social) can serve as an index of the structure and functioning of an entire ecosystem.

Indicators are believed to be an effective tool to simplify the communication process within which the results of measurement are provided to the user and for raising public awareness of environmental problems (OECD, 1994). Communication and understanding may be assisted by decision-maker and stakeholder participation in indicator selection and development. The worldwide promotion of the concept of sustainable development has led to a growing interest in actually measuring the path towards a sustainable future – commonly referred to as sustainability indicators. Participation of stakeholders within deliberative processes is seen as a key to commitment to and realization of sustainable development (for example Environment Agency, 1998). The process of making different environmental, social and economic and cultural dimensions compatible across different spatial and timescales in sets of indicators is at the core of a more integrated approach to research.

The process of identification, development, selection and communication of indicators may not only involve natural and social scientific knowledge, but also normative values developed in cultural, institutional and political contexts. Decision-makers and other stakeholders can and maybe should be involved in this process in different ways and at different stages (identification, measurement and evaluation of effects). Their involvement may also be crucial to the extent to which indicators and the ways in which they are used are accepted in different contexts.

The fourth step involves the evaluation of effects. Integrated assessment implies working with various values, reflecting different perspectives on wetland management problems. A core difficulty in integrated assessment is therefore to:

1.  relate relevant single effects, values and criteria across fields of impact in a meaningful way.
2.  make them comparable in order to be able to weight them and trade them off if necessary.

It is therefore important to identify and define all the relevant values or criteria that play a role in evaluating the effects of feasible (often already politically negotiated[4]) solutions.

Given tripartite deliberation (for example regulatory agency, experts and stakeholders) to evaluate policy and policy measures, the extent to which effects are positively or negatively related to a chosen reference situation needs to be examined.[5] This is usually done on the basis of a number of pre-selected or emergent evaluation criteria. For instance, the extent to which impacts of various policy options contribute to the realization of existing policy objectives can be examined.[6] Various criteria may play a role when making a choice between different policy options and the corresponding policy measures.

Although agencies seem to prefer to promulgate and enforce regulations based on quantitative criteria, qualitative descriptions of qualitative changes in for example community structure are often the best indicators of ecological disruption (Noss, 1990). In practice, qualitative descriptions of the intermediate changes or transitions between ecosystem states and ecosystem functions may sometimes prove to be the only way to assess the extent to which wetland management restores, maintains or enhances the integrity of an ecosystem.

Concern for public health and safety is usually one of the most important policy objectives and will generally be one of the main factors by which the effects of policy or policy measures are evaluated. Moreover, governments often believe that these safety and health concerns should apply to everybody in society. Hence, socially just policy may be another important objective. Although governments aim for safety and good health for everybody, they usually try to realize this policy at the lowest cost possible. In other words, policy options should be as cost-effective as possible. This example clearly shows that several criteria can apply simultaneously. When pursuing integrated and sustainable water resources policy, this usually means that environmental, social and economic considerations play an important role in the decision-making process, and policy and enabling measures will be scrutinized for these types of concerns. For instance, in a recent communication (COM(2000)477) from the European Commission to the European Council and Parliament, water pricing is introduced as a measure to ensure sustainable and efficient use of water. However, the communication is very clear about the way this instrument should be implemented. Economic instruments should be an integral part of a set of measures in order '*to guarantee achievement of the social, economic and environmental objectives in a cost-effective manner*'.

Once the expected or observed impacts of policy and policy measures have been evaluated on the basis of one or more criteria, the importance of each criterion in the decision-making process has to be determined, in order to be able to make a choice between policy alternatives. The degree to which various evaluation criteria will ultimately influence the decision depends on the political context (Susskind and Dunlap, 1981). Multi-criteria analysis techniques may be an important tool to support this decision-making (for an overview, see, for example, Janssen, 1994). The analytical hierarchy process (Saaty, 1980) is another helpful tool to translate qualitative judgements by decision-makers into quantitative weights. Obviously, if all effects are expressed in monetary terms, this step is not necessary.[7]

## 5   UNCERTAINTY AND SENSITIVITY ANALYSIS

Risk and uncertainty will be associated with both the physical outcomes connected with future environmental change and their social and economic consequences. Assessing the possible outcomes and the likelihood of perturbations to highly complex wetland ecosystems will inevitably be fraught with difficulty. A range of possible impacts deriving from potential management actions needs to be identified, the relevant physical effects quantified, and probabilities attached to each. A particularly important aspect relating to the uncertainty of physical effects, is the existence of thresholds beyond which disproportional and possibly irreversible effects occur. These will also be important in a social and economic sense owing to the disproportional extent of the impact and the inability to reverse the consequences in the future.

Analysis should not assume that all current physical, social and economic conditions will hold in the future. For instance, land-use changes might be predicted for the future, perhaps due to imminent regulation or long-term trends. This might affect, for example, the quantity of nitrogen in runoff and thereby the value of the wetland as a nitrogen sink. Behaviour of individuals could also adapt to change in wetland functioning, for instance with farmers changing cropping patterns as a result of increased flooding, rather than forgoing land use or yields altogether. These changes need to be incorporated into the analysis since they can influence projected effects (costs and benefits) and hence the outcome of the integrated assessment.

Uncertainty as to the correct value for environmental, social or economic variables employed and future trends can be addressed by employing sensitivity analysis or scenario analysis. Sensitivity analysis gives more than one final answer using different figures for variables employed such as the rate of discount, the extent of a function being performed and shadow pricing ratios. This provides a range of estimates within which the true figure can be expected to fall, which is less bound by particular assumptions but might result in ambiguous recommendations. Scenario analysis envisions a number of plausible future situations with a range of parameters within the valuation model, allowing a comparison of different future outcomes and policy response options. Thus an overall decision may be preferred despite a wide range of possible outcomes, although once again it may also provide more than one decision choice.

A useful distinction is between risk, to which meaningful probabilities of likely outcomes can be assigned, and uncertainty, where probabilities are entirely unknown. It has been suggested that the rate at which the future is discounted could be altered to incorporate a premium for risk (Brown, 1983). However, risk is better dealt with by attributing probabilities to possible outcomes, thereby estimating directly the expected value of future costs and benefits (Boadway and Bruce, 1984) or their 'certainty equivalents' (Markandya and Pearce, 1988), rather than in some arbitrary and often subjective addition to the discount rate which will attribute a strict (and unlikely) time profile to the treatment of risk.

As Costanza (1994, p.97) points out, 'most important environmental problems suffer from true uncertainty, not merely risk'. Such uncertainty can be considered as 'social uncertainty' or 'natural uncertainty' (Bishop, 1978). Social uncertainty derives from factors such as future incomes and technology which will influence whether or not a resource is regarded as valuable in the future. Natural uncertainty is associated with our imperfect knowledge of the environment and whether there are unknown features of it that may yet prove to be of value. This might be particularly relevant to ecosystems where the multitude of functions that are being performed have historically been unappreciated. One practical means of dealing with such complete uncertainty is, for instance, to complement a cost–benefit criterion based purely upon monetary valuation, with a Safe Minimum Standards (SMS) decision rule (Ciriacy-Wantrup, 1952; Bishop, 1978; Crowards, 1996). It is important to recognize, however, that such rules are not panaceas for complex decisions with inevitable trade-offs; both 'costs' and 'benefits' to society still have to be evaluated.

# 6   SUMMARY AND CONCLUSIONS

In order to deliver the sustainable utilization and management of wetland ecosystem resources, it is necessary to underpin management actions by a scientifically credible but also pragmatic environmental decision support system. Such a system can have the objective of economic efficiency at its heart, but still recognize other dimensions of wetland resources value and decision-making criteria. The decision support system incorporates a toolbox of evaluation methods and techniques, complemented by a set of environmental change indicators and an enabling analytical framework, thus allowing managers to identify operational decision steps. Individual projects or schemes can be appraised in their own right and clearly cost-ineffective options can be discarded. However, individual schemes and more extensive programmes will need to be placed in a wider analytical context which encompasses spatial scales up to at least the level of the catchment, and temporal scales in excess of the short run. Only in this way can a full appreciation of their effect on overall economic allocative efficiency and parallel sustainability objectives be gained.

The framework for decision support proposed in this chapter is in line with the sustainable water resources management approach advocated by the World Bank, which has at its core the adoption of a comprehensive policy framework and the treatment of water as an economic good, combined with decentralized management and delivery structures, greater reliance on pricing, environmental protection and fuller participation by stakeholders. It is recognized that the adoption of such a comprehensive framework facilitates the consideration of relationships between the ecosystem and socio-economic activities in catchments. Such a management approach requires analysis to take into account social, environmental and economic objectives; evaluate the status of wetland resources within each basin; assess the level and composition of projected demand; and take into consideration the views of all stakeholders. The advantages of such an approach are (Turner *et al.*, 2000):

- Ability to better consider both short- and long-term demands for wetland resources in an economically efficient manner.
- Ability to integrate activities and objectives that are not always feasible in separate approaches.
- Enhanced ability to manage the resources with a view to environmental issues.
- Ability to benefit from cost reductions through economies of scale.
- Ability to find efficient solutions to wetland quality and pollution problems.
- Facilitate action of reaching a consensus among the stakeholders, thereby reducing tensions and conflicts.
- Provides a means to assure equity and participation of beneficiaries and those impacted by development.
- Ability to adjust to changing priorities.
- Ability to prepare for emergencies such as floods.
- Provides a base for research and knowledge accumulation.

It is recognized that the complete adoption of such a procedure requires an institutional, financial and scientific capacity that may not be feasible in all countries (developed and developing). The aim should therefore be to move iteratively from a 'reduced form' procedure towards a comprehensive assessment over time. But certain elements are fundamental, that is, the adoption, as a minimum, of the catchment scale for analysis; the recognition of the importance of the functional approach to water uses and resources; the need for problem scoping (DPSIR) which encompasses distributional impacts; and the acceptance of economic principles for wetland valuation albeit constrained by cultural, political and other factors.

In summary then, the 'proper' appraisal of water related projects, programmes or courses of action require a comprehensive assessment of wetland ecosystem resources. In order to achieve this the analyst has to undertake the following steps:

1. On at least the catchment scale, to determine the causes of wetland ecosystem degradation/loss, in order to improve understanding of socio-economic impacts on ecosystem processes and attributes (for example with the aid of the DPSIR auditing framework).
2. Assess the full ecological damage caused by wetland ecosystem quality decline and/or loss.

3. Assess the human welfare significance of such changes, via determination of the changes in the composition of the wetland resource and ecosystem, evaluation of ecosystem functions, provision of potential benefits of these functions in terms of goods and services, and consequent impacts on the well-being of humans who derive use or non-use benefits from such a provision.
4. Formulate practicable indicators of environmental change and sustainable utilization of water resources and associated ecosystems (within the DPSIR framework).
5. Carry out evaluation analysis using monetary and non-monetary indicators (via a range of methods and techniques, including systems analysis) of alternative wetland usage and ecosystem change scenarios.
6. Assess alternative wetland uses and ecosystem conversion/development together with conservation management policies.
7. Present resource managers and policy makers with the relevant policy response options.

The steps presented here towards the development of a holistic integrated framework for socio-economic and environmental indicators are part of an integrated system aiming at the provision of transparent, meaningful and useful information. Ideally, this system should be able to support and link decision-making at different spatial and timescales with the objective of fostering the protection and sustainable management of natural resources.

## NOTES

1. According to Moscovici and Doise (1994), acts of decision, as well as acts of consenting, are above all acts of participation. For various reasons their value springs from the bond that they create between individuals and from the impression each one receives that he or she counts in the eyes of everybody as soon as he or she begins to participate. In this view, participation is considered a preliminary condition for following a goal, fulfilling a political, religious or even an economic mission. Hegel (1965, p.105) wrote: 'if people are to take an interest in something, they must be able to actively participate in it'.
2. The SPR framework is another, internationally applied, mapping tool to scope problems. It forms the basis of Ecological Risk Assessment (ERA) methods that have been developed to help manage the impacts of contaminated sites on plants, animals, and ecosystems (for example Banwart, 2000). An important difference between the DPSIR and the SPR framework is that the former focuses explicitly on the interaction between pressures exerted by human (including economic) activities and their effects on environmental and social systems. The SPR framework is somewhat more restricted to the geophysical modelling of ecological risks.
3. The OECD (1994) defines an environmental indicator as a parameter or a value derived from parameters, which points to, provides information about, describes the state of a phenomenon/environment/area, with a significance extending beyond that directly associated with a parameter value. *The UK Department of the Environment (1996)* defines indicators as quantified information, which help to explain how things are changing over time.

4.  Also in the case of (implicitly or explicitly) politically negotiated solutions – for instance, increasing tap water prices is not considered a feasible alternative as access to (tap) water is considered a basic human right to which all groups of people (low and high income) should have equal access – it will increase the transparency of the decision-making process and help the identification of relevant evaluation criteria of the impacts of feasible solutions to explicitly show the values underlying the outcome of these politically negotiated solutions.

5.  The difference between this step and the previous step corresponds, for example, to the distinction made in the literature between descriptive and normative indicators (for example Weterings and Opschoor, 1994). Descriptive indicators reflect an actual state or condition, whereas normative indicators relate this actual state or condition to a reference state or condition. Sustainability indicators are normative indicators since they intend to show how far off society is from a desired (sustainable) situation.

6.  These reference or target values may refer to 'static' normative valuation criteria, for example rarity, naturalness, diversity or degree of distortion are often used as important ecological valuation criteria, but may also refer to more 'dynamic' norms based on simple rules of thumb. Examples of such rules are that abstraction rates of renewable natural resources may not exceed regeneration rates over a certain period of time, or discharges into environmental media such as water cannot exceed the natural absorption capacity of this medium.

7.  If one of the criteria in a multi criteria analysis (MCA) is expressed in money, for instance the financial investment costs of a wetland restoration project, the weights used to trade off the various criteria scores can be interpreted theoretically as shadow prices. The outcome of the MCA is then theoretically the same as the outcome of a cost–benefit analysis (CBA) where all effects are valued through the same shadow prices. However, in practice it is usually difficult to interpret the weights in this particular way and furthermore requires a specific way of assigning weights to criteria. An important advantage of MCA techniques is that it is much easier to take into account, and trade-off effects are expressed in physical instead of monetary terms. Effects measured in physical terms do not have to be translated into money terms first through economic valuation techniques. In this way MCA allows more aspects or factors to play a role in the trade-off procedure than just the efficiency of wetland policy or management actions (the economic CBA criterion). An important disadvantage of MCA compared to CBA is that the outcome has no welfare theoretical basis or significance. In an MCA alternative, management actions are ranked relative to each other, based upon the criteria and weights included, while in the case of CBA the outcome of the evaluation of these alternative management actions can be interpreted in terms of their effect on social welfare.

# REFERENCES

Banwart, S.A. (2000), 'The impact of redox conditions on contaminant mobility and risk', paper presented at the workshop on Large Scale Drainage Basin Water Management, 17–18 November, Stockholm, Sweden.

Bergh, J.C.J.M. van den (1996*), Ecological Economics and Sustainable Development: Theory, Methods and Applications*, Cheltenham, UK and Brookfield, US: Edward Elgar.

Bishop, R.C. (1978), 'Endangered species and uncertainty: The economics of a safe minimum standard', *American Journal of Agricultural Economics*, **60**, 10–18.

Boadway, R.W. and N. Bruce (1984), *Welfare Economics*, Oxford: Basil Blackwell.

Boesch, D. (1999), 'The role of science in ocean governance', *Ecological Economics*, **31**, 189–98.

Brown, S.P. (1983), 'A note on environmental risk and the rate of discount: A comment', *Journal of Environmental Economics and Management*, **10**, 282–286.

Ciriacy-Wantrup, S.V. (1952), *Resource Conservation: Economics and Policies*, Berkeley, CA: University of California Press.

Costanza, R. (1994), 'Three general policies to achieve sustainability', in A-M Jansson, M. Hammer, C. Folke and R. Costanza (eds), *Investing in Natural Capital: The Ecological Economics Approach to Sustainability*, Washington, DC: Island Press.

Costanza, R., L. Wainger, C. Folke and K-G. Maler (1993), 'Modelling complex ecological economic systems', *Bioscience*, **43**(8), 545–55.

Crowards, T. (1996), 'Addressing uncertainty in project evaluation: The costs and benefits of safe minimum standards', Global Environmental Change Working Paper GEC 96-04, Centre for Social and Economic Research on the Global Environment (CSERGE), University of East Anglia and University College, London.

Cvetkovich, G. and T.C. Earle (1992), 'Environmental hazards and the public', *Journal of Social Issues*, **48**(4), 1–20.

de Vries, M.S. (1999), *Calculated Choices in Policy-making. The Theory and Practice of Impact Assessment*, Basingstoke, UK: Macmillan Press.

Environment Agency (1998), *Consensus Building for Sustainable Development*, Sustainable Development Publication Series SD12, Bristol.

Harremöes, P. and R.K. Turner (2001), 'Methods for integrated assessment', *Regional Environmental Change*, **2**, 57–65.

Hegel, G.W.F. (1965), *La raison dans l'histoire*, Paris: Plon.

Janssen, R. (1994), *Multiobjective Decision Support for Environmental Management*, Dordrecht: Kluwer Academic Publisher.

Janssen, M. (1996), 'Meeting targets. Tools to support integrated assessment modelling of global change', Ph.D. thesis, University of Maastricht.

Landres, P.B., J. Verner and J.W. Thomas (1988), 'Ecological uses of vertebrate indicator species: A critique', *Conservation Biology*, **2**(4), 316–28.

Lorenzoni, I., A. Jordan, M. Hulme, R.K. Turner and T. O'Riordan (2000a), 'A co-evolutionary approach to climate change impact assessment: Part I. Integrating socio-economic and climate change scenarios', *Global Environmental Change*, **10**, 57–68.

Lorenzoni, I., A. Jordan, T. O'Riordan, R.K. Turner and M. Hulme (2000b), 'A co-evolutionary approach to climate change impact assessment: Part II. A scenario-based case study in East Anglia (UK)', *Global Environmental Change*, **10**, 145–55.

Markandya, A. and D.W. Pearce (1988), 'Environmental considerations and the choice of discount rates in developing countries', Environment Department Working Paper no.3, World Bank, Washington, DC.

Mitchell, B. (1990), *Integrated Water Management: International Experiences and Perspectives*, London: Belhaven Press.

Moscovici, S. and W. Doise (1994), *Conflict and Consensus. A General Theory of Collective Decisions*, London: SAGE.

Norris, R.H. and K.R. Norris (1995), 'The need for biological assessment of water quality: Australian perspective', *Australian Journal of Ecology*, **20**, 1–6.

Noss, R.F. (1990), 'Indicators for monitoring biodiversity: A hierarchical approach', *Conservation Biology*, **4**(4), 355–64.

OECD (1994), *Environmental Indicators*, Paris: Organisation for Economic Co-operation and Development.

Parson, E.A. (1995), 'Integrated assessment and environmental policy making', *Energy Policy*, **23**(4/5), 463–75.

Rotmans, J. and M. van Asselt (1996), 'Integrated assessment: A growing child on its way to maturity', *Climate Change*, **34**, 327–36.

Rotmans, J. and H. Dowlatabadi (1998), 'Integrated assessment modelling', in S.

Rayner and E. Malone (eds), *Human Choice and Climate Change*, vol. 3; Tools for Policy Analysis, Columbus, OH: Battelle Press.

Rotmans, J., M.B.A. van Asselt, A.J. de Bruin, M.G.J. den Elzen, J. de Greef, H. Hilderink, A.Y. Hoekstra, M.A. Janssen, H.W. Köster, W.J.M. Martens, L.W. Niessen and H.J.M. de Vries (1996), 'Global change and sustainable development: A modelling perspective for the next decade', RIVM report 461502004, Bilthoven, The Netherlands.

Saaty, T.L. (1980*), The Analytical Hierarchy Process*. New York: McGraw-Hill.

Simon, H.A. (1964), 'Rationality', in J. Gould and W.L. Kolb (eds), *A Dictionary of the Social Sciences*, Glencoe, IL: The Free Press.

Simon, H.A. (1972), 'Theories of bounded rationality', in C.B. Radner and R. Radner (eds), *Decision and Organization*, Amsterdam: North Holland.

Simon, H.A. (1982), *Models of Bounded Rationality*, Cambridge, MA: MIT Press.

Susskind, L.E. and L. Dunlap (1981), 'The importance of non-objective judgements in environmental impact assessments', *Environmental Impact Assessment Review*, **2**, 335–66.

Turner, R.K. (2000), 'Integrating natural and socio-economic science in coastal management', *Journal of Marine Systems*, **25**, 447–60.

Turner, R.K., S. Subak and N.A. Adger (1996), 'Pressures, trends and impacts on coastal zones: Interactions between socio-economic and natural systems', *Environmental Management*, **20**, 159–73.

Turner, R.K. *et al.* (1998), 'Coastal management and environmental economics', *The Geographical Journal*, **164**, 269–81.

Tuner, R.K., J.C.J.M. van den Bergh, T. Suderquist, A. Barendregt, J. Van der Straaten, E. Maltby and E.C. Van Ierland (2000), 'Ecological–economic analysis of wetlands: Scientific integration for management and policy', *Ecological Economics*, **35**, 7–23.

Weber, J.-L. and P. Crouzet (1999), 'Integrated physical modelling inputs to environmental accounting. From research to implementation: Policy-driven methods for evaluating macro-economic performance', *EU RTD in Human Dimensions of Environmental Change*, report series 1999/1, DG XII, Brussels.

Weterings, R. and J.B. Opschoor (1994), 'Towards environmental performance indicators based on the notion of environmental space', *report to the Advisory Council for Research on Nature and Environment*, The Netherlands.

Weyant, J., O. Davidson, H. Dowlatabadi, J. Edmonds, M. Grubb, E.A. Parson, R. Richels, J. Rotmans, P.R. Shukla, R.S.J. Tol, W. Cline and S. Frankhauser (1996), 'Integrated assessment. Climate change 1995: Economic and social dimensions of climate change', contribution of working group III to the Second Assessment Report of the IPCC, pp. 367–96, Cambridge University Press.

# 3. Environmental indicators and sustainable wetland management

## R. Brouwer, S. Crooks and R.K. Turner

## 1 INTRODUCTION

The main objective of this chapter is to synthesize in a coherent way the wetland indicators found in the literature which aim to inform policy and decision-making concerned with sustainable natural resource management. The concept of *ecosystem integrity* will be used as the organizing principle behind the indicator framework. The concept of ecosystem integrity has recently gained in popularity and has been defined as the maintenance of system components, interactions among them and the resultant behaviour or dynamic of the system (King, 1993).[1]

In the literature, other *sustainability* concepts have been proposed as well, such as *ecosystem health* (Costanza *et al.*, 1992) or *ecosystem resilience* (Holling, 1986). The former has been defined as a system free of distress syndrome, while the latter refers to a system's ability to maintain its structure and pattern of behaviour in the presence of stress. Ecosystem integrity resembles the above mentioned concepts in that they all refer to, implicitly or explicitly, a certain minimum structural system composition required for the overall functioning of ecosystems. A lot of the subsequent debate about the usefulness of these different concepts has been dominated by semantics. For our purposes, the most important characteristic of all of these concepts for incorporation in the indicator framework is that they adopt a systems approach to the analysis of complex natural resources such as wetlands. The land–water interactions found in wetlands and their openness necessitate a management approach, which accounts for these key characteristics in a coherent and consistent way. The chapter will give an overview of existing ecological, biological, chemical and hydrological indicators to monitor and evaluate wetland ecosystem management.

## 2 ENVIRONMENTAL INDICATORS

The contemporary search for sets of indicators which inform decision-makers about existing or new environmental problems has a long history, but efforts have been intensified in the 1990s as sustainable development principles and objectives have gained prominence. Contrary to precise measurements, indicators point out a state or condition which is considered relevant for a more general phenomenon of interest, but which cannot be measured directly because of partial scientific understanding, inconvenience or lack of resources. At the Earth Summit in Rio in 1992 most countries committed themselves to develop a set of sustainability indicators to help inform government, industry, non-governmental organizations and the public about issues related to sustainable development.

In general, environmental indicators serve to reduce the complexity of environmental problems and to increase the transparancy of the possible trade-offs involved in specific policy choices. Moreover, environmental indicators are usually understood as quantifiable variables which provide information about changes in environmental conditions. The variable itself may describe an environmental state at a certain point in time and an analysis of these variables over time will provide information about the relevant changes and the rate of change. However, indicators can also be qualitative and descriptive in nature. For example, it may be difficult or impossible to reduce a complex situation into one or more with supposedly dimensional variables. The variables may be highly interrelated, making the compilation of one or more supposedly independent indicators meaningless.

Environmental indicators serve a number of purposes, two of which were mentioned above (reduce complexity and increase transparency). The OECD identifies yet another purpose, namely that of simplifying the communication process by which the results of measurement are provided to the user. When thinking of compiling and using environmental indicators, careful consideration of which specific purpose the indicator should serve is an essential first step. It drives the subsequent data requirements. Hence, the first question which has to be answered is: what does one wish to indicate and what for? This involves defining the specific environmental problem one wishes to address, identifying at which point it exists in the environmental chain from source to receptor, at which space and timescale and in which way.

Basically, environmental problems can be measured at their source, where human activities exert certain pressures on the environment (pressure indicators), at the receptor point (either human or non-human organic and inorganic), where the pressures result in a change of the quantity and quality of environmental assets (effect indicators), or somewhere in between these two (process of change indicators).

Pressure and effect indicators are the most common indicators, which were originally developed by the OECD within the so-called Driving forces–Pressures–State–Impact–Response (DPSIR) framework which highlights the different aspects of environmental problems and provides a general, internationally accepted framework for the development of environmental indicators (see Figure 1.1). Pressure indicators usually reflect human activity induced emissions, discharges, depositions or interventions (flows) into environmental media (land, air, water and living resources) over a period of time, while effect indicators (state indicators) reflect stocks of natural resources or environmental service flows at a certain point in time. On the other hand, impact indicators refer to the effects of a changed environment on human beings. A fourth type of indicator distinguished by the OECD are indicators for societal response, which are intended to show the extent to which society (government and non-government) responds to environmental changes and concerns at sector, national or international level. This includes for example the allocation of public budgets for environmental management.

The definition of the geographical- and timescale determines the indicator's aggregation level and hence the indicator's usefulness or relevance for different environmental problems. In other words, it determines the appropriate context in which the indicator can be used. In general, the indicator should provide enough detail of the specific environmental problem at hand. When aiming at a more integrated description of environmental problems, for example in terms of pressure and effect indicators as in the DPSIR framework, the geographical- and timescales do not necessarily correspond. In effect, given the dynamics present in many ecosystems, this will often not be the case. Trying to measure the parameter values at the same scale will require a number of simplifying assumptions. Pressures can be local (for example energy generation), but have a global impact (such as global warming) and vice versa (for example the impact of rising sea level on local economies).

When it comes to indicating a specific environmental problem, two types of indicators can be distinguished: descriptive and normative (Weterings and Opschoor, 1994). Descriptive indicators reflect an actual state or condition, whereas normative indicators relate this actual state or condition to a reference state or condition. Often, sustainability indicators are normative indicators since they are intended to show how far one has drifted from a desired (that is, sustainable) situation. The scaling mismatch problem is a particular concern with this type of indicator. Ecological sustainability is usually defined on a global scale in terms of the earth's life support system, whereas the time span could be thought of in terms of a natural or human system and its component parts' longevity. Both indicators have to be expressed in the same geographical and time dimensions (besides the same unit of measurement) in order to be able to combine them in one and the same indicator.

Once the objective of the environmental indicator has been established, a second important step is to ensure that the data used to construct the indicator (assuming for the moment that the data is available, up to date and reliable) is consistent with this objective. In other words, one has to find the correct or most appropriate data to fit the indicator's objective. Moreover, the way the data is statistically processed should ultimately result in an indicator that reflects what it is supposed to do. According to the OECD, the indicator should be analytically sound, that is theoretically well founded in technical and scientific terms (OECD, 1994).

Related to the issue of finding the correct or most appropriate data are the issues of data availability and data quality. Knowledge of environmental issues is often incomplete and surrounded by scientific uncertainties. It is therefore important to indicate the degree of reliability of the information provided in the environmental indicator, and to make explicit the model underlying the data collection. Moreover, most environmental indicators are published more than once and therefore require some kind of institutional structure or mechanism to regularly update the relevant data.

Finally, as information theory points out, a single word has little meaning without the rest of the sentence. Given the environmental indicator's objective, space and timescale, statistical adequacy and analytical soundness, its appropriate interpretation context should be made explicit to the user of the information. Moreover, indicators are usually normative in themselves. The choice of a specific indicator for a more general phenomenon implicitly reflects some subjective evaluation of current understanding of science and indicates at the same time policy priorities and policy paradigms. Making value judgements explicit in technical decisions means that they can be discussed and the merits of each determined.

## 3  COMBATING SCIENTIFIC UNCERTAINTY

One of the major problems when using indicators is the doubt that they actually measure features of the environment that are of interest and that they change in some meaningful way with respect to environmental change (Norris and Norris, 1995). Ideally, one indicator can be constructed that captures the whole spectrum of relevant ecosystem attributes at different levels of organization for sustainable management of that specific ecosystem, but this will rarely be the case. In fact, Landres *et al.* (1988) point out the danger of, for example, wildlife habitat management policy relying on a single indicator only, such as a species indicator. Given the complexity of natural systems, the probability is small, even with adequate research, that a single indicator can serve as an index of the structure and functioning of an entire ecosystem.

King (1993) argues that the description of a system simultaneously involves both structure and function: what are the components, how are they connected and how do they operate together? According to King, system integrity thus implies the integrity of both system structure and function, a maintenance of system components, interactions among them and the resultant behaviour or dynamic of the system. Given the emphasis on both system components and the interactions between them, the loss of system integrity has to be evaluated in the light of both structure and functioning or processes. In the context of biological diversity, Franklin *et al.* (1981) distinguished a third criterion or attribute to identify and describe ecosystems, namely ecosystem composition. Composition refers to the identity and variety of elements in a system, whereas structure refers to the physical organization of a system.

The effect of pressures exerted by human activities on ecosystems can be measured by defining the relevant indicator *spheres* for ecosystem structure, composition and function. The sustainability of natural resource management, or the impacts of environmental pressures on ecosystem integrity can subsequently be assessed in the following two ways.

First, indicators of environmental change can be related to ecological, biogeochemical and/or hydrological benchmarks, or *sustainability rules* based on natural scientific models, if available, to determine ecosystem integrity. For example, emission loads in an ecosystem can be compared to the assimilative capacity of a specific ecosystem.

Secondly, ecosystem integrity can be assessed by investigating the impact of environmental pressures on structural, compositional and functional ecosystem changes and the impact of these changes on each other. This will often be a qualitative analysis. For example, human induced stress may alter ecosystem structure or composition. The impact of this change in ecosystem structure or composition on general ecosystem functioning has to be investigated to assess ecosystem integrity.

The loss of a single system component such as the loss of a single species or population (resulting in a change of ecosystem composition and/or structure) or a change in interaction (processes) does not necessarily imply loss of system integrity. Many systems, including ecological systems, appear to be resilient to alteration of structure. Whole system function is maintained despite the structural change. Ecosystem components may perform equivalent functions, and loss of one or more may produce very little change in whole system function (Harcombe, 1977; Foster *et al.*, 1980; Rapport *et al.*, 1985; O'Neill *et al.*, 1986; Vitousek, 1986).[2] This is also called functional redundancy (King, 1993).

Although agencies seem to prefer to promulgate and enforce regulations based on quantitative criteria, qualitative descriptions of qualitative changes in for example community structure are often the best indicators of ecological disruption (Noss, 1990). In practice, qualitative descriptions of the intermediate changes or transitions between ecosystem states and ecosystem functions may sometimes prove the only way (or a very important complement to numerical indicators) to assess the extent to which wetland management restores, maintains or enhances the integrity of an ecosystem.

## 4   FRAMEWORK AND INDICATOR DOMAINS

Although a lot of research exists on different aspects of wetland ecosystems, not much of that work tries to bring these often separate pieces of investigation together under the same umbrella. Based on previous work, Angermeier and Karr (1994) provide a conceptual organization of general ecosystem integrity with five classes of interacting factors: physiochemical conditions (for example salinity, nutrients), trophic base (for example system productivity, energy content of food), habitat structure (for example spatial complexity, vegetation form), temporal variation (for example seasonality, flow regime) and biotic interactions (for example predation, parasitism). This provides a fairly comprehensive framework to derive integrity indicators. Some of these factors refer to ecosystem structure and composition, while others refer to ecosystem processes.

The only study so far focusing on indicators for wetland integrity is by Keddy *et al.* (1993). A preliminary list of six indicators for wetland integrity is drawn up: diversity, indicator guilds, exotics, rare species, plant biomass and amphibian biomass. Although this is a preliminary list, a coherent framework underlying the selection of these specific indicators is lacking. Exotics are perceived as evidence of invading organisms and are hence considered an indicator of ecosystem distress. Amphibian biomass is considered a particularly suitable indicator for wetlands. Amphibians inhabit both aquatic and terrestrial habitats, making them sensitive to a wide range of contaminants, while they are also an important food source for many higher trophic levels in wetlands and are at the same time higher invertebrate carnivores.

Wetlands occupy a transitional zone between aquatic and terrestrial ecosystems. Although there are a diverse range of wetland types, they possess a unique character in that they support a mosaic of both wet and dry environments. Because of their transitional nature, the boundaries of wetlands are often difficult to define. Wetlands do, however, share a few attributes common to all forms. Of these, hydrological structure (the dynamics of water supply, throughput, storage and loss) is most fundamental to the nature of a wetland system. It is the presence of water for a significant period of time which is principally responsible for the development of a wetland (Hughes and Heathwaite, 1995).

Given the unique interactions between water and land in wetland ecosystems, these two environmental media are used in this chapter as the two main indicator *domains*. Biodiversity is the third domain. Based on the specific indicators found in the literature, indicator sets have been compiled for each of these domains following the conceptual breakdown of ecosystems into structure, composition and function components (see Table 3.1). Although this breakdown seems to suggest that these aspects will be looked at independently,

*Table 3.1    Framework for wetland ecosystem indicators*

| Wetland domain | Ecosystem component | Indicator sphere |
|---|---|---|
| Landscape | Structure | Topology |
| | Composition | Land form and cover |
| | Function | Land use interactions |
| Water regime | Structure | Hydrology |
| | Composition | Biogeochemical water properties |
| | Function | Water constituents flux |
| Biodiversity | Structure | Food web trophic structure |
| | Composition | Keystone species and umbrella species |
| | Function | Energy transfer between trophic levels |

it is important to emphasize that it is the interdependency *within* and *between* ecosystem components and wetland domains that is of primary interest in this systems approach.

In principle, each of these wetland features and components can be monitored at their own specific, but highly interrelated temporal and spatial scales, at different levels of organization. The impacts of human activities or management intervention on wetland *ecosystems* can only be assessed if these three indicator spheres are considered together. The three wetland domains and their indicator spheres will be discussed in more detail in the following sections.

## 5    LANDSCAPE DOMAIN INDICATORS

The position of wetlands in landscape is an important emerging concept in wetland science (Bell *et al.*, 1997). Landscape refers to a mosaic of heterogeneous landforms, vegetation types and land uses (Urban *et al.*, 1987). From this, the concept of *landscape ecology* arose as an approach to introduce ecological principles within land management (Schreiber, 1990). The central focus of this new approach to ecology is described as the interrelationships between landscape structure (including composition), that is, the patterns of ecosystems across space, and landscape functioning, that is, the interactions of flows of energy, matter and species within and among the ecosystem structure (Kupfer, 1995). As such, landscapes can be seen as open systems influenced by geomorphology, that is, the arrangement and differentiation of landforms and the processes that have been or are shaping them, and pedology, that is, the processes involved in soil formation (see, for example, Gerrard, 1992).

Mitsch (1992) demonstrated that controls on wetland form and function operate at widely different spatial scales and that wetlands have different functions depending on their position in the landscape (for example, location in catchment area, surface topography).[3] The spatial scale of a regional landscape may vary from the size of a national forest or park, to the size of a physiographical region or biogeographical province. Sizeable geographical regions resulting from geomorphology and climatic regimes have characteristic wetland forms and vegetation types. Some regions contain isolated basins that are reached by vertebrates through their own efforts and are potentially affected by loss or degradation of individual basins, while others form a contiguous habitat and may be affected by reduction or fragmentation (Weller, 1988).

Noss (1983) introduced the term *regional landscape* to emphasize the spatial complexity of regions. Regionalization, that is the process of defining regions in which biophysical processes are expected to be similar, is a concept developed in the 1970s to understand and classify landscapes using spatial patterns of relevant environmental variables.[4] Nowadays, it is considered to provide an effective biophysical framework facilitating the assessment of natural biophysical conditions to manage natural resources (Perry and Vanderklein, 1996).[5] For example, water conditions cannot be separated from controlling influences of the surrounding landscape.

According to Urban *et al.* (1987), landscape assessment, by definition, requires the utilization of principles that are dictated by the hierarchy of scale and the controlling external environment of the system. Bailey (1987) calls this controlling external environment 'forcing conditions' and uses the concept of forcing conditions to establish three major levels of scale to map ecosystems: the macroscale (regional) dictated by climate, the mesoscale (landscape mosaic) dictated by land surface form, and the microscale (landscape elements) delineated by vegetation characteristics. Another hierarchy of scale of wetland variation is presented by the Committee on Characterization of Wetlands (1995), going from continental (physiographical regions) to wetland classes and sites within a wetland. *Between* wetland classes, size and connections to upland, aquatic and other wetlands are considered the main characteristic types of variations, caused by hydroperiod, soils and plant assemblages, while *within* wetlands topographical positions are caused by plant species composition, hydrological status and redoximorphic features.

Irrespective of which ecoregional classification is chosen, according to Klopatek (1988) the classification must include landform type. Landforms such as floodplains or river channels determine the boundary conditions controlling the spatial location and rate of geomorphological processes which have direct and often predictable effects on ecosystem processes (Swanson *et al.*, 1988). The ecoregional boundaries scale provides the transitional medium to the next level, that is wetland type, as defined, for example, by Cowardin *et al.* (1979). In this way, the wetland is looked upon as a landscape element.

Many variables combine to give a region its peculiar character. Different processes matter in different regions. Consequently, defining a region can be considered an integrative process using many different physiographical and biological variables (Perry and Vanderklein, 1996). Gallant *et al.* (1989) explain that the selected variables may either cause regional variations (such as climate, mineral availability, physiography) or integrate causal factors (for example soils, vegetation, land use). In the former case, climate determines for example the relative abundance and seasonality of precipitation, and mineral availability, and the characteristics of water chemistry including salinity and phosphorus levels. However, maps of causal factors alone often do not adequately indicate how these factors interact to determine, for example, water quality parameters. In the latter case, land-use maps serve for example as indicators of spatial changes in natural environmental characteristics and resource quality. Land use provides key subtleties, implying important consequences for water resource character and sensitivity to degradation, missed when measuring only climate, topography and physiography. Spatial patterns of past and current land use have for example a major influence on water quality sensitivity and land-use maps provide important indicators of those spatial patterns (Gallant *et al.*, 1989).

Topological aspects such as wetland size, shape, connectivity and distance between wetlands may have significant impacts on overall wetland ecosystem functioning (for example Swanson *et al.*, 1988; Klopatek, 1988; Johnston, 1994). For example, loss of connectivity within and between wetlands through landscape fragmentation can significantly affect nutrient processing (Johnston, 1994) or the integrity of species communities (Noss, 1983 and 1987; Merriam, 1991; Cattrijsse *et al.*, 1997). Furthermore, according to Johnston (1994), the cumulative loss of wetland function may or may not be linearly proportional to the area lost. Initial losses of wetland areas may have smaller effects on wetland function than later losses. For example, losses from watersheds containing 10 to 50 per cent wetlands have little effect on flood flow, but losses from watersheds containing less than 10 per cent have a large effect on flood flow. A similar 10 per cent threshold was found in the susceptibility of wetlands to increased loadings of suspended solids (Johnston, 1994). Hence, the impact of habitat fragmentation within the landscape is not only an alteration of size and isolation of a given ecosystem patch, but the restriction of movement of energy, matter and species in and across ecosystems. It is therefore important to be aware of the potential importance of landscape factors which might influence ecosystem functioning, including edge effects, corridor functioning and boundary dynamics (Kupfer, 1995).

Table 3.2 presents the landscape indicators found in the literature. The organization of this and the subsequent indicator tables for the two other wetland

Table 3.2  *Landscape indicators*

| Ecosystem | Indicator | Purpose/objective | Relevance for sustainable wetland management |
|---|---|---|---|
| Structure | 1. Area size | • indicate the administrative–political and natural boundaries of the wetland management area<br>• assess the overall trend in area loss over time of specific wetland forms (in combination with composition indicators)<br>• assess viability of area size dependent species communities | • effect of cumulative wetland area loss on different wetland functions (e.g. Johnston, 1994)<br>• minimum area size required for species richness (island bio-geography) (e.g. Brown and Dinsmore, 1986) |
| | 2. Connectivity | • indicate the habitat structure of the wetland ecosystem<br>• assess the relative ease of species movement<br>• assess the overall integrity and resilience of the wetland ecosystem<br>• assess impairment of overall wetland functioning | • all biological and ecological systems have a degree of resilience; they will tolerate a certain level of stress or depreda-tion, while maintaining the capacity to recover; even if individual elements of a system are destroyed, these elements can often be restored provided that the essential network of relationships that constitutes the system remains (e.g. Clayton and Radcliffe, 1996)<br>• loss of connectivity between wetlands through landscape fragmentation can significantly affect the cumulative function in nutrient processing (Johnston, 1994)<br>• effect of fragmentation on the integrity of the species community (Noss, 1983, 1987; Merriam, 1991) |
| | 3. Proximity | • indicate the relative distribution of ecosystem and landscape types<br>• assess the opportunity for species migration<br>• assess the possible influence of wetland sites on each other within and between wetlands through consideration of the distance between wetland sites | • reserves which are more isolated may experience lower rates of species immigration (Diamond, 1975); over time this may lead to a decline in species pool within an isolated system as extinctions occur<br>• marginal areas between ecosystems are often characterized by unique transitional species communities |
| | 4. Shape | • indicate the relationship between edge length and area of an ecosystem<br>• assess possible implications of edge effects on ecosystem<br>• assess implications of boundary dynamics on species | • highly convoluted ecosystems may be more susceptible to disturbance or stress because of proportionally larger edge region and exposure to external pressures (Schonewald-Cox and Bayliss, 1986; Schonewald-Cox, 1988)<br>• increased soil surface area in proportion to volume may increase rate of nutrient recycling and attenuation of hydrodynamic energies |
| | 5. Floodplain location | • access extent of transition zone between uplands and aquatic system<br>• assess wetland functioning as flood control buffer | • effectiveness of wetlands is dependent on position in catchment area (Ogawa and Male, 1986) |

| | | | |
|---|---|---|---|
| Composition | 1. Landform | • indicate the natural boundaries of wetland management sites<br>• determine wetland type of class<br>• indicate the spatial location and distribution of impact assessment and the relevant biogeochemical processes involved<br>• assess the heterogeneity of the wetland ecosystem and hence the system's suitability as habitat for ecologically sensitive species or species that utilize multiple habitat types | • landforms determine the boundary conditions controlling the spsyisl location and rate of geomorphic process which have direct and often predictable effects on ecosystem process (e.g. Swanson et al., 1988)<br>• landscape features such as heterogeneity and related features of landscape composition (proportions of particular habitats) can be major controllers of species composition and abundance and of population viability for sensitive species (e.g. Noss and Harris, 1986) |
| | 2. Vegetation cover | • indicate vegetation composition (at community level, not individual species level)<br>• identify and describe individual communities and the relationship among communities<br>• describe wetland cover type (standardization enables comparison among disparate monitoring efforts)<br>• global indicator of hydrology, water availability and water quality<br>• assess the harvest potential or wetland sites<br>• indicator of biomass and resource productivity<br>• global indicator of species communities | • monitoring the positions of ecotones at various spatial scales may be useful to track vegetation response to climate change and disruptions or disturbance regimes (Noss, 1990)<br>• strong relationship between frequently recurrent or sustained soil saturation (with water) and the development of communities dominated by plants specifically adapted for or requiring such conditions (hydrophytic vegetation); communities composed of these plant species have been used for decades to identify wetlands (CCW 1995)<br>• repeating expensive inventories of species distributions can be impractical for monitoring purposes; periodic inventories of vegetation can effectively monitor the availability of habitats over broad geographic areas; inferences about species distributions can be drawn from such inventories (Noss, 1990) |
| | 3. Soil characteristics | • assess effect of soil texture on wetland functioning such as nutrient recycling or sediment retention<br>• assess effect of chemical soil composition on wetland functioning | • floodplain soils exhibit characteristics of both sediment transport and deposition and soil formation (Gerrard, 1992)<br>• impact of nitrogen and phosphorous on eutrophication |
| Function | 1. Land-use changes | • assess land-use changes over time and hence provide insight in possible stress and disturbances<br>• global indicator of landscape processes of change | • although there is no conceptual basis for fine-scale predictions of responses that can be generalized, there are numerous general principles that predict the direction and to some degree the magnitude of ecosystem responses to a wide variety of disturbances such as road construction, agricultural practices etc. (Risser, 1988) |

indicator domains is the same. The first column shows the ecosystem component to which each indicator in the second column refers, while the third column details the purpose or objective of the indicator. The last column gives some relevant references to existing scientific research to justify the inclusion of the specific indicator.

In Table 3.2, five essential structural landscape indicators are presented. Area size, connectivity, proximity, shape and floodplain location all somehow affect wetland functioning in general or in specific areas such as nutrient processing or flood control. Landform (waterways, transitional flooding zones, terrestrial habitats and so on), vegetation cover and soil characteristics are used as indicators for landscape composition. Together they provide insight into various wetland dynamics and processes. Finally, for practical reasons and in view of the tremendous impact human activities can have on landscapes, land-use changes are included as a global indicator of landscape processes instead of focusing on microscale ecological and biogeochemical processes such as the impact of climate change on soil formation.

# 6   WATER REGIME DOMAIN INDICATORS

Water regime is central to the definition of a wetland. Water enters wetland systems by a number of mechanisms ranging from river influx, tidal inundation, land surface runoff, groundwater discharge and precipitation. Similarly, water may leave a wetland through a river flow, groundwater recharge, tidal ebbing and evapotranspiration. These flows are, by and large, extremely variable and stochastic in nature. The storage of water within a wetland system is determined by the balance of inflow and outflow relationships and the topography of the underlying basin. Storage within the main body of the wetland is very much dependent on landscape features such as the volume of accumulated sediment, transfer rate of water through the system and depth of adjacent water bodies. In fact, some wetlands may be flooded for extended periods of time, while others may only be flooded for short and infrequent intervals.

Water acts both as a stimulus and a limit to species composition and richness in wetland systems, depending on water storage and physical hydrodynamics. Alterations to hydrological conditions can have a significant impact on species composition and diversity, productivity, the exchange of organic material (import–export) and nutrient cycling within the wetland (Mitsch and Gosselink, 1993). Surprisingly, of the many thousands of vascular plant species in existence, relatively few have adapted to waterlogged soils and even fewer to waterlogged saline soils. A high water table or significant surface floodings act as a selective pressure to support vegetation communities often tolerant of anoxic soil conditions. Because of this, waterlogged soils generally support a lower species richness than less frequently flooded systems, but also an abundance of rare niche specialists.

Wetland classifications are generally based on ecology, physical and geomorphological characteristics. One of the first widely used classification systems, devised by Cowardin *et al.* (1979), divides wetlands into marine, estuarine, riverine, lacustrine and palustrine, with associated sub-classes, based on simple hydrological and geomorphological criteria. Wetland systems portray heterogeneity across a range of spatial scales from extensive landscape features down to local water table patterns and levels of water quality.

In the United States, assessment of wetland functions has become a key consideration in determining options for mitigating wetland losses through permitted development. The adopted *hydrogeomorphic* (HGM) approach classifies wetlands based on three fundamental factors that influence how wetlands function: position of the wetland in the landscape (geomorphological setting), water source (hydrology), and the flow and fluctuations of the water once in the wetland (hydrodynamics) (Brinson, 1993). HGM uses a hierarchical classification with seven major hydrogeomorphological wetland classes: riverine, depressional, slope, flat (organic soil and mineral soil) and fringe (estuarine and lacustrine). The wetland classes are then divided into geographical sub-classes. Once this has been ascertained, it is intended to use comparisons to other known and calibrated *reference* wetlands to assess wetland functioning.

Measurement of material (nutrient, sediment and biotic) budgets or mass balances between input and outputs, which take place on a range of spatial and temporal scales, are also important in characterizing water regime. Wetlands have been described as the 'kidneys of the landscape' (Mitsch and Gosselink, 1993) because of their vital role in transforming many common pollutants into harmless byproducts or into essential nutrients for further biological utilization. Quantifying, through mass balance calculations, the flow of nutrients through an open system such as a wetland is no simple task. Kadlec and Knight (1995) point out that a proper mass balance must satisfy the following conditions:

1.  The system for the mass balance must be defined carefully. The actual definition of the system is dependent on the context of the study, though a global term might be applied when the entire waterbody of a wetland is investigated. Alternatively, if only a section or particular element of the system is under investigation, an internal mass balance might be computed.
2.  The time period for the inputs and outputs must be specified. Fluxes vary across a range of temporal scales from short term tidal, to seasonal or even longer climatic event cycles. The finite period of evaluation must be put

into context with these longer term cycles if relatively accurate flux calculations are to be determined.

3.  All the inputs and outputs to the chosen system must be included. The concept of mass balance should be invoked to calculate one or a group of material fluxes.

4.  Any production and destruction reactions taking place within the wetland must be identified to take into account material changes.

5.  Waterborne constituent flows are determined by separate measurements of water flow and concentrations within the flow. As such, accurate water mass balance is a prerequisite to an accurate material flux mass balance.

6.  Where possible, it is desirable to demonstrate closure of the mass balance.

A number of studies have been undertaken to calculate water and constituent material fluxes on a range of scales from a range of environments,[6] but the controversy over whether certain wetlands actually are sinks or sources of various materials reflects the uncertainty surrounding these studies.

The adoption of a strictly hydrological approach to evaluating wetlands has its limitations, as direct evidence of hydrology is often difficult to obtain and may require monitoring over several years to identify seasonal variations. In many countries, monitoring of baseline data such as regional rainfall or tidal level exists, but care must be taken when extrapolating general regional data to a local site-specific situation.

For instance, considering coastal wetlands, tidal elevation data is available at many sites around the UK coastline. However, because of the effects of estuarine morphology and, locally, saltmarsh morphology on the progression of a tidal wave, extrapolation of a tidal elevation from a tidal station to a marsh elsewhere in the estuary is prone to considerable error. Likewise in fluvial systems, a complex network of wetlands act to store water and defuse flood events. Thus, water elevations on one floodplain need not equate to water levels elsewhere in the catchment. For extrapolation of information to be meaningful, a programme of detailed monitoring is required to provide inter-site correlation.

With these complexities in mind, it is rarely possible to find hydrological data specific to wetland systems, unless it has been subject to a specific site investigation. Fortunately, hydric soils and hydrophilic vegetation are reliable indirect indicators of wetland hydrology and can be used to infer its presence when the hydrology has not been altered. When hydrology has been altered, soil and vegetation might not be reliable indicators, and the hydrological status must be evaluated independently (National Research Council, 1995).

Hollis and Thompson (1998) point out that in hydrological studies of wetlands it is not unusual to gather data from non-standard sources such as a farmer's records, hydrological data from non-hydrological agencies, oral information from local people or photographic evidence. A major technical achievement will be to determine an average or characteristic water regime for sites on which there is no hydrological data, or for which hydrological data only covers a short time interval (National Research Council, 1995).

Many reviews acknowledge that the key hydrological factors underpinning the existence of a wetland are the rate and balance of water supply and loss and water storage (Hughes and Heathwaite, 1995). These factors control the variations in wetland character in terms of position of the water table and frequency of flooding events (Heathwaite *et al.* 1993). In a discussion of hydrological analysis requirements, Hollis and Thompson (1998) define six key hydrological variables which require monitoring for effective wetland management: water level regime, land–area–volume relationships, water balance, turnover rate, extremes and water quality.[7]

Water quality represents the compositional component of the water regime. Water richness in nutrients, oxygen, toxicants and pH levels and clarity are important in influencing wetland ecology and function. Many natural external and internal factors influence catchment water quality, including self-regulatory systems within wetlands, which act to recycle nutrients and contaminants (Mitsch and Gosselink, 1993). Increasingly though, anthropogenic factors are determining the quality of water in wetland systems. These forms of pollution may come from upstream discharges of chemicals or nutrients from outfalls and from non-point pollution sources such as runoff from agricultural land or otherwise developed areas.

A number of critical water quality impacts result from different land uses: change in suspended sediment load, organic matter and biochemical oxygen demand, bacteria, parasites and viruses, nutrient loads, heavy metals, organic toxins such as pesticides and hydrocarbons, acidification, salinization and temperature (Perry and Vanderklein, 1996). The effects of pollution on the long term sustainability of biota is not so well understood and so creation of threshold toxicant limits is difficult to ascertain, particularly if multiple pollutants are involved. The reason for this is that pollutants may act to increase the death rate or to reduce the birth rate, and up to a certain point these effects need not lead to continued population decline. Species populations may therefore withstand a certain amount of extra mortality or reduced reproduction, without declining in the long term (Newton, 1988).

In Table 3.3, three of the hydrological indicators proposed by Hollis and Thompson (1998) are presented, that is water level regime, level–area–volume relationships and water balance, to reflect the structural component of the wetland system. Composition basically reflects water quality and has been broken down into load components (sediment, organics, nutrients, toxicants, oxygen and organisms). Finally, turnover is used to indicate wetland hydrology processes.

*Table 3.3  Water regime indicators*

| Ecosystem | Indicator | Purpose/objective | Relevance for sustainable wetland management |
|---|---|---|---|
| Structure | 1. Water level regime | • describe the temporal variation in surface and sub-surface water level and reflect the relationship between water flux and wetland topography | • as diffusion of oxygen through aqueous solution is of the order of 10,000 times slower than through a porous medium, such as a drained soil, the position of the water table within a wetland is important in determining the microbial respiration and porewater geochemistry (Gambrell and Patrick, 1978), and hence macrophyte production<br>• integral component of material flux calculations<br>• depth of surface water influences availability of light to primary producers |
| | 2. Level–area–volume relationships | • describe the area flooded by waters and determine the geographical coverage of the wetland | • changes in LAVR impacts geographically on species composition and richness (Hughes and Heathwaite, 1995)<br>• essential to understand how hydrological input and outputs impact on ecological elements such as species distribution |
| | 3. Water balance | • indicate the interactions of precipitation, river flooding, groundwater discharge, tidal exchange, evapotranspiration, water abstraction, catchment management and topography on other hydrological characteristics | • frequently of inundation is a determinant of species composition and richness (Wheeler and Shaw, 1995; Hughes and Heathwaite, 1995)<br>• influences the budget of dissolved and particulate material across the wetland/catchment interface (Murray and Spencer, 1997)<br>• calculation of water balance is an important component of material budget calculations<br>• a positive water balance is essential for carbon preservation in peatlands (Mitsch and Gosselink, 1993) |
| Composition | 1. Sediment load | • indicate among and nature of sediment supplied or lost from a wetland system<br>• determine rate of sediment supply | • sedimentation rate determines topography–water level interactions in wetland systems<br>• important in determining long-term resilience of wetland to pressures such as rising sea level or subsidence<br>• the nature of the sediment may influence wetland resistance to remobilization by hydrological events and influence nature of biogeochemical interactions<br>• high sediment loads may be responsible for reduction of primary production of aquatic plants, blockage of fish gills, smothering of benthic organisms<br>• associated mobilisation of agricultural pollutants |
| | 2. Organic load | • indicate nature and supply or release of organic matter | • organic sedimentation rate influences carbon availability and below ground productivity possibly influences productivity of nearby ecosystems such as estuaries (Gordon *et al.*, 1985)<br>• microbial breakdown of untreated sewage or decaying vegetation can deplete oxygen levels within the water column, stressing oxygen dependent organisms<br>• a factor in the development of anoxia within waterlogged sediment influencing biogeochemical processes such as nutrient recycling and absorption of metals<br>• oxygen level important in the reduction of bacterial levels derived from sewage<br>• required as part of carbon flux calculations<br>• if known amount of oxygen required to degrade organic matter can estimate effect on BOD |
| | 3. Nutrient load | • indicate nature and supply or release of nutrients | • wetlands require an influx of nutrients for biomass growth |

| | | | |
|---|---|---|---|
| | | • estimate potential for eutrophication | • excess loads of nitrogen and phosphorus may stimulate algal blooms with associated impacts on biodiversity and water quality<br>• nutrients may pose a health hazard in high concentrations |
| Composition | 4. Toxicant load | • indicate potential for health implications for humans and change in organism diversity within ecosystem | • toxicant level is one of a number of stress factors which may cumulatively lead to a reduction in species diversity (Stansfield et al., 1989)<br>• although the effects of excess toxic loading are often apparent in mass mortality of organisms it is usually difficult to correlate toxicant load at subcritical levels directly with species abundance because of non-linear relationships and additive effects with other factors and toxicants (Newton, 1988) |
| | 5. Oxygen level | • indicate oxygen availability to dependent organisms<br>• indicate nature of bacterial respiration taking place and hence possible biogeochemical processes<br>• indicate the potential for metal assimilation within wetland soils | • depletion of oxygen can lead to stress on oxygen dependent organisms and reduction in species diversity<br>• presence of oxic and anoxic zones within sediment influences nutrient cycling rate (Kadlec and Knight, 1995)<br>• organic decomposition occurs most rapidly under oxic conditions<br>• redox determines mobility of inorganic pollutants, such as metals, thus determining the assimilative capacity of the wetland system and bioavailability of pollutants<br>• rate of oxygen consumption can be used to investigate rate of biogeochemical processes<br>• BOD reflects utilization of oxygen by respiration and availability to oxygen dependent organisms |
| | 6. Bacteria, viruses and water-borne parasites | • indicate potential health hazards | • globally water-borne diseases and parasites pose perhaps the greatest threat to human health, particularly in the developing world (Nash, 1993)<br>• various species of bacteria are important in the regulation of water quality by assimilating DOC (Cole and Pace, 1995), releasing nutrients during the remineralization of organic matter (Anderson, 1992) or acting as both source and sink for organic nitrogen (Goldman et al., 1987; Saunders and Purdie, 1998)<br>• bacterial breakdown of organic matter may lead to reduced oxygen levels in water |
| | 7. Temperature | • determine rate at which chemical reactions takes place both inorganically and biologically mediated | • temperature controls rates of biochemical process, determining factors such as pore water redox, primary productivity, organic decomposition and species diversity (e.g. Newman and Clausen, 1997)<br>• nitrogen flux processes such as ammonification, nitrification and denitrification are all temperature dependent (Kadlec and Knight, 1995)<br>• phosphorus absorption to substratum is temperature-correlated due to sensitivity to redox (Nichols, 1983)<br>• an important component of biochemical and geochemical mass balance and flux calculations |
| Function | 1. Turnover rate | • describe the rate at which water and constituents are transmitted through the wetland system | • turnover rate determines the throughput rate of water constituents through the wetland<br>• influences biochemical wetland properties such as nutrient accumulation and environmental quality by flushing of pollutants and water-borne organisms (Lent et al. 1997)<br>• may influence rate of sediment supply or removal from wetlands |

# 7   BIODIVERSITY DOMAIN INDICATORS

Biological diversity was abbreviated into biodiversity in the mid 1980s to capture the essence of research into the variety and richness of life on Earth (Jeffries, 1997). This variety of life can be studied at different levels: genetic variation, number of species or ecosystems. Nowadays, biodiversity is understood as consisting of more than just species diversity, although in practice it is still commonly measured by counting the number of species in an area and the turnover of species among areas (Williams and Gaston, 1994).

Biodiversity can be defined and measured from the perspective of different scientific disciplines such as systems ecology or biology at different hierarchical, spatial and temporal scales. In the two most widely cited definitions, by the American Office of Technology Assessment and the Biodiversity Convention,[8] biodiversity comprises both variety and variability and covers both biotic and abiotic complexes. The inclusion of the word 'variability' besides variety or diversity among living organisms and the emphasis on both biotic and abiotic components in both definitions illustrates the difficulty in pinpointing the concept of biodiversity to a single scale of measurement and introduces at the same time a strong analytical aspect to its measurement.

Three main biodiversity monitoring categories or levels can be distinguished in the literature (for example Noss, 1990): genetic diversity, taxonomic diversity and ecological diversity. These categories originate from distinct 'schools' or disciplines within biology and systems ecology with different emphasis or focus on biodiversity as the outcome of evolutionary and ecological processes (Jeffries, 1997). The ecological domain of biodiversity focuses mainly on populations, communities or ecosystems and their interactions with the physical environment, whereas the evolutionary domain can be defined by a focus on genetic processes and patterns and the variation they create.

Genetic and subcellular diversity includes all biodiversity expressed within individual cells plus non-cellular organisms such as viruses. Genetic variation may be driven by the physical environment, but genetic diversity is the main focus point linked to species since genetic processes could function without any environmental influence. Without genetic variation, evolution and adaptation cannot occur (Jermy *et al.*, 1995). Even when a habitat has been preserved, evolution is still going on, in the form of longer term adaptation to climatic or other environmental change or on a shorter timescale. Even in the best preserved habitats, ecological communities are dynamic entities with species interacting with each other. The measurement of genetic diversity is a rapidly evolving area (Jeffries, 1997).

Taxonomic diversity refers to species diversity and is the most popular idea behind biodiversity. Taxonomy is the theory and practice of describing the

diversity of organisms and the arrangement of these organisms into classifications. The most fundamental unit for taxonomic research is the individual
organism, while the species is widely accepted as the most basic of natural
units. However, a great deal of disagreement exists over what a species exactly
is. Two main concepts exist, which differ in emphasis on the reproductive
process and genetic correlation (Jermy *et al.*, 1995). The first one defines
species as 'groups of interbreeding natural populations isolated from other
such groups' (Mayr, 1969), while the second one defines species as 'the smallest aggregation of populations diagnosable by a unique combination of character states in comparable individuals' (Nixon and Wheeler, 1990). Given the
definition of biodiversity in the Biodiversity Convention (see note 8 at the end
of this chapter), the latter seems to be a more appropriate definition of species,
since the former excludes a large number of organisms, particularly plants,
which reproduce asexually.

After species have been defined, their classification based on a hierarchical
pattern of genetic relationships or descendence, is an important next step for
the purpose of wider extrapolation and estimation of the distribution of species
richness. Cladistic analysis or cladograms are widely accepted as providing an
efficient method for representing information about organisms and seem to be
regarded as having a firm foundation for establishing relationships between
different organisms. A cladogram is based on three main assumptions (Farris
*et al.*, 1970; WCMC, 1992): (1) features shared by organisms form a hier-
archic pattern; (2) this pattern can be expressed as a branching diagram; (3)
each branching point symbolizes the features held in common by all the
species arising from that node.

Besides the existence of a hierarchy in taxa based on genetic relationships
or descendence, another hierarchy can be found in the feeding interactions
between the biotic components of an ecosystem (also called ecological
community) as part of the food web (for example Putman, 1994). A food chain
is an energy path or linear sequence of links that depicts who eats whom or
what. Primary producers (or autotrophs) comprise the first trophic level. These
species (mainly green plants but also algae and cyanobacteria in some ecosystems) are responsible for trapping solar energy and converting it into chemical
energy and tissue biomass, which may then be utilized by the rest of the
ecosystem. All other members of the community are dependent on the primary
producers for energy, either directly or indirectly. Because some energy is used
at each trophic level and the transfer of energy between trophic levels is never
completely efficient, less energy is available at higher trophic levels.

Consumers (or heterotrophs) are animals and micro-organisms (and occa-
sionally plants) that feed on primary producers and each other. The second
trophic level is made up of primary consumers (herbivores which feed directly
on primary producers), while secondary consumers (carnivores which feed on

herbivores) comprise the third trophic level, and tertiary consumers (carnivores which feed on other carnivores) comprise the fourth. Omnivorous animals may be given partial representation in several trophic levels in proportion to the composition of their diet. Decomposers (also classified as heterotrophs) are the species which feed on and break down dead plant and animal material, making the component nutrients available to the system again. Understanding the flow of energy through an ecosystem is important for conservation and any sustainable exploitation of that system (Jermy *et al.*, 1995).

Biodiversity indicators are being compiled in massive numbers despite arguments that they are answers to questions which have not yet been articulated (for example Norris and Norris, 1995). Monitoring of biodiversity usually occurs at species level. Higher taxa can, for example, be used as an indicator to predict overall biodiversity. The use of selected species groups as indicators of overall biodiversity is attractive because if suitable indicator relationships can be shown to exist, sampling for just the selected species will greatly reduce survey costs. However, too often evidence is lacking that a relationship does exist between the indicator group and overall biodiversity (Williams and Gaston, 1994).

Adequate definition of the spatial and temporal scales on which diversity is measured is of paramount importance (Rosenzweig, 1995). For example, species-area curves support the rule that more species will be found if a larger area is sampled. Seasonal variation and corresponding migratory patterns of for example birds, on the other hand, cause diversity to oscillate through the year. The relationship between succession after natural or human induced disturbances and diversity is rather unclear. Some empirical research exists (see Rosenzweig, 1995 for an overview), but often not more than a few years is spent on monitoring communities.

Plant and animal species have also been used as indicators of environmental conditions such as water quality (Norris and Norris, 1995) or habitat quality (for example Weller, 1988). Most uncertainty seems to focus on their validity, that is, that they actually measure those features of the environment that are of interest, and that they respond in a meaningful way with respect to environmental change. However, given the complexity of natural systems, the probability is small that a single species can serve as an index of the structure and functioning of an ecological community or even an entire ecosystem (Ward, 1978; Cairns, 1986). Assuming that the relevant species–habitat relationships are adequately modelled, population density has been used as an indicator of habitat quality for that species or one or more species have been used to indicate habitat suitability for other species. Landres *et al.* (1988) identified several problems when using indicators to assess habitat quality. Weller (1988) argues that in order to derive meaningful habitat patterns and impact assessments, it is essential to understand water regimes, vegetation patterns and vertebrate habitat strategies. A single measure may be highly misleading given that the structure of vegetation and communities is dynamic.

Noss (1990) lists five categories of species that may warrant special monitoring or protection:

1.  Ecological indicators: species that signal the effects of perturbations on a number of other species with similar habitat requirements.
2.  Keystones: pivotal species upon which the diversity of a large part of the community depends.
3.  Umbrellas: species with large area requirements which, if given sufficient protected habitat area, will bring many other species under protection.
4.  Flagships: popular, charismatic species that serve as symbols and rallying points for major conservation initiatives.
5.  Vulnerables: species that are rare, genetically impoverished, dependent on patchy or unpredictable resources, extremely variable in population density, persecuted or otherwise prone to extinction in human-dominated landscapes.

Keystone species are identified by Jermy *et al.* (1995) as playing a crucial role in an ecosystem. Examples of groups which include keystone species are predators, parasites and pathogens which help to maintain population levels of prey and host species, large herbivores and termites which control ecological succession, species that create and maintain landscape features such as waterholes and wallows in arid areas, pollinators, seed dispersers and other obligate mutualists, and plants that provide a resource in time of scarcity.

Some keystone species are essential for the formation of the biotope in which they live or for ecosystem functioning. Closely related to this is the idea of guilds, that is functional groups or clusters of species interacting among themselves more strongly than with other elements of the community (for example Keddy, 1990; Putman, 1994). These species perform a similar function in a given ecosystem.

Regarding this latter point, three competing theories as to how an ecosystem might respond to loss of species diversity exist (Jermy *et al.* 1995). The 'redundant species' hypothesis suggests that there is a minimum set of species required for an ecosystem to function and that adding or losing others does not affect processes (Walker, 1992; Lawton and Brown, 1993). The 'rivet' hypothesis (Ehrlich and Ehrlich, 1981) suggests that all species are essential and that as species are lost, functioning is impaired. The 'idiosyncratic response' hypothesis, finally, suggests that functions change when diversity changes, but in an unpredictable way (Vitousek and Hooper, 1993; Lawton, 1994).

Experimental tests of these hypotheses in controlled laboratory conditions using a controlled environmental chamber (ecotron), suggest that most processes (decomposition rates, nutrient uptake and so on) vary idiosyncratically with species richness, but that both uptake of carbon dioxide and plant productivity declined as species richness declined, as predicted by the rivet hypothesis (Naeem *et al.*, 1994 and 1995). As hypothesized in systems theory, it seems that a greater number of links in a food web will provide more opportunities for checks and balances should any environmental change occur.

In Table 3.4 the traditional focus on species is reflected in the compilation of biodiversity indicators, usually because of the time and costs involved in monitoring genetic variety. However, these indicators will be complemented with relevant environmental and ecological habitat variables. This corresponds to the approach outlined by Noss (1990), whose breakdown of biodiversity into structural, compositional and functional biodiversity has been used as the overarching framework for ecosystem integrity assessment in this discussion.

In view of the importance of food chains to ecosystem structure, composition and functioning, the food web will be the central concept in the compilation of biodiversity indicators. This means that trophic levels will provide the hierarchy within this indicator sphere; while the physical environment establishes the limits to food chains and food webs as measured in the previous sections in terms of landscape and water regime indicators.

In order to determine the consequences of environmental impacts on food webs, the structure of wetland food chains has to be determined first (see Table 3.1) and secondly the impact of environmental variability (for example through human disturbance) on the food web. In terms of habitat and food support, landscape parameters such as wetland size, shape, connectivity and distances between wetlands need to be measured to evaluate potential cumulative impacts (Klopatek, 1988). Briand (1983) found that for a given number of species, the trophic linkage (connectance) in the food web is significantly lower in variable than in constant environments, that is habitats in constant environments possess longer food chains whereas those with variable environments have greater widths.

Many species are obligately dependent on wetlands, while many others facultatively use wetlands because of the proportionately higher amounts and quality of food resources present (Weller, 1988). Using one or more vertebrates to indicate environmental conditions or habitat quality (for that particular and other species) has to be based on established valid relationships between species and the environmental conditions or habitat features of interest. Indicator species often have little to say about overall environmental trends and may have deluded management authorities into thinking that all is well with an environment simply because an indicator is thriving (Noss, 1990).

Landress *et al.* (1988) address the criteria used in the past to select species

*Table 3.4  Biodiversity indicators*

| Ecosystem | Indicator | Purpose/objective | Relevance for sustainable wetland management |
|---|---|---|---|
| Structure | 1. Trophic levels of food web | • describe food chain in wetland<br>• indicate energy transfer levels | • food chain support important wetland function<br>• dependency of species on specific trophic structure<br>• important determinant in calculation of primary productivity<br>• biodiversity has a closer relationship to the amount of food resource present than to area alone (Martin and Karr, 1986) |
| Composition | 1. Key species | • indicate species richness<br>• indicate overall wildlife habitat quality<br>• indicate specific environmental conditions | • keystone species are essential for the formation of the biotope in which they live or for ecosystem functioning |
| | 2. Umbrella species | • indicate minimum wildlife habitat require-ments<br>• indicate overall species richness | • empirical evidence for the existence of minimum wetland size for particular bird species (e.g. Brown and Dinsmore, 1986)<br>• the larger the area required, the more likely it is to include the spectrum of resources needed by other organisms dependent on that particular habitat |
| Function | 1. Productivity | • biomass productivity indicator<br>• energy transfer efficiency indicator | • insight into the different mechanics and efficiency of operation at trophic levels<br>• may have profound implications for whole wetland ecosystem structure and functioning given possible links between energy flows and diversity (Odum, 1975)<br>• inherently unstable structures may in practice prove stable if energy flows through the system are high enough (DeAngelis, 1980) |

indicators for ecological or habitat assessment. From these, we will adopt the following three for the purpose of assessing overall wetland ecosystem integrity:

1.  Area requirement: if a single species is used as an indicator of habitat quality or of a community, it is commonly assumed that the species should require a large area for its territory. Ideally, the indicator would have greater area requirements than any other species in the community, because the larger the area required, the more likely it is to include the spectrum of resources needed by other organisms dependent on that particular habitat. These species are usually called umbrella species (see above). Brown and Dinsmore (1986) found empirical evidence for the existence of minimum wetland size for particular bird species (5 ha). As wetland size increases, the number of individuals and species increase in some pattern, often a sigmoid curve, as well. However, Martin and Karr (1986) showed that diversity has a closer relationship to the amount of food resource present than to area alone, another reason for making the food web a central concept in the biodiversity indicators sphere.

2.  Specialists: species vary in the range of resources or habitats used, each species falling somewhere along a specialist–generalist continuum. Odum (1971) suggested that specialists are better indicators because they are more sensitive to habitat changes. Sensitivity to environmental conditions obviously is a necessary prerequisite to the use of species as indicators of environmental change. In wetlands, Keddy *et al.* (1993) have suggested that amphibians are sensitive to a wide range of contaminants because of their semipermeable skin and the fact that they inhabit both aquatic and terrestrial habitats. However, their reliance on more than one habitat and hence exposure to a variety of possible disturbances or contaminants makes it at the same time increasingly difficult to associate their decline with one or more specific environmental condition.

3.  Residency status: since non-permanent or migratory species are subject to a variety of sources of mortality, it may be tricky to use them to indicate environmental conditions on-site. A decline in their abundance may be unrelated to habitat conditions on the breeding or foraging grounds. Permanent (not necessarily endemic) residents will hence usually be more reliable indicators. However, it is still important to take into account the spatial and temporal scale on which species density is measured such as the openness of the ecosystem and succession stages (see for example Rosenzweig, 1995). Population dynamics such as generation times or life cycles and the impact of changing environmental conditions on evolutionary change between generations must also be considered (see for example Begon and Mortimer, 1992).

Summarizing, umbrella and keystone species will be identified to indicate (1) overall wetland biodiversity, (2) wetland habitat quantity and quality and (3) environmental conditions.

Finally, the functional biodiversity component will be indicated by biomass. In wetlands, biomass appears to be an excellent indicator of trophic status (Keddy *et al.*, 1993), although Onuf and Quammen (1986) and Klopatek (1988) conclude that the primary productivity of a wetland (that is the total amount of energy captured within a community by the producer level) is not a critical variable in determining wetland food chain support. On the other hand, Odum (1975) suggested that variation in type, quantity and quality of energy flows through communities may have profound implications for its whole structure and functioning given possible links between energy flows and diversity. DeAngelis (1980) furthermore observes that inherently unstable structures may in practice prove stable if energy flows through the system are high enough. Putman (1994) considers four aspects of resource flows through communities: the amount of energy handled by the system, the efficiency of energy transfer between trophic levels, the rate or speed of energy flow and the nature of associated nutrient cycles (open or closed, sedimentary or non-sedimentary). Differences in the efficiency of energy transfer at different trophic levels offer insight into the different mechanics and efficiency of operation at these levels. Keddy *et al.* (1993) propose the use of plant biomass as a performance indicator of primary producers since it is not only relatively easy to monitor, but may also provide more information than the biomass of a few selected species in view of the response time to the cumulative effects of nutrients available over a long period of time.

# 8   DISCUSSION AND FUTURE RESEARCH

In this chapter, an overview was presented of existing models to compile environmental indicators to monitor and assess wetland management. An attempt was made to integrate existing indicators put forward in different scientific disciplines into a coherent indicator framework. The concept of ecosystem integrity was taken as an organizing principle behind the framework. The breakdown in structural, compositional and functional system components, originally proposed in the context of biodiversity assessment techniques, was used to organize the indicator sets which covered three highly interrelated domains or aspects of wetland ecosystems: landscape, water regime and biodiversity.

A set of 24 quantitative and qualitative environmental indicators was taken from the literature to assess the impact of pressures on wetland ecosystems. The organization of the indicators into three distinct fields, according to three different ecosystem components may suggest independency between indicators or indicator sets. However, in fact it is the interdependency and compatibility within and between the indicators for ecosystem components and wetland domains across different scales and hierarchies that is of primary interest and which provides the main challenge to produce a genuinely integrated indicator framework. In the sections in which the indicator sets were discussed (sections 4–6), an attempt was made to make explicit the importance of interrelatedness or interdependency. However, this could only be done in a very limited way based on current scientific understanding.

An important next step will be to assess the extent to which this framework results in useful and meaningful information in terms of the systems approach for assessing the sustainability of wetland ecosystem use and management. In other words, how compatible and comparable are the various indicators across scales and to what extent do they complement each other in order to sketch as much as possible a comprehensive and complete picture, while respecting at the same time real resource constraints (time and money) in monitoring efforts. The indicators measure different dimensions of wetland ecosystems and the comparability or amount of 'common ground' of these different indicators has to be assessed in different case studies.

In practice, many of the indicators may consist of several sub-indicators, depending on the specific wetland site or system of interest, possibly resulting in something like an indicator tree or hierarchy. Also, some indicators will be more relevant than others, again depending on the specific conditions or circumstances prevailing at different wetland sites or within specific systems. Hence, it is important to bear in mind that the indicator sets are in this sense not absolute to the overall assessment of wetland ecosystems. Their applicability, meaningfulness and usefulness, especially in relation to each other, in wetland management practices have to be considered carefully in each specific situation.

It is also important to point out that the indicators do not indicate whether or not specific management intervention or environmental change maintains ecosystem integrity. In other words, the presented indicators are not sustainability indicators. They reflect certain aspects of a system state which are considered relevant, based on scientific understanding of wetland ecosystems, in order to be able to assess the impacts of human activities or to evaluate management intervention in a comprehensive and reliable way. In order to assess sustainable use of wetlands, benchmarks or reference points are needed, which can be partly established via scientific understanding of, for example, absorption or carrying capacities of an ecosystem, but often include normative judgements about wetland conservation.

Furthermore, the selection of specific indicators is arbitrary. Besides scientific importance other selection criteria for the indicator sets presented were expected ease of observation and computation and cost-effectiveness. Ideally one would perhaps also look at genetic variety present in wetlands in order to get a comprehensive view of possible wetland degradation, but this will be a time consuming and expensive exercise. Hence our reliance, *inter alia*, on species indicators. On the other hand, very little is known about the exact role of specific species in an ecosystem and to what extent they support specific ecosystem functions.

Finally, most of the indicators presented here are state variables related to the effects of human intervention on wetland ecosystems. Land-use change in Table 3.2 is the only indicator that directly relates to an environmental pressure. When comparing the outcome of the state indicators with some targeted reference state or situation, insight is needed into the often complex relationship between cause and effect in order to be able to change (reduce) existing pressures on ecosystems. The suggested indicators may furthermore monitor environmental change at different points along a continuum from source to effect. Hence, given known interdependency, the efficiency of monitoring may be enhanced by focusing on a reduced number of selected points along this continuum.

## NOTES

1. The concept of ecosystem integrity covers various natural scientific disciplines with systems science playing an important synthesizing background role. The concept of ecosystem integrity was first introduced by Leopold (1989) and has since been defined in various ways in ecological and biological literature. Over the past decade, it has nevertheless grown in influence, suggesting a transition in societal understanding of our relationship to the physical, chemical and biological environment (Karr, 1993). Although there exists a relatively well developed body of literature about ecosystem integrity, especially for large aquatic ecosystems, there seems to be a lack of general agreement amongst experts about the meaning and relevance of the concept and the measures needed to index it.
2. For example, primary productivity or nutrient cycling may remain relatively constant while species composition changes (Harcombe, 1977; Rapport *et al.*, 1985) or dominant species are removed (Foster *et al.*, 1980).
3. Mitsch (1994) distinguishes between two hierarchical levels of analysis: the ecosystem level which covers several $km^2$ spatially and the landscape level which covers hundreds of $km^2$.
4. River basin management is a more familiar term in water resources management than ecoregional management. River basin management has become synonymous with water resources management. It is accepted that basins share similar properties and concerns and represent a logical framework from which to manage. The dominance of river basin management reflects the historical dominance of the linear, upstream–downstream orientation of hydrologists and managers. It is less suited to management of non-linear lakes, groundwaters or wetlands (Perry and Vanderklein, 1996).
5. Mitsch (1994) includes a number of examples.
6. In this study we have separated the compositional properties of water quality from the structural hydrological characteristics.
7. The Office of Technology Assessment (OTA) defines biodiversity as 'the variety and variability among living organisms and the ecological complexes in which they occur' (OTA, 1987).

8. The Biodiversity Convention at the UN Conference on Environment and Development in Rio de Janeiro in 1992 defines biodiversity as 'the variability among living organisms from all sources including terrestrial, marine and other aquatic ecosystems and ecological complexes of which they are a part: this includes diversity within species, between species and of ecosystems'.

# REFERENCES

Anderson, T.R. (1992), 'Modelling the influence of food C: N ratio and respiration on growth and nitrogen excretion in marine zooplankton and bacteria', *Journal of Plankton Research*, **14**(12), 1645–71.

Angermeier, P.L. and J.R. Karr (1994), 'Biological integrity versus biological diversity as policy directives', *BioScience*, **44**, 690–97.

Bailey, R.G. (1987), 'Suggested hierarchy of criteria for multiscale ecosystem mapping', *Landscape and Urban Planning*, **14**, 313–19.

Begon, M. and M. Mortimer (1992*), Population Ecology: a Unified Study of Animals and Plants*, Oxford: Blackwell Scientific Publications.

Bell, S.S., M.S. Fonseca and L.B. Motten (1997), 'Linking restoration and landscape ecology', *Restoration Ecology*, **5**, 318–23.

Briand, F. (1983), 'Biogeographic patterns in food web theory', in D.L. DeAngelis, W.M. Post and G. Sugihara (eds), *Current Trends in Web Theory*, ORNL-TM 5983, Oak Ridge National Laboratory, Oak Ridge, Tennessee.

Brinson, M.M. (1993), *A Hydrogeomorphic Classification for Wetlands*, Wetlands Research Program Technical Report WRP-DE-4, US Army Corps of Engineers, Waterway Experiment Station, Vicksburg, MS: Bridgham and Richardson.

Brown, M. and J.J. Dinsmore (1986), 'Implications of marsh size and isolation for marsh bird management', *Journal of Wildlife Management*, **50**, 392–97.

Cairns, J. Jr. (1986), 'The myth of the most sensitive species', *Bioscience*, **36**, 670–72.

Cattrijsse, A., R. Hederick and J.M. Dankwa (1997), 'Nursery function of an estuarine tidal marsh for the brown shrimp Crangon crangon,' *Journal of Sea Research*, **38**, 109–21.

Clayton, A.M.H. and N.J. Radcliffe (1996), *Sustainability: A Systems Approach*, London: Earthscan Publications.

Cole, J.J. and M.L. Pace (1995), 'Bacterial secondary production in oxic and anoxic fresh-waters', *Limnology and Oceanography*, **40**(6), 1019–27.

Committee on Characterization of Wetlands (CCW) (1995), in National Research Council (1995), *Wetlands; Characteristics and Boundaries*, Washington, DC: National Academy Press.

Costanza, R. (1992), 'Toward an operational definition of ecosystem health', in R. Costanza, B.G. Norton and B.D. Haskell (eds), *Ecosystem Health: New Goals for Environmental Management*, Washington, DC: Island Press.

Costanza, R., B.G. Norton and B.D. Haskall (eds) (1992), *Ecosystem Health*, Covelo, CA: Island Press.

Costanza, R., R. d'Arge, R. de Groot, S. Farber, M. Grasso, B. Hannon, K. Limburg, S. Naeem, R.V. O'Neill, J. Paruelo, R.G. Raskin, P. Sutton and M. van den Belt (1997), 'The value of the world's ecosystem services and natural capital', *Nature*, **387**: 253–60.

Cowardin, L.M., V. Carter, F.C. Golet and E.T. LaRoe, (1979), *Classification of Wetlands and Deepwater Habitats of the United States*, FWS/OBS-79/31, US Fish and Wildlife Service, Washington, DC.

DeAngelis, D.L. (1980), 'Energy flow, nutrient cycling and ecosystem resilience', *Ecology*, **61**, 764–71.

Diamond, J.M. (1975), 'The island dilemma: lessons of modern biogeographic studies for the design of natural preserves', *Biological Conservation*, **7**, 129–146S.

Ehrlich, P.R. and A. Ehrlich (1981), *Extinction: The Causes of the Disappearance of Species*, New York: Random House.

Farris, J.S., A.G. Kluge and M.J. Eckhardt (1970), 'A numerical approach to phylogenetic analysis', *Systematic Zoology*, **19**, 172–89.

Foster, M.M., P.M. Vitousek and P.A. Randolph (1980), 'The effect of Ambrosia artemisiifolia on nutrient cycling in first-year old-field', *American Midland Nature*, **100**, 106–13.

Franklin, J.F., K. Cromack and W. Denison (1981), *Ecological Characteristics of Old-Growth Douglas-Fir Forests*, USDA Forest Service General Technical Report PNW-118, Pacific Northwest Forest and Range Experiment Station, Portland, Oregon.

Gallant, A.L., T.R. Whittier, D.P. Larsen, J.M. Omernik and R.M. Hughes (1989), *Regionalization as a Tool for Managing Environmental Resources*, EPA Research and Development Report EPA/600/3-89/060, US EPA Environmental Research Laboratory, Corvallis, OR.

Gambrell, R.P. and W.H. Patrick, Jr. (1978), 'Chemical and microbiological properties of anaerobic soils and sediments', in D.D. Hook and R.M.M. Crawford (eds), *Plant Life in Anaerobic Environments*, Ann Arbor, MI: Ann Arbor Science.

Gerrard, J. (1992), *Soil Geomorphology. An Integration of Pedology and Geomorphology*, London: Chapman and Hall.

Goldman, J.C., D.A. Caron and M.R. Dennett (1987), 'Regulation of gross growth efficiency and ammonium regeneration in bacteria by substrate', *Limnology and Oceanography*, **32**(6), 1239–52.

Gordon, D.C. Jr., P.J. Cranford and C. Desplanque (1985), 'Observations on the ecological importance of salt marshes in the Cumberland Basin, a macrotidal estuary in the Bay of Fundy', *Estuarine, Coastal and Shelf Science*, **20**, 205–27.

Harcombe, P.A. (1977), 'Nutrient accumulation by vegetation during the first year of recovery of a tropical rain forest ecosystem', in J. Cairns Jr., K.L. Dickson and E.E. Herricks (eds), *Recovery and Restoration of Damaged Ecosystems*, Charlottesville: University Press of Virginia.

Heathwaite, A.L., R. Eggelsmann and K.-H. Göttlich (1993), 'Ecohydrology, mire drainage and mire conservation', in A.L. Heathwaite and K.-H. Göttlich (eds), *Mires: Process, Exploitation and Conservation*, Chichester: John Wiley and Sons.

Holling, C.S. (1986), 'The resilience of terrestrial ecosystems: local surprise and global change', in W.C. Clark and R.E. Munn (eds), *Sustainable Development of the Biosphere*, Cambridge: Cambridge University Press.

Hollis, G.E. and J.R. Thompson (1998), 'Hydrological data for wetland management', *Water and Environmental Management*, **12**(1), 9–17.

Hughes, J. and A.L. Heathwaite (1995), *Hydrology and Hydrochemistry of British Wetlands*, London: John Wiley and Sons.

Jeffries, M.J. (1997), *Biodiversity and Conservation*, London: Routledge.

Jermy, A.C., D. Long, M.J.S. Sands, N.E. Stork and S. Winser (eds) (1995), *Biodiversity Assessment: A Guide to Good Practice*, Department of the Environment/HMSO, London.

Johnston, C.A. (1994), 'Cumulative impacts to wetlands', *Wetlands*, **14**, 47–55.

Kadlec, R.H. and R.L. Knight (1995), *Treatment Wetlands*, London: Lewis Publishers.

Karr, J.R. (1993), 'Measuring biological integrity: lessons from streams', in S. Woodley, J. Kay and G. Francis, *Ecological Integrity and the Management of Ecosystems*, sponsored by Heritage Resources Centre, University of Waterloo and Canadian Parks Service, Ottawa: St. Lucie Press.

Keddy, P.A. (1990), 'Competitive hierarchies and centrifugal organization in plant communities', in J.B. Grace and D. Tilman (eds), *Perspective on Plant Competition*, New York: Academic Press.

Keddy, P.A., H.T. Lee and I.C. Wisheu (1993), 'Choosing indicators of ecosystem integrity: wetlands as a model system', in S. Woodley, J. Kay and G. Francis, *Ecological Integrity and the Management of Ecosystems*, sponsored by Heritage Resources Centre, University of Waterloo and Canadian Parks Service, Ottawa: St. Lucie Press.

King, A.W. (1993), 'Considerations of scale and hierarchy', in S. Woodley, J. Kay and G. Francis, *Ecological Integrity and the Management of Ecosystems*, sponsored by Heritage Resources Centre, University of Waterloo and Canadian Parks Service, Ottawa: St. Lucie Press.

Klopatek, J.M. (1988), 'Some thoughts on using a landscape framework to address cumulative impacts on wetland food chain support', *Environmental Management*, **12**(5), 703–11.

Kupfer, J.A. (1995), 'Landscape ecology and biogeography', *Progress in Physical Geography*, **19**, 18–34.

Landres, P.B., J. Verner and J.W. Thomas (1988), 'Ecological uses of vertebrate indicator species: a critique', *Conservation Biology*, **2**(4), 316–28.

Lawton, J.H. (1994), 'What do species do in ecosystems?', *Oikos*, **71**, 367–74.

Lawton, J.H. and V.K. Brown (1993), 'Redundancy in ecosystems', in E-D. Schultz and H.A. Mooney (eds), *Biodiversity and Ecosystem Function*, Ecological Studies no. 99, 255–270, Berlin: Springer-Verlag.

Lent, R.M., P.K. Weiskel, F.P. Lyford and D.S. Armstrong (1997), 'Hydrologic indicies for nontidal wetlands', *Wetlands*, **17**(1), 19–30.

Leopold, A. (1989), *A Sand County Almanac*, Oxford: Oxford University Press.

Martin, T.E. and J.R. Karr (1986), 'Patch utilization by migrating birds: resource oriented?', *Ornis Scandinavica*, **17**, 165–74.

Mayr, E. (1969), *Principles of Systematic Zoology*, New York: McGraw-Hill.

Merriam, G. (1991), 'Corridors and connectivity: animal populations in heterogeneous environments', in D.A. Sanders and R.J. Hobbs (eds), *Nature Conservation 2: the Role of Corridors*, Chipping Norton, NSW: Surrey Beatty and Sons, pp. 133–142.

Mitsch, W.J. (1992), 'Landscape design and the role of created, restored and natural riparian wetlands in controlling nonpoint source pollution', *Ecological Engineering*, **1**, 27–47.

Mitsch, W.J. (ed.) (1994), *Global Wetlands: Old World and New*, Amsterdam: Elsevier.

Mitsch, W.J. and J.G. Gosselink (1993), *Wetlands*, New York: van Nostrand Reinhold.

Murray, A.L. and T. Spencer (1997), 'On the wisdom of calculating annual material budgets in tidal wetlands', *Marine Ecology Progress Series*, **150**(1–3), 207–16.

Naeem, S., L.J. Thompson, S.P. Lawler, J.H. Lawton and R.M. Woodfin (1994), 'Declining biodiversity can alter the performance of ecosystems', *Nature*, **368**, 734–7.

Naeem, S., L.J. Thompson, S.P. Lawler, J.H. Lawton and R.M. Woodfin (1995), 'Empirical evidence that declining species diversity may alter the performance of terrestrial ecosystems', *Philosophical Transactions of the Royal Society, London*, Series B, **347**, 249–62.

Nash, L. (1993), 'Water quality and health', in P. Gleick (ed.), *Water in Crisis: A Guide to the World's Fresh Water Resources*, Oxford: Oxford University Press.

National Research Council (1995), *Wetlands; Characteristics and Boundaries*, Washington, DC: National Academy Press.

Newman, J.M. and J.C. Clausen (1997), 'Seasonal effectiveness of a constructed wetland for processing milkhouse wastewater', *Wetlands*, **17**(3), 375–82.

Newton, I. (1988), 'Determination of critical pollutant levels in wild populations, with examples from organochlorine insecticides in birds of prey', *Environmental Pollution*, **55**, 29–40.

Nichols, D.S. (1983), 'Capacity of natural wetlands to remove nutrients from waste-water', *Journal of Water Pollution Control*, **55**, 495–505.

Nixon, K.C. and Q.D. Wheeler (1990), 'An amplification of the phylogenetic species concept', *Cladistics*, **6**, 211–23.

Norris, R.H. and K.R. Norris (1995), 'The need for biological assessment of water quality: Australian perspective', *Australian Journal of Ecology*, **20**, 1–6.

Noss, R.F. (1983), 'A regional landscape approach to maintain diversity', *BioScience*, **33**, 700–706.

Noss, R.F. (1987), 'From plant communities to landscapes in conservation inventories: a look at The Nature Conservancy (USA)', *Biological Conservation*, **41**, 11–37.

Noss, R.F. (1990), 'Indicators for monitoring biodiversity: a hierarchical approach', *Conservation Biology*, **4**(4), 355–64.

Noss, R.F. and L.D. Harris (1986), 'Nodes, networks and MUMs: preserving diversity at all scales', *Environmental Management*, **10**, 299–309.

Odum, E.P. (1971), *Fundamentals of Ecology*, third edition, Philadelphia, PA: W.B. Saunders.

Odum, E.P. (1975), 'Diversity as a function of energy flow', in W.H. van Dobben and R.H. Lowe-McConnell (eds), *Unifying Concepts in Ecology*, The Hague: W. Junk.

OECD (1994), *Environmental Indicators*, Paris: Organisation for Economic Co-operation and Development.

Office of Technology Assessment, (OTA) (1987), *Technologies to Maintain Biological Diversity*, Washington, DC: US Government Printing Office.

Ogawa, H. and J.W. Male (1986), 'Simulating the flood mitigation role of wetlands', *Journal of Water Resource Planning and Management*, **112**, 114–28.

O'Neil, R.V., D.L. DeAngelis, J.B. Waide and T.F.H. Allen (1986), *A Hierarchical Concept of Ecosystems*, Princeton, NJ: Princeton University Press.

Onuf, C.P. and M.L. Quammen (1986), 'Coastal and riparian wetlands of the Pacific region: the state of knowledge about food chain support', workshop proceedings, National Wetlands Technical Council.

Perry, J. and E. Vanderklein (1996), *Water Quality: Management of a Natural Resource*, Oxford: Blackwell Science.

Putman, R.J. (1994), *Community Ecology*, London: Chapman and Hall.

Rapport, D.J., J.A. Regier and T.C. Hutchinson (1985), 'Ecosystem behaviour under stress', *American Naturalist*, **125**, 617–40.

Risser, P.G. (1988), 'General concepts for measuring cumulative impacts on wetland ecosystems', *Environmental Management*, **12**(5), 585–9.

Risser, P.G. (1996), 'Biodiversity and ecosystem function', in F.B. Samson and F.L Knopf (eds), *Ecosystem Management; Selected Readings*, New York: Springer-Verlag.

Rosenzweig, M.L. (1995), *Species Diversity in Space and Time*, Cambridge: Cambridge University Press.

Sanders, R. and D.A. Purdie (1998), 'Bacterial response to blooms dominated by diatoms and Emiliania huxleyi in nutrient-enriched mesocosms', *Estuarine, Coastal and Shelf Science*, **46**, 35–48.

Schonewald-Cox, C.M. (1988), 'Boundaries in the protection of nature reserves: translating multidisciplinary knowledge into practical conservation', *BioScience*, **38**, 480–86.

Schonewald-Cox, C.M. and J.W. Bayliss (1986), 'The boundary model: a geographical analysis of design and conservation of nature reserves', *Biological Conservation*, **38**, 305–22.

Schreiber K-F (1990), 'The history of landscape ecology in Europe', in I.S. Zonneveld and R.T.T. Forman (eds), *Changing Landscapes: an Ecological Perspective*, New York: Springer-Verlag, pp. 21–33.

Stansfield, J., B. Moss and K. Irvine (1989), 'The loss of submerged plants with eutrophication III. Potential roles of organochlorine pesticides: a palaeoecological study', *Freshwater Biology*, **22**, 109–32.

Swanson, F.J., T.K. Kratz, N. Caine and R.G. Woodmansee (1988), 'Landform effects on ecosystem patterns and processes', *BioScience*, **38**, 92–8.

Turner, R.K. (1991), 'Economics and wetland management', *Ambio*, 20(2), 59–63.

Urban, D.L., R.V. O'Neil and H.H. Shugart (1987), 'Landscape ecology', *BioScience*, **37**, 119–27.

Vitousek, P.M. (1986), 'Biological invasions and ecosystem properties: can species make a difference?' in H.A. Mooney and J.A. Drake (eds), *Ecology of Biological Invasions of North America and Hawaii*, New York: Springer-Verlag.

Vitousek, P.M. and D.U. Hooper (1993), 'Biological diversity and terrestrial ecosystem biogeochemistry', in E.D. Schulze and H.A. Mooney (eds), *Biodiversity and Ecosystem Function*, Ecological Studies no. 99, 3–14, Berlin: Springer-Verlag.

Walker, B.H. (1992), 'Biodiversity and ecological redundancy', *Conservation Biology*, **6**, 18–23.

Ward, D.V. (1978), *Biological Environmental Impact Studies: Theory and Methods*, New York: Academic Press.

WCMC (1992), *Global Diversity. Status of the Earth's Living Resources*, London: Chapman and Hall.

Weller, M.W. (1988), 'Issues and approaches in assessing cumulative impacts on waterbird habitat in wetlands', *Environmental Management*, **12**(5), 695–701.

Weterings, R. and J.B. Opschoor (1994), *Towards Environmental Performance Indicators Based on the Notion of Environmental Space*, report to the Advisory Council for Research on Nature and the Environment, The Netherlands.

Wheeler, B.D. and S.C. Shaw (1995), 'Plants as hydrologists? An assessment of the value of plants as indicators of water conditions in fens', in J. Hughes and A.L. Heathwaite (eds), *Hydrology and Hydrochemistry of British Wetlands*, London: John Wiley and Sons.

Williams, P.H. and K.J. Gaston (1994), 'Measuring more of biodiversity: can higher-taxon richness predict wholesale species richness?', *Biological Conservation*, **67**, 211–17.

# 4. The economics of wetland management

## R.K. Turner, R. Brouwer, T.C. Crowards and S. Georgiou

## 1  INTRODUCTION

According to Samuelson and Nordhaus (1985), economics is the study of how people and society end up choosing, with or without the use of money, to employ scarce productive resources that could have alternative uses – to produce various commodities and distribute them for consumption, now or in the future, among various individuals and groups in society. In other words, economics analyses the costs and benefits of improving patterns of resource use. Because limited resources are available to satisfy multiple social needs, resources have to be distributed as efficiently as possible to ensure maximum benefit to society. Given the fundamental preoccupation with scarcity, economics defines the conditions required to secure the most efficient alloca-tion of scarce resources in a variety of contexts.

Conservation of wetlands will be associated with opportunity costs, which are the benefits forgone from possible alternative uses of the resources that are essential to continued wetland functioning. On the other hand, going ahead with these alternative activities results in the opportunity costs of forgone benefits that would otherwise be derived from the wetland. Quantifying these benefits in a way that makes them comparable with the returns derived from alternative uses can strengthen the case for conserving wetlands and improve public decision-making (Balmford *et al.*, 2002).

Cost–benefit analysis (CBA) is carried out in order to compare the economic efficiency implications of alternative actions. The benefits from an action are contrasted with the associated costs (including the opportunity costs) within a common analytical framework. To allow comparison of these costs and benefits related to a wide range of scarce productive resources, including the various goods and services provided by wetland ecosystems, measured in widely differing units, a common numeraire is employed: money.

This is where most problems start for economic project appraisal since some resources, especially environmental resources such as wetlands, are not priced in money terms. For many goods and services provided by wetlands there is no market in which they are traded, and hence no market price is available which reflects their economic value.

As wetlands and the functions they provide become increasingly scarce, the conventional view of treating wetlands as a free resource is being increasingly questioned. The lack of pricing of wetland functions, as well as the lack of cost recovery mechanisms, has been one of the main determinants of inefficient and often inappropriate and excessive use of wetlands (conversion, excessive harvesting, pollution). As these problems mount, wetlands are increasingly being recognized as a scarce natural resource, with calls for their services to be priced appropriately. Pricing of these services is considered a necessary condition for the sustainable use of wetlands. The economic valuation of wetland use compares the willingness to pay and opportunity costs of the goods and services supplied.

## 2   PROPERTY RIGHTS AND ECONOMIC EFFICIENCY

Although wetlands perform many functions and are potentially very valuable, these values have often been ignored and wetland losses and degradation allowed to continue. Some conversion of wetlands might well have been in society's best interests, where the returns from the competing land use are high. However, wetlands have frequently been lost to activities resulting in only limited benefits or, on occasion, even costs to society (Turner, 1991; van Vuuren and Roy, 1993).

Central to the discussion of inefficiency (costs outweighing benefits) and natural resource degradation often is a proper analysis of property rights. A property right is an entitlement on the part of an owner to a resource or good and where the entitlement is socially enforced. If property rights are efficiently allocated in an economy, it can be shown that the resulting allocation of resources will maximize the sum of individuals' welfare (Just, Hueth and Schmitz, 1982). Four conditions are generally acknowledged to be required for an efficient property rights structure to exist (Tietenberg, 1992):

- Universality – all resources are privately owned and all the entitlements are completely specified.
- Exclusivity – all the benefits and costs arising from ownership of the resource must accrue to the owner.
- Transferability – owners must be able to transfer property rights to another owner in voluntary exchange.
- Enforceability – there must be a structure of penalties which prevent others from encroaching on or taking over property rights with the agreement of the owner.

Many resource problems arise because these conditions fail to be met by one or more of the various types of property rights regimes. The type of property rights regime in place has to be examined before considering any policy recommendation or investment in a particular project. The various types of property rights regimes include:

- Open access property – here property rights to the resource are not allocated or defined at all, and individuals have no incentive to conserve the resource since they have no assurance that others will do likewise.
- Common property – here resources are owned or managed by a reasonably well defined group of people, with usage rules aimed at exclusivity and backed by enforcement of those rules.
- Private property – here a right is secured to undertake a given use of the resource and a duty to refrain from socially unacceptable uses of the resource. Sometimes the exclusivity condition breaks down, resulting in third party effects, or is not possible due to joint supply of goods such as public goods.
- State property – this refers to the context where the resource rights are held by the state, and such a regime has the attraction that all externalities are potentially 'internalized'.

Table 4.1 shows the various conditions for an efficient allocation of property rights and relates them to the various types of property rights regimes in existence. As can be seen, resource problems will arise because of a failure of one or more of the various regimes to fulfil one or more of the conditions of universality, exclusivity, transferability or enforceability. Resource problems cannot, however, simply be resolved by defining property rights, since no one system is capable of dealing with all the necessary conditions, and other more general factors may be at work (for example over-reliance on single commodities, population pressure and so on).

## 3   OPPORTUNITY COSTS OF WATER AND WETLAND DEGRADATION[1]

Marginal Opportunity Cost (MOC) is a useful tool for conceptualizing and measuring the physical effects of wetland use and degradation in economic terms. MOC seeks to measure the full societal cost of an action or policy that uses a unit of a natural resource such as wetlands. Sustainable resource management requires that MOC should equate with the price that users have to pay for their resource use. If the price is less than MOC then the resource will be over-consumed or utilized. A price higher than MOC will result in the

*Table 4.1 A typology of property rights regimes and conditions for efficiency*

|  | Open access | Common property | Private property | State property |
|---|---|---|---|---|
| Universality | No | Defined for the group | Yes | No |
| Exclusivity | No | Defined for the group | Fails in the presence of externalities and public goods | No, but non-nationals excluded |
| Transferability | No | Applies to the group | Yes | No |
| Enforceability | No | Yes: legal and social sanctions | Yes: legal and social sanctions | Yes: legal sanctions |
| Overall efficiency | Very low: no incentive to conserve | Many regimes are efficient, but inherent risk of breakdown | Efficient but market failure occurs in presence of externalities and public goods | Often inefficient due to government failure |

*Source:* Pearce *et al.* (1994).

resource being under-consumed or utilized. Sustainable pricing differs from standard economic efficiency pricing in that it includes a premium to cover the costs accruing from any resource depletion.

The concept of opportunity cost is used to refer to the best alternative use to which resources can be put if they are not being used for the purpose being considered. MOC includes the following three components.

First, there are the direct costs of using wetlands, such as those related to labour and materials used to extract goods or services (for example fishing or harvesting reed). Sometimes such costs require adjustment for taxation and market imperfections in order to reflect true opportunity costs (shadow pricing). These costs will vary with the difficulty of extraction.

The second part of MOC is the external cost, which are those costs arising from the fact that changes in one component of the natural resource base have effects on other components and the efficiency with which other activities can be conducted. The value of such impacts is given by the value of the activity or commodity in its alternative use. Costs that occur in the future require discounting by a discount factor in order to make them commensurate with present day costs. While such information on marginal external costs is diffi-cult to obtain and often imprecise or incomplete, useful approximations can be made. It is the external costs arising from unsustainable resource use that are of particular interest.

The final component of MOC is concerned with the fact that if a resource is fixed in supply (non-renewable) and is experiencing a positive rate of exploitation, then use of a unit of the resource implies its non-availability for future use. As such a scarcity premium can be put on the resource, which depends on the size of the stock relative to the rate of exploitation, how strong future demand will be relative to present demand, the availability and cost of future substitutes, and the discount rate. This scarcity premium is known as the user cost (Conrad and Clark, 1987) and relates to the value of the opportunity forgone by exploiting and using the wetland in the current period rather than some time in the future. It also incorporates the fact that as a consequence of current use and exploitation, costs of future use and exploitation may be higher (for example costs of future pumping of groundwater as it becomes more and more difficult to extract the remaining water as stocks fall; or the costs of future clean-up as the stock of pollution accumulates, or the wetland's absorp-tion capacity – also a stock – decreases).

The user cost of water is often ignored, especially where wetlands are treated as an open access resource, with users behaving in an individually competitive manner. This happens for example when property rights are ill defined or not enforced. Use of the wetland is then governed by the law of capture, on a 'first come, first served' basis. Each user will try to exploit as much as possible in fear of other users exploiting the resource first, and also in the belief that the amount they themselves use is only a small proportion of the overall stock. Ignoring user costs will result in exploitation rates that exceed the optimal rate since the costs of extraction are undervalued.[2] This contrasts with the case where a single user has rights to the resource. In this case the user accounts for the user costs since he or she alone will face all the increased costs of extracting from a depleted resource in the future.

So, MOC = MDC + MEC + MUC, where MDC refers to marginal direct costs, MEC to marginal external costs and MUC to marginal user costs. Marginal user costs can also refer to a renewable resource, which is being used in a non-sustainable way.

Given its relationship to marginal cost pricing and allocative efficiency, MOC is a useful pricing principle as it forces attention on to the externalities associated with natural resource degradation, and guides pricing policy in providing incentives for allocative efficiency. Excessive resource use should be discouraged by proper marginal cost pricing. Failure to set water charges for irrigation on the basis of user benefits has, for instance, always been used as a classic cause of inefficiency in the agricultural sector (for example Repetto, 1986).

This brings us to the importance of properly valuing the socio-economic benefits derived from wetlands as an important and often necessary condition for efficient and sustainable use of wetlands.

# 4   WILLINGNESS TO PAY FOR WETLAND CONSERVATION

In economics, value is expressed as the degree to which people want to use or give up scarce resources, such as money or time, to acquire or retain something. Value exists in that sense only through the interaction between a subject (individual) and an object, and is therefore not considered as an intrinsic quality of something (Pearce and Turner, 1990). As in other social sciences, the value people attach to something is based upon a hypothesized positive relationship between their observed behaviour or verbal response and that value. In economics, an individual's value is assumed to be revealed or expressed in market behaviour and measured in money terms through the concept of an individual's willingness to pay (WTP), for instance for wetland quality improvement or wetland conservation, or willingness to accept (WTA) compensation, for instance as a result of quality decline or wetland destruction. WTP and WTA can not be used interchangeably. Although the WTP approach has become the most frequently applied and has been given peer review endorsement through a variety of studies (such as Arrow *et al.*, 1993), the question as to which concept is most appropriate basically depends upon the specific circumstances and the (traditional) property rights regime associated with the given wetland use.

Whereas the opportunity costs of wetland use or exploitation basically constitute the supply of the goods and services provided by the wetland (and the marginal opportunity costs the supply curve), WTP or WTA for wetland conservation make up the demand for these goods and services (and marginal WTP or WTA the demand curve). The marginal opportunity costs reflect the (social) costs to supply one extra unit of a wetland good or service, while marginal WTP or WTA reflects how much an individual or, if aggregated across individuals, society as a whole is willing to pay or accept in return for this one extra unit.

The concept of marginality is used by economists in relation to questions of resource allocation and scarcity. One of the main principles emerging from the literature on the economics of natural resource use is that efficient use requires that the marginal opportunity costs of use are equated to their marginal benefits (the point at which total benefits net of total costs are maximized). Although for most products the amount actually paid in the market place is given by the price of the product (though in the case of most wetland goods and services markets often do not exist or are highly imperfect), some people are willing to pay more than this price and hence receive an additional benefit over and above the amount they actually have to pay. This additional benefit is known as the consumer's surplus. A product's price and its economic value are therefore two different things, and may explain why wetlands are often said to have a very high value, but no or only a very small price.

Where goods are traded in markets, the price of a good is theoretically the product of supply and demand. Generally speaking, more of a good will be demanded the lower its price, while more of a good will be supplied the higher its price. Economists expect that marginal values decline as the service flow increases and vice versa. This is illustrated in Figure 4.1.

The market price ($P^m$) is the price at which demand matches supply, with a quantity $Q^m$ being traded. However, at quantities less than $Q^m$, some individuals would be willing to pay more than the market price (since the demand curve is higher than $P^m$), suggesting that market price alone is only a minimum estimate of the value derived. The area between the market price and the demand curve (triangle A) is the consumer's surplus, or the additional utility gained by consumers above the price paid. Total social benefits or total economic value (TEV) are therefore the expenditure (areas B + C or price multiplied by quantity) plus the consumer's surplus (area A). The total cost of producing quantity $Q^m$ is the area below the supply curve (area C). The area above the supply curve and below the market price is known as the producer's surplus, since at quantities below $Q^m$ producers would be prepared to sell for

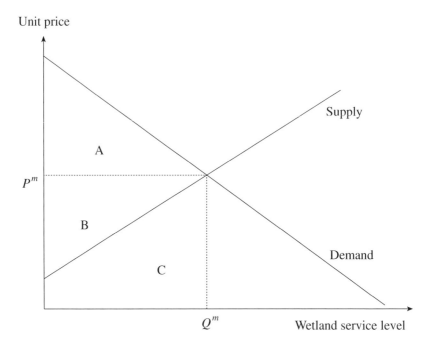

*Figure 4.1    Supply and demand curves for a continuous non-exhaustible*
*            wetland service*

less than the market price that they receive. The *net* social benefit is then the consumer's surplus (area A) plus the producer's surplus (area B).

Where the services supplied by a wetland are only available in discrete amounts and are furthermore characterized by a (known) critical threshold, total costs and benefits become infinite at this critical level (Figure 4.2). Both the supply and demand curves are vertical at this point. Total costs are infinite at this point, because the resource and the services it provides can not be replaced, repaired or substituted, or only at a relatively high cost, once the critical threshold has been passed. Total benefits are infinite at this point if the service provided is assumed to be life supporting and also valued as such by consumers. If the critical point of irreversible change is surrounded by uncertainties, for instance regarding physical cause–effect relationships, safe minimum standards (SMSs) may be used here to complement the economic cost–benefit assessment (for example Ciriacy-Wantrup, 1952; Bishop, 1978; Crowards, 1996).

SMSs are closely related to sustainability considerations (Pearce and Turner, 1990). Sustainability essentially requires that the stock of natural capital available in the future is equivalent to that available at present. The concept of sustainability has been roughly partitioned into two approaches: weak

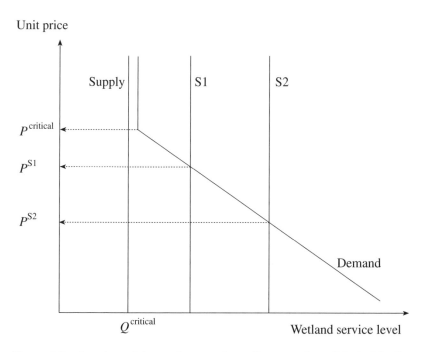

*Figure 4.2    Supply and demand curves for a discrete exhaustible (critical) wetland service*

sustainability and strong sustainability (Turner, 1993). Weak sustainability requires that the total stock of capital, whether man-made or natural, be maintained, and rests upon the assumption of substitutability between these two types of capital. Economic theory suggests that decreasing supplies of natural resources will tend to increase their price, encouraging more efficient use, substitution with other goods, and technological advancement. However, complete substitution will not always be possible due to physical limits to the efficiency and availability of substitution opportunities, the question of whether man-made capital is able to compensate fully for all the functions provided by complex ecosystems, and the existence of 'critical' natural capital and thresholds beyond which reversal is not possible or practicable. Hence the more stringent interpretation of 'strong sustainability', which requires that the total stock of natural capital be non-declining. Projects should either conserve the natural environment or ensure that losses incurred are replaced or fully compensated for in physical terms by the implementation of 'shadow projects' (Barbier, Markandya and Pearce, 1990).

It is often necessary within cost–benefit analysis to choose between alternative projects which may have different intertemporal patterns of benefits and costs extending over varying durations. Costs and benefits, which occur at different times, are made comparable in economic appraisals by converting the stream of future costs and benefits into 'present' values. This allows them to be directly compared, the difference between total benefits and costs being referred to as 'net present value' (NPV). A project is only accepted if NPV is positive.

The choice of a discount rate can have significant influence on which projects pass the cost–benefit criterion. Options that involve high initial costs and a stream of benefits far into the future, such as the creation or restoration of wetlands, are less likely to be accepted when employing a higher rate of discount. Options for which the benefits are more immediate and the costs are not incurred until far into the future, will become more viable with a higher discount rate.

A higher discount rate is also more likely to encourage more rapid depletion of non-renewable natural resources and over-exploitation of renewable natural resources, thereby reducing the inheritance of natural capital for future generations. However, lower rates of discount will tend to encourage investments that might not otherwise have been viable and could conceivably result in more rapid depletion of resources (Fisher and Krutilla, 1975). The link between the size of the discount rate and the degree to which options will impinge upon the environment is therefore sometimes ambiguous, and it is not always clear that the traditional call for lower discount rates in order to incorporate environmental concerns is generally valid.

The total economic value (TEV) of a good or service is given by the area under the demand curve. In valuing a resource such as a wetland, the TEV can be usefully broken down into a number of categories, which basically reflect different reasons or motivations in general as to why people value environmental goods and services. These are illustrated in Figure 4.3. The initial distinction is between use value and non-use value. Use value involves some interaction with the resource, either directly or indirectly. Indirect use value derives from services provided by the wetland. This might include the removal of nutrients, providing cleaner water to those downstream, or the prevention of downstream flooding. Direct use value, on the other hand, involves interaction with the wetland itself rather than via the services it provides. It may be consumptive use, such as the harvesting of reeds or fish, or it may be non-consumptive such as recreational and educational activities. There is also the possibility of deriving value from 'distant use' through media such as television or magazines, although whether or not this type of value is actually a use value, and to what extent it can be attributed to the wetland involved, is unclear.

Non-use value is associated with benefits derived simply from the knowledge that a resource, such as an individual species or an entire wetland, is

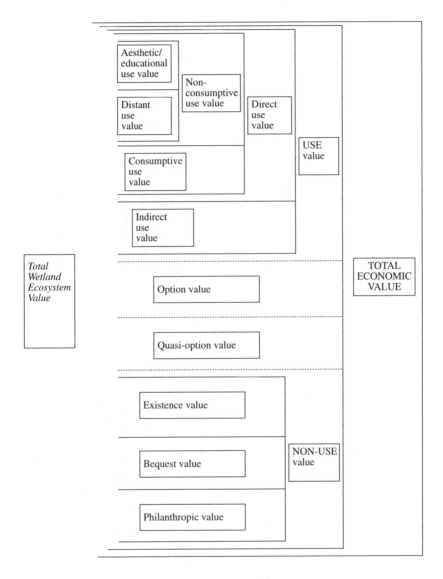

*Figure 4.3    Components of total economic value*

maintained. It is by definition not associated with any use of the resource or tangible benefit derived from it, although users of a resource might also attribute non-use value to it. Non-use value is closely linked to ethical concerns, often being linked to altruistic preferences, although for some these too stem ultimately from self-interest (Crowards, 1997). Non-use value can be split into three basic components, although these may overlap depending upon exact definitions.

Existence value can be derived simply from the satisfaction of knowing that some feature of the environment continues to exist, whether or not this might also benefit others. Bequest value is associated with the knowledge that a resource will be passed on to descendants to maintain the opportunity for them to enjoy it in the future. Philanthropic value is associated with the satisfaction from ensuring resources are available to contemporaries of the current generation.

Two other categories are option value and quasi-option value. Option value implies that an individual derives benefit from ensuring that a resource will be available for use in the future. In this sense it is a form of use value, although it can be regarded as a form of insurance to provide for possible future but not current use. Quasi-option value is associated with the potential benefits of awaiting improved information before giving up the option to preserve a resource for future use. It suggests a value in particular of avoiding irreversible damage that might prove to have been unwarranted in the light of further information. An example of an option value is in bio-prospecting, where biodiversity may be maintained on the off-chance that it might in the future be the source of important new medicinal drugs. It has been suggested that option value is less a distinct category of total value than the difference between an *ex ante* perspective yielding 'option price' (consumer surplus plus option value) and an *ex post* perspective giving expected consumer surplus, as a measure of value (Freeman, 1993).

As Figure 4.3 illustrates, TEV which encompasses these various types of value, is itself regarded as a part of the overall 'Total Wetland Ecosystem Value'. Recent advances in the development of ecological–economic models and theory all seem to stress the importance of the overall system, as opposed to individual components of that system. This points to another dimension of total environmental value, namely the value of the system itself. The economy and the environment are now jointly determined systems linked in a process of co-evolution, with the scale of economic activity exerting significant environmental pressure. The dynamics of the jointly determined system are characterized by discontinuous change around poorly understood critical threshold values.

The adoption of a systems perspective serves to re-emphasize the obvious but fundamental point that economic systems are underpinned by ecological systems and not vice versa. There is a dynamic interdependency between economy and ecosystem. The properties of biophysical systems are part of the set of constraints which bound economic activity. The constraints set has its own internal dynamics, which react to economic activity exploiting environmental assets (extraction, harvesting, waste disposal, non-consumptive users).

Feedbacks then occur which influence economic and social relationships. The evolution of the economy and the evolution of the constraints set are interdependent and 'co-evolution' is thus a crucial concept (Common and Perrings, 1992).

Private economic values may not capture the full contribution of component species and processes to the aggregate life-support functions provided by ecosystems (Gren *et al.*, 1994). Furthermore, some ecologists argue that some of the underlying structure and functions of ecological systems which are prior to the ecological production functions cannot be taken into account in terms of economic values. Total economic value will therefore underestimate the true value of ecosystems. The prior value of the ecosystem structure has been called 'primary value' and consists of the system characteristics upon which all ecological functions depend (Turner and Pearce, 1993).[3] Their value arises in the sense that they produce functions which have value (secondary value). The secondary functions and values depend on the continued health, integrity, existence, operation, and maintenance of the ecosystem as a whole. The primary value notion is related to the fact that the system holds everything together and as such has, in principle, economic value. Thus the total value of the wetland ecosystem exceeds the sum of the values of the individual functions. It can also be argued that a healthy ecosystem contains an ecological redundancy capacity and there is thus an 'insurance' value in maintaining the system at some 'critical' size in order to combat stress and shocks over time.

To summarize, the social value of an ecosystem may not be equivalent to the aggregate private total economic value of that same system's components, for the following reasons:

- The full complexity and coverage of the underpinning 'life-support' functions of healthy evolving ecosystems is currently not precisely known in scientific terms. A number of indirect use values within systems therefore remain to be discovered and valued (quasi option value, that is the conditional expected value of information).
- Because the range of secondary values (use and non-use) that can be instrumentally derived from an ecosystem is contingent on the prior existence of such a healthy and evolving system, there is in a theoretical sense a 'prior value' that could be ascribed to the system itself. Such a value would, however, not be measurable in conventional economic terms and is non-commensurate with the economic (secondary) values of the system. The operating system possesses value related to the structure and functioning properties of the system, which hold everything together. This value is more than the sum of its individual components.

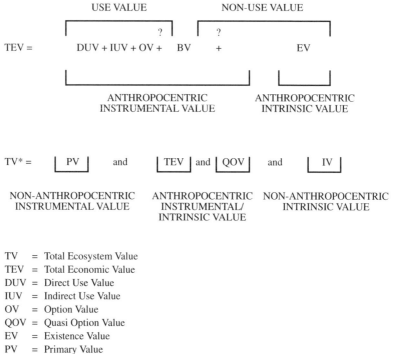

TV   = Total Ecosystem Value
TEV  = Total Economic Value
DUV  = Direct Use Value
IUV  = Indirect Use Value
OV   = Option Value
QOV  = Quasi Option Value
EV   = Existence Value
PV   = Primary Value
IV   = Intrinsic Value
BV   = Bequest Value

*Notes*
\* The separate components of TV are not additive since they reflect different dimensions of value.
? = uncertain boundaries.

*Source*:   Turner (2000).

*Figure 4.4    Total ecosystem value and total economic value*

• A healthy ecosystem also contains a redundancy reserve (Barbier, 1994), a pool of latent keystone species or processes which are required for system maintenance in the face of stress and shock.

These elements in the total ecosystem value framework (TV), with TEV being a part of TV and non-anthropocentric intrinsic value as a completely separate notion not commensurate with the other components, are laid out in Figure 4.4 and Table 4.2.

*Table 4.2   A general value typology (adapted from Hargrove, 1992)*

| | | | | |
|---|---|---|---|---|
| **Anthropocentric** | 1. Instrumental value | Total Economic Value = use value + non-use value. The non-use category is bounded by the existence value concept which has been the subject of much debate. Existence value may therefore encompass some or all of the following motivations: | Interpersonal altruism (*philanthropic* motivation and value), resource conservation to ensure availability for others; vicarious use value linked to self-interested altruism and the 'warm glow' effect of purchased moral satisfaction | |
| | | | Intergenerational altruism (*bequest* motivation and value), resource conservation to ensure availability for future generations | |
| | | | Stewardship motivation, human responsibilities for resource conservation on behalf of all nature | If existence value is defined to include stewardship and Q-altruism, then it will overlap with the next category outlined below |
| | | | Q-altruism, motivation based on the belief that non-human resources have rights and/or interests and as far as possible should be left undisturbed | |
| | 2. Intrinsic value | This value category is linked to anthropocentrism that recognizes a range of values extending beyond instrumental values and is culturally dependent | Value attribution is to entities which have a 'stake' or 'goods of their own', and 'instrumentally use other parts of nature for their own intrinsic ends . . .'. It remains an anthropocentrically related concept because it is still a human value that is ascribing intrinsic value to non-human nature ('Q-altruism') | |
| **Non-anthropocentric** | 3. Instrumental value | Entities are assumed to have sakes or goods of their own independent of human interests | Also encompasses the good of collective entities, e.g. ecosystems, in a way that is *not* irreducible to that of its members. This category may not demand moral consideration as far as humans are concerned | |
| | 4. Intrinsic value | Viewed in an objective sense, 'inherent worth' in nature, the value that an object possesses independently of the valuation of humans | A meta-ethical claim, usually involving the search for constitute rules or trump cards with which to constrain anthropocentric instrumental values and policy. It is therefore entirely separate from any human-related environmental value component | |

## 5   VALUATION TECHNIQUES

A range of valuation techniques exists for assessing the economic value of the functions performed by wetland ecosystems. These are detailed in Table 4.3. Many ecological functions produce goods and services which are not traded in markets and therefore remain unpriced. The valuation techniques presented in Table 4.3 attempt to assess the relative economic worth of these goods or services using non-market valuation techniques. More detailed information on the underlying theory and practical implementation of these techniques can be found in a number of general texts including Braden and Kolstad (1991), Bromley (1995), Freeman (1993), Hanley and Spash (1993), Pearce *et al.* (1994), Randall (1987) and Bateman and Willis (2000).

An important distinction to make is between those valuation techniques which estimate benefits directly and those which estimate costs as a proxy for benefits. For instance, estimating Damage Costs Avoided, Defensive Expenditures, Replacement/Substitute Costs or Restoration Costs as part of an economic valuation exercise suggests that the costs are a reasonable approximation of the benefits that society attributes to the resources in question. The underlying assumption is that the benefits are at least as great as the costs involved in repairing, avoiding or compensating for damage. These techniques are widely applied because of the relative ease of estimation and availability of data, but it is important to be aware of the limitations in terms of the information they convey with respect to economic benefits.

Where market prices exist for resources, these may have to be adjusted for market distortions such as taxes or subsidies to provide shadow prices, but otherwise they are likely to provide a relatively simple means of assessing economic value. However, theoretically these estimations based on market prices are still not the same as the total economic value, since they do not include the consumer surplus.

Approaches related to market analysis include the assessment of productivity losses that can be attributed to changes in the ecosystem and the incorporation of the ecosystem as one of the inputs into the production function of other goods and services. Investment by public bodies in conserving ecosystems may represent a surrogate for aggregated individual willingness to pay and hence social value. These 'public prices' paid for resources have been used to approximate the value society places upon them, as for instance the costs of designating an ecosystem as a nature reserve.

In the absence of market prices, two theoretically valid benefit estimation techniques are hedonic pricing or the travel cost method. These are

# Table 4.3  Valuation methods

| Valuation method | Description | Direct use values | Indirect use values | Non-use values |
|---|---|---|---|---|
| Market analysis | Where market prices of outputs (and inputs) are available. Marginal productivity net of human effort/cost. Could approximate with market price of close substitute. Requires shadow pricing. | ✓ | ✓ | |
| Productivity losses | Change in net return from marketed goods: a form of (dose-response market analysis. | ✓ | ✓ | |
| Production functions | Ecosystem treated as one input into the production of other goods: based on ecological linkages and market analysis. | | ✓ | |
| Public pricing | Public investment, for instance via land purchase or monetary incentives, as a surrogate for market transactions. | ✓ | ✓ | ✓ [2] |
| Hedonic Price Method (HPM) | Derive an implicit price for an environmental good from analysis of goods for which markets exist and which incorporate particular environmental characteristics. | ✓ | ✓ | |
| Travel Cost Method (TCM) | Costs incurred in reaching a recreation site as a proxy for the value of recreation. Expenses differ between sites (or for the same site over time) with different environmental attributes. | ✓ | ✓ | |
| Contingent Valuation Method (CVM) | Construction of a hypothetical market by direct surveying of a sample of individuals and aggregation to encompass the relevant population. Problems of potential biases. | ✓ | ✓ | ✓ |
| Damage costs avoided | The costs that would be incurred if the ecosystem function were not present, e.g. flood prevention. | | ✓ | |
| Defensive expenditures | Costs incurred in mitigating the effects of reduced environmental quality. Represents a minimum value for the environmental function. | | ✓ | |
| Relocation costs | Expenditures involved in relocation of affected agents or facilities: a particular form of defensive expenditure. | | ✓ | |
| Replacement/substitute costs | Potential expenditures incurred in replacing the function that is lost, for instance by the use of substitute facilities or 'shadow projects'. | ✓ | ✓ | ✓ [3] |
| Restoration costs | Costs of returning the degraded ecosystem to its original state. A total value approach; important ecological, temporal and cultural dimensions. | ✓ | ✓ | ✓ [3] |

*Notes*

1. Indirect use values associated with functions performed by an ecosystem will generally be associated with benefits derived off-site. Thus, methodologies such as hedonic pricing and travel cost analysis, which necessarily involve direct contact with a feature of the environment, can be used to assess the value of indirect benefits from the ecosystem.

2. Investment by public bodies in conserving ecosystems can be interpreted as the total value attributed to the ecosystem by society. This could therefore encapsulate potential non-use values, although such a valuation technique is an extremely rough approximation of the theoretically correct economic measure of social value, which is the sum of individual willingness to pay.

3. Perfect restoration of the ecosystem or creation of a perfectly substitutable 'shadow project' ecosystem, which maintains key features of the original, might have the potential to provide the same non-use benefits as the original. However, cultural and historical aspects as well as a desire for 'authenticity' may limit the extent to which non-use values can be 'transferred' in this manner to newer versions of the original. This is in addition to spatial and temporal complexities involved in the physical location of the new wetland or the time frame for restoration.

based on preferences being revealed through observable behaviour, and are restricted in their application to where a functioning market exists, such as that for property in the case of hedonic pricing, or where travel to the site is a prerequisite to deriving benefit, such as with recreational visits in the travel cost method.

Contingent valuation, based on surveys that elicit 'stated preferences' and has the potential to value benefits in all situations, including non-use benefits that are not associated with any observable behaviour. However, the legitimacy of contingent valuation methods and results is still contested (for example Foster, 1997; Brouwer *et al.*, 1999), especially in the context of non-use values, and conducting a contingent valuation survey can sometimes be a lengthy and resource-intensive exercise.

It may not always be necessary to initiate a new study in a project to determine how the economic welfare of individuals might be affected by some environmental change. If a similar project has previously been undertaken elsewhere, estimates of its economic consequences might be usable as an indicator of the impacts of the new project. Such an approach has been termed 'benefits transfer' because the estimates of economic benefits are 'transferred' from a site where a study has already been completed to a site of policy interest (Brouwer, 2000). The benefits transferred from the study site could have been measured using any of the direct or indirect valuation techniques outlined above.

There are broadly speaking two main approaches to benefits transfer:

1. Transferring average benefit estimates. Here it is assumed that changes in welfare experienced on average by individuals at existing sites are equal to those that will be experienced at the new site. Previous studies are used to estimate the consumer surplus or average WTP of individuals engaged in, say, recreational activities of various kinds. The value of a 'person-day' for each recreational activity at existing sites is multiplied by the forecast change in the number of days at the new site, to obtain estimates of the aggregate economic benefits of recreation at the new site.
2. Transferring adjusted average benefit values based on benefit functions. Here the mean unit values of the existing studies are adjusted before transferral to the new site in order to better reflect the conditions at the new site. These differences might be in socio-economic characteristics of households, in the environmental change being looked at or the availability of substitute goods and services and so on.

Benefits transfer is still in its infancy, in part because for many environmental policy issues only a limited number of high quality valuation studies have been completed. However, it is potentially a very important and useful estimation approach, as it could feasibly provide accurate and robust benefit estimates at a fraction of the cost of a full-blown valuation study.

# 6 ECONOMIC VALUATION OF WETLAND ECOSYSTEM FUNCTIONS

Wetlands provide various functions which are beneficial to society. A distinction can be made between hydrological, biogeochemical and ecological functions.

Hydrological functions refer to the wetland's ability to store flood waters, the interactions between ground and surface waters and the storage of sediments:

- Flood water detention: the short and long term detention and storage of waters from overbank flooding and/or slope runoff.
- Groundwater recharge: the recharge of groundwater by infiltration and percolation of detained flood water into an aquifer.
- Groundwater discharge: the upward seepage of groundwater to the wetland surface.
- Sediment retention: the net retention of sediments carried in suspension by waters inundating the wetland from river overbank flooding and runoff from a contributory area.

Biogeochemical functions of a wetland refer to the export and storage of naturally occurring chemical compounds that can have significant effects on the quality of the environment:

- Nutrient retention: the storage of excess nutrients (nitrogen and phosphorus) via biological, biochemical and geochemical processes in biomass (living and dead) and soil mineral compounds of a wetland.
- Nutrient export: the removal of excess nutrients (nitrogen and phosphorus) from a wetland via biological, biochemical, physical and land management process.
- *In situ* carbon retention: the retention of carbon in the form of partially decomposed organic matter or peat in the soil profile due to environmental conditions that reduce rates of decomposition.
- Trace element storage and export: the storage and removal of trace elements from a wetland via biological, biochemical and physical processes in the mineral compounds of wetland soils.

Ecological functions relate primarily to the maintenance of habitats within which organisms live:

- Ecosystem maintenance: the provision of habitat for animals and plants through the interaction of physical, chemical and biological wetland processes (including habitat and biological diversity).
- Food web support: the support of food webs within and outside a wetland through the production of biomass and its subsequent accumulation and export.

The socio-economic benefits derived from these functions can be measured in a variety of ways, as shown in the previous section. In doing so, the following steps can be distinguished:

1. Identification of the goods and services involved.
2. Assessment of their provision level (including quality).
3. Identification of the groups of people in society who benefit from them (or will be suffering a loss when they are removed, destroyed or degraded).
4. Identification of the possible values attributed to them by these different groups in society.
5. Selection of the appropriate economic valuation technique(s).
6. Estimation of the total economic value.

The choice of valuation method that can be employed to estimate the economic value of the good or service (step 5) will often be up to the analyst to decide. While some methods are theoretically preferable to others (see previous section), other 'second best' measures may often be easier to determine in practice. The choice of method is likely to depend, in part, on time, resources and data available for the investigation. An overview of the wetland ecosystem functions and valuation methods used so far in assessing their socio-economic benefits is given in Table 4.4.

The indirect use benefits from flood water detention mainly refer to potential damage avoided downstream. Besides the calculation of avoided damage costs, defensive expenditures related to flood warning or avertive action, the replacement or substitution costs of building dykes if the wetland is removed, hedonic pricing studies have looked at the influence of risks of flooding on property prices whereas contingent valuation studies have been used to estimate public WTP for flood protection.

Ground (and surface) water recharge and discharge may include non-use values when water supplies are maintained for the sake of future generations. Based on market analysis, production function approaches and the calculation of replacement costs, the direct and indirect use value of wetlands for drinking water purposes and irrigation in agriculture have been estimated. Hedonic

Table 4.4 Valuation methods used to estimate the socio-economic benefits of wetland ecosystem functions (adapted from Crowards and Turner, 1996)

| Wetland ecosystem function | Direct use values | Indirect use values | Non-use values | Economic valuation method |
|---|---|---|---|---|
| *Hydrological functions* | | | | |
| Flood water detention | ✓ | ✓ | | HP, CV, ADC, DE, RC |
| Groundwater recharge/discharge | ✓ | ✓ | ✓ | MA, PF, HP, TC, CV, RC |
| Sediment retention | ✓ | ✓ | | ADC |
| *Biogeochemical functions* | | | | |
| Nutrient retention/export | ✓ | ✓ | ✓ | MA, PF, HP, TC, CV, DE, RC |
| Trace element storage and export | ✓ | ✓ | ✓ | MA, PF, HP, TC, CV, DE, RC |
| *In situ* carbon retention | ✓ | ✓ | ✓ | ADC |
| *Ecological functions* | | | | |
| Ecosystem maintenance | ✓ | ✓ | ✓ | MA, HP, TC, CV, RC |
| Food web support | ✓ | ✓ | ✓ | MA, RC |

*Notes*
MA: Market Analysis    CV: Contingent Valuation    PF: Production Function
HP: Hedonic Pricing    DE: Defensive Expenditures    ADC: Avoided Damage Costs
TC: Travel Cost    RC: Replacement Costs (Shadow Project)

pricing studies have investigated the effect of access to water on property prices. Travel cost and contingent valuation studies have examined the recreational benefits associated with instream flow levels.

The direct and indirect benefits of wetlands retaining sediments from flood water and runoff water have been mainly estimated in terms of damage avoided (for example recreation, navigation, agriculture).

The direct and indirect use benefits from nutrient and trace element retention and export mainly refer to maintaining or improving water quality for various reasons, including drinking water and recreation. Market analysis and production function approaches were used to estimate the value of clean water on human health and commercial fishing (forgone earnings). Defensive or avertive expenditures incurred by households have been assessed to avoid exposure to contaminated (ground)water supply. Replacement cost studies looked at the costs of equivalent waste water treatment methods. Travel cost studies have been used to assess the value of improved water quality at recreational sites, while hedonic pricing studies investigated the impact of differing water qualities on residential housing prices. Contingent valuation studies have assessed WTP for protecting and improving (ground)water quality for a variety of reasons (drinking water, health, recreation, habitat preservation and so on), including non-use motivations such as bequest or existence values.

The socio-economic value of a wetland's capacity to store carbon (peat accumulation) has been estimated through exercises looking at the damages caused by climate change. Although these studies only assessed the indirect use value involved, the storage of carbon may also have non-use value (for example reducing climate change for the sake of future generations).

The socio-economic benefits of wetlands producing biomass (fish, reed and so on) have been evaluated through market analyses and replacement cost estimations of shadow projects. Restoration cost studies have looked at the costs related to rehabilitating the ecology of wetlands (reed beds, cleaning up pollution and so on). Hedonic pricing studies have been carried out to assess property prices in and near wetlands. Travel cost studies have estimated the recreational expenditures for waterfowl hunting, birdwatching, fishing and so forth. Finally, contingent valuation surveys have been used to estimate the use and non-use values, separately or at the same time, through public WTP for species and habitat preservation. Appendix 4.1 presents a selection of empirical studies and their valuation findings.

# APPENDIX 4.1

## Table A4.1 Valuation empirical studies

| Bibliographic study characteristics | | | | Study Characteristics | | | | Estimate value characteristics: | | | |
| Authors | Title | Bibliographical details | Year | Issue addressed in study/General Function–Use identification | Valuation technique | Year of data collection | Measurement unit | Mean/Total | Water system: Groundwater/ surface water | Spatial scale | Country |
|---|---|---|---|---|---|---|---|---|---|---|---|
| Bateman, L., et al. | 'A Contingent Valuation Study of the Norfolk Broads' | Report to the National Rivers Authority | 1992 | Average WTP to preserve present landscape\n\nFunction–Use: Habitat, Non-use value | CV | | English pounds per person per year | Use values: 78–105 Non-use values of local population: 14:7 Non-use values of the rest of GB:4:8 | Broads | Regional | United Kingdom |
| Bateman, I.J., I.H., Langford, R.K. Turner, K.G. Willis and G.D. Garrod. | 'Elicitation and Truncation Effects in Contingent Valuation Studies' | Ecological Economics, 2, 161–79 | 1995 | Analysis of methods of eliciting WTP in a CV study of flood protection of a UK wetland | CV | 1991 August, September | English pounds/years | | Wetlands | Local | United Kingdom |
| Bergstrom, J.C., J.R. Stoll, J.P. Titre, and V.L. Wright | 'Economic Value of Wetlands-Based Recreation' | Ecological Economics, 2, 129–47 | 1990 | Wetlands loss and recreational value\n\nFunction–Use: Recreation | CV | 1986–1987 | Dollars, per user | 360 | Wetlands | Regional | USA |
| Breaux, A., S. Faber and J. Day | 'Using Natural Coastal Wetlands Systems for Wastewater Treatment: An Economic Benefit Analysis' | Journal of Environmental Management, 44, 285–91 | 1995 | Wetland value for waste treatment use\n\nFunction–Use: Industrial Supply | RC | | Dollars per year per film | (a. Value represents annualized cost saving to the firm from using a more extensive discharge dispersion system on a 6.2 acre wetlands site: 26700;- (b. Estimate is wetland's treatment value per acre, including all plants' capitalized cost savings and based on treatment systems with a 25year lifetime (low estimate): 6231 | Wetlands | Local | USA |

Table A4.1 (continued)

| | Bibliographic study characteristics | | | Study Characteristics | | | | Estimate value characteristics: | Water system: | | |
|---|---|---|---|---|---|---|---|---|---|---|---|
| Authors | Title | Bibliographical details | Year | Issue addressed in study/General Function–Use identification | Valuation technique | Year of data collection | Measurement unit | Mean/Total | Groundwater/ surface water | Spatial scale | Country |
| Broadhead, C., J.P. Amigues, B.Desaigues, and J. Keith | 'Riparian Zone Protection: The Use of the Willingness to Accept Format (WTA) in a Contingent Valuation Study' | Paper presented at the World Congress of Environmental and Resource Economists in Venice, Italy | 1998 | In 1997, a study was financed by the French Ministry of Environment to evaluate the costs of preserving riparian habitat on the banks of the Garonne River. The CVM was used to study households that currently own land on the banks of the river. More precisely, a WTA was used to estimate the loss to owners for no longer being able to farm riverbank areas actively. Results of this study are reported and analysed in this paper. | CV | 1997 | FF/ha/year | Mean WTA for program 1373FF/ha | River | Regional | France |
| Brouwer, R. and L.H.G. Slangen | 'Contingent Valuation of the Public Benefits of Agricultural Wildlife Management: The Case of Dutch Peat Meadow Land' | European Review of Agricultural Economics, 25, 53–72 | 1998 | To provide a conservative estimate of the public benefits of agricultural wildlife management on Dutch peat meadow land and to provide a monetary estimate of the public benefits of management agreements. Function–Use: Habitat, Rare or Endangered Species | CV | 1994 | Dutch guilders and years | WTP: South Holland/ Friesland/Limburg/ total: 131,4/113.6/ 64.5/124.5 | Ditch | Regional | Nether-lands |
| Cooper, J. and J.B. Loomis | 'Testing whether Waterfowl Hunting Benefits Increase with Greater Water Deliveries to Wetlands' | Environmental and Resource Economics, 3(6), 545–561 | 1993 | Impact on recreational waterfowl hunting benefits of an increase in refuge water supplies to levels necessary for biologically optimal refuge management | TC | 1990 | US $ per acre-foot of additional water supply | 0.93–20.40 (OLS), 0.64–14.05 (Poisson) | Wetlands | Regional | USA |

96

| Author | Title | Journal | Year | Method | Date | Units | Value | Description | Habitat | Scale | Country |
|---|---|---|---|---|---|---|---|---|---|---|---|
| Cooper, J.C. | 'Using the Travel Cost Method to Link Waterfowl Hunting to Agricultural Activities' | *Cahiers d'Economie et Sociologie Rurales*, 35, 5–26 | 1995 | TC | 1988 | US $ per hunter day and total for Kesterson | 55.41 | Impact of contaminated irrigation runoff on waterfowl hunting benefits. Function–Use: Recreation, Agricultural Supply | Wetlands | Regional | USA |
| Cordell, H.K. and J.C. Bergstrom | 'Comparison of Recreation Use Values Among Alternative Reservoir Water Level Management, Scenarios | *Water Resources Research*, 29 (2), 249–258 | 1993 | CV | 1988/1989 | US $ per individual (>=12 years old) for access to TVA reservoirs per year | 41.70–75.05 | Recreational benefits of three water level management alternatives in comparison to other use values (hydropower, flood control, etc.) Function–Use: Flooding, Recreation, Hydro power Generation | Lake (reservoir) | Regional | USA |
| Costanza, R., S.C. Farber and J. Maxwell | 'Valuation and Management of Wetland Ecosystems' | *Ecological Economics*, 1, 335–61 | 1989 | MV | 1983 | Dollars per acre / Dollars per acre per year | (a Present value of the marginal product of an acre of wetland through production of five commercial fishery products (brown and white shrimp, menhaden, oyster, and blue crab) is reported. 3% was used for discounting: 845; (b Estimated value of annual average product of an acre of march and open water area is reported. This estimate may overvalue the wetland since average product is generally lower than marginal product, the more appropriate. | Coastal wetlands in Louisiana Function–Use: Commercial Fishing | Wetlands | Regional | USA |

## Table A4.1 (continued)

| | Bibliographic study characteristics | | | | Study Characteristics | | | | | | | |
|---|---|---|---|---|---|---|---|---|---|---|---|---|
| Authors | Title | Bibliographical details | Year | Issue addressed in study/General Function–Use identification | Valuation technique | Year of data collection | Measurement unit | Estimate value characteristics: Mean/Total | Water system: Groundwater/ surface water | Spatial scale | Country |
| Dalecki, M.G., J.C. Whitehead and G.C. Blomquist | 'Sample Non-Response Bias and Aggregate Benefits in Contingent Valuation: an Examination of Early, Late, and Non-respondents' | *Journal of Environmental Management,* 38: 133–43. | 1993 | Wetland preservation<br><br>Function–Use: Wetland Habitat | CV | 1990 | $/person/year | (a. Individual median WTP estimate for wetland preservation of the first wave (response rate = 24%): 24.4; (b. Individual median WTP estimate for wetland preservation of the fourth wave (response rate = 67%): 6.54. | Wetlands | Regional | USA |
| Foster, V., I.J. Bateman and D. Harley | 'Real and Hypothetical Willingness to Pay for Environmental Preservation: A Non-Experimental comparison' | In *Environmental Valuation Economic Policy and Sustainability: Recent Advances in Environmental Economics* Melinda Acutt and Pamela Mason (eds). Northampton, MA: Edward Elgar, 35–49 | 1998 | Land purchases, species preservation, and habitat conservation<br><br>Function–Use: Habitat Rare or Endangered Species | MV | 1995 | Pounds sterling per mailing<br><br><br>Pounds sterling | (a. Reported value is the mean donation per mailing to the RSPB fund raiser. The fund raising appeal was for the land purchase of maritime health habitat in Ramsey Island in 1992. This is the average donation (includes returned and not returned): £1.73/mailing; (b. Reported value is the total value of donations for the RSPB fund raiser. The fund raising appeal was for the protection of reedbed habitat for bittern in 1993: £268 430. | Wetlands | National | United Kingdom |

98

| Author | Title | Source | Year | Method | Year | Description | Units | Notes | Resource | Scale | Country |
|---|---|---|---|---|---|---|---|---|---|---|---|
| Gren, I.M. | 'Alternative Nitrogen Reduction Policies in the Malar Region, Sweden' | Ecological Economics, 7(2), 159–72 | 1993 | RC | 1991 | Denitrification functions of wetlands Function–Use: Habitat | SEK millions (1 US $ = SEK 5.8); SEK/Kg N | (a. Value is the total cost of restoring wetlands that reduce the load of nitrogen by 1194 tons. Significant cost reduction for nitrogen abatement can be attained through restoring wetlands: 49; (b. Value is the high-end estimate for the marginal cost of abating 1 Kg of nitrogen through restoring wetlands. Significant cost reduction for nitrogen abatement can be attained through restoring wetlands. | Wetlands | Regional | Sweden |
| Gupta, T.R. and J.H. Foster | 'Economic Criteria for Freshwater Wetland Policy in Massachusetts' | American Journal of Agricultural Economics, 57(1), 40–45 | 1975 | DF | 1972 | Function–Use: Recreation Multiple uses/benefits associated with wetlands (value of wildlife, visual-cultural benefits, water supply, and flood control benefits of wetlands) | Dollars per acre per year | (a. Value represents average benefits from flood control for low quality acres: 10; (b Value represents average benefits from flood control for high quality acres: >80 | Wetlands | Regional | Jordan |
| Heimlich, R. E. | 'Costs of an Agricultural Wetland Reserve' | Land Economics, 70(2), 234–46 | 1994 | RC | 1982 | Wetlands converted from cropland | Dollars per acre | (a. Value is the high estimate of the marginal costs of 5 million acres of wetland reserve: 1184; (b. Value is the high estimate of the total average cost (in $/acre) that minimizes reserve costs for wetland reserve of 1 million acres: 286. | Wetlands | National | USA |

| Bibliographic study characteristics | | | | Study Characteristics | | | | Estimate value characteristics: | Water system: Groundwater/ surface water | Spatial scale | Country |
|---|---|---|---|---|---|---|---|---|---|---|---|
| Authors | Title | Bibliographical details | Year | Issue addressed in study/General Function–Use identification | Valuation technique | Year of data collection | Measurement unit | Mean/Total | | | |
| Klein, R.J.T. and I.J. Bateman | 'The Recreation Value of Cley Marshes Nature Reserve: An Argument against Managed Retreat?' | *Water and Environmental Management*, 12, 280–85 | 1998 | The main aim of this study is to provide an estimate of the recreational value of the Cley Reserve. Function–Use: Recreation, Habitat | CV | 1996 | A: In UK pounds, per household, per year or per visit. B. In UK pounds, per party per annum | WTPfee (incl., Zero-bids in UK pounds): 1.58; WTPfee (excl.): 2.22; WTPtax (incl.): 48.15; WTPtax (excl.): 62.08 | Reserve | Regional | United Kingdom |
| Kosz, M. | 'Valuing Riverside Wetlands: The Case of the Conau-Auen National Park' | *Ecological Economics*, 16, 109–27 | 1996 | The aim of this paper is briefly to review the main results of the cost–benefit analysis concerning all the variables that depend on direct anthropocentric use, including energy production with hydroelectric power stations, shipping ground water protection, stabilization of the river bed to stop channel erosion, visitors' benefits, forestry, farming, fishing, hunting and the cost of establishing a national park. This was done because there was a plan to build one or more hydroelectric power stations in the area under study, the Donau-Auen. This was operationalized by 4 different development projects (1) Establishing a national park in all easily available areas (not included in the WTP value. (2) Founding a national park in all available areas including | CV | 1993 (June and July) | ATS 1993 a year | 2a) 919, 80; 2b) 329, 25; 3a) 694,9; 3b) 122,21: 4a) 689,85; 4b) 69, 63 | River | Regional | Austria |

| Author | Title | Journal | Year | Description | Method | Date | Units | Values | Geography | Scale | Country |
|---|---|---|---|---|---|---|---|---|---|---|---|
| Mannesto, G. and J.B. Lommis | 'Evaluation of Mail and In-Person Contingent Value Surveys: Results of a Study of Recreational Boaters' | Journal of Environmental Management, 32, 177–90 | 1991 | private property, concept of hydraulic engineering including extensive measures artificially changing the waterway to avoid further river bed erosion. (3) Construction of a hydro-electric power station near Wolfsthal. (4) Construction of a hydroelectric power station near Wildungsmauer. (The last project is higher in magnitude compared to the third). Wetland loss  Function–Use: Recreation | CV | Interview data drom 29 August to 9 October 1987; Mailing data also in this same period. | $ and concerning the mail back list: 25% increase or 50% increase of total delta wetlands. | 1a) 69.80; 1b) 37.12; 1c) 37.85; 2a) 59.27; 2b) 39.47; 2c) 33.14 | Delta LAKE BAY | Regional | USA |
| Miyata, Y. and H. Abe | 'Measuring the Effects of Flood Control Project: Hedonic Land Price Approach' | Journal of Environmental Management, 42, 389–401 | 1994 | Aim is to measure the effects of a flood control project planned for the Chitose River Basin in Japan by evaluating the reduction in expected physical flood damage derived by construction and improvement of flood control facilities.  Function–Use: Flooding | HP | 1990 | Yen per $Km^2$ cm and area | The total annual average cost of the flood control unit project for the Chitose River (in million yen): case 1: project cost/annual average cost: 0/0; case 2: 96787/4898; case 4: 201848/10214; case 5: 267405/13531; case 6: 310366/15705. Total benefit: Ebvetsu: 5032.0/146.3; Chitose; 12499.2/336.0; Eniwa: 24460.3/497.2; Hiroshima: 8191.5/615.9; Nanporo: 7479.2/138.2; Naganuma: | River basin, Catchment | Regional | Japan |

Table A4.1  (continued)

| Bibliographic study characteristics | | | | Study Characteristics | | | | Estimate value characteristics: | Water system: Groundwater/ surface water | Spatial scale | Country |
|---|---|---|---|---|---|---|---|---|---|---|---|
| Authors | Title | Bibliographical details | Year | Issue addressed in study/General Function–Use identification | Valuation technique | Year of data collection | Measurement unit | Mean/Total | | | |
| Roberts, L.A. and J.A. Leitch | 'Economic Valuation of Some Wetland Outputs of Mud Lake, Minnesota, South Dakota' | Agricultural Economics Report No. 381, Department of Agricultural Economics, North Dakota State University, USA | 1997 | The purpose of this study was to approximate some economic values of Mud Lake, a managed 'wetland' on the border between Minnesota and South Dakota, to provide information to promote more efficient and effective management of Mud Lake and its wetlands. This is done by evaluating some selected outputs: flood control, water supply, fish and wildlife habitat, recreation and aesthetics, and disamenities to water quality. The DVM was used to evaluate fish and wildlife habitat, recreation and aesthetics. Water quality was valued by estimating the extra | CV | 1995 | $ per year per acre | 26390.2/288.4; total: 84052.4/300.5. The corresponding total cost is estimated as 310.4 billion yen and the total estimated benefit computed from the land price variations is 84 billion yen, thus the flood control project under this study may be deemed as a less cost-efficient project. Flood control: total: $440; Water supply/ conservation; $94; WTP regarding fish/ wildlife habitat, recreation, and aesthetics: 1) $7; 2) $8, 3) $6 | Lake | Regional | USA |

102

| Author | Title | Year | Journal | Description | Method | Year | Units | Value notes | Topic | Scale | Location |
|---|---|---|---|---|---|---|---|---|---|---|---|
| Stevens, T.H., S. Benin and J.S. Larson | 'Public Attitudes and Economic Values for Wetland Preservation in New England' | 1995 | *Wetlands*, **15**(3), 226–31 | costs of water treatment, flood control by damages prevented, and water supply by estimating a residual return to public wear utilities. Function–Use: Recreation, Flooding. Wetlands in New England. Function–Use: Flooding | CV | 1993 | Dollars per respondent | (a. Value is the high end estimate of respondents' yearly WTP to protect New England wetlands that provide flood protection water supply and pollution control: 80.41; (b. Value is the low end estimate of respondents' yearly WTP to protect New England wetlands that provide flood protection, water supply and pollution control: 73.89. | Wetlands | National | New England |
| Steever, W.J., M. Callaghan-Perry, A. Searles, T Stevens and P. Svoboda | 'Public Attitudes and Values for Wetland Conservation in New South Wales, Australia' | 1998 | *Journal of Environmental Management*, **54**(1), 1–14 | Wetland conservation. Function–Use: Habitat | CV | 1996 | Australian dollars/person/ year for 5 years | (a. Value represents median WTP for the pooled sample. Value from the pooled sample omits those respondents who did not express WTP: 100;(b. Value represents aggregate value for wetlands in New South Wales, Australia, assuming a WTP per household of A$17.10 and 2.23 million households inthe state: 38. | Wetlands | Regional | Australia |
| van Kooten, G.C. | 'Bioeconomic Evaluation of Government Agricultural Programmes on Wetland Conversion' | 1993 | *Land Economics*, **9**(1), 27–38 | Wetlands providing migratory waterfowl habitat and recreation opportunities. Function–Use: Agricultural Supply | OM | 1988 | Dollars per acre per year | Marginal value of water-fowl habitat as cropland per acre year is reported. Government subsidy of $4.50 per bushel of grain and an average yield of 30 bushels/acre were assumed (land has no livestock value): 37.97. | Wetlands | Regional | USA |

Table A4.1 (continued)

Study Characteristics

| | | Bibliographic study characteristics | | | | | | Estimate value characteristics: | Water system: Groundwater/ | | |
|---|---|---|---|---|---|---|---|---|---|---|---|
| Authors | Title | Bibliographical details | Year | Issue addressed in study/General Function–Use identification | Valuation technique | Year of data collection | Measurement unit | Mean/Total | surface water | Spatial scale | Country |
| Whitehead, J.C. | 'Measuring Willingness to Pay for Wetlands Preservation with the Contingent Valuation Method' | Wetlands 10(2), 187–201. | 1990 | Preservation of a bottomland hardwood forest wetland  Function–Use: Habitat | CV | 1989 | $/household/year | Value measures meanWTP for wetland preservation estimated from log-linear form of model: 6.31 | Wetlands | Local | USA |
| Whitehead, J.C. | 'Environment Interest Group Behaviour and Self-Selection Bias in Contingent Valuation Mail Surveys' | Growth and Change, 22(1), 10–21 | 1991 | Wetland preservation  Function–Use: Habitat | CV | 1989 | $/person/year | (a. Value is the average a WTP per person/year in the general sample for the preservation of the Clear Creek wetland area (assuming 15% of the general population belongs to an environmental interest group): 4. 12; (b. Value is the average WTP per person/year in the environmental interest group sample for the preservation of the Clear Creek wetland area: 42.83. | Wetlands | Local | USA |
| Willis, K.G. | 'Valuing non-market wildlife commodities: An evaluation and comparison of benefits and costs'. | Applied Economics, 22, 13–30. | 1990 | WTP for the preservation of the current state of the wetlands  Function–Use: Recreation, Habitat | CV | | £/ha | (a. total use value: 44; (b total non-use value: 807. | Wetlands | Regional | United Kingdom |

# NOTES

1. Adapted from Pearce and Markandya (1989).
2. El Serafy (1989) developed another approach, which is also called the user cost approach, to estimate the depreciation of the stock of natural capital in green accounting procedures based on the concept of Hick's income. The user costs in the text refer to the value of the resource as if it had not been exploited (Pearce and Turner, 1990).
3. Similar value concepts found in the ecological–economics literature are 'inherent value' (Farnworth *et al.*, 1981), 'infrastructure value' (Costanza *et al.*, 1997), and in the context of biodiversity conservation, 'contributory value' (Norton, 1986).

# REFERENCES

Arrow, K., R. Solow, P.R. Portney, E.E. Leamer, R. Radner and Schuman (1993), *Report of the NOAA Panel on Contingent Valuation*, report to the General Council of the US National Oceanic and Atmospheric Administration Resources for the Future, Washington, DC.

Balmford, A. *et al.* (2002), 'Economic reasons for conserving wild nature', *Science*, **297**, 950–53.

Barbier, E.B. (1994), 'Valuing environmental functions: Tropical wetlands', *Land Economics*, **70**(2), 155–73.

Barbier, E.B., A. Markandya and D.W. Pearce (1990), 'Environmental sustainability and cost–benefit analysis', *Environment and Planning A*, **22**, 1259–66.

Bateman, I.J. and K.G. Willis (eds) (2000), *Valuing Environmental Preferences*, Oxford: Oxford University Press.

Bishop, R.C. (1978), 'Endangered species and uncertainty: The economics of a safe minimum standard', *American Journal of Agricultural Economics*, **60**, 10–18.

Braden, J.B. and Kolstad, C.D. (eds) (1991), *Measuring the Demand for Environmental Quality*, Amsterdam: North-Holland.

Bromley, D.W. (ed.) (1995), *The Handbook of Environmental Economics*, Oxford, UK and Cambridge, MA: Blackwell.

Brouwer, R. (2000), 'Environmental value transfer: State of the art and future prospects', *Ecological Economics*, **32**, 137–52.

Brouwer, R., N. Powe, R.K. Turner, I.H. Langford and I.J. Bateman (1999), 'Public attitudes to contingent valuation and public consultation', *Environmental Values*, **8**(3), 325–47.

Ciriacy-Wantrup, S.V. (1952), *Resource Conservation: Economics and Policies*, Berkeley, CA: University of California Press.

Common, M. and C. Perrings (1992), 'Towards an ecological economics of sustainability', *Ecological Economics*, **6**, 7–34.

Conrad, J.M. and C.W. Clark (1987), *Natural Resource Economics: Notes and Problems*, Cambridge: Cambridge University Press.

Costanza, R., R. d'Arge, R. de Groot, S. Farber, M. Grasso, B. Hannon, K. Limburg, S. Naeem, R.V. O'Neill, J. Paruelo, R.G. Raskin, P. Sutton and M. van den Belt (1997), 'The value of the world's ecosystem services and natural capital', *Nature*, **387**, 253–60.

Crowards, T. (1996), *Addressing Uncertainty in Project Evaluation: The Costs and Benefits of Safe Minimum Standards*, Global Environmental Change Working Paper GEC 96-04, Centre for Social and Economic Research on the Global Environment (CSERGE), University of East Anglia and University College London, UK.

Crowards, T.C. (1997), 'Nonuse values and the environment: Economic and ethical motivations', *Environmental Values*.

Crowards, T.C. and R.K. Turner (1996), *FAEWE Sub-project Report: Economic Valuation of Wetlands*, Centre for Social and Economic Research on the Global Environment (CSERGE), University of East Anglia and University College London, UK.

El Serafy, S. (1989), 'The proper calculation of income from depletable natural resources', in Y.J. Ahmad, S. El Serafy and E. Lutz (eds), *Environmental Accounting for Sustainable Development*, Washington, DC: World Bank.

Farnworth, E.G., T.H. Tidrick, C.F. Jordan and W.M. Smathers (1981), 'The value of ecosystems: An economic and ecological framework', *Environmental Conservation*, **8**, 275–82.

Fisher, A. and J.V. Krutilla (1975), 'Resource conservation, environmental preservation, and the rate of discount', *Quarterly Journal of Economics*, **89**, 358–70.

Foster, J. (ed.) (1997), *Valuing Nature? Economics, Ethics and Environment*, London and New York: Routledge.

Freeman, A.M.I. (1993), *The Measurement of Environmental and Resource Values*, Washington, DC: Resources for the Future.

Gren, I-M., C. Folke, R.K. Turner and I. Bateman (1994), 'Primary and secondary values of wetland ecosystems', *Environmental and Resource Economics*, **4**, 55–74.

Hanley, N. and C.L. Spash (1993), *Cost–Benefit Analysis and the Environment*, Aldershot, UK and Brookfield, US: Edward Elgar.

Hargrove, C. (1992), 'Weak anthropocentric intrinsic value', *The Monist*, **75**(2), 183–207.

Just, R., D. Hueth and A. Schmitz (1982), *Applied Welfare Economics and Public Policy*, Englewood Cliffs, NJ: Prentice Hall.

Norton, B.G. (1986), *Towards Unity Among Environmentalists*, Oxford: Oxford University Press.

Pearce, D.W. and A. Markandya (1989), 'Marginal opportunity cost as a planning concept in natural resource management', in G. Schramm and J. Warford (eds), *Environmental Management and Economic Development*, London: Johns Hopkins University Press.

Pearce, D.W. and R.K. Turner (1990), *Economics of Natural Resources and the Environment*, Hemel Hempstead, UK: Harvester Wheatsheaf.

Pearce, D., D. Whittington, S. Georgiou and D. James (1994), *Project and Policy Appraisal: Integrating Economics and Environment*, Paris: OECD.

Randall, A. (1987), *Resource Economics: An Economic Approach to Natural Resource and Environmental Policy*, New York: John Wiley and Son.

Repetto, R. (1986), *Skimming the Water: Rent Seeking and the Performance of Public Irrigation Systems*, Washington, DC: World Resource Institute.

Samuelson, P. and W. Nordhaus (1985), *Economics*, New York: McGraw-Hill.

Tietenberg, T.H. (1992), *Innovation in Environmental Policy: Economic and Legal Aspects of Recent Developments in Liability and Enforcement*, Aldershot, UK and Brookfield, US: Edward Elgar.

Turner, R.K. (1991), 'Economics and wetland management', *Ambio*, **20**, 59–63.

Turner, R.K. (1993), 'Sustainability: Principles and practice', in R.K. Turner (ed.), *Sustainable Environmental Economics and Management: Principles and Practice*, London: Belhaven Press.

Turner, R.K. (2000), 'The place of economic values in environmental valuation', in I.J. Bateman and K.G. Willis (eds), *Valuing Environmental Preferences*, Oxford: Oxford University Press.

Turner, R.K. and D.W. Pearce (1993), 'Sustainable economic development: Economic and ethical principles', in E.B. Barbier (ed.), *Economics and Ecology: New Frontiers and Sustainable Development*, London: Chapman and Hall.
van Vuuren, W. and P. Roy (1993), 'Private and social returns from wetland preservation versus wetland conversion to agriculture', *Ecological Economics*, **8**, 289–305.

# 5. A meta-analysis of wetland ecosystem valuation studies[1]

## R. Brouwer, I.H. Langford, I.J. Bateman and R.K. Turner

## 1   INTRODUCTION

This chapter addresses the socio-economic values of the various functions performed by wetland ecosystems. Environmental economists have developed a variety of techniques for measuring such values of which the contingent valuation (CV) method is probably the most widely applied in contemporary research. CV is a survey method where individuals are presented with information about specific environmental changes, and their perception, attitudes and preferences regarding these changes are elicited. In order to measure the effect of the suggested changes on people's welfare, respondents are typically asked for either their willingness to pay (WTP) or their willingness to accept (WTA) compensation for the gains or losses involved (Mitchell and Carson, 1989). Of these options the WTP approach has become the most frequently applied and has been given peer review endorsement through a variety of studies (see, for example, Arrow *et al.*, 1993). When aggregated across those who will be affected by the suggested environmental changes, this stated WTP amount is used as a socio-economic indicator of the environmental values involved.

Given the substantial indirect, often off-site, use and non-use values involved, wetlands have been the focus of attention in several CV studies (Crowards and Turner, 1996). Many of these studies try to estimate the total economic value of wetlands. Total economic value consists of use and non-use values (Pearce and Turner, 1990). CV is the only economic method to date which is able, in principle, to account for possible non-use motivations underlying people's value statements. Whereas use values refer to the values associated with the actual use of the various goods and services wetlands provide, non-use values are unrelated to any actual or potential use of these goods and services.

In this chapter, the main findings of CV studies of wetlands in temperate climate zones in developed economies will be investigated. The main objective is to quantify the socio-economic values associated with wetland ecosystem functioning in a *meta-analysis* of wetland CV studies, supplementing qualitative analyses provided for example by Gren and Söderqvist (1994) or Crowards and Turner (1996). Natural and social science are brought together by relating the various hydrological, biogeochemical and ecological wetland functions to the societal benefits derived from these functions and the socio-economic values attached to these benefits.

## 2   METHODOLOGY

The results from 30 different CV studies of wetlands in temperate climate zones in developed economies were compared and synthesized in a meta-analysis. Only very few tropical wetland valuation studies exist (Barbier, 1993). Tropical wetland studies are excluded from the meta-analysis presented here because of the enormous differences between population samples in developed and developing countries regarding socio-cultural and demo-graphic–economic characteristics.

Since the beginning of the 1990s, meta-analysis has been playing an increasingly important role in environmental economics research (van den Bergh *et al.*, 1997). Originally a technique used in experimental medical treatment and psychotherapy, meta-analysis is the statistical evaluation of the summary findings of empirical studies, helping to extract information from large masses of data in order to quantify a more comprehensive assessment. It enables researchers to explain differences in outcomes found in single studies on the basis of differences in underlying assumptions, standards of design and/or measurement. As such, meta-analysis is an important extension of quantitative analyses and can be seen as a supplement to qualitative analysis.

Compared to qualitative analysis, important advantages of meta-analysis are that on the 'input' side it does not prejudge research findings on the basis of the original study's quality, while it avoids a differential subjective weighting of studies in the interpretation of a set of findings on the 'output' side (Glass *et al.*, 1981). However, one drawback is that it may be biased towards including significant study results only, since it may well be that insignificant study results will not be published. Furthermore, multiple results from the same study are often treated as individual, independent observations without explicit testing for intra-study correlation (Wolf, 1986).

In the field of environmental valuation, meta-analyses have focused on a range of environmental issues from outdoor recreation to urban air pollution, based on single or multiple valuation techniques. The increase in meta-analytical research seems to be triggered principally by (1) increases in the available number of environmental valuation studies, (2) the seemingly large differences in valuation outcomes as a result of the use of different research designs (Carson *et al.*, 1996), and (3) the high costs of carrying out environmental valuation studies which tend to increase policy maker demand for transferable valuation results.

Meta-analysis enables researchers to identify criteria for valid environmental value transfer or to test the convergent validity of value estimates. In the first case the data set is entirely used to determine the factors which help to significantly explain variances in valuation outcomes. In the second case the data set can be split for example in two parts, one of which is used for the first purpose and another to test whether the value estimates based on the significant factors fall within the confidence interval of the other half's estimates.

Environmental value transfer is commonly defined as the transposition of monetary environmental values estimated at one site (study site) through market based or non-market based economic valuation techniques to another site (policy site). The most important reason for using previous research results in new policy contexts is cost-effectiveness. Applying previous research findings to similar decision situations is a very attractive alternative to expensive and time consuming original research in order to inform decision making quickly.

The criteria for selecting studies for environmental value transfer suggested in the literature focus on the environmental goods involved, the sites in which the goods are found, the stakeholders and the study quality (Desvousges *et al.*, 1992). However, very little published evidence exists of studies that test the validity of environmental value transfer. Moreover, in the few studies that have been carried out, the transfer errors are substantial (Brouwer, 2000).

As more information about factors influencing environmental valuation outcomes becomes available, for instance through the meta-analysis presented here, transfers across populations and sites seem to become more practicable, using either existing (secondary) information only or supplementing this information with new original (primary) data.

## 3   DATA SET AND STUDY CHARACTERISTICS

The list of wetland CV studies included in the meta-analysis is presented in Table 5.1. Most studies have been published in journals. Half of all studies were carried out between 1985 and 1989, with most being published in the first three years of the 1990s. One study was carried out in the 1970s, 19 in the 1980s and 10 in the 1990s.

Besides the inclusion of published and significant results, Table 5.1 illustrates two other problems in this meta-analysis. First, a number of people have been involved in several studies and related publications. This may result in an

*Table 5.1   Studies included in the meta-analysis*

| | Authors | Type of Publication[a] | Study Year | $n$[b] |
|---|---|---|---|---|
| 1 | Bateman *et al.* (1995) | journal article (EE) | 1991 | 3 |
| 2 | Bergstrom, Stoll, Titre and Wright (1990) | journal article (EE) | 1986 | 1 |
| 3 | Bishop and Boyle (1985) | consultancy report | 1985 | 2 |
| 4 | Bishop, Boyle and Welsh (1987) | journal article (TAFS) | 1985 | 7 |
| 5 | Brouwer and Slangen (1998) | journal article (ERAE) | 1994 | 3 |
| 6 | Carson and Mitchell (1993) | journal article (WRR) | 1983 | 3 |
| 7 | Cooper and Loomis (1991) | book chapter | 1987 | 3 |
| 8 | *Cummings, Ganderton and McGuckin (1994)* | journal article (AJAE) | 1992 | 2 |
| 9 | Desvousges, Smith and Fisher (1987) | journal article (JEEM) | 1981 | 21 |
| 10 | Farber (1988) | journal article (JEM) | 1984 | 1 |
| 11 | Garrod and Willis (1996) | journal article (JEPM) | 1993 | 4 |
| 12 | Green and Tunstall (1991) | journal article (AE) | 1986 | 1 |
| 13 | Greenley, Walsh and Young (1981) | journal article (QJE) | 1976 | 4 |
| 14 | Silvander (1991) | dissertation | 1989 | 2 |
| 15 | Jordan and Elnagheeb (1993) | journal article (WRR) | 1991 | 2 |
| 16 | Kaoru (1993) | journal article (ERE) | 1989 | 1 |
| 17 | Kosz (1996) | journal article (EE) | 1993 | 1 |
| 18 | Lant and Roberts (1990) | journal article (EPA) | 1987 | 6 |
| 19 | Loomis *et al.* (1991) | book chapter | 1989 | 10 |
| 20 | Loomis (1987) | journal article (WRR) | 1985 | 1 |
| 21 | Olsen, Richards and Scott (1991) | journal article (Rivers) | 1989 | 3 |
| 22 | *Phillips, Haney and Adamowicz (1993)* | journal article (CJAE) | 1991 | 2 |
| 23 | Sanders, Walsh and Loomis (1990) | journal article (WRR) | 1983 | 2 |
| 24 | Schultz and Lindsay (1990) | journal article (WRR) | 1988 | 1 |
| 25 | Spaninks (1993) | MSc thesis | 1993 | 3 |
| 26 | Spaninks, Kuik and Hoogeveen (1996) | scientific report | 1995 | 2 |
| 27 | Sutherland and Walsh (1985) | journal article (LE) | 1981 | 2 |
| 28 | Whitehead and Blomquist (1991) | journal article (WRR) | 1989 | 6 |
| 29 | Willis (1990) | journal article (AE) | 1986 | 2 |
| 30 | Willis, Garrod and Saunders (1995) | journal article (JEM) | 1992 | 2 |

*Notes*

Year of publication in parentheses.

[a] Clarification of abbreviations:

| | | | |
|---|---|---|---|
| AE: | Applied Economics | JEEM: | Journal of Environmental Economics |
| AJAE: | American Journal of Agricultural | | and Management |
| | Economics | JEM: | Journal of Environmental Management |
| CJAE: | Canadian Journal of Agricultural | JEPM: | Journal of Environmental Planning and |
| | Economics | | Management |
| EE: | Ecological Economics | LE: | Land Economics |
| ERAE: | European Review of Agricultural | QJE: | The Quarterly Journal of Economics |
| | Economics | TAFS: | Transactions of the American Fisheries |
| ERE: | Environmental and Resource | | Society |
| | Economics | WRR: | Water Resources Research |
| EPA: | Environment and Planning A | | |

[b] Number of observations taken from each study.

*authorship* effect. Learning from previous studies, authors may use similar, perhaps slightly adapted survey designs in subsequent studies. Secondly, 103 data points (observations) were extracted from 30 studies. This corresponds, on average, to three or four observations per study. More than half of all studies provided one or two observations. Outliers are the studies by Loomis *et al.* (1991) and Desvousges *et al.* (1987), providing 10 and 21 observations respectively. Studies provided more than one observation mainly because of the use of split survey samples targeting different wetland user and non-user groups and testing different survey designs.

The possibility that results from the same study may cluster together, for example as a result of identical survey design or sample population, and that results from some studies may be more variable than others was tested and accounted for in the meta-analysis (see section 4 below).

Although the studies included in the analysis focus primarily on wetlands or wetland type areas, the specific WTP questions addressed in each study cover a large continuum of activities, actions or projects related to wetlands, but in some cases (approximately a third of all studies) also to water resources in general. These values were kept in the analysis because they referred directly to the hydrological wetland functions distinguished in the analysis and were considered reliable estimates for these functions. The WTP questions range from outdoor recreational activities like birdwatching or fishing, to groundwater protection and complete wildlife habitat preservation. Two thirds of the studies were carried out in the USA, the rest in Europe. Half of the European studies were carried out in the UK.

Separating the heterogeneous complex of hydrological, biogeochemical and ecological functions performed by the wetlands considered in each study in the meta-analysis was very difficult. Based on the various functions addressed in the reviewed studies, a simple distinction was therefore first of all made between four main wetland ecosystem functions: flood control, water generation, water quality support and wildlife habitat provision (Figure 5.1). Secondly, the main function valued in each study was assigned to one of each of these four groups. Hence, each study was categorized as addressing one of these four main wetland functions, unless a study explicitly generated distinct values for different wetland functions.

Obviously, wetland ecosystem structures and processes and the functions they provide are highly interrelated, making it very hard, and in some cases impossible, to distinguish between individual functions. They often go hand in hand and attempts to separate them, for example for economic valuation purposes in order to avoid double counting, are liable to be arbitrary. This implies that double counting is a real problem and attempts to aggregate up to system level values are fraught with difficulties.

Also, in the case of the human benefits derived from the wetland functions

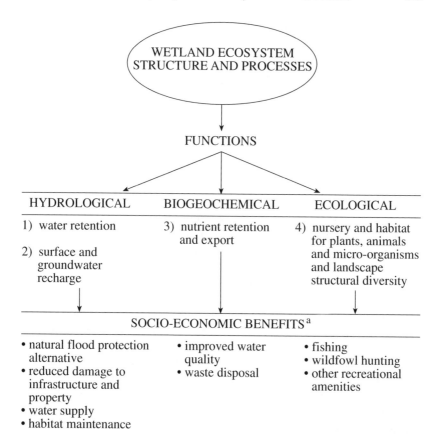

*Figure 5.1*    *Main wetland functions identified in the meta-analysis and their derived socio-economic benefits*

involved, complete separation of direct and indirect use and non-use benefits is difficult. Only in a third of all studies could a single benefit flow be identified, in all other cases wetland functions provided multiple benefits.

Most studies (70 per cent) asked respondents for the use and non-use values attached to the benefits derived from wetland functions. One study (Schultz and Lindsay, 1990), elicited future use value only (option value), while another (Greenley *et al.*, 1981) focused, among others, on the *ex ante* 'option price' of being able to make a better informed judgement in the future based on more information becoming available regarding water quality.

In eight studies an attempt was made to break down the stated total economic value *ex post* in the questionnaire into the various components distinguished in the literature, for example use, option, philanthropic, bequest, stewardship and existence value. In two water quality studies (Carson and Mitchell, 1993; Desvousges *et al.*, 1987), respondents were presented *ex ante* with a 'value card' which described the main reasons why water quality might be valued. In another two studies use and non-use values were elicited separately, either by the use of different questionnaires (Bishop *et al.*, 1987) or the use of separate questions for use and non-use values in the same questionnaire (Greenley *et al.*, 1981).

Finally, two study quality indicators were included in the analysis: one for the quality of the studies included in the meta-analysis and one for the quality of the meta-analysis itself. The quality of individual studies is indicated by the study response rate and the quality of the meta-analysis by the so-called scope test. Both indicators are found back in the NOAA's 'burden of proof' requirements (Arrow *et al.*, 1993).[2]

A high non-response, either to the entire survey instrument or the valuation question, raises concern regarding the study's representativeness, and questions the validity of the survey design employed and the extent to which the valuation scenario in the questionnaire was comprehensible and credible. The scope test refers to the sensitivity of WTP measures to changes in the provision level of the goods and services being valued, that is the difference between reference and target provision levels. In order to conform with neoclassical consumer theory, responses should also reveal a smaller WTP for smaller amounts of an environmental commodity provided by an environmental programme.

Very few studies reported the extent of protest bids and other questionable responses in the survey. Although most studies mention the survey response rates, it is in many cases not clear what these response rates actually represent or which criteria have been used to exclude responses from further analysis. Where such information was available, protest bids and questionable responses were excluded from the response rates.

In order to carry out a scope test, the size of the affected study site and the difference between the reference and the target levels of environmental service provision in the CV scenarios of environmental change should ideally be considered. However, in two thirds of all studies no information is provided about the size of the area involved. In about one third of all studies, the study site size was estimated using geographical maps. Problems accumulate when also aiming to include the difference between the reference and target levels of the various wetland functions distinguished in the environmental scenarios in each study. The multi-dimensional nature of these functions makes a comparison between studies impossible. Hence, instead an ordinal 'relative size' variable was compiled, referring to the share of each study site in the country's total stock of wetlands.

## 4   THE MODEL

The structure of the data used in the meta-analysis is complex. WTP values are generated by different studies, carried out in different geographical locations using different valuation formats. Using the summary statistics of these different studies in a pooled sample, the usual conditions required for Ordinary Least Squares (OLS) regression are likely to be violated. In order to account for heteroscedasticity, a Generalized Least Squares (GLS) regression technique called multilevel modelling was used (Langford, 1994; Langford *et al.*, 1999).[3] Given the shape of the distribution of the WTP amounts, a logarithmic transformation was used. Hence, for the log (WTP) amounts of the studies $Y$, the GLS model is:

$$Y = X\beta + Z\theta \tag{5.1}$$

where $X\beta$ consists of the design matrix $X$ and associated parameters $\beta$ and represent the mean or fixed effects of the explanatory variables on the dependent variable $Y$. However, whereas in OLS regression there is a single vector of error terms or residuals, here a more complex variance structure may be modelled where the values of residuals are dependent on explanatory variables included in the design matrix $Z$ for the random part of the model (Z-Theta). For example, using one explanatory variable for simplicity, model (5.1) can be written as:

$$y_i = \beta_0 + \beta_1 x_{1i} + u_i + v_i x_{1i}, \begin{bmatrix} u_i \\ v_i \end{bmatrix} \sim N\left( \begin{bmatrix} 0 \\ 0 \end{bmatrix}, \begin{bmatrix} \sigma_u^2 & \sigma_{uv} \\ \sigma_{uv} & \sigma_v^2 \end{bmatrix} \right) \tag{5.2}$$

where $u_i$ is the residual associated with the intercept $\beta_0$, and $v_i$ is the residual associated with the slope parameter $\beta_1$ of $x_1$. While the variance of the responses in OLS is determined by a single residual term, in the basic GLS model the variance is dependent on the explanatory variable:

$$\text{var}(y_i) = \sigma_u^2 + 2\sigma_{uv}X_1 + \sigma_u^2 X_1^2 \tag{5.3}$$

This can be done for any number of variables, hence making the variance of the responses a complex function of the explanatory variables, accounting for heteroscedasticity. This turns out to be highly relevant, as there are significant differences, for example, in the variance of responses within different studies (intra-study effects). Using the subscript $j$ to label different studies, the basic previous GLS model can be rewritten as:

$$y_{ij} = \beta_0 + \beta_1 x_{1ij} + u_{ij} + v_{ij}x_{1ij} + s_j, \begin{bmatrix} u_i \\ v_i \end{bmatrix} \sim N\left( \begin{bmatrix} 0 \\ 0 \end{bmatrix}, \begin{bmatrix} \sigma_u^2 & \sigma_{uv} \\ \sigma_{uv} & \sigma_v^2 \end{bmatrix} \right), s_j = N(0, \sigma_s^2)$$

(5.4)

where $\sigma_s^2$ the variance parameter that describes the differing variability of estimates within different studies. This latter model will be referred to as the 'extended' model in the results section.

## 5   RESULTS

A first step in the meta-analysis was to make stated average WTP amounts in each study comparable. The response variable is average WTP per household per year for the preservation of specific wetland aspects. After expressing WTP in national currencies in terms of their 1990 purchasing power, these national currencies were converted in the International Monetary Fund's (IMF) Special Drawing Rights (SDRs), which is the Fund's official monetary unit of account (IMF, 1996). Average WTP for wetland function preservation found in all studies taken together is 62 SDRs.[4] The median is considerably lower, namely 34 SDRs.

The breakdown of WTP values according to a number of possible explanatory factors is presented in Table 5.2. Mean WTP values have been calculated for (1) wetland types as identified by Dugan (1990); (2) main wetland functions; (3) relative wetland size; (4) the different value types elicited in the studies (use and/or non-use values); (5) the continent where the wetland sites are found; (6) the way people were asked to pay for wetland function preservation in the CV survey as part of the institutional setting of the wetland conservation programmes (for example through general income taxation or otherwise); and (7) the way the WTP question was elicited in the CV survey (for example in an open-ended question or otherwise).

The calculated differences in mean WTP for each of these categories are statistically significant at the 5 per cent significance level or stronger (see the outcomes of the chi-square test statistic in the last column of Table 5.2). The range of values (minimum and maximum) found for the factor levels across studies is considerable.

Mean WTP per household is more or less the same for salt and fresh water

*Table 5.2  Summary statistics*

| | Mean WTP (SDRs) | Standard Error | Min (SDRs) | Max (SDRs) | $n^a$ | $\chi^2$ (p<)[b] |
|---|---|---|---|---|---|---|
| **Wetland Type** | | | | | | 15.2  (0.05) |
| *Salt water* | 56.2 | 27.2 | 19 | 137 | 4 | |
| marine | 22.7 | 3.7 | 19 | 26 | 2 | |
| lagoonal | 136.6 | – | – | – | 1 | |
| lake | 42.8 | – | – | – | 1 | |
| *fresh water* | 58.9 | 6.1 | 1 | 267 | 97 | |
| riverine | 71.7 | 13.7 | 1 | 267 | 38 | |
| lacustrine | 36.8 | 9.4 | 12 | 88 | 9 | |
| palustrine | 36.9 | 4.3 | 9 | 117 | 31 | |
| groundwater | 125.7 | 24.3 | 99 | 174 | 3 | |
| *fresh and salt water* | 237.5 | 106.2 | 131 | 344 | 2 | |
| **Wetland Function** | | | | | | 7.8  (0.05) |
| flood control | 92.6 | 24.4 | 24 | 177 | 5 | |
| water generation | 21.5 | 6.8 | 3 | 59 | 9 | |
| water quality | 52.5 | 5.9 | 9 | 174 | 43 | |
| biodiversity | 76.1 | 12.8 | 1 | 344 | 46 | |
| **Relative Wetland Size** | | | | | | 13.1  (0.01) |
| very large | 86.9 | 17.6 | 19 | 177 | 8 | |
| large | 70.3 | 21.6 | 12 | 344 | 16 | |
| medium | 67.0 | 8.9 | 3 | 267 | 58 | |
| small | 29.5 | 13.2 | 1 | 137 | 13 | |
| very small | 53.4 | 13.8 | 24 | 105 | 6 | |
| **Value Type** | | | | | | 6.1  (0.05) |
| use value | 68.1 | 8.4 | 9 | 344 | 50 | |
| non-use value | 35.5 | 4.8 | 12 | 78 | 13 | |
| use and non-use values | 63.8 | 12.9 | 1 | 267 | 40 | |

*Table 5.2 (continued)*

| | Mean WTP (SDRs) | Standard Error | Min (SDRs) | Max (SDRs) | $n^a$ | $\chi^2$ ($p<$)[b] |
|---|---|---|---|---|---|---|
| **Country** | | | | | | -3.0  (0.003)[c] |
| USA and Canada | 70.8 | 7.8 | 3 | 344 | 80 | |
| Europe | 32.8 | 8.4 | 1 | 177 | 23 | |
| **Payment Mode** | | | | | | 27.4  (0.001) |
| income tax | 121.3 | 18.1 | 2 | 267 | 22 | |
| entrance fee/private fund | 28.6 | 5.7 | 1 | 137 | 28 | |
| product prices | 47.8 | 8.9 | 3 | 174 | 22 | |
| combination of 1 and 3 | 42.8 | 6.3 | 9 | 117 | 26 | |
| trip expenditures | 102.9 | 6.8 | 89 | 112 | 3 | |
| not specified | 237.5 | 106.2 | 131 | 344 | 2 | |
| **Elicitation Format** | | | | | | 10.1  (0.01) |
| open-ended | 37.4 | 6.5 | 1 | 137 | 35 | |
| dichotomous choice | 91.2 | 17.1 | 3 | 344 | 29 | |
| iterative bidding | 78.5 | 14.9 | 9 | 244 | 20 | |
| payment card | 47.1 | 8.4 | 10 | 174 | 19 | |

*Notes*
[a] The number of observations does not sum up to 103 in all cases as a result of missing values.
[b] Outcome of the non-parametric Kruskal–Wallis test statistic which has approximately a chi-squared distribution under the null hypothesis of equal average WTP in all groups.
[c] Outcome of the non-parametric Mann–Whitney test statistic for 2 independent samples which has approximately a standard normal distribution under the same null hypothesis.

wetlands. However, the number of observations for salt water wetlands is very low. Almost all observations refer to fresh water wetlands. Within fresh water wetlands, the value of wetlands fed by rivers (riverine) is twice as high as the value of lakes and ponds (lacustrine) or marshes and swamps (palustrine). Groundwater is valued most, although the number of observations is again low.

The wetland function flood control generates the highest mean WTP, followed by wildlife habitat provision and landscape structural diversity (labelled 'biodiversity' in Table 5.2). Surface and groundwater recharge (labelled 'water generation' in Table 5.2) has the lowest value. As expected, larger sites result in higher WTP. An inconsistency is found between the categories 'small' and 'very small'.

Use values associated with wetland functions are almost twice as high as non-use values. However, a combination of the two is not equal to their sum, suggesting some non-linear relationship between the two. Socio-psychological and related factors underpinning so-called embedding effects, where the sum of the valuations placed on the parts of a commodity exceeds that for the whole (Bateman *et al.*, 1997), may be one important reason.

North-Americans are WTP, on average, more than Europeans. Since average income data for the survey samples is missing in most of the studies reviewed, the country in which the wetland sites are found and the CV surveys were carried out is used as an indicator for income differences to account for people's capacity to pay.

Income taxation as a payment vehicle generates the highest average WTP value, followed by stated WTP over and above actual trip expenditures to visit a wetland site (use value). The latter is part of a set of payment mechanisms which present wetland functions to respondents as a private good, that is to be 'consumed' by the individual who is being interviewed by asking her to pay for example an entrance fee. On the other hand, general income taxation is expected to prompt responses which consider the implications of wetland preservation for society at large, not just for the individual (Mitchell and Carson, 1989; Blamey, 1995). Hence, the higher WTP value elicited through this payment mechanism is expected to reflect more than private use values only.[5]

The high value for non-specified payment modes is due to outliers and the very low number of observations. Calculating through the value of wetland function preservation in existing product prices yields a significantly higher mean WTP than the establishment of a private fund or raising entrance fees.

Finally, corresponding to previous research results (for example McFadden, 1994; Bateman *et al.*, 1995; Willis *et al.*, 1995), the open-ended elicitation format yields a significantly lower WTP than other formats. The dichotomous choice format (yes or no to a given bid amount) yields the highest average

WTP, followed by the iterative bidding procedure (yes or no to a sequence of bid amounts). Possible explanations are the larger numbers of non-responses or protest responses OE tends to produce (Desvousges *et al.*, 1983) or the uncertainty experienced in answering the unfamiliar WTP question for non-market goods and services in an open-ended format (Bateman *et al.*, 1995).

The findings for the basic and extended GLS model in which we account for study-level effects are presented in Table 5.3. Only those variables are included that are statistically significant at the 0.1 level.

The fixed part of the model represents the fixed or mean effects of each variable, as for an OLS regression model, while the random part displays the variance and covariance parameters that model heteroscedasticity.

The estimates for the regression results are obtained through Maximum Likelihood techniques (for example Maddala, 1983). The outcome of the like-lihood ratio test ($\chi_{14}^2 = 96.51$; $p < 0.01$) rejects the null hypothesis of zero effects for all explanatory variables. A pseudo R-squared was calculated from the log likelihood (LL) function. The outcome corresponds with the goodness-of-fit measures usually found in CV studies. Since the pseudo R-squared lacks the straightforward explained variance interpretation of R-squared in OLS regression (Hamilton, 1993), it is used here as a rough indicator for the model's goodness-of-fit. The estimated models account for approximately 37 per cent of the observed variability in the mean WTP values found in individual studies.

For the fixed part of the basic and extended model, the estimated coefficients in the semi-log function represent the constant proportional rate of change in the dependent variable per unit change in the independent variables (Johnston, 1984). Hence, the coefficient estimated for the dummy variable 'Payment vehicle' in the basic model reflects, *ceteris paribus*, an almost twice as high average WTP for an increase in income tax than for any other payment vehicle. Compared to other elicitation formats, WTP is reduced, on average, by 41 per cent (*ceteris paribus*) when using studies in a value transfer exercise, which are based on an open-ended WTP question.

The basic model also indicates that study location has a significant impact on average WTP. The dummy variable has a value of one if the research took place in North America and of zero if in Europe. As shown before, average WTP is substantially higher in North America than in Europe.

The parameter estimates for the four main wetland functions are particularly interesting. These functions are found to have a statistically significant role in explaining variance in average WTP. The size of the estimated parameters indicates that average WTP is, as before, highest for flood control, but this time, whilst controlling for other explanatory factors, it is followed by water genera-tion and water quality, and is lowest for the wetland function biodiversity supply. The latter is used as the baseline category in the regression analysis in

Table 5.3  GLS results for the basic and extended model

| Fixed Effects | | Basic Model | | Extended Model | |
|---|---|---|---|---|---|
| Parameter | Parameter Definition | Estimate | Standard Error | Estimate | Standard Error |
| Constant | intercept | 3.356*** | 0.100 | 3.311*** | 0.247 |
| Payment vehicle | dummy: 1 = income tax / 0 = other | 1.880*** | 0.265 | 1.576*** | 0.362 |
| Elicitation format | dummy: 1 = open-ended / 0 = other | –0.411** | 0.130 | –0.376* | 0.183 |
| Country | dummy: 1 = North America / 0 = other | 1.861*** | 0.217 | 1.629*** | 0.363 |
| Response rate (1) | dummy: 1 = 30–50% / 0 = other | –2.253*** | 0.326 | –1.722*** | 0.451 |
| Response rate (2) | dummy: 1 = >50% / 0 = other | –1.904*** | 0.333 | –1.461** | 0.450 |
| Flood control | dummy: 1 = flood control / 0 = other | 1.477*** | 0.240 | 1.134* | 0.456 |
| Water generation | dummy: 1 = water generation / 0 = other | 0.691* | 0.342 | 0.441 | 0.479 |
| Water quality | dummy: 1 = water quality / 0 = other | 0.545[†] | 0.282 | 0.659* | 0.327 |

*Table 5.3 (continued)*

| Random Effects | | Estimate | Standard Error | Estimate | Standard Error |
|---|---|---|---|---|---|
| **Between Studies** | | | | | |
| $\sigma^2_{constant}$ | variance | – | – | 0.160* | 0.071 |
| **Between Average WTP** | | | | | |
| $\sigma^2_{constant}$ | variance | 0.059* | 0.029 | 0.045 | 0.028 |
| $\sigma_{payment\ vehicle,\ constant}$ | covariance | 0.020 | 0.043 | 0.001 | 0.036 |
| $\sigma_{country,\ constant}$ | covariance | 0.689** | 0.222 | 0.351** | 0.129 |
| $\sigma_{country,\ payment\ vehicle}$ | covariance | -0.707** | 0.226 | -0.345*** | 0.134 |
| $\sigma_{flood\ control,\ constant}$ | covariance | -0.013 | 0.050 | 0.027 | 0.060 |
| $\sigma_{water\ generation,\ constant}$ | covariance | -0.637** | 0.227 | -0.266† | 0.153 |
| $\sigma_{water\ quality,\ constant}$ | covariance | -0.424† | 0.231 | -0.188 | 0.135 |
| $LL_{unconstrained}$ | | -83.907 | | -81.874 | |
| Pseudo R-squared | | 0.365 | | 0.380 | |
| $N$ | | 92 | | 92 | |

*Notes*

As a result of missing values for explanatory variables, the number of observations is reduced from 103 to 92.

† = significant at 0.10   ** = significant at 0.01

* = significant at 0.05   *** = significant at 0.001

order to avoid multicollinearity. The positive parameter estimates for the three other wetland functions indicate that these functions generate higher values than the baseline function biodiversity supply.

This suggests the prominence of use over non-use motivations underpinning stated WTP amounts. The distinction between use and/or non-use values does not have a significant impact on average WTP, probably because the corresponding variance is already accounted for by the distinction between wetland functions. Also, relative wetland size is statistically not significant.

Higher response rates, a rough indicator of better overall study quality, appear to result in significantly lower average WTP than low response rates. A practical explanation may be that low response rates are sometimes biased towards including a relatively large number of sample respondents with a greater interest than average in environmental protection and corresponding WTP.

The model's random effects can be used to (1) model heteroscedasticity and (2) investigate the suitability of using specific CV results in a value transfer exercise. This will be explained below.

The interpretation of the random effects is as follows: the variance of the constant in the basic and extended model is the variance associated with the baseline case, that is where the value of all the explanatory variables is zero. The variance of, for example, North American studies in the basic model is $(0.059 + 2*0.689) = 1.437$. Hence, North American studies are more variable than European ones. In this way heteroscedasticity can be modelled in the basic model. Another example is North American studies using income taxation as a payment vehicle:

$$\sigma^2_{\text{country, payment vehicle}} = 0.059 + 2*0.689 + 2*0.020 - 2*0.707 = 0.023$$

The last term in this equation is the covariance between payment vehicle and country. So, wetland CV studies based on income taxation in the US appear to have a particularly low variance.

Accounting for study level effects in the basic model significantly reduces the sample variance or standard deviation of average WTP in the extended model ($\chi^2_1 = 4.06$; $p < 0.05$). The extended, multilevel model accounting for the random effects between studies hence provides a significant improvement over conventional meta-analysis by allowing for the hierarchical structure of data implicit in clustering of multiple results from single studies. As expected, having explained some of the variance in the model by study-level effects, the random effects between log(WTP) amounts have decreased, except for the covariance between flood control and the intercept.

However, in the extended model the fixed effects have slightly decreased, while the significance level of half of the explanatory variables is lower. The only increase is seen in the significance of the wetland function 'water quality'. The wetland function water generation has become statistically insignificant and has switched places with the function 'water quality supply' in the order of size, suggesting that the results must be viewed with some caution when properly accounting for intra-study variability.

If low variance is considered an estimate of quality in the sense that study results are better suited for comparison and hence can be more readily put together in a value transfer exercise, then it can be concluded that *on the whole* studies using income taxation as a payment vehicle are better suited than other payment vehicles, and that studies valuing wetland biodiversity tend to be less variable than studies valuing wetlands in their capacity of generating water or maintaining water quality.

## 6   DISCUSSION AND CONCLUSIONS

Estimates for socio-economic use and non-use values attached to different hydro-ecological and biogeochemical wetland functions were compared and synthesized in a meta-analysis of wetland CV studies. The meta-analysis provides insights into the factors that have to be considered when attempting to transfer environmental values on the basis of CV studies. A statistically significant breakdown of WTP values for four main wetland functions was presented. Although single ecosystem characteristics or functions are given meaning and value within existing ecosystem structures, the distinction between functions is essential for a valid transfer of the economic values generated within an ecosystem's primary self-organizing capacity. It reduces the risk of double counting when attempting to assess a natural resource's total economic value on the basis of different valuation studies.

From an anthropocentric point of view the size of the estimated parameters in the estimated basic model is as expected. Average WTP is highest for flood control, because of the possible risks to life and livelihood as a result of flooding and the capacity of wetlands to reduce this risk, followed by water supply and water quality and finally the provision and maintenance of biodiversity. However, these results have to be handled with care for a number of reasons.

Ecosystem structures and processes provide a heterogeneous complex of highly interrelated socio-economic functions. The analysis presents a simple and arbitrary breakdown of these functions into independent components. The distinction between four main wetland functions also does not necessarily correspond with people's perception of the various functions wetlands perform, which depends upon their own knowledge and experience with the resource. It is people's perception of a good's characteristics or functions that influences their attitudes and behaviour, not necessarily the good's 'objective' characteristics (for example Adamowicz *et al.*, 1997). Finally, accounting for intra-study variability, the statistical analysis produces slightly different results regarding the significance and size of the effect of the main functions on the WTP values. The low number of observations also has to be taken into consideration.

On the other hand, the study progressed meta-analytical research in environmental economics by providing a statistical multilevel model which accounts for the clustering of results from the same studies (for example as a result of identical survey design or sample population) and for the fact that results from some studies may be more variable than others. In the GLS models used, the variance and covariance estimators not only enabled us to model heteroscedasticity, but also provided important background information for environmental value transfer.

Finally, although considerable effort has been put into specifying the characteristics of the environmental functions and correspondingly the environmental goods and services involved, other important aspects, which may have helped to explain differences in valuation outcomes, remain undefined. This is a common problem in meta-analyses in the field of environmental valuation as a result of insufficient and inadequate information provided in published valuation studies. Relevant information about the samples' socio-economic characteristics is missing in many studies, let alone respondents' socio-psychological and cultural characteristics.

In meta-analysis, inferences are made on the basis of information on global statistics, such as the mean and standard deviations of parameter estimates. These may or may not describe individual behaviour adequately. In order to overcome this potential problem and to increase the study's validity and reliability, a logical next step would be to gather more information about sample population characteristics by complementing the analysis with the underlying individual responses. This will provide an important test of the appropriateness of meta-analysis as an instrument to synthesize CV outcomes for the purpose of value transfer.

## NOTES

1. This chapter is based on work which has originally been published as Brouwer *et al.* (1999).
2. In 1992, the National Oceanic and Atmospheric Administration (NOAA) commissioned a prestigious 'Blue-Ribbon Panel' of economists and survey specialists, co-chaired by Nobel laureates Kenneth Arrow and Robert Solow, to investigate the CV method. After carefully considering a wide range of issues, the panel's report gave the method a qualified bill of health, but only if studies were conducted to a rigorous set of guidelines. The panel identified a subset of issues which it called 'burden of proof' requirements.
3. The GLS regression was carried out using the package MLN (Rasbash and Woodhouse, 1995).
4. By the end of 1995, one SDR approximately equalled one and a half US dollars.
5. Obviously, 'users' of specific wetland functions, for instance people who visit a wetland site

for recreational fishing or boating, may also hold values related to their non-use (for example preservation for future generations).

# REFERENCES

Adamowicz, W., J. Swait, P. Boxall, J. Louviere and M. Williams (1997), 'Perceptions versus objective measures of environmental quality in combined revealed and stated preference models of environmental valuation', *Journal of Environmental Economics and Management*, **32**, 65–84.

Arrow, K., R. Solow, P.R. Portney, E.E. Leamer, R. Radner and H. Schuman (1993), 'Report of the NOAA panel on contingent valuation', *Federal Register* (January 15), **58**(10), 4601–14.

Barbier, E.B. (1993), 'Sustainable use of wetlands. Valuing tropical wetland benefits: Economic methodologies and applications', *The Geographical Journal*, **159**(1), 22–32.

Bateman, I.J., I.H. Langford, R.K. Turner, K.G. Willis, G.D. Garrod (1995), 'Elicitation and truncation effects in contingent valuation studies', *Ecological Economics* **12**(2), 161–79.

Bateman, I.J., A. Munro, B. Rhodes, C. Starmer and R. Sugden (1997), 'Does part–whole bias exist? An experimental investigation', *Economic Journal*, **107**(441), 322–32.

Bergh, J.C.J.M van den, K.J. Button, P. Nijkamp and G.C. Pepping (1997), *Meta-analysis in Environmental Economics*, Dordrecht: Kluwer Academic Publishers.

Bergstrom, J.C., J.R. Stoll, J.P. Titre and V.L. Wright (1990), 'Economic value of wetlands-based recreation', *Ecological Economics*, **2**, 129–47.

Bishop, R.C. and K.J. Boyle (1985), 'The economic value of Illinois Beach State Nature Reserve', Consultancy Report, Madison, Wisconsin.

Bishop, R.C., K.J. Boyle and M.P. Welsh (1987), 'Toward total economic valuation of Great Lakes fishery resources', *Transactions of the American Fisheries Society*, **116**, 339–45.

Blamey, R.K. (1995), *Citizens, Consumers and Contingent Valuation: An Investigation into Respondent Behaviour*, Ph.D. dissertation, Australian National University, Canberra.

Brouwer, R. (2000), 'Environmental value transfer: State of the art and future prospects', *Ecological Economics*, **32**, 137–52.

Brouwer, R. and L.H.G. Slangen (1998), 'Contingent valuation of the public benefits of agricultural wildlife management: The case of Dutch peat meadowland', *European Review of Agricultural Economics*, **25**, 53–72.

Brouwer, R., I.H. Langford, I.J. Bateman and R.K. Turner (1999), 'A meta-analysis of wetland contingent valuation studies', *Regional Environmental Change*, **1**(1), 47–57.

Brouwer, R., I.H. Langford, I.J. Bateman, T.C. Crowards and R.K. Turner (1997), 'A meta-analysis of wetland contingent valuation studies', Global Environmental Change Working Paper 97-20, Centre for Social and Economic Research on the Global Environment (CSERGE), University of East Anglia and University College London, UK.

Carson, R.T. and R.C. Mitchell (1993), 'The value of clean water: The public's willingness to pay for boatable, fishable, and swimmable quality water', *Water Resources Research*, **29**(7), 2445–54.

Carson, R.T., N.E. Flores, K.M. Martin and J.L. Wright (1996), 'Contingent valuation and revealed preference methodologies: Comparing the estimates for quasi-public goods', *Land Economics*, **72**, 80–99.

Cooper, J. and J.B. Loomis (1991), 'Economic value of wildlife resources in the San Joaquin Valley: Hunting and viewing values', in A. Dinar and D. Zilberman (eds), *The Economics and Management of Water Drainage*, Dordrecht: Kluwer.

Costanza, R., R. d'Arge, R. de Groot, S. Farber, M. Grasso, B. Hannon, K. Limburg, S. Naeem, R.V. O'Neill, J. Paruelo, R.G. Raskin, P. Sutton and M. van den Belt (1997), 'The value of the world's ecosystem services and natural capital', *Nature*, **387**, 253–60.

Crowards, T. and R.K. Turner (1996), *FAEWE Sub-Project Report: Economic Valuation of Wetlands*, Centre for Social and Economic Research on the Global Environment (CSERGE), University of East Anglia and University College London, UK.

Cummings, R.G., P.T. Ganderton and T. McGuckin (1994), 'Substitution effects in CVM values', *American Journal of Agricultural Economics*, **76**, 205–14.

Desvousges, W.H., V.K. Smith and M.P. McGivney (1983), 'A comparison of alternative approaches for estimating recreation and related benefits of water quality improvements', report to the US Environmental Protection Agency, Washington, DC.

Desvousges, W.H., V.K. Smith and A. Fisher (1987), 'Option price estimates for water quality improvements: A contingent valuation study for the Monongahela River', *Journal of Environmental Economics and Management*, **14**, 248–67.

Desvousges, W.H., M.C. Naughton and G.R. Parsons (1992), 'Benefit transfer: Conceptual problems in estimating water quality benefits using existing studies', *Water Resources Research*, **28**(3), 675–83.

Dugan, P.J. (ed) (1990), *Wetland Conservation: A Review of Current Issues and Required Action*, The World Conservation Union, Gland, Switzerland.

Farber, S. (1988), 'The value of coastal wetlands for recreation: An application of travel cost and contingent valuation methodologies', *Journal of Environmental Management*, **26**, 299–312.

Garrod, G.D. and K.G. Willis (1996), 'Estimating the benefits of environmental enhancement: A case study of the river Darent', *Journal of Environmental Planning and Management*, **39**(2), 189–203.

Glass, G.V., B. McGaw and M.L. Smith (1981), *Meta-Analysis in Social Research*, Beverly Hills: Sage.

Green, C.H. and S.M. Tunstall (1991), 'The evaluation of river water quality improvements by the contingent valuation method', *Applied Economics*, **23**, 1135–46.

Greenley, D.A., R.G. Walsh and R.A. Young (1981), 'Option value: Empirical evidence from a case study of recreation and water quality', *The Quarterly Journal of Economics*, 657–73.

Gren, I.-M. and T. Söderqvist (1994), *Economic Valuation of Wetlands: A Survey*, Beijer Discussion Paper Series No.54, Beijer Institute, Stockholm.

Hamilton, L.C. (1993), *Statistics with Stata 3*, Belmont, CA: Duxbury Press.

IMF (1996), *International Financial Statistics Yearbook*, International Monetary Fund.

Johnston, J. (1984), *Econometric Methods*, third edition, New York: McGraw-Hill.

Jordan, J.L. and A.H. Elnagheeb (1993), 'Willingness to pay for improvements in drinking water quality', *Water Resources Research*, **29**(2), 237–45.

Kaoru, Y. (1993), 'Differentiating use and nonuse values for coastal pond water quality improvements', *Environmental and Resource Economics*, **3**, 487–94.

Kosz, M. (1996), 'Valuing riverside wetlands: The case of the "Donau-Auen" National Park', *Ecological Economics*, **16**, 109–27.

Langford, I.H. (1994), 'Using a generalised linear mixed model to analyse dichotomous choice contingent valuation data', *Land Economics*, **70**(4), 507–14.

Langford, I.H., I.J. Bateman, A.P. Jones, H.D. Langford and S. Georgiou (1998), 'Improved estimation of willingness to pay in dichotomous choice contingent valuation studies', *Land Economics*, **74**(1), 65–75.

Langford, I.H., M. Morris, A.-L. McDonald, H. Goldstein, J. Rasbash and T. O'Riorden (1999), 'Simultaneous analysis of individual and aggregate responses in psychometric data using multilevel modelling', *Risk Analysis*, **19**, 669–77.

Lant, C.L. and R.S. Roberts (1990), 'Greenbelts in the cornbelt: Riparian wetlands, intrinsic values, and market failure', *Environment and Planning A*, **22**, 1375–88.

Loomis, J.B. (1987), 'Balancing public trust resources of Mono Lake and Los Angeles' water rights: An economic approach', *Water Resources Research*, **23**(8), 1449–56.

Loomis, J.B., M. Hanemann, B. Kanninen and T. Wegge (1991), 'Willingness to pay to protect wetlands and reduce wildlife contamination from agricultural drainage', in A. Dinar and D. Zilberman (eds), *The Economics and Management of Water Drainage*, Dordrecht: Kluwer.

Maddala, G.S. (1983), *Limited-Dependent and Qualitative Variables in Econometrics*, Cambridge: Cambridge University Press.

McFadden, D. (1994), 'Contingent valuation and social choice', *American Journal of Agricultural Economics*, **76**, 689–708.

Mitchell, R.C. and R.T. Carson (1989), *Using Surveys to Value Public Goods: The Contingent Valuation Method*, Washington, DC: Resources for the Future.

Olsen, D., J. Richards and R.D. Scott (1991), 'Existence and sport values for doubling the size of Columbia river basin salmon and Steelhead runs', *Rivers*, **2**(1), 44–56.

Pearce, D.W. and R.K. Turner (1990), *Economics of Natural Resources and the Environment*, Hemel Hempstead, UK: Harvester Wheatsheaf.

Phillips, W.E., T.J. Haney and W.L. Adamowicz (1993), 'An economic analysis of wildlife habitat preservation in Alberta, *Canadian Journal of Agricultural Economics*, **41**, 411–18.

Randall, A. (1986), 'The possibility of satisfactory benefit estimation with contingent markets', in R.G. Cummings, D.S. Brookshire and W.D. Schulze (eds), *Valuing Environmental Goods: An Assessment of the Contingent Valuation Method*, Totowa, NJ: Rowman and Allanheld.

Rasbash, J. and G. Woodhouse (1995), *MLn Command Reference*, London: Institute of Education, University of London.

Sanders, L.D., R.G. Walsh and J.B. Loomis (1990), 'Toward empirical estimation of the total value of protecting rivers', *Water Resources Research*, **26**(7), 1345–57.

Schkade, D.A. and J.W. Payne (1994), 'How people respond to contingent valuation questions: A verbal protocol analysis of willingness to pay for an environmental regulation', *Journal of Environmental Economics and Management*, **26**, 88–109.

Schultz, S.D. and B.E. Lindsay (1990), 'The willingness to pay for groundwater protection', *Water Resources Research*, **26**(9), 1869–75.

Silvander, U. (1991), 'The willingness to pay for angling and ground water in Sweden', Ph.D. dissertation, The Swedish University of Agricultural Sciences, Uppsala.

Smith, V.K. (1992), 'On separating defensible benefit transfers from "Smoke and Mirrors" ', *Water Resources Research*, **28**(3), 685–94.

Spaninks, F.A. (1993), 'Een Schatting van de Sociale Baten van Beheersovereenkomsten met behulp van de Contingent Valuation Methode', M.Sc. dissertation,

Department of Agricultural Economics and Policy, Wageningen Agricultural University, The Netherlands.

Spaninks, F.A., O.J. Kuik and J.G.M. Hoogeveen (1996), 'Willingness to pay of Dutch households for a natural Wadden Sea. An application of the contingent valuation method', Report E-96/6, Institute for Environmental Studies, Amsterdam.

Sutherland, R.J. and R.G. Walsh (1985), 'Effect of distance on the preservation value of water quality', *Land Economics*, **61**(3), 281–91.

Tolba, M.K. and O.A. El-Kholy (1992), *The World Environment 1972–1992*, London: Chapman and Hall, on behalf of the UN Environment Programme.

Turner, R.K. (1992), 'Policy failures in managing wetlands', in *Market and Government Failures in Environmental Management*, Paris: OECD.

Whitehead, J.C. and G.C. Blomquist (1991), 'Measuring contingent values for wetlands: Effects of information about related environmental goods', *Water Resources Research*, **27**(10), 2523–31.

Willis, K.G. (1990), 'Valuing non-market wildlife commodities: An evaluation and comparison of benefits and costs', *Applied Economics*, **22**, 13–30.

Willis, K.G., G.D. Garrod and C.M. Saunders (1995), 'Benefits of environmentally sensitive area policy in England: A contingent valuation assessment', *Journal of Environmental Management*, **44**, 105–25.

Wolf, F.M. (1986), *Meta-Analysis*, Beverly Hills: Sage.

# 6. Social and deliberative approaches to support wetland management[1]

## R. Brouwer, R.K. Turner, S. Georgiou, N. Powe, I.J. Bateman and I.H. Langford

## 1 INTRODUCTION

Monetary economic valuation of the environment has been both supported and heavily criticized in the social science literature and by policy practitioners. The use of cost–benefit analysis (CBA) in environmental policy making and contingent valuation (CV) as an extension of traditional CBA has stimulated an extensive debate.[2] For most critics, the neo-classical economic value theory underlying CBA and CV is overly restrictive. The assumptions underlying the theory are considered too narrow to properly describe the environmental values people hold, the process of preference construction, or the way individual values are aggregated into a social value. Other criticism seems to originate from fears that the economic efficiency (net benefit) criterion is being promoted as a meta decision-making criterion. Some of the critics consider environmental valuation more as a social process relying upon social agreements (for example Sagoff, 1988; Jacobs, 1997) and as such only loosely tied, if at all, to technical valuation methods and techniques.

Environmental economists are accused of blind adherence to an outmoded neo-classical economic theory lacking empirical verification and political consensus. For some of the critics, the supposed biases and practical inconsistencies found in CV surveys further undermine the validity and modern relevance of neo-classical economic value theory.

Much of the debate about the use of CV in CBA is conditioned by ethical and implicit value judgements held by various protagonists (Turner, 1978). First, there is the question whether the utilitarian ethic underlying economic efficiency is considered an appropriate basis for dealing with the allocation of scarce resources, including the environment. It is argued that this approach is too restrictive because it disregards important issues like the distribution of resources and non-anthropocentric values. Secondly, and related to this first point is the question of whether environmental systems, including their intrinsic values, ought to be valued in monetary terms. Thirdly, there is the question of how environmental values should be elicited, either through CV or alternative approaches. In order to keep the debate in context and transparent, these normative issues should be laid out and considered carefully.

In this chapter, we review the literature which supports the need for a socio-cultural group-based approach to human behaviour, including valuation. The issues surrounding values elicitation and their incorporation into the decision-making process are also considered. A spectrum of more deliberative and inclusionary approaches (DIPs) to decision-making can be identified, ranging from information provision and consultation exercises of various sorts (inclu-sionary processes) to fully fledged participatory processes in which stake-holders are a component of the decision-taking mechanism. Supporters of DIPs argue that through experiencing such contexts, individuals 'learn' more about citizenship and collective responsibilities for, among other things, the environment. Individuals become immersed in a 'social learning process' and the facilitation of this process brings benefits in terms of 'better' decision-making in complex and uncertain contexts, better information dissemination and transparency and a building of trust and accountability in contemporary society (see Figure 6.1).

We will present the results of a study that tried to address some of these questions in *post*-survey group discussions by asking respondents who participated in a CV survey about their opinions and views on the survey, the meaning of their answers, the usefulness of their answers for actual decision-making, especially their willingness to pay (WTP) state-ments, and their preferences for the two types of public consultation they had been involved in, that is the individual survey approach and the group discussion. The study's main objective was to assess the validity of the CV method by means of qualitative social research. The implicit assumption underlying the CV method, that people are able to express their feelings, opinions, attitudes, beliefs, norms and values individually within a single economic measure, was explored in *post*-CV survey focused group discus-sions, commonly known as focus groups. Respondents who participated in the CV survey were invited to attend a group discussion in order to elicit their feelings towards the overall approach taken. Discussants were also encouraged to detail the meaning and accuracy of responses and to high-light any further issues they considered relevant to the study undertaken. Before presenting details of the case study, we first take a closer look at group-based as opposed to individual-based behavioural theories and approaches.

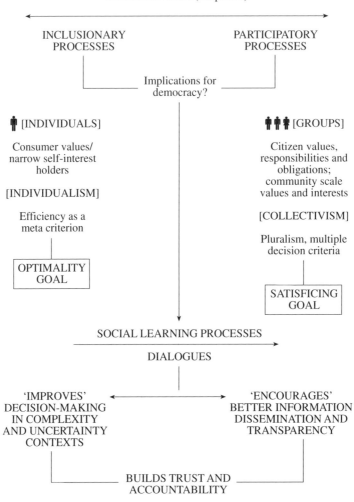

*Figure 6.1    Social and deliberative approaches to support management and policy making*

## 2    SOCIO-CULTURAL GROUP-BASED METHODOLOGIES

A full understanding of human activities requires an analysis of individual behaviour in a social setting. Boland (1982) criticizes the individualistic nature (methodological individualism) of neo-classical economic theory with its emphasis only on individuals as decision-makers in any explanation of social phenomena. In contrast to the individualistic approach, methodological holism requires social theories to be grounded in the behaviour of irreducible groups of individuals (Blaug, 1980). A further approach, 'structuralism', (Kay, 1982) considers the links and interactions between groups as well as in the groups themselves. Individuals must be considered as members of social identities and social values. It is also true to say that some degree of social interaction has been introduced into economic theory dealing with, for example, game theory and group dynamics and that experimental economics explicitly relies jointly on the findings of psychology and economics.

Although psychological processes occur only in the individual, the individual does not think and act in the same way irrespective of whether he or she is or is not a member of a group. Action in groups may differ greatly from individual action. An individual may be part of several different wholes, or groups, and may differ according to the whole or group to which he or she belongs in the given situation. Membership in a group refers to belonging in a psychological sense. The individual has a different role and function according to the group (whole) to which he or she belongs, and will not be expected to behave in the same way in different group situations. Group members experience a sense of belonging and common sense of identity, and have affective, cognitive or behavioural psychological effects on each other (Brown, 1996).

Groups have the power to influence individuals' behaviour, their experience, and their joint constructions of reality, as well as having properties that seem to belong to themselves. The perspective of experimental social psychology provides the dominant viewpoint about what happens in groups, with a large body of research showing that being in a group and subject to group processes clearly does have an influence on individuals, even when the group is largely simulated. The emphasis then is on the cognitive and motivational changes that occur within individuals when they become group members. The norms, roles, emotions and communication patterns generated by the group feed back on individuals, giving rise to emergent properties of groups, which then become more than the sum of the individuals making them up. Groups will thus seem to possess a character of their own which will be conferred to their members. The members of the group will gain a social identity and validation as a result of their membership.

In a group situation it is meaningful to speak of 'group forces' or 'group motives'. Conscious identification of an individual with his or her group is one instance of the effectiveness of such forces. Being subject to the same stimuli and the same requirements of the situation is another instance. Reciprocal reinforcement of motives of different individuals belonging to the same group, 'social facilitation', is a common phenomenon, in economic as in any other interpersonal behaviour.

Various social influence processes have been considered to be operating within groups. The presence of others may have an effect on judgements that can be carried over to later situations. Work by Asch (1952) considered group pressure towards conformity and the fact that a majority of people in a group situation may be in a position to sway the minority in the group. Milgram (1974) considered the difference between obedience and conformity in groups. Conformity was seen as going along with one's peers in a group, while obedience was considered with respect to a person in authority in a hierarchical situation (though both involve abdication of responsibility). Using the view that influence of one person over another arises from social power and status rather than from a psychological 'need' to be acceptable to others, Milgram was able to show that group membership may shield the individual from demands and pressures emanating from the leader of an experiment. Moscovici *et al.* (1969) found that in certain circumstances a minority was able to exert influence on the majority in a group. The extent to which this takes place will depend on factors such as the style of argument, whether the minority is considered part of the 'in-group' or viewed as an 'out-group', and whether the minority's opinions are gaining acceptance outside the group.

In addition to groups to which one belongs there are 'reference groups' from which an individual may derive standards for his or her behaviour. Both group belonging and reference groups play a role in behaviour. Such reference groups come into play when people express socially desirable answers in response to survey questions. In comparative groups, comparison with others is a strong and continuing feature of personal behaviour. Judgements about status and self-esteem, and the process of self-actualization, usually entail some degree of social interaction and interpersonal comparison. The comparisons provide a yardstick by which judgements can be made. Goals are often set and expectations formed by reference to others. Social comparisons therefore must play a central part in any analysis of motivation. Studies of social comparison and consumer behaviour (Baxter, 1988) have established that group pressures can indeed exert an influence on an individual's perceptions, and that in the absence of objective norms and standards, an individual will turn to other people for guidance on what the norms should be, and may adopt the norms of a group to which he or she aspires (normative groups).

An alternative to the social psychological view, the psychodynamic approach considers the effects of group membership from a different set of assumptions about the psychological processes involved and about the nature of the individuals and their relation to groups (Morgan and Thomas, 1996). Here unconscious motives, unconscious communications and the processes of identification and projection give rise to many of the effects seen in groups. The approach attempts to add understanding of more subtle and unconscious kinds of learning, and the construction of realities and selfhoods.

The social psychological experimental approach focuses on the objective search for truth using controlled experiments, in which variables are operationally defined and manipulated, and behaviour observed and measured. As such it is restricted in the kinds of phenomena that can be observed since it does not allow for the scope of interactions and happenings that can take place and which are characteristic of group settings in most everyday contexts. The psychodynamic approach meanwhile goes behind observable behaviours, and considers group life in terms of meanings, subjective experiences and the emotions of group members.

We have discussed perspectives on groups and processes within groups. These included social influence processes based on the experimental social psychology perspective, and the psychodynamic approach, which stresses unconscious processes. Leaving aside for a moment the question of group processes we consider from a group perspective the representations (or constructions) that people use to understand the world, the evaluations which go along with them, and the actions that such representations allow. Such representations and evaluations can be considered from an individualistic perspective using the notion of attitudes and beliefs. However, we now look at the dependence of such evaluations on the widely shared images of how the world operates, generated in turn from social interactions. The representations must be considered as part of a broader social and political process.

The use of attitudes in experimental work on social cognition has been attacked by the advent of recent social constructionist approaches (Wetherall and Maybin, 1996). Traditional attitude research has viewed attitudes as atomistic and unrelated to one another, though some attempts have been made to consider their often-patterned nature. There has also been the problem of treating attitudes as personal possessions and specific to individuals, when in fact many attitudes are not unique but shared by many people. We thus need to address the failure to consider the organization of attitudes into clusters and systems, and we need to examine the relationship between collective views and individual attitudes. The theory of social representations (Moscovici, 1976) is one approach that attempts to address these problems.

The basic idea of social representations theory is that people come to understand the social world using mental images (social representations) and clusters which are shared by members of a social group. Such representations are one of the things that distinguish one group from another. The representations originate and evolve in conversations between people and circulate in the media. They act as a guide providing a code for communication and evaluation of whether something is good or bad. The concept of attitudes remains, but now acts as a secondary phenomenon underpinned by social representations.

Further problems nevertheless arise with the concept of attitudes; people's evaluations may vary greatly with any particular context, thus giving rise to the view that they are not expressions of one consistent underlying attitude. Following on from this problem is the question of what the role of such evaluations is in terms of what people do with them. How expression of attitudes (evaluative discourse) is used in everyday situations has not been considered in traditional attitude work.

Discursive psychology (Edwards and Potter, 1992) considers the element of interaction, in terms of talk and discourse, which goes on within social life. It is concerned with looking at how society and culture shape the construction of events, along with the psychological implications for evaluation and representation. It views people's talk and their texts as social practices in their own right. Actions, constructions, rhetoric and the building of versions of the world are related to building versions of the self. Representations are used in the performance of actions, with specific elements in the representation contributing to the performance of the action.

We now consider group approaches and how they relate to environmental valuation and decision-making.

## 3   ENVIRONMENTAL VALUE ELICITATION AND UTILIZATION IN DECISION-MAKING

We have seen that the individual-based values of neo-classical economic theory have been criticized and considered to provide an inadequate description of the environmental values people hold, and the process by which preferences are constructed. Looking at individual preferences is atomistic, and the uncertainties and ambivalence found in many ordinary explanations are treated as oddities and inconsistencies. Studies often confine people's choices to predetermined categories and rarely attempt to get people to interpret events. Qualitative analysis is rarely undertaken.

The value-free claim of positive neo-classical economics is that it treats preferences and values of economics agents as neutral and makes no prescriptions about how they ought to behave: this has come under attack. It is instead argued that rationality and self-interest are ideologically consequential, legitimizing selfishness as the natural state of the world. As such they cannot be considered neutral. Etzioni (1988) has been particularly influential here and criticizes the reality, lack of humanity and reductionism of the rationality and self-interest of neo-classical economic theory. Rather, he argues that choices are made and motivated by people's value system and beliefs usually in a non-dispassionate way. In addition to selfishness, there exists moral obligation.

Problems arise in the manner in which individual values are aggregated to give a social value, and the acceptance of utilitarianism and with it the net-benefit criterion, implicitly rejects other possible decision criteria. Alternative ethical perspectives include egalitarianism, paternalism, the notion that individuals have rights to some minimum level of subsistence, and the idea that humans possess moral interests or rights (see Turner and Pearce, 1993 for a detailed discussion). Although some critics have argued that all values are anthropocentric and usually instrumental, they maintain that the economic approach reflects a partial view of values. For example, deep ecologists and others (Sagoff, 1988) reject the motivational assumption that value is solely given by the individual and reflects individual preferences. The environmentalist positions argue that the values expressed are not necessarily economic in nature. Instead people may be expressing their held values. According to Lockwood (1997) there are three ways in which such values can be rationally expressed. First, he argues that one might be able to choose between alternatives without being able to rank them. However, it would seem that the mere action of choice would imply that a ranking has been made. Secondly, alternatives can be ranked and trade-offs made. Third, alternatives can be ranked, but trade-offs are not acceptable (for example lexicographic preferences). If environmental values are considered to be non-compensatory in this way then the environmental positions lead to the advocacy of sustainability standards or constraints, which to some extent do away with the need for valuation of specific components of the environment or health. It is still necessary, however, to quantify the opportunity costs of such standards; or to quantify the costs of current, and prospective environmental health risk protection and maintenance measure.

Sociologists, anthropologists and some economists look at values not from the perspective of individual behaviour but rather from a social perspective. More generally, the relations between society and values have to be examined at the deeper level of what in anthropology is called culture. Economic anthropologists have stressed the importance of cultural values, and the fact that cultures will differ in their economic organization, complexity and values. Critics also argue that psychological laws like their economic counterparts are subservient to culture and history. People's values, preferences and behaviour, and their interpretation, are also determined culturally. Anthropology considers each culture to be a system in synchronous equilibrium, built up progressively in the course of evolution, and with strongly related subsystems. The characteristics of each culture are important since it will influence the types of personalities liable to have access to various roles. In addition, there is the question of the interaction between the society and the individual in the process of the double construction of individual personalities and of the culture itself. Economics must therefore incorporate a wider view of reality incorporating social culture. These other perspectives mean that there will be a more comprehensive understanding of the costs and benefits of actions. This can be easily understood in the context of the social and longer-term effects of individual preferences and behaviour that misperceive costs and benefits. More informed individual and institutional decisions may require a societal conscience. Individual choices and social well-being do not always correspond, such that there is a justification for a 'public interest' point of view and values. Public education, national defence and so on, are examples of social choice products where 'public interest' values are implied. Egalitarian points of view also emphasize the social and communal nature of human behaviour and the possibility of a social contract (Rawls, 1971).

A more collectivist approach can be adopted which allows for the recognition of 'generalized obligations' towards other members of society (Turner and Pearce, 1993). From such a collectivist viewpoint, all value is still anthropocentric, but is not restricted to the satisfaction of preferences of individuals. Rather, it is argued that individuals also hold 'considered preferences', which they express after careful deliberation. Sagoff (1988) makes a distinction between respondents acting as consumers in a market context as prescribed by economic theory, and respondents acting as citizens in a social choice context. Given their role as citizens, individuals will be influenced by held values, attitudes and beliefs regarding public good provision. It is thus argued that public environmental decision-making contexts prompt people to act under their citizen role, and thus individual-based approaches to valuation are inappropriate for such contexts. Individuals may hold both private (self-interested) and public or social (in the public/group/community interest) preferences. However, it is now thought that a continuum of behaviour exists in which either role will be more or less dominant depending on the specific context, and where individual self-interest is balanced against community-based interests (Brouwer *et al.*, 1999). In this way humans play a multidimensional role, acting as both socially responsible citizens and as self-interested consumers, rather than just either one.

Property rights, social choices and moral concerns now become intertwined with values in the debate over the 'proper' extent of the market in decision-making (O'Neill, 1997). There are different views on how decision-making procedures are or should be organized. O'Neill (1997) argues that commercial norms and the market place should not be extended to cover all forms of public goods. The argument here is that public preferences reflect opinions or beliefs, and so can be considered to be different from private preferences, which reflect desires or wants. Public preferences are thus not reflected in the market place, and so monetary cost–benefit analysis fails to incorporate them. Cultural theorists also argue that different preferences for decision-making procedures for different issues will arise as cultural views on social relations differ. Lockwood (1997) also recognizes that at the same time as advocating the use of market-based methods of value expression, it is important to identify alternative modes of value expression so that the non-compensatory values discussed above, for example, have a fair hearing and due consideration of them can be taken into account in the decision process.

O'Neill (1997) suggests an increased role for deliberative institutions in resolving the economy–environment/health conflict, and greater consideration of the social and economic conditions necessary to sustain them. To some extent social values are nevertheless incorporated in legislation that has gone through the political process, a process that reflects not only economic considerations, but also cultural, social, ethical and scientific aspects. Emphasizing these non-economic factors gives rise to a fixed-standard, strong sustainability approach to environmental policy (Turner, 1993).

The different views regarding environmental decision-making procedures and how they are or should be organized have different implications for the use of individual-based approaches to environmental valuation as opposed to deliberative group approaches. If environmental valuation is seen more as a social process that operates through social agreements then it is argued that the individual-based valuation methods and techniques such as contingent valuation will not capture the elements of this process. Some authors (Clarke *et al.*, 2000) have also conducted empirical investigations which question the role of contingent valuation as a method of decision-making, because of the difficulty faced by respondents in framing a reply, so that they often feel coerced into giving a monetary amount. In addition respondents also challenged claims that CV was a democratic process ensuring that public attitudes were incorporated into policy decisions. These authors argue that decisions should be based on social consensus about appropriate standards and rational choices rather than the values found in CV studies. They propose as an alternative, deliberative and participatory group approaches, such as 'citizen's juries' and focus group meetings. These are characterized as qualitative data-producing, deliberative collective processes that allow for the fact that preferences and values are dependent on interactive social processes and cultural factors, as simulated in the group discussions. Qualitative data-producing methods have previously been suggested as useful addenda to the more quantitative techniques used in the individual approaches (Chilton and Hutchinson, 1999).

The background and dynamic social context in which people perceive the presented environmental problem, relate it to their personal experiences and beliefs, norms and values and shape it into a new or existing preference structure is clearly important. Under the individual-based approaches such as contingent valuation, it is outcomes that are relevant, however, as captured by a one-time 'snapshot' of preferences. Questions regarding the meaning of environmental objects and the process of valuation are not usually considered (Jorgensen and Syme, 1995). Rather the objective in CV studies is to obtain willingness to pay estimates in a manner that is consistent with the requirements of cost–benefit analysis. Nevertheless, even then it is difficult to conceive of a satisfactory policy-related cost–benefit study that can set aside such questions as the public's impressions of the role of government in public good provision, issues about equity between social groups, considerations regarding the public's ability to affect public decision-making outcomes, and so on (Jorgensen, 1999).

Despite claims to the contrary, group approaches must, in our view, encompass an economic focus, in the sense that the elements of the options considered in any decision choice will have been traded off against one another (either explicitly or implicitly) in making the decision; that is, as mentioned earlier there are opportunity costs associated with the choice, both at the individual and collective level.

The different approaches to environmental valuation will produce quite different types of information, and have relative strengths and weaknesses in different decision-making settings. Nevertheless, they also have the potential to provide complementary analysis and results when used as part of a mixed methodological design. The type of information that is required by decision-makers to aid a decision, as well as the public's ability and desire to deliver such information will determine the extent to which either or both approaches can and should be used. There is considerable debate regarding the degree to which the single monetary measure expressed in cost–benefit type studies can capture the feelings, attitudes, norms, beliefs, values and preferences of individuals. The deliberative approaches, it is claimed, allow respondents to develop their views and express more considered 'true' preferences, which accurately reflect their interests and well-being, free of the errors, biases and inconsistencies often found using CV surveys. However, there are problems with the deliberative and participatory approaches.

Deliberation can be considered to be prone to bias and errors as a result of herding behaviour and dominant personalities within a group. 'Considered' preferences found after deliberation may thus be no better than the 'unconsidered' preferences found in CV surveys (Cookson, 2000). Further problems relate to the representativeness of participation, problems of a common language of understanding, equity issues concerning information accessibility and strategic bargaining positions, as well as a lack of a firm institutional basis (O'Riordan *et al.*, 1997). It has also been argued that the deliberative approach places too much emphasis on the subjective judgement of the investigator in setting the agenda for deliberation and discussion (Cookson, 2000). Taking this type of view further, Brouwer *et al.* (1999) claims that while CV research has been criticized for imposing a market construct and context on respondents, the use of the deliberative approach is open to the problem of what Bhaskar (1989) calls 'Critical Realism'. Here the research process becomes both a scientific and political 'transformational intervention', rather than a mechanism for reproducing the underlying social relationships.

In choosing between the approaches it is important to consider the extent to which the information is both meaningful and representative. Usually the more detailed the information the less representative it is, and vice versa. As far as decision-making is concerned the question remains as to whether in-depth information is more useful than that of a broader (representative) nature. Three core questions need to be considered when deciding upon an appropriate approach. First, one must consider which approach delivers the types of information decision-makers are looking for in the specific public policy domains. Second, we need to know which approach the public themselves prefer as a decision-making procedure in the different public policy domains. Finally, one must consider which type of information the public are willing and able to provide in the different public policy domains.

It is not always clear what kind of information decision-makers want. Furthermore, politicians will 'manipulate' information to serve their own purposes. This raises the issue of public trust in science and the need for openness in making explicit the assumptions used in formulating inferences from the decision-making approaches. The issue of what type of procedure is preferred by the public, and their ability and willingness to provide information remain open research questions. We now turn to some case study research which has examined the role of focus groups in wetland valuation and management processes.

## 4    THE ROLE OF FOCUS GROUPS IN ENVIRONMENTAL VALUATION

Parallel to a shift in academic interest in social deliberation in environmental policy and decision-making, focus groups are becoming an increasingly popular technique in the field of environmental valuation (for example Desvousges and Frey, 1989; Desvousges *et al.*, 1992; Hutchinson *et al.*, 1995; Hanley *et al.*, 1997). Focus group discussions use techniques originally proposed in sociology, but which have since been systematically developed in marketing research and have more recently been used as a tool for political campaigning and public policy-making (Johnson, 1996). In focus groups, a small number of individuals are brought together to discuss one or more topics as a group. Compared to the personal interview, the dynamics of the meeting are clearly very different (Churchill, 1987). In the individual interview the flow of information is mainly one way (from the respondent to the interviewer), whereas in the focus group setting there is interaction and feedback within the group discussion. The social context is therefore broader: each individual is exposed to the ideas of the others and submits his or her ideas to the group for consideration.

In focus groups, the role of the researcher is to moderate, listen, observe and analyse the process of social interaction (for example Krueger, 1998). The purpose of bringing about social interaction can differ considerably. CV researchers have tended to use focus groups in auxiliary fashion as illuminating, but exploratory, with results that are not suitable for aggregation and generalization across a population. Typically, focus groups are carried out as a series. Multiple groups with similar participants are needed to detect patterns and trends across groups. A single group study can be risky since there may be various factors that may cause a group to produce atypical results. Group polarization, extensively tested in social-psychology (for example Isenberg, 1986; Mackie, 1986; Pavitt, 1994), may be one such important factor. In groups, individuals may shift their views, opinions, attitudes and preferences to the more extreme side of the perceived group consensus after being exposed to the average view(s) held by the group, because of social comparison (Festinger, 1954) or persuasive arguments (Pavitt, 1994).

In CV studies, focus groups are usually used to explore people's general knowledge about the subject of interest, their perception and understanding of the subject. The aim is to help the CV researcher to determine how much information to present and how to present it in a given context, as well as how to refine the questions used in the survey (for example Desvousges *et al.*, 1984; Hoehn, 1992). Recently, in-depth group discussions have been used to explore respondent perceptions of the survey after participation (Burgess *et al.*, 1998).[3]

The study by Burgess *et al.* seriously questions the role of CV in environmental decision-making by arguing that people come up with a monetary amount because of the coercive interview situation or people's trust in the expertise held by those asking the questions. Burgess *et al.* conclude that decisions about the environment should be based on social consensus about appropriate standards and acceptable choices rather than on the individual WTP amounts elicited in CV surveys. Their critique is in our view heavily conditioned by the problems with the specific CV survey used as an exemplar. This was experimental in nature and therefore not established 'best practice' (Garrod, personal communication, 1998). Nevertheless, the in-depth group discussion does offer CV researchers a different perspective on the elicitation of environmental values and seems to be relevant to a comprehensive appraisal of the CV method.

The use of group discussions, usually over a longer period of time, as an alternative to the survey-based CV approach to elicit environmental values,[4] offers more of a process-oriented approach to environmental valuation. By contrast, CV gives a 'snapshot' of people's attitudes, preferences and values. In the former approach, the process underlying and leading to the environmental values people hold or are asked to express is emphasized, while in the latter approach only the end result at a certain point in time is monitored without paying much attention to the relevant background or context in which the values have come about. The use of group discussions is more in line with a social constructivist approach (for example Berger and Luckman, 1967), where knowledge and preferences are understood to be dependent upon social processes and cultural factors as simulated in group discussions. As such, it provides the opportunity to open up the process by which respondents perceive the presented environmental problem, relate it to their personal experiences, beliefs, norms and values, and shape it into a new or existing preference structure. Furthermore, for the purpose of validating CV research it provides the researcher with the opportunity to go into more detail about the actual meaning of answers in terms of respondents' motivations and the effect of the given broader social context.[5]

In the study reported here, respondents who participated in a CV survey were invited to attend group discussions about the survey and the overall approach taken. The qualitative data made available in these group sessions was analysed based on majority views. The use of majority views reflects a social constructivist perspective on the group discussions, while at the same time it provides a very useful device with which to analyse qualitative data.

After the group discussion, participants were asked to fill out a short questionnaire consisting of 12 questions about their perception of the group discussion in relation to the survey, their perception of the CV survey and the valuation questions in particular, and their general views on the natural environment and public consultation. This provided additional quantifiable information about individual group members' private perception of the CV survey, the valuation questions and the group discussion, in addition to the group majority views on these issues.

It is important to point out here that the group discussions were moderated by environmental economists trying to get a better understanding of survey participant perception and understanding of a specific CV survey. This should be borne in mind when we present the results below. The data communicated in qualitative social research can be looked at from numerous perspectives and hence, as mentioned, does not have a single meaning. The majority views found in each group are the views as monitored by the researchers, either through explicit prompting by the moderator during the group discussions or the assistant-moderator's notes on the overview grid. An overview grid was used which listed all the relevant issues to be discussed during the group meetings. For each issue, the assistant-moderator noted whether it was brought up in a prompted or unprompted way. Participant understanding of and agreement about the key issues was noted in terms of whether there was a minority, majority or unanimity vote.

The focus groups followed a large-scale CV survey which investigated public attitudes and preferences to a flood alleviation scheme for the Norfolk and Suffolk Broads, a large wetland area in East Anglia in the UK. The Broads is a National Park in all but name. It benefits from being part of a wider family of specially protected areas, including the National Parks, but also has the advantage of its own tailor-made legislation in order to deal with specific issues in the area (see Chapter 10 in this volume). The CV survey aimed, among other things, to provide a valid and reliable monetary estimate of the recreational and amenity benefits enjoyed by visitors to the Broads. This monetary estimate was part of an extended cost–benefit assessment of a flood alleviation scheme for the area centred on the strengthening of the Broads river embankments.

The questionnaire used in the CV survey was extensively tested before application and was to a large extent based on a previous survey carried out in the same area (Bateman *et al.*, 1992 and 1993). In this previous study, no significant problems were encountered with the questionnaire design or the valuation questions: the non-response to the valuation questions (including protest bidders) was less than 5 per cent. Before the questionnaire was used in the 1996 study, it was tested in three focus group sessions to explore people's general understanding of the subject matter. Subsequently, 100 face-to-face interviews were undertaken. This pre-survey research led to several adjustments to the information and questions in the questionnaire. Finally, the actual survey consisted of just over 2100 face-to-face interviews of Broads visitors at 10 different sites and was followed up by seven focus group discussions with 52 survey participants.

The CV study focused on user willingness to pay (WTP) to prevent flooding. Hence, it is primarily the area's 'use value' that was being estimated, although possible 'non-use' motivations may have been underlying WTP responses as well. Interviewing was carried out at recreational sites throughout the Norfolk and Suffolk Broads in the summer of 1996 on a random 'next to pass' basis. Visitors to the sites were approached in the open-air and asked if they would participate in a 20-minute interview conducted by the University of East Anglia. In total, 2114 questionnaires were successfully completed.

The questionnaire started off by asking respondents about their visit intensity, travel time, sites visitation, the activities they undertake and aspects they like or dislike about the Broads. Next, information about the possibility of saline flooding was presented by the interviewer, with the aid of a story-board which was taken to the interview sites. On the board, a map showed the extent of possible saline flooding, while carefully selected photographs depicted the landscape and ecology changes after persistent saline flooding.[6] After reading out the information and taking respondents through the map and pictures on the board, respondents were asked whether they had any questions. If they had, further clarification was given. Questions were anticipated based on the pilot survey and each interviewer had a standard list of answers to these possible questions. Respondents were then given more time to look at the board if they wanted to.

After this information had been presented, respondents were asked about their previous knowledge of the issues involved, that is, possible flooding in the Broads. Subsequently, they were informed about the current funding of the existing river embankments protection system through general taxation and were asked whether they agreed in principle with an increase in their taxes (irrespective of the exact amount) to ensure that the improved flood alleviation scheme would be implemented. If they did not agree, they were asked for their reasons. Asking respondents for the reasons why they disagree with the principle of stating a WTP amount, or why they are able to state a specific payment is considered of paramount importance in the assessment of the validity of the survey and the meaningfulness of individual replies. Furthermore, on the basis of this question the CV researcher is able to classify respondents either as protest or non-protest bidders.

The actual WTP question following the principle question consisted of a follow-up bidding procedure. The bid amounts were derived from the open-ended elicitation format used in the pilot study and hence were considered fairly representative of what people would consider paying. Finally, at the end of the questionnaire respondents were asked about their feelings towards the payment vehicle (general taxation), their trust in the responsible authority designated to implement the scheme, the perceived realism of the proposed scheme and about a number of demographic and socio-economic characteristics of their household.

The target group for the post-survey group discussions were respondents who agreed to give their name and telephone number after the survey which enabled the University to verify, if necessary, the respondent's participation in the survey. In order to keep the organization of these group meetings feasible in terms of keeping them near respondents' place of residence, only respondents who lived in or around the Broads area were contacted. This means that only one specific group of Broads users from the CV survey has been included in the focus groups, that is local residents who can be expected to have a better than average interest in the area and to be rather well informed about the issues at stake.

On the basis of the available phone numbers and postcodes, seven group meetings were organized at different places in Norfolk (two in Great Yarmouth, two in Norwich and two in Acle) and Suffolk (one in Lowestoft). Sixty respondents from and around Great Yarmouth who left their name and phone number, 59 respondents from and around Norwich, 68 respondents from and around Acle and 45 respondents from and around Lowestoft were contacted and invited to attend a group meeting to further discuss the issues brought up during the interview.

A standard approach was used to invite and inform people about the purpose of the meeting. They were offered £25 to attend a two-hour meeting. The financial incentive to participate was mentioned right at the start of the telephone call in order to avoid possible self-selection and to get as much of a cross-section of the sample population as possible. Once people agreed by phone to come to a meeting (52 of the 232 respondents contacted), they were sent a formal letter of invitation, additional information about the purpose of the meeting and, as a reminder, a blank copy of the questionnaire they filled out.

A number of selection criteria for the compilation of the groups were formulated before the groups met, the most important ones being (1) whether or not a respondent was in favour in principle of raising general taxes to implement the flood alleviation scheme and (2) an equal number of women and men in each group. However, the limited number of available telephone numbers and the low response resulted in two groups consisting of respondents who all agreed with the principle question, but no group consisting of respondents who all disagreed. Instead, five mixed groups had to be compiled. Overall, most people (81 per cent of the 52 post-survey participants) agreed in principle to pay for the proposed scheme. Fifteen per cent said no to the principle question in the CV survey and 4 per cent did not know or were unsure. In terms of the actual bid amounts and the WTP question, 90 per cent of those respondents who agreed to the principle question also said yes to the starting bid which ranged between £1 and £500 per year. Of these 38 respondents, two said no to the higher follow-up bid (which was £500 in those two cases). Almost all respondents who said no to the starting or follow-up bid explained that they could not afford the payment. Only one respondent considered flood protection to be a government task and not a legitimate question for an individual to take responsibility for, even though he agreed first with the principle of raising general taxes to prevent the area from flooding.

Getting an equal share of men and women in each group meeting proved difficult. First, if a man telephoned respondents at home to invite them to attend a follow-up meeting, this resulted in a very low response from women. However, if a woman phoned, a much higher number of women agreed to come along. Secondly, in three groups four women only agreed to come to the meeting if they could also bring their husband, even though they were told explicitly that the meetings were meant to consist of people who participated in the survey only. Hence, four husbands were present at three meetings and participated in the group discussion. Only in the first group was the presence of the two husbands perceived (by the moderator and assistant-moderator) as biasing the discussion. Both men were very talkative, while their wives kept silent most of the time. Similar distortions of group meetings consisting of married couples have been reported by Krueger (1994).

A summary of the participant characteristics is presented in Table 6.1. Every group included at least two people who were members of an environmental group or nature conservation organization. However, in three of the seven groups, the majority of group members were not. Fifty-three per cent of all participants were full-time employed and 80 per cent of the remainder were retired. Groups 3 and 5 had a high proportion of retired people. Most group members were aged between 35 and 54 years (47 per cent) and had a gross income of between £7500 and £30 000 per year (63 per cent).

A standard discussion protocol was drawn up to facilitate the group meeting and tested and adjusted in two group meetings with UEA students before the actual meetings with the survey participants. The standard protocol addressed the main issues to be discussed at each meeting and included prompts to selective issues if they were not brought up spontaneously by the group members. The main structure of each meeting is presented in Table 6.2. The questions in Table 6.2 were presented to the group by the group moderator for discussion.

Both the survey and the group discussion focused on the preservation of the current Broads landscape and amenities and the impact of persistent saline flooding on recreational experiences in the Broads. This was made explicit by the group moderator in the group discussions whenever the use of the WTP results in an extended CBA of the flood alleviation scheme was explained, or other relevant issues to the CBA were brought up, such as flood damage costs to existing infrastructure and private properties.

Overall, the meetings lasted between two and three hours and were taped. The assistant moderator was responsible for taping the session and taking notes of what people said during the discussion. In order to (i) facilitate the assistant moderator's note-taking work, (ii) increase the transparency of the meeting and (iii) aid interpretation of the results, an overview grid was developed and tested in the two pilot focus group meetings. The overview grid listed all the relevant issues to be discussed during the meeting, the assistant moderator's notes on whether a particular issue was brought up prompted or unprompted, and whether a majority agreement was reached.

At the end of each meeting participants were asked to fill out a brief questionnaire individually. The questionnaire consisted of 12 short questions regarding participant perception of the focused group discussion in relation to the survey, his or her perception of the CV survey and the valuation questions in particular, and his or her general views about public consultation.

Two types of results can be highlighted. Given the debate in literature about the 'significance' of divergent individual or minority views, the presentation of the majority views found in the groups will be followed by an overview of

Table 6.1 Focus group participant characteristics

| | Sex | Age group | Occupation/ employment | Income group | Environment group member | Principle question | Starting bid | WTP | Follow-up bid | WTP |
|---|---|---|---|---|---|---|---|---|---|---|
| Group 1 | woman | 35–44 | full time | 10,000–15,000 | GP/FoE | yes | 60 | yes | 75 | yes |
| | man | 18–24 | student | <5,000 | no | yes | 200 | yes | 500 | no |
| | man | 18–24 | full time | 5,000–7,500 | no | yes | 200 | yes | 500 | no |
| | man | 45–54 | full time | 20,000–30,000 | no | yes | 10 | yes | 15 | yes |
| | woman | 18–24 | unknown | 7,500–10,000 | no | yes | 40 | yes | 50 | yes |
| | man | 65–74 | retired | 10,000–15,000 | no | yes | 500 | no | 200 | no |
| | woman | 45–54 | full time | 15,000–20,000 | RSPB | yes | 30 | yes | 40 | yes |
| | woman | 65–74 | retired | 5,000–7,500 | RSPB | yes | 60 | yes | 75 | yes |
| | woman | 45–54 | full time | 10,000–15,000 | RSPB/NT/GP/FoE | yes | 25 | yes | 30 | yes |
| Group 2 | man | 45–54 | full time | 30,000–34,000 | WWF | yes | 10 | yes | 15 | yes |
| | man | 75+ | retired | 40,000–50,000 | NT | yes | 5 | yes | 10 | yes |
| | woman | 55–64 | retired | <5,000 | no | yes | 50 | yes | 60 | yes |
| | man | 55–64 | full time | 15,000–20,000 | WWF | yes | 150 | yes | 200 | yes |
| | man | 25–34 | full time | 7,500–10,000 | no | yes | 30 | yes | 40 | yes |
| | man | 65–74 | retired | 10,000–15,000 | RSPB | yes | 200 | yes | 500 | yes |
| | man | 35–44 | full time | 20,000–30,000 | no | yes | 40 | yes | 50 | yes |
| | woman | 55–64 | retired | <5000 | local nature trust | yes | 15 | yes | 20 | yes |
| Group 3 | man | 65–74 | retired | 5,000–10,000 | no | no[1] | – | – | – | – |
| | man | 65–74 | retired | 20,000–30,000 | RSPB/NT | yes | 60 | yes | 75 | yes |
| | man | 65–74 | retired | 7,500–10,000 | NT | yes | 150 | no | 100 | no |
| | woman | 35–44 | full time | 30,000–40,000 | no | yes | 10 | yes | 15 | yes |
| | man | 35–44 | full time | 15,000–20,000 | no | no[1] | – | – | – | – |
| | woman | 55–64 | retired | Missing | RSPB | no[2] | – | – | – | – |
| | woman | 55–64 | retired | Missing | NT/NNT/GP/FoE | yes | 25 | yes | 30 | yes |
| Group 4 | woman | 45–54 | full time | 15,000–20,000 | GP/FoE | yes | 20 | yes | 25 | yes |
| | man | 35–44 | full time | 40,000–50,000 | NT/GP/FoE | yes | 5 | yes | 10 | yes |
| | man | 25–34 | full time | 7,500–10,000 | no | yes | 1 | yes | 5 | yes |

| Sex | Age | Employment | Income | Environment group | | | | | |
|---|---|---|---|---|---|---|---|---|---|
| man | 65–74 | full time | 20,000–30,000 | no | no[3] | – | – | – | – |
| woman | 45–54 | full time | 20,000–30,000 | no | yes | 150 | yes | 200 | yes |
| man | 45–54 | full time | 10,000–15,000 | NT | yes | 500 | yes | 1000 | yes |
| man | 45–54 | full time | 20,000–30,000 | GP/FoE | yes | 60 | yes | 75 | no |
| **Group 5** | | | | | | | | | |
| woman | 18–24 | full time | 50,000–75,000 | RSPB/BS/local trust/GP/FoE/WWF | yes | 500 | no | 200 | no |
| man | 65–74 | retired | 20,000–30,000 | no | yes | 5 | yes | 10 | yes |
| man | 65–74 | retired | 7,500–10,000 | no | yes | 25 | yes | 30 | yes |
| woman | 18–24 | full time | <5,000 | no | don't know | 25 | don't know | 20 | don't know |
| man | 25–34 | full time | 20,000–30,000 | no | no[3] | – | – | – | – |
| woman | 55–64 | retired | 7,500–10,000 | no | yes | 1 | yes | 5 | yes |
| woman | 65–74 | retired | <5,000 | no | yes | 60 | yes | 75 | yes |
| man | 65–74 | retired | 30,000–40,000 | NT | no[4] | – | – | – | – |
| **Group 6** | | | | | | | | | |
| man | 35–44 | full time | 20,000–30,000 | local nature trust | yes | 15 | yes | 20 | yes |
| woman | 45–54 | full time | 30,000–40,000 | local nature trust | yes | 1 | yes | 5 | yes |
| man | 45–54 | retired | 10,000–15,000 | RSPB/NT/NNT | yes | 150 | yes | 200 | yes |
| man | 45–54 | retired | 10,000–15,000 | no | yes | 15 | yes | 20 | yes |
| man | 35–44 | full time | 15,000–20,000 | no | no[1] | – | – | – | – |
| man | 45–54 | full time | 15,000–20,000 | GP/FoE/WWF | yes | 100 | yes | 150 | yes |
| **Group 7** | | | | | | | | | |
| man | 35–44 | full time | 20,000–30,000 | no | no[2] | – | – | – | – |
| man | 45–54 | homemaker | 7,500–10,000 | no | yes | 40 | yes | 50 | yes |
| man | 45–54 | full time | 20,000–30,000 | NT | yes | 60 | yes | 75 | yes |
| man | 35–44 | carer | 10,000–15,000 | no | yes | 25 | yes | 30 | yes |
| woman | 45–54 | part time | 10,000–15,000 | no | yes | 100 | yes | 150 | yes |
| woman | 45–54 | full time | 10,000–15,000 | WWF | yes | 500 | no | 200 | no |
| man | 45–54 | full time | 15,000–20,000 | no | don't know | 5 | yes | 10 | yes |

*Notes*

Reasons for not agreeing with the principle question:
[1] Cannot afford to pay any more taxes
[2] Don't want to write a blank cheque for this scheme
[3] Scheme should not be funded through general taxation
[4] Government responsibility to protect the Broads from flooding

Environment Groups:
GP: Green Peace; WWF: World Wildlife Fund
FoE: Friends of the Earth; NT: National Trust
RSPB: Royal Society of the Protection of Birds
BS: Broads Society; NNT: Norfolk Naturalist Trust

*Table 6.2   Focus group protocol*

---

1. *Reception* of group members, introduction of each group member to the moderator and the assistant moderator and the other group members

2. *Introduction*
   - participation experiences in the Broads
   - importance attached to the area
   - awareness of the problems facing the Broads
   - ideas of their own about how the Broads should be managed in view of these problems

2. *Specific research problem (1)*
   - remind participants of the board used and the information presented during the survey
   - ask participants whether they have questions about the board or information supplied

4. *Deepening (1)*
   - how do participants feel about the flood alleviation scheme
   - ability to make a choice in favour or against the scheme
   - how do participants feel about the fact that the scheme is going to be financed through increased income taxes, implying that each of them will be affected; if they disagree, ask them who should pay and why
   - trust in the way the scheme is going to be financed
   - understanding of the bidding procedure
   - what do the stated bid amounts participants are willing to pay actually reflect; does this amount of money reflect what they consider the conservation of the Broads worth? Why do participants consider it important to pay the stated bid amounts for the scheme?

5. *Specific research problem (2)*
   - outline of the contingent valuation approach of asking individuals for their willingness to pay for environmental protection and/or enhancement programmes and the use of the aggregate results in informing actual environmental decision-making
   - ask participants whether they have questions about this approach and the way the results are used as input in environmental decision-making

6. *Deepening (2)*
   - how do participants feel about this approach; how do they feel about being involved in this approach, knowing that the information they provide will be part of the information decision-making process?
   - do participants consider this an acceptable approach; is this the best approach? Do they feel capable of participating in this approach? Do they think the general public is capable of being involved in this approach? Do they feel their responses are a reliable source of information? To what extent are their responses accurate?
   - if participants disagree with the approach, how should  decision-makers be informed, or how should environmental decision-making take place; should it be a consultation of the government by experts? Should it be a public referendum? Should it be a deliberative process between citizens and/or stakeholders similar to the discussion they are part of now?

7. *Finalizing*
   - any other issues participants would like to discuss or issues raised by the group that the group moderator would like to come back to.

8. *Filling out of a short questionnaire by group members individually*

---

individual or minority views considered relevant to the specific CV research. Both the majority and minority view findings will be complemented by results from the questionnaire filled out by the group participants after the group discussion. In two of the seven groups, a majority considered the overall approach of asking people for their individual WTP to elicit the environmental values they hold as not acceptable and inappropriate. The main reason given for this position was that the flood alleviation scheme and its consequences were too complex to be able to make a decision on in the available interview time. A majority in these two groups said that the CV survey should specify in more detail how the problems could be dealt with, who will be affected and who will pay. The implication here is that discussants felt that they did not have enough information at hand to give a meaningful answer.

On the other hand, in five of the seven groups, a majority considered the overall approach acceptable and suggested that the answers were meaningful and accurate enough to inform actual decision-making. However, discussants emphasized that the answers to the WTP question can be considered valid and useful only as long as the money is really spent on the flood alleviation scheme to protect the wetland area. This illuminates the importance of public trust in the institutional context in which solutions are presented in CV surveys.

The analysis of the individual group members' responses to the questionnaire following the group discussion also did not indicate the scale of rejection of the CV methodology as described by Burgess *et al.* (1998). Two thirds of all group participants thought that asking people whether or not they were willing to pay an amount of money for the flood alleviation scheme would help decision-makers in their appraisal of the scheme. A further 21 per cent disagreed and felt the CV results were not useful for policy, while 12 per cent did not know or were unsure.

Ninety per cent of all participants furthermore stated that they felt comfortable about being asked to express their opinions and feelings towards the proposed scheme during the face-to-face interview. Almost 75 per cent felt comfortable being asked to express the importance they attached to the scheme in monetary terms. Of the remainder, 8 per cent stated that they did not feel very comfortable and 2 per cent stated they were not comfortable at all. The other 15 per cent did not know or were unsure.

Specific majority views found in individual groups supporting the CV approach in this specific context of recreational amenities associated with a flood alleviation scheme, confirmed that the WTP statement related to the specific scheme and was not prompted because the environment was considered a cause worth paying for. However, a majority of respondents in one group claimed that the costs of the flood alleviation scheme influenced their answer. In general, this finding would limit the usefulness of the CV estimates for CBA: there is a risk of double counting since the estimated benefits derived from the area's recreational amenities are net of the costs of the flood alleviation scheme.

In almost every group a significant number of people considered the specific river bank flood alleviation schemes in a broader context, either in combination with efforts to strengthen the Norfolk and Suffolk coastal defences or in the National Park management context. Even though respondents were asked to look at the specific flood alleviation scheme in isolation, in six groups the problem of strengthening the river embankments was considered in combination with flood alleviation efforts in the coastal zone. In all groups, at least one person brought up the issue of tidal barriers which various agencies have proposed over the years. In four groups the problem was considered explicitly in a longer term framework, and it was thought that more structural measures beyond the mere strengthening of the river embankments were required. In these groups a majority agreed that the problem had to be solved at the source, that is, nearer to the coast where the salt water enters the Broads rivers in the first place. Some participants considered it useless to discuss the river embankment schemes in isolation. In one group one person argued that the coastal defences should have been explicitly included in the scheme. In six of the seven groups the problem of rising sea level as a result of global warming was brought up as an important problem for the area. The participants in most groups were well informed about the issue of flood defence. The flooding disaster in the area in 1953 causing the deaths of many people was still fresh in the minds of the older participants.

The majority of group participants considered the outcome of the proposed schemes in the Norfolk and Suffolk Broads to be fairly to very important to them personally (90 per cent) and fairly to very important to the nation as a whole (80 per cent). In three of the seven groups, the Broads were called a national asset, requiring central government intervention for various reasons. The most important reason brought up in five groups was that many more places in the UK suffered from environmental problems, like the Broads, and required some kind of protection. In four of these groups, the Broads were compared with other National Parks and the problems they face. In one group, three of the seven participants considered the problem presented to them a national issue in the sense that it concerned the countryside in general. In another five groups the costs of the schemes involved were considered too high to be borne by local residents and visitors only. Only the central Government was considered capable of raising the amounts of money necessary to implement the flood alleviation scheme.

Although in six of the seven groups a majority or all members agreed that national taxation is the most appropriate payment vehicle for this specific problem, whenever trust in the Government was brought up by the group moderator, a consistent (over all groups) group behaviour was displayed:

people started to laugh. A large majority of people had no or very little trust in the Government. In only two groups did someone give the new Labour Government the benefit of the doubt. In another group only one person considered the Broads Authority a good institution with a coherent view on the future of the Broads. Although most groups consisted of rather well informed local residents, in two groups a few people did not know who was responsible for the Norfolk and Suffolk Broads. In five groups participants brought up the issue of the boat toll which boat owners paid to the Broads Authority. In three of these groups a few people had little trust in how the Broads Authority was spending the money. This corresponded with a more general distrust about the payment vehicle, that is national taxation: in five groups a majority of people felt that they would have no control whatsoever over whether their money actually would be spent on the Norfolk and Suffolk Broads or any other environmental asset in the UK. One group unanimously agreed that one body should be set up to finance the schemes through central government taxation.

There are indications that preferences had been 'constructed' during the face-to-face interview. In two groups, a majority agreed that only during the interview did the extent of the problems become clear. The information provided in the survey made respondents reflect on the importance of the area. This finding has been suggested as invalidating the CV method as a revealed preference approach, which assumes that preferences are already in place and fixed, and behaviour is explained with the help of these preferences. However, strictly speaking, CV is not a revealed but an expressed preference approach, reflecting a behavioural intention, not behaviour itself. Moreover, forming preferences and values on the basis of the information supplied is not specific to CV, but a more general phenomenon in communication consistent with findings in socio-psychological research of decision-making (Schkade and Payne, 1994).

A majority in all groups stated that the group discussion had improved their understanding of the questionnaire and had made them feel more capable of making a decision about the flood alleviation scheme in terms of whether or not they were WTP a specific bid amount. When asked whether they wished to change their previous answers in the CV survey after the group discussion, a majority in all groups said no. Only three respondents in one group (a minority in this group) said they would have changed their answers after the group discussion. This group and three other groups were given the opportunity to change their individual answers to the valuation questions in the questionnaire after the group discussion. Only one of the three people who said they would change their answers after the group discussion did so. In three groups the participants agreed unanimously that they did not want to change their previous answers and saw no need to fill out the valuation questions again.

In five of the seven groups, a majority preferred both personal interviews and group discussions as the most appropriate type of public consultation for this specific environmental problem. Only one group preferred a group discussion to the personal interviews and one group was undecided. In this latter group, half of the participants stated a preference for a group discussion, while the other half preferred both. A majority in six groups felt a need to discuss the flood alleviation scheme with others. Only in one group did a majority of participants not express this need. When asking respondents who they would like to discuss the specific environmental problem with, a majority in four groups ticked 'experts' in the questionnaire. A majority in two groups cited other local residents affected by the flood alleviation scheme as possible extra consultees. Although a majority in all groups considered the area a national asset deserving the same level of protection as other national parks in the UK, only three participants felt a need to discuss the issue of flood alleviation in this area with other UK citizens.

Finally, respondents claimed to have had sufficient time to consider and answer the questions during the interview. No indication was found that respondents felt coerced, either to participate in the survey or to answer the questions according to interviewer expectations.

In almost every group one or two group members were present who had an outspoken opinion about the valuation questions or who were confused about the follow-up bid questions. In group 1, one person said that it was not necessary to ask for a monetary amount to express one's feelings. On the other hand, another person in the second group felt that asking for a monetary amount was proper, because it evoked a 'straightforward' answer to a 'straightforward' question. Two individuals in group 2 had problems with the follow-up bid amounts, mistakenly thinking that the individual bids would be summed. They also related the bid amounts to the costs of the schemes, thinking that they were asked the second amount because the first amount was not enough to cover the costs.

Also in group 3, one person argued that the bid amounts were meaningless after he discovered that they were not related to the costs of the scheme. Another person thought that the questionnaire did not say exactly what she was paying for. The same two issues were brought up again in group 4 by two other people. One of these two regarded the bid amount he was presented with as 'good value for money', a result which was also found by Burgess *et al.* (1998), hence relating the bid amount to the actual implementation of the scheme.

In group 5, one person asked 'how can you put a value on the Broads?'. He suggested that the costs of different options should be compared and the least costly option favoured, also a result found by Burgess *et al.* (1998). In group 6, one person considered the recreational amenities 'very hard to value'. Another person in that same group, however, had fewer problems with the approach, arguing that 'you have to make the decision somehow'.[7] In the context of the follow-up bid, two people felt pushed into answering the second bid. Both said that they had some idea, but that they did not have an exact amount in mind and needed more time to consider the second bid.

In group 7, one person argued that the money amounts elicited during the personal interview were meaningless because at the time of the interview he was only considering the specific environmental problem in the Broads. Afterwards he also considered other issues worth paying for, environmental and non-environmental, local and national ones. Hence, this person's answers to the valuation questions can be interpreted as an overestimation, since substitutes were not considered explicitly during the interview. On the other hand, this reaction can also be interpreted as a partial rejection of the CV methodology. Partial, because the person in question did understand the need to make a decision somehow, but argued that there were simply too many important causes for him to give to in order to be able to decide exactly how much to spend on this specific problem.

## 5   DISCUSSION AND CONCLUSIONS

In the case study, support was found for the individual WTP-based approach, but respondents also favoured a participatory deliberative approach to inform the environmental decision-making process. Mixed views were encountered, suggesting that a combination of both approaches may be most appropriate. A majority of group participants preferred personal interviews combined with group discussions as the most appropriate type of public consultation for this specific environmental problem.

In a majority of groups, the information provided through the CV survey, including the WTP statements, was considered meaningful and accurate enough to be used as input into real decision-making. The problem of persistent saline flooding was considered in a wider spatial and temporal context than the CV research had originally envisaged, which may have affected respondent definition of the specific environmental goods involved, that is the recreational amenities found in the Broads. However, it is important to keep in mind that the focus groups consisted of well informed local residents, most of whom have some vested private interest in the area and who could consequently be expected to (be able to) consider the issue of flood alleviation in the wider context of, for example, coastal protection. The scope of this research was limited in that we were unable to address the question as to whether other interviewed visitors living outside the area perceived the flood alleviation problem in the same detail as the local residents in the focus groups.

Furthermore, the uncertainty experienced by many people in the context of general taxation, that is, whether their money would actually be spent on the flood alleviation scheme, is inherent to the payment vehicle which the respondents claimed to prefer in the first place. During the pre-testing of the survey, in the actual survey and in the focus group discussions, a vast majority of respondents considered central government taxation the most appropriate way to finance the scheme. Given the response in the focus groups, an earmarked income tax might have taken away some of people's possible reservations against the context in which their willingness to pay was elicited. Although respondents exhibited these reservations in the post-survey research, one group (group 7) unanimously agreed that when answering the WTP question during the main survey, they assumed that the money would indeed be spent on the scheme. In three groups, including the latter group, a majority suggested that the funds should be made available nationally, but allocated regionally. A local body should be made responsible for the actual spending of the money, which corresponds to the current *status quo*.

As a number of respondents felt that they had learnt from the group discussions, they were given the opportunity to complete the WTP component of the questionnaire again, in the group and privately. Despite our concerns about the sensitivity of responses to the social context and hence the additional different social perspectives provided by different group participants, a majority of group participants claimed that their answers had not changed after the group discussion. This can be interpreted in a number of ways. That the individual WTP estimates appear to be robust in this broader social context and reliable for inclusion in decision-making may seem an obvious interpretation. However, the fact that respondents did not change their WTP statements has to be considered carefully given that (i) most respondents agreed with the principle of paying extra general taxation to ensure implementation of the flood alleviation scheme, and (ii) most respondents had vested interests in the area and hence were keen to communicate the message to policy-makers that the area had a high value to them. In most groups, people seemed to understand the relationship between this value and the opportunity they were offered to express this value in terms of their WTP. But this finding is subject to a number of possible caveats. There were indications that at least for some of the respondents their WTP was conditioned (i) by a wider spatial and temporal context, (ii) by their feelings about how much trust they had in the 'system' actually spending the money on the scheme, and (iii) by the interpretation of the bid amounts in terms of the costs of the scheme and therefore as 'good value for money' instead of total economic value. Consequently, if the WTP responses were not well defined or respondent behaviour was ambivalent as a result of the complexity of the decision-making situation, they may have been difficult to shift. The combined impact of these caveats on the overall findings is to leave them short on providing full support for neo-classical economic theory predictions and resulting values.

This result raises questions about the role of information and the social context in which environmental values are elicited, as well as about the compatibility of different types of information. Our findings cannot be regarded as formal proof that the CV approach generates the same information as a more deliberative elicitation approach for environmental values. More research is needed since the individual and group-based approaches place the whole process of eliciting environmental values, monetized or not, in different social settings and therefore provide us with different kinds of information. Typically, qualitative research will provide in-depth information on fewer cases, whereas quantitative procedures will allow for more breadth of information across a larger number of cases. A combination of both approaches offers future promise for environmental valuation.

The use of either or both approaches depends on the type of information policy-makers are looking for in specific policy domains, but also the type of information the public is able to deliver and how much the public is willing to participate in public consultation. In this respect, it is furthermore important to distinguish clearly between social and social scientist preferences for different approaches of public consultation. The individual survey-based approaches to environmental valuation and the deliberative stakeholder group approaches are rooted in different views on how decision-making procedures are or should be organized. Different cultural views on social relations are assumed to give rise to different preferences towards decision-making procedures for different kinds of issues, including environmental ones (see, for example, Rayner, 1984 in the context of risk management). These cultural foundations can be found underpinning the different approaches to environmental valuation. While CV research has been criticized for imposing a market construct and context on respondents, the recent use of focus groups linked to public decision-making may be equally suspect from a 'critical realism' point of view (Bhaskar, 1989). The group discussion may not be mere consultation or a mechanism to reproduce underlying social relationships, but rather more of a 'transformational intervention', at once scientific and political. It is therefore just as open to manipulation and steering.

In CV research, deliberative and inclusionary research has an essential role to play and is in some studies already playing that role. In the pre-survey stage it can be used to identify the stakeholders involved, to identify the type of information considered appropriate to facilitate the conflict resolution process, and to explore different stakeholders' general knowledge and understanding of the environmental issues involved. All this helps the researcher to determine, together with the stakeholders, how and how much information to present in the questionnaire. Important ethical and moral judgements associated with the specific environmental problem will become apparent in this stage of the research.

In the post-survey stage, deliberation or qualitative social research can be used for two main purposes:

(i)   To provide insights into the process by which respondents answered the way they did;
(ii)  To discuss the survey results with the different stakeholders involved and relate these to the decision(s) to be made.

In this latter case, CBA and CV as an extension to CBA are merely components of the overall decision-making process which will be based on a balancing of multiple criteria and supporting information. The individual survey-based approaches also have an essential role to play in deliberative and inclusionary approaches to environmental valuation by opening up the social process regarding the environment–economy trade-offs at different decision-making levels. Individuals are expected to be 'consumers' and 'citizens' simultaneously much of the time. The suggested dichotomy (Sagoff, 1988) is not as sharply drawn in reality and rather unnatural since individuals are more likely to behave along a continuum rather than to form two mutually exclusive groups. Depending on the specific context, either role will be more or less dominant, as individual self-interest is balanced against community-based interests. The participatory approaches to environmental valuation will gain in terms of transparency and meaningfulness if these different dimensions are made explicit, something for which the CV method has been developed and extensively tested in specific environmental domains over the past 15 to 20 years. This quantifiable information can play its part in the facilitation of the overall, real world, multi-criteria decision-making process.

## NOTES

1.  This chapter is based on work which has originally been published as Brouwer *et al.* (1999).
2.  CV is a collective term for various survey-based environmental valuation approaches.
3.  Burgess and her colleagues distinguish between in-depth group discussions and focus groups. Contrary to focus groups, in-depth group discussions do not have a protocol. Group members are given a broad theme and asked to discuss this theme amongst themselves. The group moderator does not drive the discussion. He or she only hands over the theme and allows the discussion to flow as it will (Burgess, personal communication, 1998). Focus groups, on the other hand, have a more directed discussion within certain degrees of freedom (for example Morgan, 1993; Krueger, 1994). The topics for discussion prompted by the moderator are predetermined and sequenced after careful consideration and development.
4.  Sometimes also referred to as a 'Citizen's Jury' (for example Aldred and Jacobs, 1997).
5.  For this purpose, verbal protocol analysis, an in-depth personal interview technique, could also have been used and would perhaps have been a more appropriate method given the individualistic basis underlying CV. However, like CV this approach does not include the broader social context in which environmental values may be elicited.
6.  The information and photographs were carefully compiled and selected with the help of the

natural scientists working at the School of Environmental Sciences at the University of East Anglia.
7.  A majority in group 6 considered the WTP question 'the best value one can get at'.

# REFERENCES

Aldred, J. and M. Jacobs (1997), *Citizens and Wetlands*, report of the Ely Citizen's Jury, mimeo, Centre for the Study of Environmental Change, Lancaster University, UK.

Asch, S.E. (1952), 'Effects of group pressure upon modification and distortion of judgments', in G.E. Swenson, T.M. Newcomb and E.L. Hartley (eds), *Readings in Social Psychology*, New York: Holt, Rinehart and Winston.

Bateman, I.J., I.H. Langford, K.G. Willis, R.K. Turner and G.D. Garrod (1993), 'The impacts of changing willingness to pay question format in contingent valuation studies: An analysis of open-ended, iterative bidding and dichotomous choice formats', GEC Working Paper 93-05, Centre for Social and Economic Research on the Global Environment (CSERGE), University of East Anglia and University College London, UK.

Bateman, I.J., K.G. Willis, G.D. Garrod, P. Doktor, I.H. Langford and R.K. Turner (1992), 'Recreational and environmental preservation value of the Norfolk Broads: A contingent valuation study', mimeo, Environmental Appraisal Group, University of East Anglia, UK.

Baxter, J.L. (1988), *Social and Psychological Foundations of Economic Analysis*, London: Harvester Wheatsheaf.

Berger, P. and T. Luckman (1967), *The Social Construction of Reality*, New York: Anchor Books.

Bhaskar, R. (1989), *Reclaiming Reality: A Critical Introduction to Contemporary Philosophy*, London: Verso.

Blaug, M. (1980), *The Methodology of Economics: Or How Economists Explain*, Cambridge: Cambridge University Press.

Boland, L.A. (1982), *The Foundations of Economic Method*, London: George Allen and Unwin.

Brouwer, R., N. Powe, R.K. Turner, I.J. Bateman and I.H. Langford (1999), 'Public attitudes to contingent valuation and public consultation', *Environmental Values*, **8**, 325–47.

Brown, H. (1996), 'Themes in experimental research on groups from the 1930s to the 1990s', in M. Wetherell (ed.), *Identities, Groups and Social Issues*, London: Sage.

Burgess, J., J. Clark and C.M. Harrison (1998), 'Respondents' evaluations of a CV survey: A case study based on an economic valuation of the Wildlife Enhancement Scheme, Pevensey Levels in East Sussex', *Area*, **30**(1), 19–27.

Chilton, S.M. and W.G. Hutchinson (1996), 'Message or myth? The contribution of focus groups to the contingent valuation process', staff paper, Centre for Rural Studies, The Queen's University of Belfast, Northern Ireland.

Chilton, S.M. and W.G. Hutchinson (1999), 'Do focus groups contribute anything to the contingent valuation process?, *Journal of Economic Psychology*, **20**(4), 465–83.

Churchill, G.A. Jr. (1987), *Marketing Research; Methodological Foundations*, fourth international edition, Chicago, IL: Dryden Press.

Clark, J., J. Burgess and C.M. Harrison (2000), 'I struggled with this money business: respondents' perspectives on contingent valuation', *Ecological Economics*, **33**, 45–62.

Cookson, R. (2000), 'Incorporating psycho-social considerations into health valuation: an experimental study', *Journal of Health Economics*, **19**, 369–401.

Desvousges, W.H. and J.H. Frey (1989), 'Integrating focus groups and surveys: examples from environmental risk studies', *Journal of Official Statistics*, **5**(4), 349–63.

Desvousges, W.H., V.K. Smith, D.J. Brown and D.K. Pate (1984), *The Role of Focus Groups in Designing a Contingent Valuation Survey to Measure the Benefits of Hazardous Waste Management Regulation*, RTI Project no. 2505-13, Research Triangle Institute, North Carolina.

Desvousges, W.H., F.R. Johnson, R.W. Dunford, K.J. Boyle, S.P. Hudson and K.N. Wilson (1992), *Measuring Non-use Damages Using Contingent Valuation: An Experimental Evaluation of Accuracy*, Research Triangle Monograph 92-1. Research Triangle Institute, North Carolina.

Edwards, D. and J. Potter (1992), *Discursive Psychology*, London: Sage.

Etzioni, A. (1988), *The Moral Dimension*, New York: The Free Press.

Festinger, L. (1954), 'A theory of social comparison processes', *Human Relations*, **7**, 117–40.

Hanley, N., D. MacMillan, R.E. Wright, C. Bullock, I. Simpson, D. Parsisson and R. Crabtree (1997), *Contingent Valuation Versus Choice Experiments: Estimating the Benefits of Environmentally Sensitive Areas in Scotland*, paper presented at the annual conference of the Agricultural Economics Society, Edinburgh.

Hoehn, J.P. (1992), 'Natural resource damage assessment and contingent valuation: issues and research needs', staff paper, Michigan State University.

Hutchinson, W.G., S.M. Chilton and J. Davis (1995), 'Measuring non-use value of environmental goods using the contingent valuation method: problems of information and cognition and the application of cognitive questionnaire design methods', *Journal of Agricultural Economics*, **46**(1), 97–112.

Isenberg, D.J. (1986), 'Group polarization: a critical review and meta-analysis', *Journal of Personality and Social Psychology*, **50**(6), 1141–51.

Jacobs, M. (1997), 'Environmental valuation, deliberative democracy and public decision-making institutions', in J. Foster (ed.), *Valuing Nature?*, London: Routledge.

Johnson, A. (1996), 'It's good to talk: the focus group and the sociological imagination', *The Sociological Review*, **44**(3), 517–38.

Jorgensen, B.S. (1999), 'Comments on Chilton and Hutchinson: focus groups in the contingent valuation process: a real contribution or a missed opportunity', *Journal of Economic Psychology*, **20**, 485–9.

Jorgensen, B.S. and G.J. Syme (1995), 'Market models, protest bids, and outliers in contingent valuation', *Journal of Water Resources Planning and Management*, **121**, 400–401.

Kay, N.M. (1982), *The Evolving Firm: Strategy and Structure in Industrial Organization*, London: Macmillan.

Krippendorff, K. (1980), *Content Analysis: An Introduction to Its Methodology*, Beverly Hills, CA: Sage.

Krueger, R.A. (1994), *Focus Groups: A Practical Guide for Applied Research. Thousand Oaks*, Beverly Hills, CA: Sage.

Krueger, R.A. (1998), *Moderating Focus Groups. Focus Group Kit No. 4*, Thousand Oaks, CA: Sage.

Lockwood, M. (1997), 'Integrated value theory for natural areas', *Ecological Areas*, **20**, 83–93.

Mackie, D.M. (1986), 'Social identification effects in group polarization', *Journal of Personality and Social Psychology*, **50**(4), 720–28.

Milgram, S. (1974), *Obedience to Authority*, London: The Tavistock Institute.

Morgan, D.L. (1993), *Successful Focus Groups: Advancing the State of the Art*, Newbury Park, CA: Sage.

Morgan, H. and K. Thomas (1996), 'A psychodynamic perspective on group processes', in M. Wetherell (ed.), *Identities, Groups and Social Issues*, London: Sage.

Moscovici, S. (1976), *La Psychoanalyse: Son Image et Son Public*, Paris: Presses Universitaires de France.

Moscovici, S., E. Lage and M. Naffrechoux (1969), 'Influence of a consistent minority on the response of a majority in a colour perception task', *Sociometry*, **32**, 365–80.

O'Neill, J. (1997), 'Managing without prices: the monetary valuation of biodiversity', *Ambio*, **26**(8), 546–50.

O'Riordan, T., C. Marris and I. Langford (1997), 'Images of science underlying public perceptions of risk', in J. Ashworth and C. Sanford (eds), *Risk, Science and Policy*, London: Royal Society.

Pavitt, C. (1994), 'Another view of group polarizing: the reasons for one-sided argumentation', *Communication Research*, **21**(5), 625–42.

Rawls, J. (1971), *A Theory of Justice*, Oxford: Oxford University Press.

Rayner, S. (1984), 'Disagreeing about risk: the institutional cultures of risk management and planning for future generations', in S. Halden (ed.), *Risk Analysis, Institutions and Public Policy*, New York: Associated Faculty Press.

Sagoff, M. (1988), *The Economy of the Earth*, Cambridge: Cambridge University Press.

Schkade, D.A. and J.W. Payne (1994), 'How people respond to contingent valuation questions: a verbal protocol analysis of willingness to pay for an environmental regulation', *Journal of Environmental Economics and Management*, **25**, 88–109.

Turner, R.K. (1978), 'Cost–benefit analysis: a critique', *Omega*, **7**, 411–19.

Turner, R.K. (1993), 'Sustainability: principles and practice', in R.K. Turner (ed.), *Sustainable Environmental Economics and Management: Principles and Practice*, London: Belhaven Press.

Turner, R.K. and D.W. Pearce (1993), 'Sustainable economic development: economic and ethical principles', in E.B. Barbier (ed.), *Economics and Ecology: New Frontiers and Sustainable Development*, London: Chapman and Hall.

Wetherall, M. and J. Maybin (1996), 'The distributed self: a social constructionist perspective', in R. Stevens (ed.), *Understanding the Self*, London: Sage and The Open University.

PART II


Case studies of ecological–economic
approaches to wetland ecosystem management

# 7. Environmental and economic assessment of the location of wetland buffers in the landscape for nutrient removal from agricultural runoff

## M. Blackwell and E. Maltby

## 1 INTRODUCTION

In Europe, wetland degradation and loss has been prolific in the last century, largely as a result of increasing agricultural development and pollution (Jones and Hughes, 1993) with little regard to conservationist arguments for protection because of, for example, habitat and species rarity. However, because of the observed loss of many ecological and hydrological services formerly provided for free by wetlands and the consequent environmental and economic costs of this loss, wetland protection and conservation has become an internationally important issue (Maltby *et al.*, 1992).

In any wetland a number of processes may be occurring to a greater or lesser extent. These may be of a physical, chemical, biological or ecological nature and examples of such processes include water storage, denitrification and plant uptake of nutrients. As a consequence of such processes, wetlands provide valuable goods and services. The process of water storage gives a wetland the function of flood attenuation, while the processes of denitrification and plant nutrient uptake may contribute to water quality maintenance through the removal of nutrients from surface water and shallow groundwater. Plant uptake of nutrients may also result in the performance of other functions such as support of the food web and wildlife habitat, demonstrating that an individual process may contribute to a variety of wetland functions.

This chapter focuses on the value of wetland buffer zones in environmental and economic terms for the removal of $NO_3^-$ (nitrate) from agricultural runoff. A buffer zone is a naturally or semi-naturally vegetated area situated between agricultural land and a surface water body, acting to protect the water body from harmful impacts such as high nutrient, pesticide or sediment loadings that might otherwise result from land use practices. It offers protection to a water body through a combination of physical, chemical and biological processes. The degree to which this protection is provided depends on a number of factors including the size, location, hydrology, vegetation and soil type of the buffer zone (Dosskey *et al.*, 1997; Leeds-Harrison *et al.*, 1996), as well as the nature of the pressure by which the water body is threatened.

Potential pollutants such as $NO_3^-$ are stored or removed by a variety of processes, particularly by plant uptake and bacterial processes in the soil such as denitrification. Plant uptake represents a temporary store and harvesting may be required for complete removal of pollutants from the system, while denitrification represents a direct loss of nitrogen. The precise nature and rates of the processes operating in a buffer zone will depend at least in part on the geomorphological setting and hydrological regime of the zone (Dosskey *et al.*, 1997; Correll, 1997), which controls rates and types of processes. For example, denitrification occurs optimally under anaerobic conditions typically found in wetlands (Gilliam *et al.*, 1997; Blackwell, 1997), while sediment retention is often more effective on well drained land (Dillaha and Inamdar, 1997; Dillaha *et al.*, 1988). A buffer zone may provide additional benefits such as bank stabilization, flood water detention and wildlife habitat. However, appropriate location of a buffer zone is vital for optimal performance of a desired function.

In the United Kingdom (UK), the current protocol for the implementation of buffer zones is described by both the Environment Agency (Environment Agency, 1996) and the then Ministry of Agriculture, Fisheries and Food (MAFF, 1997). Generally it is recommended that buffer zones should be located in riparian areas adjacent to main water courses and extend to between 5m and 30m in width. The Water Fringe Habitat Scheme Option (MAFF, 1997) provides one of the few sources in the UK from which funding may be acquired for the implementation of riparian buffer zones. However, the scheme is voluntary and funding is restricted to six pilot areas.

Although models for buffer zone designs such as REMM (Riparian Ecosystem Management Model) (Lowrance *et al.*, 1998) and RiMS (Riparian Management Systems) (Isenhart *et al.*, 1995) have been developed, they represent a rather rigid approach to the establishment of buffer zones in riparian regions, particularly for the prevention of $NO_3^-$ pollution. Merot and Durand (1997) describe a number of buffer zone-related models, some of which include non-riparian locations and indicate that none of them are sufficiently developed for practical application due to the large amounts of empirical data required for their validation.

Research has indicated though that the establishment of buffer zones alongside rivers and streams can be an effective measure in preventing $NO_3^-$ from reaching water bodies (Ambus and Christensen, 1993; Cooper, 1990; Haycock and Burt, 1993; Weller *et al.*, 1994). Comparisons of the efficacy of such zones and their cost effectiveness have shown that, as a solution to the problem of excess $NO_3^-$, buffer zones are favoured above other preventive measures such as Nitrate Sensitive Areas (Burt and Trudgill, 1993; Haycock, 1993; Johnes and Burt, 1993; DoE, 1986).

However, while riparian buffer zones are sometimes highly effective at removing $NO_3^-$ from diffuse sources such as shallow groundwater or surface runoff, they are often bypassed where natural hydrological flows are intercepted by ditches or drains, which are common features in the UK landscape (Goudie, 1986). Furthermore, a riparian buffer zone can be rendered ineffective for $NO_3^-$ removal from water draining agricultural land upslope (Leeds-Harrison *et al.*, 1996). In such cases, it may prove more cost-effective to establish buffer zones in association with ditches or areas of discharge that may be acting as zones of enhanced denitrification (Blackwell and Maltby, 1998). Similar conclusions have been drawn from work by Haycock and Muscutt (1995), who reported that while 85 per cent of some sub-catchments of the River Avon in Hampshire in the UK were served by effective riparian buffer strips, 60 per cent of polluting material in the river was delivered by roads and drains that effectively bypassed them.

Current policy for the establishment of wetland buffer zones does not consider the role of landscape features such as oxbow lakes, ditch overland flow zones or footslope seepage zones which may be located at substantial distances from the river bank or outside of riparian zones. These areas are often important for the removal of $NO_3^-$ from surface and ground waters. Recommendations for locating buffer zones are therefore being made without fully understanding the potential effectiveness of alternative locations. An analysis of the cost effectiveness of possible alternatives is expected to improve the allocation of scarce financial resources by directing them towards the most efficient buffer zone location.

In this chapter, two examples are presented of alternatively-located, non-riparian buffer zones for $NO_3^-$ removal in the catchment of the River Tamar in north-west Devon in the UK. Their environmental and economic efficiency with regard to $NO_3^-$ removal from agricultural runoff, particularly by denitrification, is compared with nearby conventional riparian buffer zone locations.

## 2   DESCRIPTION OF THE FIELD STUDY SITES

The two case studies involve data collected from Tetcott Barton, which is situated on the eastern bank of the River Tamar, at a point where the river is of stream order 5, and the floodplain is approximately 200 m wide. The first 100 m of floodplain from the river carries deep, well drained silty soils (cambisols) and is used for pasture, while the next 100 m comprises poorly drained silty soils (fluvisols) recently cultivated for flax production. The adjacent footslopes

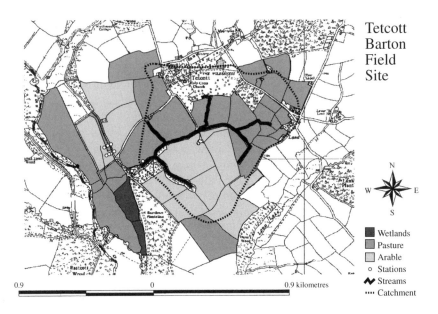

Tetcott
Barton
Field
Site

Wetlands
Pasture
Arable
○ Stations
⋎ Streams
···· Catchment

0.9                    0                         0.9 kilometres

*Figure 7.1    Map of the field study site*

have poorly drained soils of low permeability (dystric gleysols), supporting willow scrub and tall herb fen. The backslope comprises more permeable brown soils (dystric cambisols) used for arable cropping, with woodland on the steeper sections (Figure 7.1).

## 2.1    Case Study 1: In-stream Wetland Buffer Zone

This example involves the comparison of the efficiency of a conventional buffer zone with either one of two potential alternative buffer zones for the removal of $NO_3^-$ from a second order stream draining an agricultural catchment. Tetcott Stream Wetland 1 (TSW1 in Figure 7.2) is a small area of wetland (625 m$^2$) situated adjacent to Tetcott Stream, comprising great tussock sedge fen (NVC S3/CORINE 53.217). Tetcott Stream Wetland 2 (TSW2 in Figure 7.2) is similar to TSW1 in that both are located on the footslope/floodplain boundary, but TSW2 is much larger, covering an area of 3.50 ha, with tall herb fen (NVC M27/CORINE 37.1). Towards its south-eastern extremity, strong groundwater discharge occurs. The possibility exists to divert the stream through either one or both of the wetlands. A second simple diversion would allow the stream to discharge into TSW2 at its north-eastern extremity. Surrogate measurements and assays were carried out from which potential

$NO_3^-$ removal rates from the stream water by denitrification within the wetlands were calculated and used to assess the potential effectiveness of diverting the stream and providing the wetlands with the opportunity to act as buffer zones for the stream.

Monitoring stations were established at three locations within the catchment. The first was situated within TSW1 (station TS1 in Figure 7.2), one of the areas to be used as an alternative buffer zone. The second was located in an existing, narrow (2 m wide) conventional buffer zone (station TS2 in Figure 7.2), and comprised rush pasture, while the third station (TS3 in Figure 7.2) was located a short distance perpendicularly upslope from the buffer zone in an area of improved, heavily grazed pasture. Measurements made at station TS2 were assumed to be representative of soils within a buffer zone 2 m wide throughout the whole of the stream catchment. This zone is referred to as station zone TS2 (that is the conventional buffer zone) and occupies a total area of 15 592 m$^2$ within the sub-catchment. Similarly, station zone TS3 was delineated throughout the sub-catchment, with its upper boundary being equal to the distance of TS3 from the stream, and its lower boundary delineated by the upslope boundary of station zone TS2. Station zone TS3 covers an area of 26 764 m$^2$. These two station zones are shown in Figure 7.2.

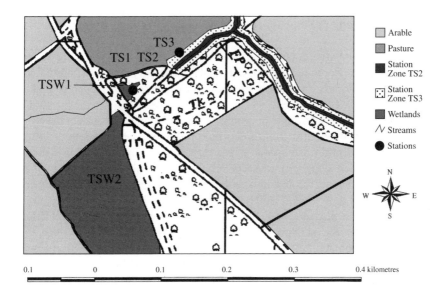

*Figure 7.2    Details of Tetcott stream study site*

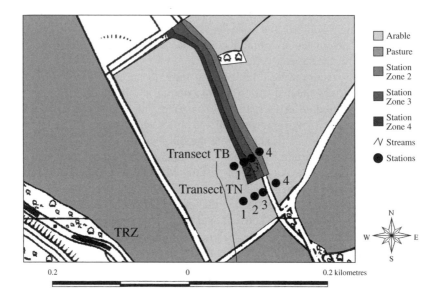

*Figure 7.3    Transects, stations and station zones in the footslope buffer
              zone*

## 2.2   Case Study 2: Slope/Floodplain Boundary Wetland Buffer Zone

The alternative buffer zone in this case study is situated approximately 200 m
from the main river in the footslope/floodplain boundary area (see Figure 7.3).
It comprises an area of shallow groundwater discharge downslope of arable
land.

Conventionally, a buffer zone would be situated along the banks of the river
and this alternative buffer zone area would potentially be subject to drainage
and improvement for use as arable land or pasture. Eight monitoring stations
were established along two transects through the footslope/floodplain boundary area, one passing through an area of wetland acting as an alternative buffer
zone (referred to as Tetcott Buffer (TB) transect in Figure 7.3) and one passing through an adjacent area that has been improved for flax production
(referred to as Tetcott Non-buffer (TN) transect in Figure 7.3), so that the
impact of reclamation for crop production could be examined.

The location of the four TB stations was determined by a combination of
geomorphology, soil, vegetation and land use along the transect. TB4 was
established on the backslope at the upslope boundary of the buffer zone, adjacent to an arable field from which much of the water passing through the

buffer zone is likely to have emanated. Soils were relatively well drained (dystric cambisols) and the vegetation comprised mainly hawthorn scrub (NVC W21/CORINE 31.812) and oak woodland (NVC W10/CORINE 41.21,51). TB3 was situated at the backslope/footslope boundary in an area of poorly drained soils (dystric gleysols) and the vegetation was predominantly alder/willow woodland (NVC W1,2,5,6,7/CORINE 44.9). TB2 was situated in the foot-slope/floodplain boundary where soils were also poorly drained dystric gleysols and the vegetation was predominantly tall herb fen (NVC M27/CORINE 37.1, 53.2). Station TB1 was situated on the floodplain in an area of backland, where the soils were poorly drained silty fluvisols, and the area was cultivated with flax. Stations on the TN transect were established in corresponding positions, the main difference being that TN1–3 had been cultivated for flax.

In addition, a monitoring station was established in the area that represents a conventional buffer zone location (referred to as Tetcott Riparian Zone (TRZ) station in Figure 7.3) adjacent to the river, in a field of improved pasture with deep, well drained, silty brown alluvial soils (cambisols).

## 3  METHOD

Measurements of soil environment variables and the collection of soil water samples were carried out over a one-year period at each monitoring station from mid December 1997 to mid December 1998. Details of the variables measured are shown in Table 7.1. Denitrification assays were carried out at ambient soil temperatures, while potential denitrification assays were carried out over a range of temperatures.

Daily soil temperatures are predicted from a linear regression equation relating soil temperatures measured during field monitoring to daily soil temperatures measured as part of the Natural Environment Research Council's Environmental Change Network programme at the nearby IGER North Wyke Research Station. Stream discharge is determined from stage measurements via a linear regression equation. Details of the methods applied follow in the next section.

## 4  RESULTS

### 4.1  Case Study 1: In-stream Wetland Buffer Zone

#### 4.1.1  Stream data
The estimated daily discharge, $NO_3^--N$ concentration and $NO_3^--N$ load in Tetcott stream during the study period are presented in Figure 7.4. The

*Table 7.1    Environmental variables measured*

| Variables | Measurement frequency | Method | References |
|---|---|---|---|
| Topsoil pH | Bi-monthly | Russell pH probe attached to a Hanna HI 9025 microprocessor | Maltby *et al.*, 1996 |
| Topsoil temperature | Bi-monthly | Temperature probe attached to a Hanna HI 9025 microprocessor | Maltby *et al.*, 1996 |
| Water table depth | Bi-monthly | Measured using an electronic water sensor in a piezometer installed to 80cm depth | Maltby *et al.*, 1996 |
| Soil water $NO_3^-$ concentration | Bi-monthly | Samples collected using ceramic cup interstitial water samplers at 10cm and 40cm depth[1]. Samples analysed using a Skalar SAM segmented flow auto-analyser[2] | [1]Grossman and Udluft, 1991 [2]Blackwell, 1997 |
| Denitrification | Seasonally | Acetylene blockage technique | Yoshinari and Knowles, 1976 adapted by Blackwell, 1997 |
| Potential denitrification | Two assays performed | Acetylene blockage technique using $NO_3^-$ amended water incubated at three different temperatures | Blackwell, 1997 |
| Stream stage | Bi-weekly | Stage board installed in stream | Maltby *et al.*, 1996 |
| Stream discharge | On four occasions over a range of discharges | Flow meter used to determine flow across stream | Maltby *et al.*, 1996 |
| Stream water $NO_3^-$ concentration | Daily | Samples collected using Epic 1011 portable waste water samplers. Samplers were analysed using a Skalar SAM segmented flow autoanalyser | Blackwell, 1997 |

estimated regression equation used to predict the discharge from stage is presented in equation (7.1).

$$\text{Log discharge (litres sec}^{-1}) = 0.231 \times \text{stage (cm)} - 3.356 \qquad (7.1)$$

($r^2 = 0.9925$)

Generally, concentrations are low with the EC maximum limit for $NO_3^-$-N in drinking water of 11.3 mg l$^{-1}$ (EC8/778a) never being exceeded. The maximum concentration measured was 10.37 mg l$^{-1}$ $NO_3^-$-N and the minimum 1.05 mg l$^{-1}$ $NO_3^-$-N. The mean over the whole monitoring period was 5.15 mg l$^{-1}$

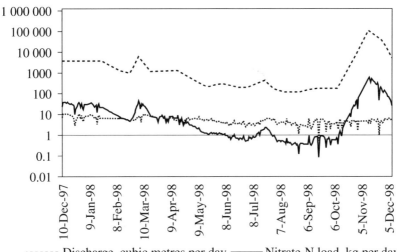

······ Discharge, cubic metres per day ——— Nitrate-N load, kg per day
·········· Nitrate-N concentration, mg per litre

*Note*:   Vertical axis is log scale.

*Figure 7.4    Discharge, $NO_3^-$-N concentrations and $NO_3^-$-N load in Tetcott
              stream*

$NO_3^-$-N. No distinct seasonal variations are apparent, although there does appear to be a general decrease in $NO_3^-$-N concentration during the monitoring period.

Daily $NO_3^-$-N loads (calculated by multiplying discharge by $NO_3^-$-N concentration) in Tetcott stream vary greatly. A distinct seasonal pattern is apparent with a late summer minimum of 0.09 kg $NO_3^-$-N $d^{-1}$, an early winter maximum of 589.36 kg $NO_3^-$-N $d^{-1}$ and a mean for the whole monitoring period of 30.41 kg $NO_3^-$-N $d^{-1}$. The pattern of $NO_3^-$-N loads closely follows that of discharge due to the relatively small variations in $NO_3^-$-N concentrations in comparison to the relatively large variations in discharge. This is demonstrated by the statistically highly significant correlation between these two variables ($r^2 = 0.98$).

### 4.1.2   Potential denitrification results for the alternative buffer zone TSW1

The results of two potential denitrification assays carried out with soil cores sampled from TSW1 to investigate the effects of diverting the stream through this wetland are shown in Figure 7.5. Denitrification rates generally were

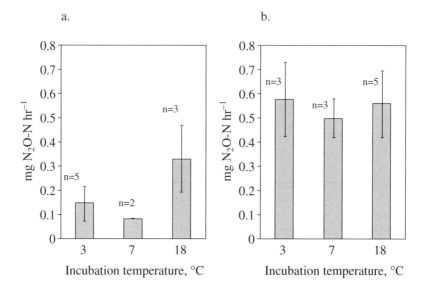

*Figure 7.5   Potential denitrification rates in TSW1 using (a) 4 mg l⁻¹*
*NO₃⁻-N amended water and (b) 10 mg l⁻¹ NO₃⁻-N amended*
*water*

much higher in the assay using 10 mg l$^{-1}$ NO$_3^-$-N amended water than in the
assay using 4 mg l$^{-1}$ NO$_3^-$-N amended water. These concentrations were
chosen as they represent the maximum and the approximate mean concentrations measured in the stream. The standard error bars indicate the high variability in the results.

In the assay carried out with 4 mg l$^{-1}$ NO$_3^-$-N amended water, the influence
of temperature was important, although surprisingly, the lowest mean value of
0.081 mg N$_2$O-N m$^{-2}$ hr$^{-1}$ was derived from the samples incubated at 7°C, and
not those at 3°C as would be expected. Similar results were observed in the
assay using 10 mg l$^{-1}$ NO$_3^-$-N amended water, with the lowest mean denitrification rate of 0.499 mg N$_2$O-N m$^{-2}$ hr$^{-1}$ again being measured in the 7°C incubation. However, this time the highest rate of 0.575 mg N$_2$O-N m$^{-2}$ hr$^{-1}$ was
measured in the 3°C incubation.

### 4.1.3   Calculation of the NO$_3^-$-N loads potentially removed by alternative buffer zone TSW1

The NO$_3^-$-N loads potentially removed by denitrification in TSW1 were calculated from a linear multiple regression equation derived from soil temperature
in TSW1 and stream water NO$_3^-$-N concentration data:

$$\text{Soil Temperature at TS1W1 (°C)} = 0.871 \times \text{Soil Temperature}$$
$$\text{at N. Wyke (°C)} - 0.139 \qquad (7.2)$$

$(r^2 = 0.873)$

Subsequent to the calculation of daily temperatures, the mean daily rate of denitrification in TSW1 was calculated from a linear multiple regression equation using the results from the potential denitrification assay, temperature and $NO_3^-$-N load as the control variables. This equation is shown below (equation 7.3).

$$D = (0.0076 \times T) + (0.0604 \times C) - 0.1290 \qquad (7.3)$$

$(r^2 = 0.903)$
where:
D = Denitrification Rate (mg $N_2$O-N m$^{-2}$ hr$^{-1}$)
T = Temperature TSW1 (°C)
C = Concentration of $NO_3^-$-N in stream (mg l$^{-1}$)

The denitrification rates predicted from this equation were then used to calculate the amount of $NO_3^-$-N in the stream water potentially removed by TSW1 if the stream were diverted. This was done by multiplying the predicted hourly denitrification rate per square metre by the area of the wetland in metres (625 m$^2$) times 24 (hours in a day). These results are shown in Figure 7.6.

The amount of $NO_3^-$-N potentially removed in TSW1 does not vary as greatly as the load in the stream, with a maximum daily amount of 0.008 kg $NO_3^-$-N and a minimum of 0.000kg $NO_3^-$-N potentially being removed by TSW1. Unlike temperature, there is no apparent seasonal trend with both lowest and highest rates of removal predicted in the winter months.

The largest percentage of potential $NO_3^-$-N removal (0.77 per cent) is predicted to occur in the summer months when loads are low due to low discharges despite high $NO_3^-$ concentrations, and denitrification rates are high due to high temperatures. However, the predicted percentage of $NO_3^-$-N load removed generally is very low, with a minimum of zero, and never exceeding 0.8 per cent. These predictions suggest that if the stream were diverted through wetland TSW1, it is unlikely that at any time a significant reduction of the $NO_3^-$-N load of the water in Tetcott stream would occur as a result of denitrification.

### 4.1.4   Calculation of the $NO_3^-$-N loads potentially removed by alternative buffer zone TSW2

An alternative scenario to diverting Tetcott Barton stream through wetland TSW1 is to divert it through wetland TSW2 (see Figure 7.2). In order to investigate the

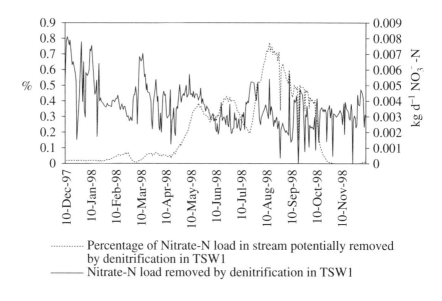

--------- Percentage of Nitrate-N load in stream potentially removed
          by denitrification in TSW1
———— Nitrate-N load removed by denitrification in TSW1

*Figure 7.6    Daily amount of $NO_3^-$-N in Tetcott stream potentially removed*
*by denitrification and percentage of daily $NO_3^-$-N load removed*
*in TSW1*

potential effects of such an action, the denitrification predictions calculated for
TSW1 were simply multiplied in proportion to the area of TSW2. This is
deemed a reasonable action given the close proximity of the two wetlands and
their similar geomorphic location. However, they do differ slightly in vegetation and therefore probably in current nutrient status, although this should not
be significant as both wetlands would potentially receive a new and similar
nutrient supply via the stream. The predicted results are shown in Figure 7.7.

The pattern of the potential amount of $NO_3^-$-N removed daily throughout
the year is the same as for TSW1, but the scale of removal is somewhat different, with up to 0.45 kg $d^{-1}$ $NO_3^-$-N being removed. Expressed as a percentage
of the $NO_3^-$-N load in the stream, these results are relatively high, with up to
44 per cent of the $NO_3^-$-N load in the stream potentially being removed by
denitrification.

### 4.1.5    Economic valuation of $NO_3^-$ removal in alternative buffer zones TSW1 and TSW2

Using the results presented above, monthly economic values for the amount of
$NO_3^-$-N removed by denitrification in each of the two wetlands have been
calculated using the Replacement Cost method (see Chapter 4). The results are

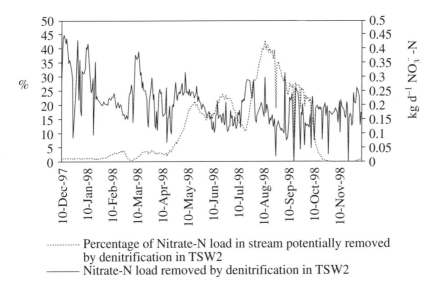

----------- Percentage of Nitrate-N load in stream potentially removed
by denitrification in TSW2
———— Nitrate-N load removed by denitrification in TSW2

*Figure 7.7*    *Daily amount of $NO_3^-$-N in Tetcott stream potentially removed*
*by denitrification and percentage of daily $NO_3^-$-N load removed*
*in TSW2*

presented in Table 7.2. The economic values are calculated by determining the
cost of removal of the amount of $NO_3^-$-N by a commercial technological
method. The system used for this comparison is the BioDen™ system
produced by Nitrate Removal Technologies, which claims to have the latest
and cheapest $NO_3^-$-N removal technology available.

The economic value of $NO_3^-$-N is based upon operating and maintenance
costs. Capital equipment costs are not incorporated in the valuation. Operating
and maintenance costs alone provide a value of £6.78 kg$^{-1}$ $NO_3^-$-N removed
(1999 prices).[1]

Adding up the predicted monthly amounts yields an annual economic value
of $NO_3^-$-N potentially removed by the alternative buffer zones TSW1 and
TSW2 of £10.40 and £581.50 respectively.

### 4.1.6    Denitrification results for the conventional buffer zone

Results from denitrification assays carried out at stations TS2 and TS3 in different seasons throughout the study period are shown in Figure 7.8. On all occa-
sions denitrification rates at TS3 are similar to or higher than those within the
conventional buffer zone at TS2. Rates at TS3 range from a minimum of
0.056 mg $N_2O$-N m$^{-2}$ hr$^{-1}$ in December 1997 to a maximum of 0.409 mg

Table 7.2 Loads and economic values of $NO_3^-$-N potentially removed in TSW1 and TSW2

| Month | Mean daily amount $NO_3^-$-N potentially removed in TSW1, kg | Mean daily amount $NO_3^-$-N potentially removed in TSW2, kg | Mean daily % $NO_3^-$-N load in Tetcott Stream potentially removed by denitrification in TSW1 | Mean daily % $NO_3^-$-N load in Tetcott Stream potentially removed by denitrification in TS1W2 | Monthly value of potential $NO_3^-$-N removal by denitrification in TSW1, £ | Monthly value of potential $NO_3^-$-N removal by denitrification in TSW2, £ |
|---|---|---|---|---|---|---|
| Dec-97 | 0.006 | 0.339 | 0.021 | 1.169 | 1.27 | 71.30 |
| Jan-98 | 0.005 | 0.275 | 0.021 | 1.167 | 1.03 | 57.81 |
| Feb-98 | 0.004 | 0.201 | 0.051 | 2.837 | 0.75 | 42.23 |
| Mar-98 | 0.005 | 0.269 | 0.044 | 2.448 | 1.01 | 56.52 |
| Apr-98 | 0.003 | 0.190 | 0.070 | 3.905 | 0.71 | 39.98 |
| May-98 | 0.004 | 0.242 | 0.287 | 16.097 | 0.91 | 50.94 |
| Jun-98 | 0.003 | 0.160 | 0.345 | 19.348 | 0.60 | 33.64 |
| Jul-98 | 0.004 | 0.198 | 0.313 | 17.523 | 0.74 | 41.69 |
| Aug-98 | 0.003 | 0.172 | 0.650 | 36.450 | 0.64 | 36.08 |
| Sep-98 | 0.003 | 0.170 | 0.483 | 27.096 | 0.64 | 35.66 |
| Oct-98 | 0.003 | 0.157 | 0.181 | 10.134 | 0.59 | 33.02 |
| Nov-98 | 0.003 | 0.174 | 0.002 | 0.089 | 0.65 | 36.45 |
| Dec-98 | 0.004 | 0.220 | 0.008 | 0.432 | 0.82 | 46.17 |

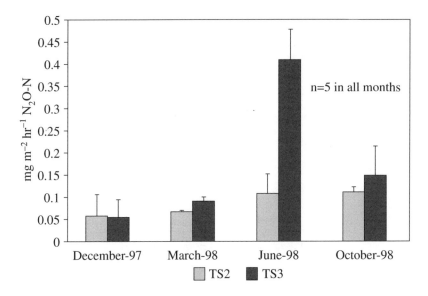

*Figure 7.8    Denitrification rates measured at TS2 and TS3*

$N_2O$-N $m^{-2}$ $hr^{-1}$ in June 1998, indicating a typical seasonal trend. Rates at TS2 generally are lower, ranging from a minimum of 0.058 mg $N_2O$-N $m^{-2}$ $hr^{-1}$ in December 1997 to a maximum of 0.111 mg $N_2O$-N $m^{-2}$ $hr^{-1}$ in October 1998, and hence do not demonstrate as strong a seasonal trend or as much variability as rates measured at TS3.

### 4.1.7    Soil water $NO_3^-$-N concentrations and volumes

The values of soil water $NO_3^-$-N concentrations measured in samples collected from interstitial porous cup (PC) water samplers at depths of 10 cm (PC10) and 40 cm (PC40) at stations TS2 and TS3 are shown in Table 7.3. Concentrations generally are low, all being less than 1 mg $l^{-1}$ $NO_3^-$-N. The minimum concentration was measured in the sample collected from PC10 at TS3 in January 1998 when no $NO_3^-$-N was detected, while the highest concentration of 0.564 mg $NO_3^-$-N was measured in the sample collected from PC40 at TS3 in November 1998. The change in $NO_3^-$-N concentration in the soil water between monitoring stations TS3 and TS2 is also shown in Table 7.3.

Water table depths were recorded in 80 cm deep piezometers (P80) at each station. These results are presented in Table 7.4. The fluctuation in the water table is greater at TS3 than at TS2, reaching a maximum depth of 50 cm in May 1998 at TS3, while the maximum water table depth recorded at TS2 was 17 cm in the same month. For much of the year the water table at both stations was recorded within 10 cm of the soil surface.

Table 7.3  *Soil water NO$_3^-$-N concentrations at TS2 and TS3*

| Month | TS2 | | TS3 | | Change in NO$_3^-$-N Conc. from TS3 to TS2, mg l$^{-1}$ | |
| | NO$_3^-$-N Concentration mg l$^{-1}$ PC10 | NO$_3^-$-N Concentration mg l$^{-1}$ PC40 | NO$_3^-$-N Concentration, mg l$^{-1}$ PC10 | NO$_3^-$-N Concentration, mg l$^{-1}$ PC40 | PC10 | PC40 |
|---|---|---|---|---|---|---|
| November-97 | – | 0.052 | 0.031 | 0.564 | – | –0.512 |
| January-98 | 0.002 | 0.020 | 0.000 | 0.120 | +0.002 | –0.100 |
| March-98 | 0.003 | 0.015 | 0.110 | 0.017 | –0.107 | –0.002 |
| May-98 | 0.003 | 0.011 | – | 0.026 | – | –0.015 |
| July-98 | 0.055 | 0.050 | – | 0.049 | – | +0.001 |
| October-98 | 0.010 | – | 0.025 | 0.007 | –0.015 | – |

Table 7.4 *Water table depth, soil water volumes and $NO_3^-$-N loads at TS2 and TS3*

| Month | Depth of water table below surface (cm) measured in P80 cm | | Volume of water passing through station zone in whole buffer, litres/day | | $NO_3^-$-N load passing through top 40 cm of soil in each station zone, g/day | |
|---|---|---|---|---|---|---|
| | TS2 | TS3 | TS2 | TS3 | TS2 | TS3 |
| November-97 | 9 | 2 | 67,681 | 125,127 | 3.520 | 70.057 |
| January-98 | 1 | 3 | 85,146 | 121,723 | 1.700 | 14.610 |
| March-98 | 8 | 9 | 69,864 | 102,077 | 1.050 | 1.735 |
| May-98 | 17 | 50 | 28,382 | 0 | 0.312 | – |
| July-98 | 12 | 37 | 61,131 | 9,878 | 3.057 | 0.484 |
| October-98 | 13 | 3 | 58,948 | 121,834 | – | 0.852 |

The total volume of water passing through the top 40 cm of the soil in each of the two station zones was calculated from soil hydraulic conductivity measurements, using a technique described by Boast and Kirkham (1971) where water table depth is measured in 80 cm piezometers over the length of the station zone (that is equal to 4228 m, twice the total length of the stream in the Tetcott stream catchment). Soil hydraulic conductivities measured in the soils at TS2 and TS3 were 0.051 m d$^{-1}$ and 0.077 m d$^{-1}$ respectively, both of which would be classed as slow (Boast and Kirkham, 1971).

The volume of water passing through the top 40 cm of the soil at station TS3 generally was higher than that passing through TS2, except in the summer when the water table drops below 40 cm. This is probably explained by the occasional presence of springs a short distance upslope of the buffer zone TS2, which form small areas of overland flow passing directly across the buffer zone, reducing the interaction of the water with the soil and consequently the effectiveness of the buffer zone. These springs probably result from the lower hydraulic conductivity of the soil at TS2 than upslope at TS3.

The $NO_3^-$-N loads passing through the top 40 cm in each station zone were calculated from the volume of water passing through the top 40 cm of soil in each zone and the $NO_3^-$-N concentration in samples collected from PC40s (Table 7.4). Although there are gaps in the data, it is apparent that during winter the $NO_3^-$-N loads passing through TS3 are greater than those passing through TS2, while the opposite holds during summer. However, this is mainly caused by the volume of water passing through the zones and less by variations in $NO_3^-$-N concentrations.

### 4.1.8   Calculation of the $NO_3^-$-N loads removed by the conventional buffer zone

Two approaches are used to calculate the amount of $NO_3^-$-N removed in the conventional buffer zone TS2 and the upslope zone TS3.

In the first approach, the denitrification measurements at TS2 have been extrapolated to estimate the total quantity of $NO_3^-$-N removed in the whole buffer zone over a period of one year. In the second approach, the amount of $NO_3^-$-N removed between TS3 and TS2 has been calculated from soil water $NO_3^-$-N concentration data. These results have been extrapolated to provide information about current removal rates in the zone between TS3 and TS2.

There are several problems associated with the extrapolation of both these data sets, mainly owing to the low number of monitoring stations and the large temporal gaps between the collection of samples and readings, as well as the assumption that process rates are consistent throughout the catchment within each station zone. The maximum $NO_3^-$-N load potentially removed by the conventional buffer zone has not been examined in this study, and the actual amounts estimated are likely to be underestimates of the potential removal as a result of the low $NO_3^-$-N concentrations received by the buffer zone. Based upon both approaches, quantities of $NO_3^-$-N removed are calculated seasonally and annually (Table 7.5).

The amount of $NO_3^-$-N removed by denitrification in the conventional buffer zone is estimated as 6.415 kg $yr^{-1}$, while the observed amount of $NO_3^-$-N loss from soil water samples between TS3 and TS2 is estimated as 3.645 kg $yr^{-1}$.

### 4.1.9 Economic valuation of $NO_3^-$ removal in the conventional buffer zone

Table 7.5 also presents the economic values of these removed quantities, using the same method as before (replacement costs). The annual economic values based on the conventional buffer zone are £43.50 $yr^{-1}$ and £24.70 $yr^{-1}$ for the conventional buffer zone and the zone between TS3 and TS2 respectively. Converting these total annual values to economic values per hectare, they are significantly lower than the economic values calculated for the alternative buffer zones TSW1 and TSW2. The economic benefits of the conventional buffer zone TS2 for nitrate removal are £27.90 $ha^{-1}$ $yr^{-1}$, while these benefits are almost six times higher (£166.00 $ha^{-1}$ $yr^{-1}$) for TSW1 and TSW2.

When comparing the economic values from alternative land uses (Table 7.6), corn production appears to be most profitable. The economic values are based on 1999 price levels and were obtained from the land manager, who is also the tenant farmer at Tetcott Barton. The economic values are all net of the land's rental price which was £111.20 $ha^{-1}year^{-1}$ (including the economic values for using the land for nitrate removal). The economic value per hectare is negative when using the land in the conventional way as a buffer zone for nitrate removal. However, it has to be kept in mind that the estimation of the economic value for nitrate removal may be an underestimation of the real value since it is based on (1) operating and maintenance costs only, not on capital costs, and (2) cost estimates instead of benefit estimates in terms of willingness to pay (see Chapter 4). On the other hand, buffer zone maintenance costs are assumed negligible here.

Net economic values are positive when converting the areas in alternative wetland buffer zones, mainly as a result of the higher $NO_3^-$-N removal rates by denitrification of these alternatives. Hence, contrary to the conventional buffer zone, the economic value of the alternative wetland buffer zones for $NO_3^-$-N removal is positive, but less than when using the wetland for agricultural purposes.

Table 7.5 Calculated $NO_3^-$-N loads removed in the conventional buffer zone and the zone between TS2 and TS3

| Season | Month of data collection | | Amount $NO_3^-$-N removed in season by denitrification, kg | Value, £ | Amount $NO_3^-$-N removed from soil water between TS3 and TS2, kg | Value, £ |
|---|---|---|---|---|---|---|
| | Denitrification | Soil water $NO_3^-$-N Conc. | | | | |
| Winter | Dec-97 | Nov-97 and Jan-98 | 1.089 | 7.38 | 3.678 | 24.94 |
| Spring | Mar-98 | Mar-98 | 1.239 | 8.40 | 0.061 | 0.41 |
| Summer | Jun-98 | May-98 and Jul-98 | 2.009 | 13.62 | −0.118 | −0.80 |
| Autumn | Oct-98 | Oct-98 | 2.078 | 14.09 | 0.024 | 0.16 |
| Totals | | | 6.415 | 43.49 | 3.645 | 24.71 |

Note: As no sample was collected from PC 40 cm in the autumn of 1998 at TS2, the $NO_3^-$-N concentration measured in PC 10 cm (0.010 mg $l^{-1}$) at this station was used to calculate the amount of $No_3^-$-N removed from soil water between TS3 and TS2 in this season.

184

*Table 7.6  Economic values associated with different wetland uses*

| | | Economic value | | |
| --- | --- | --- | --- | --- |
| | | | Alternative buffer zone | |
| | | Conventional buffer zone | TSW1 | TSW2 |
| Land use | £/ha/year | £/year | £/year | £/year |
| *Agriculture* | | | | |
| – Sheep | 86.5 | 134.9 | 5.4 | 303.0 |
| – cattle (beef) | 197.7 | 308.2 | 12.4 | 692.5 |
| – Flax | 247.1 | 385.3 | 15.4 | 865.6 |
| – Corn | 333.6 | 520.1 | 20.9 | 1168.9 |
| *Nitrate removal* | | | | |
| – Conventional buffer zone | –83.3 | –129.9 | –5.2 | –291.8 |
| – Alternative TSW1 | 54.7 | 85.3 | 3.4 | 191.6 |
| – Alternative TSW2 | 54.8 | 85.4 | 3.4 | 192.0 |

*Note*:   Money amounts are based on 1999 prices.

## 4.2   Case study 2: Footslope Wetland Buffer Zone

### 4.2.1   Denitrification results

The results from the denitrification assays carried out with samples collected at each monitoring station in different seasons throughout the study period are shown in Figure 7.9. The results vary considerably, but a general seasonal trend of high rates in the summer and autumn and low rates in the winter and spring is exhibited at all stations. The highest rate measured was 1.832 mg $N_2O$-N m$^{-2}$ hr$^{-1}$ in the autumn of 1998 at station TRZ, the conventional riparian buffer zone location. The lowest measurement was also made at this location. No denitrification could be detected in the winter of 1997.

While it is difficult to determine any specific trends among stations with the seasonal data, trends become apparent in the mean data shown in Figure 7.10. Denitrification rates exhibit a general decreasing trend downslope through the buffer zones with a minimum rate of 0.091 mg m$^{-2}$ hr$^{-1}$ $N_2O$-N at TB2 and a maximum rate of 0.120 mg m$^{-2}$ hr$^{-1}$ $N_2O$-N at TB4. A similar trend is exhibited along the TN transect, although the mean rate of 0.087 mg m$^{-2}$ hr$^{-1}$ $N_2O$-N measured at TN4 is lower than those at TN3 (0.100 mg m$^{-2}$ hr$^{-1}$ $N_2O$-N) and TN2 (0.089 mg m$^{-2}$ hr$^{-1}$ $N_2O$-N). The mean rate at the conventional buffer zone TRZ of 0.488 mg m$^{-2}$ hr$^{-1}$ $N_2O$-N is much higher than the mean rate measured at any other station. This is mainly the result of one exceptionally

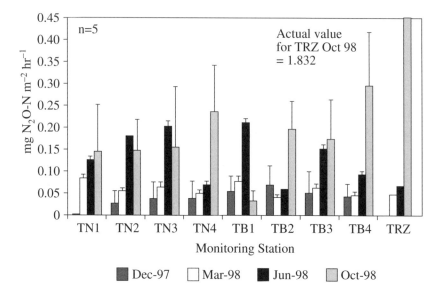

*Figure 7.9    Denitrification rates measured in footslope and conventional buffer zones*

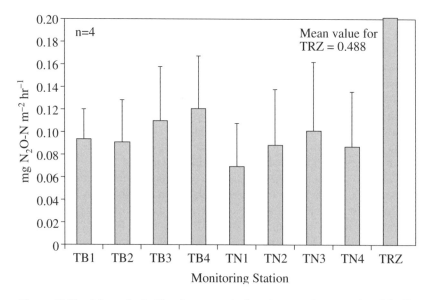

*Figure 7.10    Mean denitrification rates in footslope and conventional buffer zones*

high measurement made in October 1998, whereas in all other seasons the denitrification rates were among the lowest recorded.

### 4.2.2 Soil water $NO_3^-$-N concentrations and volumes

The values of soil water $NO_3^-$-N concentrations measured in samples collected from interstitial porous cup (PC) water samplers at depths of 10 cm (PC10) and 40 cm (PC40) at all stations are shown in Table 7.7, while mean values are presented in Figure 7.11. Gaps in the data sets are mainly the result of water samples not being collected owing to dry soil conditions. At location TRZ no samples were successfully collected at all because of the dry nature of the soil at this location. The water table never rose above a depth of 80 cm at this station.

It was possible to calculate mean annual $NO_3^-$-N concentrations in samples collected from porous cup interstitial water samplers at both 10 cm (PC10) and 40 cm (PC40) depth. These results are shown in Figure 7.11. There is a general trend for high concentrations in the soils at the upslope edge of the buffer zone, with a rapid decrease in concentration through the buffer zone at both depths. The concentrations in the samples collected in the TN transect are higher than those in the TB transect, probably as a result of more direct inputs of $NO_3^-$-N in the form of fertilizer.

### 4.2.3 Calculation of the $NO_3^-$-N loads removed in footslope and conventional buffer zones

Table 7.8 shows that station zone 3 removes most $NO_3^-$ by denitrification. This is not only because of its slightly larger size compared to the other two zones, but also because denitrification rates are relatively high all year round, whereas rates are more variable at the other two station zones. The highest denitrification rate measured was 0.296 mg m$^{-2}$ hr$^{-1}$ $N_2O$-N in the autumn at station TB4 and coincides with the greatest load of $NO_3^-$-N removed in any of the alternative buffer zones.

### 4.2.4 Economic valuation of $NO_3^-$ removal in the conventional and alternative buffer zones

The total amount of $NO_3^-$-N removed annually through denitrification in the alternative buffer zone appears to be relatively low, totalling 7.747 kg. Multiplying this amount by the fixed economic price of £6.78 per kilogram (see section 4.1.5) yields an economic value of £52.52 year$^{-1}$.

According to Table 7.8, the conventional buffer zone TRZ is more efficient both economically and environmentally, mainly as the result of one exceptionally high measurement in the autumn of 1998. A 20 m wide conventional buffer zone of the same length as the footslope buffer zone apparently is able to remove three times as much $NO_3^-$-N as the alternative buffer zone over the

*Table 7.7   Soil water NO$_3^-$-N concentrations*

| Station | TB1 | | TB2 | | TB3 | | TB4 | | TN1 | | TN2 | | TN3 | | TN4 | |
|---|---|---|---|---|---|---|---|---|---|---|---|---|---|---|---|---|
| Month | PC10 | PC40 | PC10 | PC40 | PC10 | PC40 | PC10 | PC40 | PC10 | PC40 | PC10 | PC40 | PC10 | PC40 | PC10 | PC40 |
| Nov-97 | 0.088 | 0.017 | 0.051 | | 0.837 | 0.011 | | | 0.055 | 0.046 | 0.001 | 0.046 | 3.666 | 28.101 | | 74.751 |
| Jan-98 | | | | | 0 | 0 | | | 0.566 | 0.01 | 0 | 0.074 | 2.997 | 4.964 | 8.776 | 13.079 |
| Mar-98 | 0.312 | 0 | 0 | 0 | | 2.247 | 5.941 | 24.89 | 0.111 | 0.024 | 0.003 | 0.099 | | 0.079 | | |
| May-98 | 0.012 | 0 | | 0 | | 0.01 | | | | 0.004 | | 0.245 | | 0.256 | | |
| Jul-98 | | 0.057 | | 0.045 | | 0.206 | | | | 0.057 | | 0.048 | | 0.045 | | |
| Oct-98 | 0.084 | 0.001 | | 0 | | 0.091 | 5.193 | | | 0.004 | 0.007 | 0 | | 0 | 54.115 | 26.597 |
| Means | 0.124 | 0.015 | 0.0255 | 0.009 | 0.4185 | 0.4275 | 5.567 | 24.89 | 0.074 | 0.024167 | 0.00275 | 0.085333 | 3.3315 | 5.574167 | 31.4455 | 38.14233 |

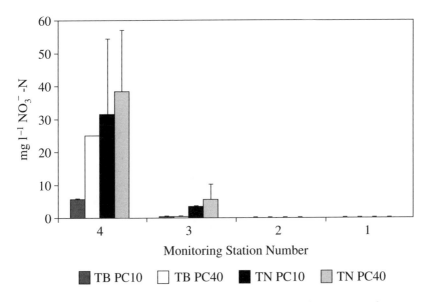

*Figure 7.11    Mean annual NO$_3^-$-N concentrations in soil water samples*

period of one year. Consequently, its economic value is also three times that of the alternative buffer zone (using the fixed price mentioned above). The annual value of the conventional buffer zone of £161.93 is equivalent to £289.20 ha$^{-1}$. Subtracting the rental price of land of £111.20 ha$^{-1}$, a net economic value results of £178.00 ha$^{-1}$.

Conversion of the annual economic value of the alternative buffer zone into a per hectare value amounts to £64.40 ha$^{-1}$. Subtracting the land rental fee from this, a negative net economic value of –£46.80 ha$^{-1}$ year$^{-1}$ results. Hence, whereas the net economic value in the first case study was positive for the alternative buffer zones and negative for the conventional buffer zone, it is exactly the other way around in the second case study.

## 5    DISCUSSION AND CONCLUSIONS

In this study only one specific element of water quality improvement which can be performed by various buffer zones has been examined. The importance of NO$_3^-$ supply to denitrification rates was demonstrated by the assay results in section 4.1.2, where the incubations with 10 mg l$^{-1}$ NO$_3^-$-N amended water produced higher rates of denitrification than those with 4 mg l$^{-1}$ NO$_3^-$-N amended water.

Table 7.8  NO₃⁻-N loads removed in alternative and conventional buffer zones

| Station | Size (ha) | Denitrification rate (mgN₂O-N m⁻² hr⁻¹) | | | | NO₃⁻-N loads removed (kg) | | | | Total removed (kg/year) | Economic value (£/year) |
|---|---|---|---|---|---|---|---|---|---|---|---|
| | | Winter | Spring | Summer | Autumn | Winter | Spring | Summer | Autumn | | |
| 4 | 0.2691 | 0.0429 | 0.0483 | 0.0934 | 0.2962 | 0.249 | 0.287 | 0.555 | 1.741 | 2.832 | 19.20 |
| 3 | 0.3197 | 0.0527 | 0.0635 | 0.1522 | 0.1741 | 0.364 | 0.448 | 1.074 | 1.216 | 3.102 | 21.03 |
| 2 | 0.2271 | 0.0689 | 0.0423 | 0.0578 | 0.1961 | 0.338 | 0.212 | 0.29 | 0.973 | 1.813 | 12.29 |
| Total | 0.8159 | – | – | – | – | 0.951 | 0.947 | 1.919 | 3.93 | 7.747 | 52.52 |
| TRZ | 0.56 | 0 | 0.0491 | 0.0703 | 1.8321 | 0 | 0.607 | 0.869 | 22.407 | 23.883 | 161.93 |

*Note:* Values for TRZ represent a buffer zone 20 m wide and the same length as the footslope buffer zone (280 m).

Variations in denitrification rates with temperature exhibited in the two assays do not follow the pattern of increase expected with increasing temperature (Nommik, 1956; Bailey, 1976). This is probably the result of the high spatial variability associated with denitrification in soils (Parkin, 1987) and the relatively low number of replicates used in the assays (for practical reasons). Small differences in rates between the 3°C and 7°C assays would be expected as at these temperatures, rates generally are reported as being very low, while at 18°C a large increase in denitrification rates would be expected (Nommik, 1956; Bailey, 1976), as seen in the results using the 4 mg l$^{-1}$ NO$_3^-$-N amended water.

Also the higher denitrification rates at TS3 than at TS2 (section 4.1.6) can probably be attributed to the fact that denitrification rates at TS2 are limited by NO$_3^-$ supply. TS3 receives direct inputs of NO$_3^-$ both from fertilizer applications and excreta from animals since the area is used as pasture for grazing, and any NO$_3^-$ deposited on the soil is likely to be removed before it reaches the buffer zone at TS2 by either plant uptake or denitrification as the soil conditions at this station are conducive to denitrification for much of the year.

In case study 2, the declining denitrification rates down through the buffer zone probably reflects the trend of declining NO$_3^-$ concentrations in the soil water along the transect, with rates decreasing as they become limited by NO$_3^-$ availability, despite the more suitable, anaerobic soil conditions for denitrification at stations TB3 and TB2.

While the rates of NO$_3^-$ removal by denitrification in the alternative buffer zone are not especially high, the buffer zone's performance is impressive, as indicated by the results obtained from soil water samples. Although the data set was not consistent enough to allow calculation of NO$_3^-$-N loads removed by all processes within the buffer zone, comparisons of concentrations of NO$_3^-$ in samples collected at each station demonstrate a rapid and large amount of removal as the soil water passes through the buffer zone to station TB2. It is likely that other processes such as plant uptake and assimilation by microorganisms in the soil are also important. It may also be the case that some dilution by deeper groundwater discharging at the site contributes to the rapid decline observed in NO$_3^-$-N concentrations down the transect.

However, denitrification may be more important than the figures imply, owing to possible problems associated with the sampling methodology, spatial and temporal variability in rates and the acetylene blockage technique itself (see Blackwell, 1997). Furthermore, one should keep in mind that the figures relate solely to the value of NO$_3^-$-N removal by denitrification and do not take into account the value of NO$_3^-$-N removal by any other process or any other value that the wetland may have. If the stream were diverted, it is likely that the amount of NO$_3^-$-N removed from the surface water would be much higher since other processes such as plant uptake and assimilation by soil organisms would also occur in addition to denitrification.

Plant uptake of N can be very high in temperate wetlands, with uptake rates of 38.1 g $Nm^{-2}$ $yr^{-1}$ having been measured in similar wetlands in Devon by Van Oorschot (1994). Using this rate, N uptake rates of 0.065 kg N $d^{-1}$ in TSW1 and 3.657 kg $d^{-1}$ in TSW2 would be feasible. While much of this N uptake probably would be in the form of $NH_4^+$-N, a large proportion is likely to involve $NO_3^-$-N. Moreover, these figures are uptake rates in the summer when they are generally much higher, whereas in the winter they are negligible. Hence, it can make a considerable difference to the buffer zones' $NO_3^-$-N removal efficiency and economic value. The wetlands will have other values, some of which will be related to water quality improvement such as sediment removal, BOD reduction, hydrological support for rivers and removal of heavy metals, pesticides and herbicides.

In case study 2, the amount of $NO_3^-$-N removed by denitrification in the conventional buffer zone is relatively high. However, these results should be viewed with caution. The high mean denitrification rate is the product of one high measurement made in October 1998, and although the measurement is likely to be 'real' (as opposed to containing a potential measurement bias), it is possible that this result is a very short lived period of denitrification, brought on by a wetting front passing through the soil as a result of heavy rainfall immediately prior to the collection of soil cores. Similar phenomena have been reported by Patrick and Wyatt (1964).

The stations on the two alternative buffer zone transects would have been less susceptible to such effects due to their wetter nature, so the heavy rainfall would not have considerably changed the soil environmental conditions. While the denitrification rate was high at this time, the source of the $NO_3^-$ in the soil is most probably an accumulation resulting from internal cycling, and not the result of a major diffuse pollution source such as that received by the alternative footslope buffer zone.

The footslope buffer zone actually performs the function of $NO_3^-$ removal from an external source, as well as simply transforming $NO_3^-$ as part of its natural internal N-cycle. Water emanating from arable fields that may be polluted or that have high $NO_3^-$ concentrations would not interact with the conventional buffer zone owing to its interception and transportation directly to the main river by drainage ditches in the floodplain or by passing at depth through permeable substrate. Water draining from fields in the floodplain may pass through the soil of the conventional buffer zone, but this is likely to happen at some depth. Several authors have reported denitrification at depth within floodplain soils (Cooper, 1990; Fustec *et al.*, 1991 and Pinay *et al.*, 1994), but denitrification is less likely to occur, often because of low carbon concentrations and short residence time resulting from the presence of highly permeable alluvial gravels.

While it is possible that some of the reductions in $NO_3^-$ concentrations in the soil water through the buffer zone may be the result of dilution by $NO_3^-$ deficient groundwater, the trend in denitrification rates tends to support the theory that much of the $NO_3^-$ is lost through denitrification. Whatever the process, the net result is a dramatic reduction in $NO_3^-$ concentration through the buffer zone, reflected in the low concentrations measured in water samples collected monthly from the drainage ditch located at the footslope boundary. These range from 0.083 mg l$^{-1}$ $NO_3^-$-N up to 4.053 mg l$^{-1}$ $NO_3^-$-N, but might have been much higher if the buffer zone were not present. Water from this ditch flows directly into the main river Tamar, some 200 m away, and if this alternatively located buffer zone were to be drained or degraded, it is likely that much higher concentrations of $NO_3^-$, resembling those measured in the soil water at TB4, would be present in this ditch water. The establishment of a conventional riparian buffer zone on the main river would do little to ameliorate the $NO_3^-$ load entering the river from this ditch.

Finally, it is not the intention of this work to promote alternative buffer zone locations in preference to conventional riparian buffer zones. It is widely acknowledged that the continuous, linear habitats in river corridors provided by the latter perform many useful functions in addition to that of $NO_3^-$ removal. In this research, the role of alternative buffer zones in the landscape is seen as enhancing and increasing not only the environmental efficiency of the functions performed by conventional buffer zones, but also the economic efficiency. Although they do not represent a tangible financial source of income to the land manager, alternative buffer zones can be economically more efficient than conventional buffer zones.

In this study, it has also been shown that the economic value of buffer zones in general comes very close to the economic value of using the wetland for agricultural grazing purposes, based on a limited economic pricing procedure. The economic values of arable land are much higher than the calculated economic values for $NO_3^-$ removal. However, one has to keep in mind that the geomorphological and soil characteristics of the wetlands, especially when buffer zones are adjacent to the river, often do not allow intensive arable activities.

Extending the economic pricing procedure to include other potential benefits, such as real cost savings of water purification and waste water treatment for public water suppliers, the net economic value is expected to increase further. Careful planning and assessment of the functioning of buffer zones in the landscape is required to optimize their use for environmentally and economically beneficial purposes, and to prevent the destruction of currently existing, potentially useful buffer zones which may be situated at some distance from main water bodies.

## NOTE

1. This is based on the removal of 10 mg $l^{-1}$ $NO_3^-$-N at a flow rate of 1.51 $ls^{-1}$. This is comparable to the discharge in the Tetcott stream for much of the summer period, although well below the discharge estimated in the winter months. The estimate nevertheless provides a generally representative figure. Obviously, if the capital costs of the equipment are incorporated, the value of the $NO_3^-$ removal function is greatly increased.

## REFERENCES

ALIS, (Arizona Legislative Information System) (1997), http://www.azleg.state.az.us.

Ambus, P. and S. Christensen (1993), 'Denitrification variability and control in a riparian fen irrigated with agricultural drainage water', *Soil Biology and Biochemistry*, **25**(7), 915–23.

Bailey, L.D. (1976), 'Effects of temperature and root on denitrification in a soil', *Canadian Journal of Soil Science*, **56**, 79–87.

Barbier, E.B., M. Acreman and D. Knowler (1997*), Economic Valuation of Wetlands: A Guide for Policy Makers and Planners*, Gland, Switzerland: Ramsar Convention Bureau.

Blackwell, M.S.A. (1997), 'Zones of enhanced denitrification in river marginal wetlands', unpublished Ph.D. thesis, Geography Department, Royal Holloway University of London, UK.

Blackwell, M.S.A. and E. Maltby (1998), 'Zones of enhanced denitrification', in A.J. McComb and J.A. Davis (eds), *Wetlands for the Future, Proceedings of INTECOL's V International Wetlands Conference*, Adelaide, Australia: Gleneagles Press.

Boast, C.W. and D. Kirkham (1971), 'Auger Hole seepage theory', *Soil Science Society of American Proceedings*, **35**(3), 365–73.

Brinson, M.M. (1993), 'A hydrogeomorphic classification for wetlands', Technical Report WRP-DE-4, US Army Engineer Waterways Experiment Station, Vicksburg, MS, USA.

Brown, S., M.M. Brinson and A.E. Lugo (1979), 'Structure and function of riparian wetlands', in R.R. Johnson and J.F. McCormick (eds*), Strategies for Protection and Management of Floodplain Wetlands and other Riparian Ecosystems*, US Forest Service Technical Report, WO–12, pp. 17–31.

Burt, T.P. and S.T. Trudgill (1993), 'Nitrate in groundwater', in T.P. Burt, A.L. Heathwaite and S.T. Trudgill (eds), *Nitrate; Processes, Patterns and Management*, Chichester, UK: John Wiley and Sons, pp. 213–38.

Cooper, A.B. (1990), 'Nitrate depletion in the riparian zone and stream channel of a small headwater catchment', *Hydrobiologia*, **202**,13–26.

Cooper, J.R., J.W. Gilliam and T.C. Jacobs (1986), 'Riparian areas as a control of nonpoint pollutants', in D.L. Correll (ed.), *Watershed Research Perspectives*, Washington, DC: Smithsonian Institutes Press, pp. 166–92.

Correll, D.L. (1997), 'Buffer zones and water quality protection: General principles', in N.E. Haycock, T.P. Burt, K.W.T. Goulding and G. Pinay (eds) *Buffer Zones: Their Processes and Potential in Water Protection*, Harpenden, UK: Quest Environmental.

Dillaha, T.A. and S.P. Inamdar (1997), 'Buffer zones as sediment traps or sources', in N.E. Haycock, T.P. Burt, K.W.T. Goulding and G. Pinay (eds), *Buffer Zones: Their*

*Processes and Potential in Water Protection*, Harpenden, UK, Quest Environmental.

Dillaha, T.A., J.H. Sherrard, D. Lee, S. Mostaghimi and V.O. Shanholtz (1988), 'Evaluation of vegetative filter strips as a best management practice for feed lots', *Journal of the Water Pollution Control Federation*, **60**, 1231–8.

DoE (1986), 'Nitrate in water', a report of the Nitrate Co-ordination Group, London: HMSO.

Dosskey, M.G., R.C. Schultz and T.M. Isenhart (1997), 'Agroforestry', Notes 1–5, http://waterhome.tamu.edu/texasyst/agroforestynotes/afnote3.htm.

Environment Agency (1996), *Understanding Buffer Strips: An Information Booklet*, Bristol: EA.

Findlay, D.C., G.J.N. Colborne, D.W. Cope, T.R. Harrod, D.V. Hogan and S.J. Staines (1984), 'Soils and their use in South West England', Soil Survey of England and Wales, bulletin no. **14**, Harpenden, UK.

Fustec, E., A. Mariotti, X. Grillo and J. Sajus (1991), 'Nitrate removal by denitrification in alluvial ground water: role of a former channel', *Journal of Hydrology*, **123**, 337–54.

Gilliam, J.W., J.E. Parsons and R.L. Mikkelsen (1997), 'Nitrogen dynamics and buffer zones', in N.E. Haycock, T.P. Burt, K.W.T. Goulding and G. Pinay (eds), *Buffer Zones: Their Processes and Potential in Water Protection*, Harpenden, UK: Quest Environmental.

Goudie, A. (1986), *The Human Impact on the Natural Environment,* (second edition), Oxford: Basil Blackwell.

Graf, W.L. (1985), 'The Colorado River', *Resource Publications in Geography, Association of American Geographers*, Washington, DC.

Groffman, P.M. (1994), 'Denitrification in freshwater wetlands', *Current Topics in Wetland Biogeochemistry*, **1**, 15–35.

Groffman, P.M., E.A. Axelrod, J.L. Lemunyon and W.M. Sullivan (1991), 'Denitrification in grass and forested vegetated filter strips', *Journal of Environmental Quality*, **20**, 671–4.

Grossman, J. and P. Udluft (1991), 'The extraction of soil water by the suction cup method: a review', *Journal of Soil Science*, **42**, 83–93.

Harrod, T.R. (1981), 'Soils in Devon V: Sheet SS61 (Chulmleigh)', *Soil Survey Record*, **70**, Harpenden, p. 183.

Haycock, N.E. (1993), 'Buffer zones: a hydrologist's viewpoint', paper presented to South-West England Soils discussion group, 8 December.

Haycock, N.E. and T.P. Burt (1993), 'Role of floodplain sediments in reducing the nitrate concentration of subsurface run-off: a case study in the Cotswolds, UK', *Hydrological Processes*, **7**, 287–95.

Haycock, N.E. and A.D. Muscutt (1995), 'Landscape management strategies for the control of diffuse pollution', *Landscape and Urban Planning*, **31**, 313–21.

Isenhart, T.M., R.C. Schultz, J.P. Colletti and C.A. Rodrigues (1995), 'Design, function, and management of integrated riparian management systems', in *Proceedings of the National Symposium on Using Ecological Restoration to Meet Clean Water Act Goals*, USEPA, Chicago, IL, March, pp. 93–102.

Johnes, P.J. and T.P. Burt (1993), 'Nitrate in surface waters', in T.P. Burt, A.L. Heathwaite and S.T. Trudgill (eds), *Nitrate: Processes, Patterns and Management*, New York: John Wiley, pp. 141–67.

Jones, T.A. and J.M.R. Hughes (1993), 'Wetland inventories and wetland loss studies: a European perspective', in M. Moser, R.C. Prentice and J. van Vessem (eds),

*Waterfowl and Wetland Conservation in the 1990s*, IWRB Special Publication No. 26, IWRB, Slimbridge, UK, pp. 164–70.

Leeds-Harrison, P.B., J.N. Quinton, M.J. Walker, K.S. Harrison, S.F. Tyrrel, J.M. Morris and T. Harrod (1996), *Buffer Zones in Headwater Catchments*, report on MAFF/English Nature Buffer Zone Project CSA 2285, Silsoe, UK: Cranfield University.

Lowrance, R.R. (1992), 'Groundwater nitrate and denitrification in a coastal plain riparian forest', *Journal of Environmental Quality,* **21**, 401–5.

Lowrance, R.R., L.S. Altier, R.G. Williams, S.P. Inamdar, D.D. Bosch, J.M. Sheridian and D.L. Thomas (1998), 'The riparian ecosystem management model: simulator for ecological processes in riparian zones', *proceedings of the First Federal Interagency Hydrologic Modeling Conference*, Las Vegas, NV, April.

MAFF (1997), *The Habitat Scheme, Water Fringe Areas*, Information Pack, London: MAFF Publications.

Maltby, E., P.J. Dugan and J.C. Lefeuvre (eds) (1992), 'Conservation and development: the sustainable use of wetland resources', *proceedings of the Third International Wetlands Conference, Rennes, France*, 19–23 September, 1988, Gland, Switzerland: IUCN.

Maltby, E., D.V. Hogan and R.J. McInnes (1996), 'Functional analysis of European wetland ecosystems, final report – phase one', EC DGXII STEP Project, Royal Holloway University of London, UK: RHIER.

Merot, P. and P. Durand (1997), 'Modelling the interaction between buffer zones and the catchment', in N.E. Haycock, T.P. Burt, K.W.T. Goulding and G. Pinay (eds), *Buffer Zones: Their Processes and Potential in Water Protection*, Harpenden, UK: Quest Environmental.

Minshall, G.W., W.S.E. Jensen and W.S. Platts (1989), 'The ecology of stream and riparian habitats of the Great Basin region: a community profile', *US Fish and Wildlife Service, Biological Reports*, **85** (7.24), 142.

Mitsch, W.J. and J.G. Gosselink (1993), *Wetlands*, second edition, New York: Van Nostrand Reinhold.

Nommik, H. (1956), 'Investigations on denitrification in soil', *Acta Agriculturae Scandinavica* VI, **2**, 195–228.

van Oorschot, M.M.P. (1994), 'Plant production, nutrient uptake and mineralisation in river marginal wetlands: the impact of nutrient additions due to former land use', in W.J. Mitsch (ed.), *Global Wetlands: Old World and New*, New York: Elsevier Science, pp. 133–50.

Parkin, T.B. (1987), 'Soil microsites as a source of denitrification variability', *Soil Science Society of America Journal*, **51**, 1194–9.

Patrick, W.H. Jr. and R. Wyatt (1964), 'Soil nitrogen loss as a result of alternate submergence and drying', *Soil Science Society of America Proceedings*, **28**, 647–53.

Peterjohn, W.T. and D.L. Correll (1984), 'Nutrient dynamics in an agricultural watershed: observations on the role of a riparian forest', *Ecology*, **65**, 1466–75.

Pinay, G., N.E. Haycock, C. Ruffinoni and R.M. Holmes (1994), 'The role of denitrification in nitrogen removal in river corridors', in W.J. Mitsch (ed.), *Global Wetlands: Old World and New*, New York: Elsevier, pp. 107–16.

Reddy, K.R., W.H. Patrick Jr. and R.E. Phillips (1978), 'The role of nitrate in determining the order and rate of denitrification in flooded soil: experimental results', *Soil Science Society of America Journal*, **42**, 268–72.

Rolston, D.E. (1986), 'Limitations of the acetylene blockage technique for field measurements of denitrification', in R.D. Hauck and R.W. Weaver (eds), *Field*

*Measurement of Dinitrogen Fixation and Denitrification*, pp. 73–91, SSSA Special Publication Number 18, *Soil Science Society of America*, Madison, USA.

Schnabel, R.R. (1986), 'Nitrate concentrations in a small stream as affected by chemical and hydrologic interactions in the riparian zone', in D.L. Correll (ed.), *Watershed Research Perspectives*, Washington, DC: Smithsonian Institutes Press, pp. 263–82.

Schultz, R.C., J.P. Colletti, T.M. Isenhart, W.W. Simpkins, C.W. Mize and M.L. Thompson (1995), 'Design and placement of a multi-species riparian buffer strip system', *Agroforestry Systems*, **29**, 201–26.

Vought, L.B-M., J. Dahl, C. Lauge-Pedersen and J.O. Lacoursiere (1994), 'Nutrient retention in riparian ecotones', *Ambio*, **23**, 342–8.

Weller, D.E., D.L. Correll and T.E. Jordan (1994), 'Denitrification in riparian forests receiving agricultural discharges', in W.J. Mitsch (ed.), *Global Wetlands: Old World and New*, New York: Elsevier Science.

Williams, R.D. and A.D. Nicks (1993), 'A modeling approach to evaluate best management practices', *Water Science Technology*, **28**(3–5), 675–8.

Yoshinari, T. and R. Knowles (1976), 'Acetylene inhibition of nitrous oxide reduction by denitrifying bacteria', *Biochemical and Biophysical Research Communications*, **69**, 705–10.

# 8. Ecological and socio-economic evaluation of wetland conservation scenarios[1]

## M.S. Skourtos, A.Y. Troumbis, A. Kontogianni, I.H. Langford, I.J. Bateman and S. Georgiou

## 1   INTRODUCTION

In recent times, Mediterranean wetlands have been destroyed and degraded to a great extent. Their loss and/or degradation in the 20th century amounts to 73 per cent of marshes in Greece, 86 per cent of the most important wetlands in France, 60 per cent of wetlands in Spain and 15 per cent of lakes and marshes in Tunisia (MEDWET, 1996). The reasons for this have been the prevention of water-borne diseases, the development of agricultural land and the expansion of cities.

Fundamental changes have occurred in our understanding of the functions and values of wetlands, and these have prompted many recent international efforts to protect and sustainably use the Mediterranean wetlands. Today, nearly 100 Mediterranean wetland sites have been listed as being of international importance under the Ramsar Convention. Since 1991, these efforts have been coordinated through MEDWET, a partnership between the European Commission, the Ramsar Bureau, the governments of France, Greece, Spain, Italy, Portugal and several non-governmental organizations. MEDWET is an initiative for concerted action, joint fund raising and mutual co-operation in wetland conservation policy. It adopts the 'wise use' imperative of the European Union, but also takes explicitly into account a number of factors considered to affect specifically the management of Mediterranean wetlands, namely:

- poverty and economic inequality
- pressure from population growth, immigration and mass tourism
- social and cultural conflicts

The Venice Declaration, detailing MEDWET's strategy for the period 1996–2006, states the necessity of increasing knowledge and raising awareness of wetland values and functions throughout the Mediterranean. For this purpose, MEDWET advocates collaboration with organizations and institutions experienced in the field of identification, quantification and assessment of the economic values of wetland functions and benefits, with a view to adapting and applying existing techniques at Mediterranean wetlands (MEDWET, 1998).

The main objective of this case study was the evaluation of alternative scenarios for the future development of the Kalloni wetland on the island of Lesvos, Greece, using both ecological risk analysis and monetary valuation as assessment methods. In this chapter we focus on the evaluation of preservation versus development scenarios estimated via the contingent valuation method (Mitchell and Carson, 1989; Bateman and Turner, 1993; Bateman and Willis, 1999), informed by the ecological risk analysis. Qualitative analysis of focus groups is also applied in order to understand stakeholders' perception of risks and developmental potentials. In addition, a rating exercise was conducted amongst the various development/preservation scenarios in order to determine the most preferred of the alternative scenario options using a non-monetary based choice exercise, and to test the consistency of this choice with the monetary valuation.

This chapter describes in detail the analysis of the social, environmental and economic impacts of future development options in Kalloni. The following section describes the background to the environmental and management issues of Kalloni Bay, and section 3 describes the methods of analysis used and their rationale. Section 4 details the quantitative results from the questionnaire survey, and section 5 describes the qualitative analysis of stakeholder focus groups. Sections 6 and 7 provide a general discussion of the results obtained and reflects on the usefulness of a mixed methodological approach to environmental valuation. Section 8 brings together the main conclusions of the study.

## 2　BACKGROUND TO THE CASE STUDY

Administratively, the Kalloni wetland complex belongs to the Prefecture of Lesvos, Greece, and extends to the periphery of the communities of Agra, Parakoila, Keramion, Kalloni, Agia Paraskeyi, Basilika, Arisvi, Lisvori and Polichnitos. The drainage basin of the wetland also includes the communities of Anemotia, Dafia, Napi, Pelopi, Stipsi, Ypsilometopon and Kapi. Under new legislation anticipating the integration of small communities into municipalities, the communities of Arisvi, Dafia, Kalloni, Keramion and Parakoila have recently merged together with the municipality of Kalloni.

The Kalloni wetland is one of the most important wetland sites in the

Aegean archipelago. The gulf of Kalloni is located in the south-eastern part of the island of Lesvos (longitude 28° 11′–28° 13′, latitude 38° 12′–39° 13′N). The gulf is a closed, shallow bay (20 km long, 10 km wide, average depth 10 m) connected to the open Aegean sea through a 4 km long narrow channel. The wetland extends over a large part ($\approx$ 50%) of the bay (11 000 ha) where the well known salt pans (2630 ha) play an important role. Part of the wetland is also the coastal area surrounding the bay with a complex of shallow brackish zones, small freshwater marshes, salt marshes and salt pans. The catchment area of the wetland includes olive groves, Pinus forests and shrub lands. Ecologically, the Kalloni wetland is considered as an important bird area, is classified as a CORINE biotope and ranks among the very first areas to be included in the NATURA 2000 network in Greece. The region is extremely important for its variety of birds and wildfowl with 259 bird species already registered in the area, of which 32 are listed in Annex 1 of the EU Directive 79/409. The role of the Kalloni wetland here is three-fold: it functions as a wintering, reproduction and migration station for the birds. Kalloni Bay is furthermore one of the most important fishing grounds in Greece, especially for oyster, and a most promising site for the development of aquaculture. Besides its ecological value, Kalloni wetland is a tourist attraction with a prominent birdwatching tradition. The sea-part of the wetland is well known for its richness in benthic organisms, endemic fish stocks and oysters.

The Kalloni Bay wetland is a prime example of a complex, multifunctional environmental asset under pressure. The wetlands are under pressure from increased population requirements, and plans for new housing have gradually stimulated the clearance of natural and semi-natural forested areas. This trend has been exacerbated by the extension of agricultural projects subsidized by the European Union (through the Regional Mediterranean Programmes), and by the recent push for tourist development in the area. The island economies and ecosystems in the Northern Aegean face important structural problems from the increasing globalization of trade and opening up of markets, especially within the borders of the European Commission. The lack of suitable policy measures designed to counterbalance the fragile economic structure in the region and to take into account the social, environmental and distributional issues inherent in the marginalization of their societies are increasingly apparent. In fact, the very notion of 'common market' can be seen as running counter to the islands' main feature, that is their spatial isolation and compartmentalization (Spilanis, 1998).

Amidst a wealth of legal and administrative provisions, Greek environmental policy is to a great extent characterized as 'symbolic' and lacking in contextual detail. The record of wetland protection in Greece reveals a significant implementation gap (Papadimitriou, 1995), and agricultural subsidies and uncontrolled construction activity have led to gradual decline and degradation of natural ecosystems.

Recent reports, undertaken mainly on behalf of the Ministry of the Environment, draw attention to this fact and propose a conservation strategy based on the development of ecotourism and a suitable zoning of human activities (Kilikidis, 1992). However, these were met with suspicion and strong resistance from both local authorities and social groups. Constrained economic activity in favour of wetland preservation was at that time a socially unacceptable option, and the only conceivable policy goal was the regulation of fisheries through quotas and seasonal fishing prohibitions. However, the situation is slowly changing. A number of factors have contributed to this, such as:

- A growing awareness of the ecological importance of wetlands
- A growing awareness of a wetland's importance for the local tourist sector
- A gradual adaptation of the institutional framework towards more decentralized environmental jurisdictions.

These developments have culminated in the establishment of a number of important conservation principles (Lazaretou, 1995):

- The Greek State is constitutionally recognized as the trustee of today's and future generations' right to a healthy environment.
- The precautionary principle 'to prevent any kind of loss of the natural resource' is also recognized by the Higher State Court as a guideline for state intervention.
- NGOs, Municipalities, Associations of Attorneys at Law and the Technical Chamber of Greece, are all granted the legal right of bringing environmental disputes to the court.
- The possibility of mitigation banking is introduced whenever the degradation or conversion of a wetland area is deemed unavoidable.

Based on these principles, a specific *National Wetlands Strategy* is currently under preparation by the Ministry of the Environment. The strategy aims at operationalizing the notion of 'wise use' of wetland resources in Greece, incorporating basic precautionary principles in other policy areas (transport, agriculture and tourism) and, last but not least, sensitizing public opinion about the importance of wetland resources.

According to the EU's Directive 92/43/COM, the Kalloni region is included in the national inventory of sites eligible to be classified as Areas of European Community interest. The Kalloni wetland is also included in the Pan

European ecological network of protected areas known as NATURA 2000, and is further classified as a 'zone of special conservation' (section 4.4). The Greek environmental framework law 1650/96 (section 21.1) also states the necessity of legal protection of an ecologically important area, and the appropriateness of specific measures taken should be documented with the Specific Environmental Assessment (SEA). However, in spite of these regulations, no specific legal status currently exists for the Kalloni wetland, although owing to changes in public attitudes towards the wetland, a distinct administrative and legal framework for the protection of the Kalloni wetland is slowly emerging. Therefore, within commissioned studies for land-use planning in Lesvos (financed by the Ministry of the Environment), proposals have been made for the establishment of specific *Zones of Land-Use Control* for Kalloni Bay. These include specific targets for controlling urban development, designation of the coastal area of the bay as a 'most ecologically sensitive area' and zones where only activities associated with the functioning of the salt pans and aquaculture are permitted. The study detailed here was undertaken in the light of these new management initiatives.

## 3   DATA COLLECTION AND METHODS: ECOLOGICAL ANALYSIS AND MANAGEMENT SCENARIOS

Three main techniques were used to evaluate the management options for Kalloni Bay. First, an ecological analysis was performed to identify realistic scenarios and current risks and pressures on the wetlands, followed by a large scale questionnaire survey of residents and visitors to the area which examined preferences for four different management scenarios. Thirdly, four stakeholder focus groups were convened with important interest groups in the area. A description of these three stages of the research follows.

Ecological analysis was performed using an 'ecosystem valuation model', the objective of which was to identify the ecological value of landscape elements of the Kalloni wetland and its catchment area. This model focused on the sensitivity of the natural habitats of the Kalloni catchment to further disturbance by human activities. The areas which have already been heavily disturbed, such as area or point settlements and annual cropland, have already lost much of their biodiversity and ecosystem function value in comparison to natural habitats. These would therefore be minimally affected by more intense human activity, at least from an ecological perspective. On the other hand, remnants of natural habitats would be highly susceptible to degradation by man-caused activities and area reduction. Environmental cartography using satellite images was combined with ecological surveys conducted in the region to build a GIS from which different outcome scenarios could be generated. These informed the choice of management scenarios.

The ecosystem value model is presented in a tabular format. Four columns are used to indicate the assumptions of the model, the environmental/ecological factors inserted in the GIS database, and weights (scores) assigned to each of them. The first column indicates the explanatory variable under consideration. The second column identifies the specific class of data of the explanatory variable under consideration. For example, nine different coded vegetation types are used in the analysis. The third and fourth columns identify the scores assigned to each of the specific factors or classes. The third column identifies the score assigned when the specific class was incident in a cell, the fourth when it was proximate to a cell.

The ecosystem value, in this model, is related to both taxonomic diversity of communities (flora and fauna) and primary function(s) of ecosystems (for example primary production or energy transfer). The estimation of the ecological value of the entire Kalloni catchment will permit the delineation of areas of increasingly greater ecological value because of the spatial variation in ecosystem function and in species richness of major flora and fauna groups, such as birds, reptiles and amphibians and plants.

The core assumption of the model concerns the sign of variation of the ecological value in case of a disturbance. An area is considered here as highly sensitive in ecological terms if a modification or change in wetland use will potentially result in a greater or more significant loss of productivity and biodiversity. Consequently, the ecosystem value model focues on the sensitivity of the natural habitats of the Kalloni catchment to further disturbance by man. Through use of the model outputs, areas of sensitivity can be identified for protection through such measures as conservation and buffering.

Assumptions of the model, which served to refine the concepts of productivity and diversity for the study area included:

- The forested areas represent remnants of the most diverse climax communities for the areas.
- Woodlands and wet grasslands are remnants of less diverse climax communities.
- Other natural vegetation communities are ecologically more diverse and productive than the simplified plant communities of agricultural and urban settings.
- Water or proximity to water enhances the ecological productivity of an area.
- Ecological edges or ecotones are the most productive portion of natural plant communities because of enhanced diversity resulting from the proximity of other communities.

- Proximity to roads and settlements tends to reduce ecological value because of the increased likelihood of man-caused disturbance.

The scoring procedure is based on three criteria:

1. **Criterion of rarity**: The score of a vegetation type is a function of its area and productivity. Vegetation types of smaller area receive higher scores.
2. **Criterion of naturalness**: Natural vegetation types receive higher score than semi-natural and man-made types.
3. **Criterion of productivity**: Vegetation types with high productivity receive a higher score than areas of low productivity.

In structuring the ecosystem value model the major factors considered include vegetation type, stream hierarchy, slope, biodiversity per habitat type, existing roads and settlements. Habitat/land use type is the basic factor considered because it most closely relates to ecological diversity and productivity. As was mentioned previously, the specific vegetation types were each assigned an initial weighted score, which reflects their relative diversity/productivity value. The other factors considered were used to modify these initial scores through a process of addition or subtraction. Streams and proximity to larger streams give an additional score because they represent a water source. Larger perennial streams give a higher score than the smaller intermittent streams. Steeper slopes were assigned a higher score because they tended to discourage man-caused intrusion. A separate sub-model was also used to identify and add scores for ecological edge conditions. The roads and settlements-related factors were subsequently modelled throughout the study area and the resulting scores subtracted in order to reduce ecological value because of proximity to human disturbance.

The resulting final scores are indicative of relative ecosystem values throughout the study area. Areas of highest value correspond to the most diverse vegetation types which had a reliable water supply and which were also distant from sources of human disturbance. The lowest value scores were assigned to agricultural and settlement areas. For mapping purposes, the entire range of scores was grouped into five categories of ecosystem value.

Multiple preliminary runs of the model were used to estimate its sensitivity to the scoring scale and its accuracy in comparison to the field reality. Expert judgement was used to estimate whether the predicted ecological value in the composite map of 'ecological value' of the Kalloni wetland corresponded to the present status of the wetland. The ecosystem value model yielded the results presented in Table 8.1 concerning the area extent of the zones characterized by each class of value. The range of variation of the ecological value in the entire Kalloni catchment, measured in cumulative score units, is from –6 to +18.

*Table 8.1   Area extent of the different classes of ecosystem value in the Kalloni catchment*

| Ecosystem value of the Kalloni wetland | Area (ha) | % |
|---|---|---|
| –6 | 2 | 0.00 |
| –5 | 27 | 0.06 |
| –4 | 41 | 0.09 |
| –3 | 82 | 0.18 |
| –2 | 107 | 0.24 |
| –1 | 139 | 0.31 |
| 0 | 216 | 0.48 |
| 1 | 247 | 0.55 |
| 2 | 331 | 0.73 |
| 3 | 782 | 1.73 |
| 4 | 1585 | 3.51 |
| 5 | 2548 | 5.65 |
| 6 | 3686 | 8.17 |
| 7 | 5093 | 11.28 |
| 8 | 5113 | 11.33 |
| 9 | 6052 | 13.41 |
| 10 | 6521 | 14.45 |
| 11 | 4952 | 10.97 |
| 12 | 4430 | 9.81 |
| 13 | 2338 | 5.18 |
| 14 | 708 | 1.57 |
| 15 | 92 | 0.20 |
| 16 | 26 | 0.06 |
| 17 | 7 | 0.02 |
| 18 | 11 | 0.02 |
| Total | 45 136 | 100.00 |

The classes covering the largest areas are those with moderately high total scores. Less than 2 per cent of the total area corresponds to values above 14. Similarly, only restricted areas correspond to values of 0 or less. Overall, a positive total score, reflecting the absence of large urban centres, industrial areas, intensive land use and other sources of negative impacts on biodiversity, characterizes the whole catchment.

The effects of land-use change on the biodiversity and the ecosystem value of the wetland have been examined under two assumptions:

1.  Doubling of the urban areas in Kalloni: the extension of settlements is assumed to affect wetland-type habitats (assumption I).
2.  Gradual and unidirectional change of wetland habitat patches to other uses: the simulated changes ranged from 0 to 100 per cent (assumption II).

The first assumption is a simulation of a policy attempting to relocate the economic activities at the centre of the island, through the development of the town of Kalloni as the commercial pole and the construction of a new airport in the lowlands of the wetland catchment's area. The second assumption is a simulation of the 'laissez-faire' policy, where changes are produced 'randomly' in space after the reaction of individual landowners to economic development policies.

Figure 8.1 shows the change in the percentage of the different ecosystem value classes (relative to the total study area, that is the entire Kalloni catchment). Significant decline is observed in relatively high ecosystem values (10 to 16). On the other hand, zones characterized by low ecosystem value (–3 to +3) present equivalent increase, in other words the spread of settlements leads to an increase of the areas of low ecosystem value. These results may appear as obvious. However, two counterintuitive conclusions may be drawn from them. The first concerns the magnitude of changes in value under assumption I; the second concerns the importance of the scale of observation for the evaluation of the change for biodiversity.

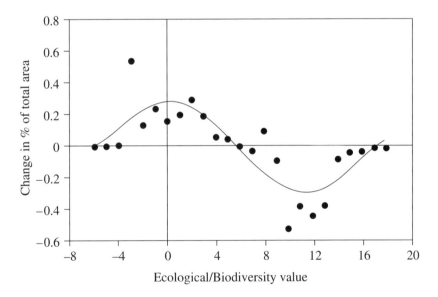

*Figure 8.1   Ecological value as a function of percentage land-use change*

At the catchment scale, a gradual change in wetland area yields a very low overall change in the ecosystem value of the area. However, under this assumption the core of the wetland habitats is lost. This apparent contradiction is scale-dependent. A recalculation of the same values within the lowland part of the wetland only, gives a different view of the importance of the loss of the wetland.

The scenarios for future development of the Kalloni wetland were designed to refer to the lowland, coastal area of the region and to a time horizon up to the year 2010. We therefore concentrated on possible land-use changes around the bay for the next decade, assuming that these medium term changes will influence the long term pattern of development in the watershed of the wetland in such a way that they will be practically irreversible. The scenarios used in the study were composed of a number of exogenous factors, common for all scenarios, and of a number of specific, endogenous provisions. The exogenous factors were:

- The rate of population change. We assumed that the general rise of living standards in the region, in combination with increasing unemployment in the urban centres, would stop the loss of human resources from the island and would contribute to a moderate population increase in the Kalloni Bay area;
- The inflow of EU funds for structural investments in the region will continue to play an important role, based on increasingly reliable frameworks for environmental impact assessment;
- The legal protection of the forested areas. We assume that areas which have already been characterized as forests continue to be protected as such. Accordingly we exclude forests from the variables included in our scenarios.

The endogenous factors included in the different scenarios were:

- The degree and the kind of support which is expected for the tourist sector;
- The degree and the kind of support for the protection of the wetlands and the wildfowl population;
- The degree and the kind of support for housing development in the region;
- The importance of agriculture and livestock raising in the region.

Using the information from the ecological analysis of the Kalloni wetland, land-use changes and their impacts on the biodiversity of the region were made realistic. Furthermore, we also ensured that the scenarios presented answer meaningful economic questions. Four development/conservation scenarios were finally chosen for evaluation. These were as follows:

1.  Status quo (SQ): land-use attributes were described as staying at their current (1998) levels;
2.  Scenario A: wetland and built areas increase modestly while the area of agricultural land decreases. Birdwatching and associated tourism are expected to increase;
3.  Scenario B: the housing area is approximately doubled and wetland areas more than halved. Consequently, there is a large loss of habitat for birds in the area. Birdwatching possibilities will be severely reduced and the associated tourism is practically expected to cease;
4.  Scenario C: a modest reduction in agricultural land is used to more than double the built area. The wetland areas remain the same, though the loss in agricultural land is expected to lead to a modest loss in species of birds, and some reduction in associated tourism is also expected.

## 4   THE CONTINGENT VALUATION SURVEY

In order to test whether the questionnaire was adequate, a pilot survey analysis was undertaken prior to the main study, particularly in respect of the wording of the questionnaire and valuation scenario. Data collection was carried out by face-to-face interview, with each interview lasting approximately 30–45 minutes. The survey was conducted over the period 3 May 1998 to 29 August 1998, and the total sample size was 330 people. The results of this pilot survey are given in Skourtos *et al.* (1999).

The main survey questionnaire consisted of a number of sections. Respondents were first asked some general questions on their attitudes concerning the major problems facing the local area, and how they viewed environmental issues relative to these. Next, respondents were asked about their familiarity with the wetland and their perceptions of the issues involved. This included questions about their use of the area, how long they spent there and why, and if they knew which areas make up the Kalloni wetland. Respondents were also asked how attractive they rated the landscape of Kalloni, how they rated Kalloni Bay as a habitat for wildlife, and what they considered to be the main risks facing the area.

The valuation section followed, in which the respondents were given information about the present day condition of Kalloni Bay. They were then asked to rate how happy they were with the present state of the bay on a Likert type scale which ranged from 0 = dreadful (could not get worse) to 100 = superb (could not get better). Descriptions were then given of the scenarios A, B and

C mentioned above. This included a graphic representation of the scenarios and status quo on a large information board, made up using digital imaging and manipulation techniques.

Respondents were then asked to rate these three scenarios on the same Likert scale as above. After a quick consistency and cross check to see that respondents had understood what was being asked, the questionnaire moved onto the monetary valuation exercise. Here, the respondents were asked to value the most favoured scenario from the ranking (rating) exercise, that is, the one with the highest rating given by them on the Likert scale.

A payment principle question was used to first see if respondents were, in principle, in favour of paying at least some amount in order to finance their preferred scenario option. Those who were not in favour of any amount were asked to state their reasons for this answer. Those who were in favour were asked to state (as an open-ended amount) the maximum amount of money that they would be willing to pay every three months for the next two years to finance their preferred scenario. They were then asked to state their main reason for their answer. The payment vehicle used for each scenario was an increase in water bills collected every three months for a period of two years, with the resulting fund being administered by the Public Water and Sewerage Corporation of Kalloni, which would supervise the execution of the necessary works required by each scenario. Following this, if respondents gave a positive response to the payment principle question, they were asked to state what amount in drachmas they would be willing to pay.

Finally, respondents were asked a number of questions regarding their socio-economic characteristics in order to provide information on representativeness of the sample, and for the willingness to pay bid function analysis. The interviews were carried out using a random selection procedure at a variety of locations in the Kalloni Bay area. The main survey was again carried out by face-to-face interview, each lasting between 30 and 45 minutes. The survey was conducted over the period 10 July until 24 September 1998, with a total sample of 914 respondents.

## 5   FOCUS GROUP ANALYSIS

An important component of most valuation studies is a follow-up appropriation study of environmental benefits and costs (Munasinghe, 1992). These benefits and costs can be discussed at three different spatial scales: local, national/regional and global/transnational. Evidence shows that economic benefits are limited on a local scale, increase somewhat on a regional/national level and then become potentially substantial on a transnational/global scale. The economic costs follow an opposite trend, from being locally significant, regionally and nationally moderate and globally small. The incentives to protect the environment seem therefore regionally very weak and regionally/nationally only moderate. The aim in this study was to address this important issue by combining the economic valuation surveys with a general stakeholder analysis and identification of environmental pressures using the methodology of focus groups, based on previous research by the authors (Langford *et al.*, 1999; Brouwer *et al.*, 1999).

The stakeholder analysis was designed to identify conflicting uses of environmental assets, the conceptualization of conflicts on the basis of property rights allocations among social groups, regions and nations, and, last but not least, to aid the understanding of the institutional mechanisms by which costs and benefits are appropriated. The conceptualization of the conflicts on the basis of the notion of property rights has to take into account the fact that property regimes are often undefined and/or of a mixed nature in the Kalloni area. This fact poses a number of questions relating to traditional class divisions, property ownership by potentially conflicting social groups, and the real nature of the environmental debate in Kalloni Bay. Is it simply a forum for expressing dissatisfaction and asserting influence over property rights issues?

A number of conflicts in the use of the Kalloni wetland are apparently the result of the unco-ordinated character of its use. The specificity of the management problem of the Kalloni wetland lies in the early and latent nature of the risks for the region which neither the state nor the local people and their organizations seem to be conscious about. The region has failed to face up to the unavoidable structural changes that the Greek state and EC Regional Directives want to introduce, while the population aspires to a development path similar to the one taken by most successful Greek island economies.

As a first step towards understanding the stakeholders' positions on the issue of management of the Kalloni wetland, we applied the focus group technique in order to identify the underlying goals, risk perceptions and the ranking of alternatives by four social groups. The aim was to elicit stakeholders' perceptions that are of interest for the subsequent survey in a number of ways (Desvouges and Frey, 1989):

- in determining the proper order and magnitude of information
- in targeting respondents who may have difficulties answering the survey questions
- in identifying troublesome language or terms
- in developing payment cards or other visual aids
- in identifying the proper extent of the population affected
- in sorting out realistic scenarios

The purpose behind the focus groups was therefore twofold:

1. to aid the development of the questionnaire survey; and
2. to gain important insights into the attitudes and motivations towards the Kalloni wetlands of important stakeholder groups.

## 6 FINDINGS: CONTINGENT VALUATION SURVEY

For the main survey, 52 per cent of the sample were residents in the Kalloni area, and 38 per cent were visitors either on day trips or holidays. Of those interviewed, 40.8 per cent rated the current landscape as 'very attractive', with only 3.2 per cent making a negative judgement. The most important risks to Kalloni Bay and surrounding wetlands were thought to come from waste water (mentioned by 58 per cent of respondents) and industrial waste (52 per cent). Municipal waste (41 per cent), aquaculture (32 per cent) and hunting (29 per cent) were also mentioned as posing risks.

The respondents were asked to rate the four options on a scale of 1 to 100 in desirability, these specifically being given as:

- Scenario A: an increase in wetland and tourist accommodation, with a decrease in agricultural land – 12 new species of birds come to the wetland, birdwatching-associated tourism increases;
- Scenario B: more than half the wetland is drained for new housing, hotels and holiday homes, agricultural land remains unchanged. Seventy-eight species of birds leave the area, birdwatching-associated tourism ceases;
- Scenario C: housing and tourist accommodation increase and agricultural land decreases, leading to the loss of nine species of birds. The area of wetland remains unchanged;
- Scenario SQ: maintenance of the status quo, which involves reversing the incremental damage caused to the wetland by rubbish tipping, encroachment and illegal sand removal, with the establishment of protected areas.

Table 8.2 gives summary statistics for the rating of each scenario, showing that on average scenario A was rated most highly, followed by the status quo, scenario C and finally scenario B.

We cannot directly analyse the rating scores given, as people may interpret the scale in different ways, for example a score of 30 given by one person may mean something different to a score of 30 given by another person. However, we can compare whether one option is preferred above another in a qualitative sense, so for each respondent, we have six pieces of information on their preference for: A versus SQ, B versus SQ, C versus SQ, A versus B, A versus C and B versus C. In addition, there may be ties, where the respondent shows

*Table 8.2    Summary statistics from the scenario rating exercise*

| Scenario | Mean rating (95% confidence intervals) | Median rating |
|---|---|---|
| Status Quo | 54.0 (52.8–55.2) | 50 |
| A | 72.18 (70.8–73.6) | 80 |
| B | 23.33 (21.9–24.7) | 20 |
| C | 45.6 (44.0–47.1) | 50 |

indifference between two scenarios. Hence, we used a nominal logistic regression analysis for each piece of information, where we simultaneously model, for example, the preference for A compared to SQ and also the indifference between A and SQ compared to choosing SQ as the preferred scenario. However, here we only report the results where a definite preference between scenarios was shown.

Table 8.3 gives the results of the multiple logistic regression analyses, with the logit of the preference for scenario A as the response variable. The symbols in the table refer to the significance of each explanatory variable, with a plus sign indicating a positive association, and a minus sign a negative association.

*Table 8.3    Multiple logistic regression analysis for preference between scenarios*

| Variable | A vs. SQ | B vs. SQ | C vs. SQ | A vs. B | A vs. C | B vs. C |
|---|---|---|---|---|---|---|
| ENVPROT | + | | | | | − |
| LNOTLESB | + | | | | | |
| ATTRACT | − − | | | | | |
| BIRDS | + + + | − − | | + + + | + + + | |
| KALBAD | + + + | + + + | + + + | | | |
| KALGOOD | | | − − − | | | |
| FEMALE | + | | | + | + + + | |
| WASTEWAT | | + | | | | |
| EDUC>6 | | − | − | + + + | | |
| INCOME | | − − | | | | − − − |
| BUILD | | | − | | | |
| AQUACULT | | | | + + + | | − − |
| AWARE | | | | | | − − − |

*Note:    $+/- = p < 0.05$, $+ +/- - = p < 0.01$, $+ + +/- - - = p < 0.001$.*

Comparing A with SQ: The multiple regression shows that the ecologically friendly scenario A is likely to be chosen by those who believe in the importance of environmental protection and have an interest in birds, but who have a negative perception of the current state of the environment. Hence, these perceptions reflect a stated need for change. Visitors from outside the island are more likely to favour scenario A, perhaps because their reason for visiting Kalloni is likely to be linked to attractiveness of the environment. Females are more likely to prefer scenario A to the status quo, perhaps because the male population is more likely to be concerned with economic outcomes. Belief that Kalloni is already an attractive environment is associated with a preference for the status quo over scenario A.

Comparing B to SQ: Scenario B describes an increase in development at the expense of the wetlands compared to the status quo scenario, which maintains wetlands at their current level. A concern over waste water as a risk to the area was positively associated with choice of scenario B, reflecting the concerns of pro-development focus groups with stakeholders such as hotel owners and the construction industry. However, a concern over the impacts of aquaculture on the area was negatively associated with choice of scenario B over the status quo. There was a strong negative association with interest in birdlife of the wetlands, and relationships with income and education were also negative, but a strong positive association with believing the environment was currently poor, again suggesting a desire for change, but for different reasons than for choosing scenario A. Basically, choosing option B over status quo reflects the motivations of some local people with low education and income for the economic development of the Kalloni Bay area, suggesting that the poorest sector of the population are more concerned with economic development than conservation.

Comparing C to SQ: Scenario C comprised a less radical development option than scenario B with the wetlands remaining the same, but some agricultural land and hence bird species being lost to urban expansion. The main predictor for choosing scenario C over the status quo was again a belief that the environment around Kalloni was poor, and choosing the status quo scenario was associated with belief that the environment is already good. Interest in birds was not an important issue in this choice. Interestingly, belief that building and construction were important issues in the area was negatively associated with choice of scenario C, perhaps reflecting the opposition of some people to the loss of agricultural land to urban development.

Comparing A to B: These two scenarios were the most contrasting, with scenario A describing ecologically friendly expansion of the wetlands, and scenario B describing an increase in development at the expense of the wetlands. The main predictors for choice of scenario A in the multiple regressions were interest in birds, being educated and being female, plus an interest in aquaculture which may be seen as a less environmentally threatening economic activity than mass tourism.

Comparing A to C: Interest in environmental protection and birds and being female were associated with preference for scenario A.

Comparing B to C: Interest in environmental protection predicted preference for scenario C over the development scenario B, as did higher income, awareness of environmental issues, and a lack of interest in transport and aquaculture. This again suggests that poorer people, with concerns over economic matters, are less likely to be interested in the environment, and more likely to choose option B.

Respondents were also asked to value their most preferred scenario, firstly via a payment principle question asking whether or not they would be prepared, in principle, to pay some amount for their preferred scenario, then via a willingness to pay that amount. Summary results of the responses are given in Table 8.4.

As can be seen a majority of respondents is in favour of an increase in water bills for achieving the preferred option in all cases except scenario B. Chi-squared analysis indicated that there was a significant relationship between payment principle response and the scenario being considered (Pearson chi-squared = 57.2, 3 degrees of freedom, $p < 0.000$).

Logistic regression analyses were carried out comparing a willingness to participate against a refusal to participate, and the results are given in Table 8.5, in the same format as Table 8.3.

Payment principle for A: Belief that environmental protection was an important issue for the Kalloni area predicted a willingness to participate, as did an interest in birds. Younger, more educated people were more willing to pay, as were females and members of environmental groups.

*Table 8.4  Summary of payment principle and WTP responses*

| | | Scenario | | |
|---|---|---|---|---|
| | Status quo | A | B | C |
| Payment principle (% 'Yes') | 53.8 | 77.6 | 41.9 | 57 |
| Mean WTP (Greek Drs) (95% confidence intervals) | 6054 (3367–8741) | 10 041 (8511–11 571) | 6166 (–793–13 127) | 9630 (5690–13 571) |
| Median WTP | 3000 | 5000 | 1000 | 3000 |
| Sample size considering each scenario | 91 | 643 | 43 | 136 |

*Table 8.5    Multiple logistic regression analysis for willingness to pay in principle responses*

| Variable | Scenario A | Scenario C | Scenario SQ |
|---|---|---|---|
| ENVPROT | + | | |
| BIRDS | + + | + | |
| FEMALE | + | | |
| EDU>6 | + + + | + | |
| AGE<30 | + + | | + + |
| ENVGROUP | + | | |
| UNEMP | | + | |
| AWARE | | | + + |

*Note:    +/– = p < 0.05, ++/– – = p < 0.01, + + +/– – – = p < 0.001.*

Payment principle for B: No significant predictor variables (note that there were only 43 people who chose scenario B as their most preferred).

Payment principle for C: Willingness to pay in principle was positively associated with a belief that unemployment was an important issue for the Kalloni area – scenario C includes urban expansion at the expense of agricultural land, which could lead to improved economic opportunities. An interest in birds and a higher education were also associated with a willingness to pay in principle.

Payment principle for SQ: For those who chose the status quo as the most preferred scenario, belief in the importance of environmental protection predicted a willingness to participate. It must be remembered that scenario SQ is not a 'do nothing' scenario, but involves reversal of the current decline in the status of the wetlands to maintain them at their current standard, by waste removal, and prevention of sand extraction and encroachment. Interestingly, younger people under 30 years old were also more willing to pay for this scenario if they had chosen it as their most favoured.

Participants who answered positively to the willingness to pay in principle question for their most favoured scenario were then asked what extra amount they would be willing to pay every three months for the next five years. Table 8.4 shows mean WTP amounts. Highest WTP was for Scenario A. An analysis of variance (ANOVA) found that we could not reject the null hypothesis that the four scenario population means are equal. However, the Kruskal–Wallis non-parametric test indicated that we could reject the null hypothesis of identical population medians (chi-squared = 16.3 with 3 degrees of freedom, $p = 0.001$).

The natural logarithms of these bid amounts were then used as response

*Table 8.6    Multiple logistic regression analysis for WTP amounts*

| Variable | Scenario A | Scenario B | Scenario C | Scenario SQ |
|---|---|---|---|---|
| ENVPROT | | | | + |
| BIRDS | | | | – – |
| KALBAD | | – | | |
| KALGOOD | | | + | |
| EDU>6 | + | | | |
| INCOME | + + + | | | |
| LOCECON | – | | | |
| WETCONS | + | + | + | |
| NATENV | | | | + + |
| HOLREC | – – – | | | |
| LSKALA | | | + + | |
| LKALLONI | | | + + | |
| RECESS | | | – | |

*Note:*   $+/– = p < 0.05$, $++/– – = p < 0.01$, $+ + +/– – – = p < 0.001$.

variables in normal regression models for each scenario, the results being shown in Table 8.6.

Willingness to pay for A: Respondents were more likely to pay higher amounts for scenario A if they were more educated, of higher income and interested in wetland conservation. However, interest in the local economy was negatively associated with willingness to pay amounts, as was visiting the area for recreation or holidays. Hence, it seems that of the majority of respondents who chose scenario A, the more educated, higher income people living in the Kalloni area are most likely to express their support via willingness to pay: perhaps these are the people who can most afford and are most committed to conservation because of their geographical proximity and higher social status.

Willingness to pay for B: Only 15 people responded positively to being willing to participate in the funding of scenario B, so the results must be interpreted with caution. Belief that the environment around Kalloni was poor at present was associated with higher amounts, but surprisingly, so was pledging the money for wetland conservation. This could be interpreted as a self-interested motivation in preserving some wetlands for tourism.

Willingness to pay for C: Belief in the importance of economic recession as an issue in the area was associated with lower willingness to pay amounts. However, those living in Kalloni village or the port of Kalloni (Skala Kalloni) were willing to pay higher amounts, perhaps because this scenario directly benefited them via urban expansion. Belief that the environment of the area was basically good, and pledging the money for wetland conservation were associated with higher amounts.

Willingness to pay for SQ: An interest in environmental protection and being in favour of enhancing the environement were associated with higher willingness to pay amounts. Interestingly, interest in birds was negatively associated with size of payment – the status quo scenario included the loss of nine species of birds due to urban expansion onto agricultural land.

## 7 FINDINGS: FOCUS GROUP ANALYSIS

Four focus group interviews were undertaken in the summer of 1998, comprising representatives of local fishermen, building constructors, hotel owners and elected representatives of villages in the Kalloni Bay area. The discussions were between 1.5 and 2.5 hours long, and participants were invited by telephone or fax. A series of general questions relating to the wetlands was prepared for each group, and these formed the focus of the group discussion. The focus groups were organized in accordance with guidelines given by Morgan (1988), and Stewart and Shamdasani (1990).

Three representatives of local fishermen were invited to the group discussion. However, only two attended, one from Kalloni (male, over 50 years old) and one (male, about 30 years old) from Parakoila a sub-division of Kalloni, who was particularly interested in shellfish. The representative from the village of Polychnitos refused to attend due to potential conflicts of interest with fishermen in Kalloni.

The representatives had a perception of Kalloni Bay as being the centre of the island, and that the sea was very rich and there was a responsibility to preserve this richness. In association with this perception of value was a negative view of outsiders, from other islands and from Italy, who would come and exploit a very local resource. The representatives believed that they had a responsibility towards the bay, but also rights over use of the bay.

Discussion was focused around the value of the bay, and issues surrounding it such as the development of aquaculture and the problem of pollution from agricultural practices. The representatives acknowledged that bad fishing practices had led to depletion of fishing stock in the past, and accepted that the state had passed laws to make fishing more sustainable. However, they felt there was also a need to address the problems of chemical pollution of the bay from fertilizers and pesticides, and noted changes in the quality of the bay which they attributed to farming practices. Aquaculture was also perceived as a negative development leading to further pollution of the bay.

Their perceptions of the wetlands were framed in terms of it being a natural habitat for fish and shellfish, which, like the rest of the bay, is under threat from pollution. However, they felt it was not their responsibility to talk to the farmers, but that of local government officials. The younger representative from Parakoila believed that many of the problems of the past, involving conflict and division between different groups of local fishermen, could be resolved by the younger people working together towards a common aim.

The hotel owners' focus group comprised six people, five who owned hotels in the area (four males and one female) and one male who was president of a local development company. The president was not invited to the focus group, but came of his own accord. This group provided the most vivid discussion, mostly about the potential for the development of tourism and the problems of waste disposal regarding the wetlands and the bay. Some of the group members were farmers as well as hotel owners, but did not acknowledge that the pollution problems of the bay were linked to use of agrochemicals. Overall, the group perceived the problems of the Kalloni area in terms of development potential, and in some respects had a negative perception of the wetlands as this was land that was unsuitable for building, and because high water levels may threaten existing buildings.

The group stated categorically that they had no responsibility for improvements in the natural habitat of the area, and problems such as high water levels were not their fault, but simply natural phenomena that they had to accept. However, they also commented that high water levels were 'a curse' and wanted more land to be drained. They later acknowledged that their perceptions of the wetland were changing – in previous years they had seen the wetlands as 'useless land', but they were now beginning to see the potential of the wetlands in attracting tourists.

Concern was expressed about the conflicts between 'eco-tourism' and mass tourist activities. The group was against the building of large hotels and favoured the development of smaller units, and a mixture of activities for tourists, such as building of a marina. One group member who came from Crete suggested the building of self-contained tourist villages, as they have in Crete. In contrast to the fishermen, who did not mention the possibility of building a new airport for the area, there was significant discussion about this issue, and disagreement about the consequences of building a new airport. Some group members thought it was a good idea as tourists would arrive in greater numbers, and gain easier access to the area. However, other members pointed out that the building of the airport could harm the wetlands, and the birds would leave, having negative consequences for tourism in the longer term.

The group of elected representatives (subsequently referred to as 'mayors') of local villages comprised four individuals, all males over 50 years old from the municipalities of Kalloni, Agia Paraskevi, Polychnitos and Basilika. The mayor of Kalloni was very dynamic compared to the others, and provided a number of interesting if speculative ideas concerning future development of the Kalloni area, and insisted that the new airport need not affect the wetlands. The other mayors tended to focus on very local problems, such as scarcity of water resources, poor road access, and limited development opportunities. They all favoured development of the new airport to move the focus of the island towards its centre, around Kalloni, and away from Mytilene, the capital city of Lesvos.

About a third of the discussion focused on the problems of pollution and waste management, such as agrochemicals and waste treatment – a waste treatment plant had been constructed, but was not in use. The wetlands were seen as an important local resource, and the mayors accepted they had a responsibility for preserving the wetlands as a natural asset but framed this in terms of future economic development. The mayor of Kalloni stated that the wetlands were pleasant, but should be restricted to certain areas, similar to parks, so they could be enjoyed but not interfere with future building developments. Hence, the wetlands were perceived as one of a number of important land uses, which should have defined boundaries, and should certainly not be expanded at the expense of other important land uses. The mayors also discussed the problems of property rights, as ownership of some areas of wetland is uncertain, and commented that this issue needed resolving in some way.

The building constructors group comprised four individuals (three males and one female) between 40 and 50 years old. They were mostly concerned about wastes being generated by development and polluting the bay. They extract sand from the bay, and realized this was a destructive activity and damaged the wetland, but would not acknowledge it was their fault – they had to extract sand as part of their legitimate commercial activities. Responsibility was also accepted for the lowering of ground water levels, as more people were coming to the area and using water as a result of building construction. Again, this was not seen as a source of blame – it was simply an inevitable consequence of a natural desire for development and the result of legitimate economic processes. The group was in favour of further development, but unsure what direction this development should take. They were concerned that both tourism and agriculture should be considered in future plans, and there were trade-offs to be made between the two.

## 8   DISCUSSION AND CONCLUSIONS

It is important to set the focus group discussion in the context of the social processes operating in the Kalloni Bay area. Soon after the researchers started making phone calls to invite participants to the focus groups, everyone in the locality knew about the research project and was discussing it. The participants therefore had prepared themselves to face the researchers from the University department in Mytilene, and indeed, one participant arrived uninvited, as commented on earlier. Participants therefore stressed their interest in environmental issues and the hotel owners in particular wanted to show how much they cared about the wetlands and the birds that visited there. It was pointed out that local people had helped in a recent book written about the birdlife on the wetlands.

Nevertheless, the focus groups revealed important differences in the social constructions made by different stakeholders on the wetlands and their place in the culture and economy of the Kalloni area. The issue of local people having rights over local resources was an important theme, and participants thought that problems and conflicts should be resolved locally. However, different stakeholders were reluctant to enter into discussions with each other – for example, the refusal of the fishermen's representative from Polychnitos to participate in the focus group. There was, in general, a belief that all the different activities involving the wetlands such as tourism, agriculture and fishing could co-exist – many local people combine occupations such as being farmers and hotel owners. However, the links between the consequences of different activities were not always accepted, for example, farmers refused to make the connection between use of fertilizers and pesticides on their fields and pollution of the bay. The uncertainty over property rights and responsibility was also a major area of concern, and inappropriate uses of land on one property were acknowledged as having detrimental effects on adjacent properties. Farmers in Agia Paraskevi owned a lot of the land around Kalloni, and there were important differences in the social perceptions of people coming from Kalloni and Agia Paraskevi. People in Kalloni were seen as being rather carefree, and interested in having a good time, while those in Agia Paraskevi were seen as hard working and industrious. Land around Kalloni has been acquired by people in Agia Paraskevi by purchase or through marriage, and hence it may be that people from the two villages have different motivations behind their perceptions of the wetland.

We believe that our study contains some important information for the economic analysis of value of wetland areas. First, it can be seen that using the different scenarios, and from focus group discussions with relevant stakeholders, there is tremendous diversity in the motivations of different individuals and groups, and for the economic information to be relevant, this complexity must be investigated thoroughly. However, this does not mean that it is useless to attempt an economic analysis of value. It was clearly apparent from the focus groups and interviews that the great majority of people were quite willing and able to express economic preferences that were based on sound logic – after all, local people have been exploiting the economic potential of the wetland for centuries. However, when attempting to place an economic value on the wetland, competing motivations and needs must be explored. For example, the local mayors valued the wetlands as a tourist potential that should be managed as a 'park', with strictly defined boundaries and distinct uses. For the building constructors, the wetland was a nuisance, but even they could profit from increased exploitation of the wetland for tourism, and, as mentioned earlier, many people had not one but a combination of occupations.

Beyond this, it can also be seen that people are quite capable of functioning, in terms of 'utility', as both citizens and consumers (Sagoff, 1988). As citizens, they do feel responsibility for their environment, though this is often expressed in very different ways, as the focus groups demonstrated. However, these responsibilities are also to themselves as consumers of the wetland's economic potential. This again does not mitigate against an economic analysis, but calls for a more detailed and profound analysis than simply asking everybody their willingness to pay; property rights, conflicting interests of different villages and user groups and the tension between local and more global needs are all real and apparent issues to be considered. By employing a mixed methodology, we have gone some way to uncovering some of these complexities, and we have collected information on the preferences of individuals and focus groups which we believe is of genuine use to policy makers.

## NOTE

1. Sections of this chapter are based on work first published as Kontogianni *et al.* (2000).

## REFERENCES

Bateman, I.J. and R.K. Turner (1993), 'Valuation of the environment, methods and techniques: the contingent valuation method', in R.K. Turner (ed.), *Sustainable Environmental Economics and Management: Principles and Practice,* London: Belhaven Press.

Bateman, I.J. and K.G. Willis (1999), *Valuing Environmental Preferences: Theory and Practice of the Contingent Valuation Method in the US, EC and Developing Countries*, Oxford: Oxford University Press.

Brouwer, R., N. Powe, R.K. Turner, I.J. Bateman and I.H. Langford (1999), 'Public attitudes to contingent valuation and public consultation', *Environmental Values*, **8**, 325–47.

Desvousges, W.H. and J.H. Frey (1989), 'Integrating focus groups and surveys: examples from environmental risk studies', *Journal of Official Statistics*, **5**, 349–63.

Kilikidis, S. (1992), 'The Wetland of Kalloni Bay (Lesvos Island)', commissioned by YPEXODE, University of Thessalonika, Greece.

Kontogianni, A., M.S. Skourtos, I.H. Langford, I.J. Bateman and S. Georgiou (2000), 'Integrating stakeholder analysis in non-market valuation of environmental assets', *Ecological Economics*, **37**, 123–38.

Langford, I.H., S. Georgiou, R.J. Day and I.J. Bateman (1999), 'Comparing perceptions of risk and quality with willingness to pay: a mixed methodological study of public preferences for reducing health risks from polluted coastal bathing waters', *Risk, Decision and Policy*, **4**(3), 201–20.

Lazaretou, T. (1995), *The Legal Protection of Wetlands in Greece*, Athens: Papazisis Editions.

MEDWET (1996), *Mediterranean Wetland Strategy 1996–2006*, http://www.iucn.org/.

MEDWET (1998), *A Strategy for Mediterranean Wetlands*, Thessalonika.

Mitchell, R.C. and R.T. Carson (1989), *Using Surveys to Value Public Goods: The Contingent Valuation Method*, Washington, DC: Resources for the Future.

Morgan, D.L. (1988), 'Focus groups as qualitative research', *University Series on Qualitative Research Methods 1*, Beverley Hills: Sage.

Morgan, D.L. and R.A. Krueger (1993), 'When to use focus groups and why', in D.L. Morgan (ed.), *Successful Focus Groups: Advancing the State of the Art*, Newbury Park: Sage.

Munasinghe, M. (1992), 'Biodiversity protection policy: environmental valuation and distribution issues', *Ambio*, **21**(3), 227–36.

Papadimitriou, G. (1995), 'Directive 92/43/COM in Greek Legislation. Its importance for conservation of natural habitats and wild flora and fauna', in *WWF, Natura 2000, The Application of European Directive 92/43/COM in Greece, Proceedings*, Athens, Greece.

Sagoff, M. (1988), *The Economy of the Earth*, Cambridge: Cambridge University Press.

Skourtos, M.S., A.I. Troumbis, A. Kontogianni, T. Akriotis and M. Simeonidis (1999), *ECOWET Project: Functions, Values and Dynamics, Final Report, Greek Case Study*, University of the Aegean, Mytilini, Lesvos, Greece.

Spilanis, J. (1998), *Specificity and Development Potential of the Greek Island Space*, report to the Ministry of Finance, Mytilini, Lesvos, Greece.

Stewart, D.W. and P. Shamdasani (1990), *Focus Groups: Theory and Practice*, Newbury Park: Sage.

# 9. Wetland creation: socio-economic and institutional conditions for collective action[1]

## T. Söderqvist and T. Lindahl

## 1 INTRODUCTION

Wetlands are today an uncommon feature in the main agricultural districts in Sweden. Although exact figures of the amount of wetlands converted to agricultural land are not available, it is estimated that peat land with a peat depth of at least 30 centimetres converted to arable land constituted about a quarter of the fourfold increase in arable land during the 19th century (Löfroth, 1991; SCB, 1996a). To what extent wetlands without peat, or with a peat depth of less than 30 centimetres, have been converted is not known with certainty. A substantial conversion is however likely to have taken place since 30–60 per cent of today's arable land in the main agricultural regions is systematically pipe-drained (Löfroth, 1991; SCB, 1996b).

The conversion of wetlands to agricultural land is not difficult to understand in view of the fact that there has always been a strong emphasis on increased and cost-effective food production in Swedish agriculture. However, in recent years increased attention is paid to the drawbacks of wetland loss. The goods and services provided by wetlands to society, such as nitrogen reduction and flood water detention, are more and more emphasized (Gren et al., 1994; Ewel, 1997; Mitsch and Gosselink, 2000; Turner et al., 2000).

In Sweden, the role of wetlands in nitrogen reduction has been relatively well studied and has become well-known, in particular in the context of the deteriorating ecological conditions of the Baltic Sea and the ensuing search for reductions in the load of nutrients to the Baltic Sea. Atmospheric and water-borne emissions of nitrogen and phosphorus to the Baltic Sea increased considerably during the 20th century. Estimates suggest a fourfold increase due to human activities for nitrogen and an eightfold increase for phosphorus (Larsson et al., 1985). The eutrophication caused by this inflow of nutrients involves an increased primary production and, consequently, more dead organic matter, the decomposition of which consumes oxygen. Eutrophication is expected to have a negative impact on human welfare. For example, more turbid water, algal blooms and a changed composition of the algae flora may discourage people from engaging in seaside recreation, while the increased frequency of anoxic conditions may affect fishery (Hansson and Rudstam, 1990).

Concern about the ecological conditions of the Baltic Sea resulted in 1988 in a ministerial agreement to reduce the nutrient emissions by 50 per cent by 1995 (Swedish Cabinet Bill 1990/91:90). However, although various measures have been taken, the objective was not met in Sweden, nor the majority of the other countries situated around the Baltic Sea and the North Sea. Additional efforts to reduce nutrient emissions have therefore been proposed and under-taken, including the restoration and creation of wetlands (SEPA, 1997, 2002; Swedish Cabinet Bill 2000/01:130). The presence of denitrification processes in a wetland make it a potentially effective means to reduce nitrogen (Jansson *et al.*, 1998; Leonardson, 1994). The attention paid to wetlands' nitrogen reduc-tion capacity also helped to understand that wetlands are not an isolated entity in the landscape. When wetlands are converted to another type of land, or when wetlands are restored or created, this is likely to have consequences for other ecosystems, including marine ones such as the Baltic Sea. It is therefore crucial to be aware of how wetlands are biogeophysically linked to surrounding ecosystems (Jansson *et al.*, 1998 and 1999; Rockström *et al.*, 1999; Lundberg, 1999; Lundberg and Moberg, 2001).

Using wetlands to reduce nutrient loads to the sea is also likely to be an interesting option from an economic point of view. Research findings indicate that nutrient abatement programmes should include this measure in order to be cost-effective (Gren, 1993; Gren *et al.*, 1997a,b), that is total abatement costs for accomplishing a given reduction of the nutrient load to the sea are reduced if conventional measures such as improved sewage treatment and changes in agricultural practices are combined with wetland creation.

After a long history of significant wetland losses, the past decade has in fact shown an increase in the share of wetland areas in the Swedish agricultural landscape as a result of the restoration and creation of wetlands. There are a number of reasons for this new tendency to restore and create wetlands.

First of all, Swedish agri-environmental policy has gradually become more concerned about nutrient emissions from agriculture. For example, changed agricultural practices have been encouraged and in some Swedish agricultural districts wetland creation has been introduced as one of several nutrient abate-ment measures. Secondly, wetland creation initiatives have also been nourished by an increased attention to the loss of biological diversity in the agricultural landscape. Thirdly, land conversion as a means of reducing agricultural produc-tion has been encouraged in Swedish agricultural policy. Finally, some wetlands have also been created as a result of individual initiatives based on an

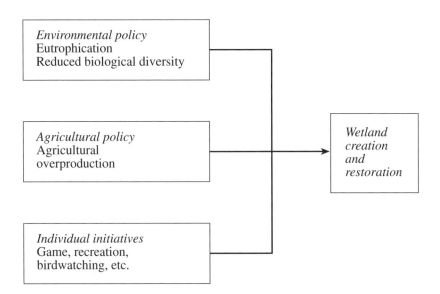

*Figure 9.1    Forces encouraging wetland restoration and creation in Sweden*

interest in game and birdwatching. The main forces encouraging wetland restoration and creation are summarized in Figure 9.1.

In this chapter, the socio-economic and institutional conditions for wetland creation in the context of agri-environmental policies will be addressed in more detail.

## 2    AGRI-ENVIRONMENTAL POLICY AND WETLAND CREATION[2]

Introducing wetland creation as an alternative means to abate nutrient emissions from agricultural land and the provision of other socially valued ecosystem services implies that current land uses have to be changed and may hence involve considerable opportunity costs (see Chapter 4). The conversion of agricultural land to wetlands is an example of a rather swiftly introduced new policy *objective*, which is not necessarily accompanied by a new policy *strategy*. Policy strategies may be divided into three broad groups: regulative, economic and communicative strategies, see Table 9.1, each associated with a number of policy instruments that can be introduced for realizing the policy objectives (Eckerberg *et al.*, 1995; Vedung, 1996). Tradition plays an important role in the choice of a policy strategy. Furthermore, the policy strategy is

*Table 9.1     Three different policy strategies and their associated instruments*

| Policy strategies | Regulative | Economic | Communicative |
|---|---|---|---|
| Policy instruments | Permits<br>Rules<br>Prohibitions<br>Sanctions | Taxes<br>Charges<br>Permit markets<br>Subsidies | Information<br>Advice<br>Education<br>Negotiation |

likely to be rooted in a certain institutional setting and show a high degree of persistency (Winter, 1994).

In Swedish agricultural policy, there has always been heavy reliance on communicative policy strategies. Information, education and advice are common policy instruments, typically in combination with other instruments. For example, information is necessary for disseminating the purpose and existence of other policy instruments. Economic policy instruments introduced in the agricultural sector to meet environmental objectives are often 'carrots' such as subsidies (as opposed to 'sticks' such as taxes and levies). The choice for this specific policy strategy design can largely be attributed to the corporative tradition in Swedish agricultural policy. Box 9.1 expands on this by providing a brief history of Swedish agricultural policy.

---

## BOX 9.1   SWEDISH AGRICULTURAL POLICY – A BRIEF HISTORY

Modern Swedish agricultural policy has its origin in an agreement between the Social Democratic Party and the Agrarian Party in 1933. The Agrarian Party accepted fiscal interventions as suggested by the social democrats in return for measures to raise and stabilize farmers' income. Income maintenance was the prime objective. In view of this, import protection and price supports for the agricultural sector were introduced. The price setting reflected a corporative structure, where the government determined prices of agricultural products after negotiations with the agricultural sector. This was further formalized by legislation in 1947, when a more comprehensive agricultural policy was launched. Three goals of the agricultural policy were now defined:

1. national food supply: Swedish farmers should be capable of fully meeting the population's nutritional needs.
2. income maintenance: a family farm of 10–20 hectares should have a net income comparable to a skilled industrial worker's earnings.
3. dynamic efficiency: there should be a simultaneous increase in agricultural output and shift of labour to the fast-growing industrial sector in order to increase national economic growth.

While there were some changes in specification and relative priority, these goals characterized agricultural policies until the 1980s.

Another component of the corporative tradition is the fact that farmers' organizations have always been closely connected and highly involved in the formulation and implementation of policy (Eckerberg and Niemi-Iilahti, 1997:49). Farmers' involvement in the policy process is facilitated by the dominance of one organization: the Federation of Swedish Farmers (LRF). In 1999, the members of LRF comprised 122 000 individuals, 50 corporate associations and 16 industry organizations. The individual farmer is usually linked through personal membership and via membership of the corporate associations. The associations have about 300 000 members. Swedish associations of farmers outside the LRF are relatively very small.

Given the goals mentioned above, Swedish agricultural policy seemed very successful until the 1970s. Due to mechanization and rationalization, the agricultural production increased despite the fact that a large number of people left farming for other occupations, the gap between farm incomes and industrial wages narrowed, and Sweden attained self-sufficiency or surplus in most basic foods. Domestic food prices were, however, far above international levels, and as a response to public opinion, the government lowered prices by introducing food subsidies in 1973. In addition, excess production became an increasingly costly problem, since governmental export subsidies paid the difference between international and domestic prices.

A growing national debt and the increasing importance of environmental issues on the political agenda triggered a substantial revision of agricultural policies in the 1980s and the beginning of the 1990s. The corporative tradition of negotiated prices was abandoned and replaced by a market-oriented process where prices were to be gradually reduced to a level decided by supply and demand. Environmental protection and nature conservation became official agricultural policy goals in 1984. Policy instruments were introduced that contributed both to a reduced agricultural production and environmental benefits, such as fees and levies on fertilizers and agricultural chemicals, and to financial support for nature conservation efforts such as the protection of meadows and pasture land.

To some extent, this revision of Swedish agricultural policy corresponds to the development of the EU agricultural policy (CAP). Self-sufficiency and equity for farmers and consumers dominated policy until the early 1980s, when environmental problems together with excess grain production started to receive more attention. The CAP reform in 1992 involved the integration of agricultural and environmental policies. While the Swedish agricultural policy reform was more far-reaching in market-orientation, the parallels in policy change facilitated the harmonization between the Swedish national policy and CAP when Sweden joined the EU in 1995.

The revised agricultural policy in Sweden also involved the introduction in 1989 of subsidies for wetland creation. Conversion of arable land to wetlands as a way of reducing agricultural production seems to have been in focus at the outset. There was however a gradual increase in the attention paid to wetlands' provision of environmental benefits. Two environmental issues that seem to have triggered this attention were the eutrophication of the seas and the decline in biodiversity in the agricultural landscape.

*Sources*:   Swedborg (1980), Holmström (1988) and Lindahl (1998).

Turning to policy implementation, two contrasting approaches can be identified (Table 9.2). The top-down approach presumes a hierarchical organization with dominant public governance. Governmental bodies are divided into sectors, which are responsible for their specific fields only. On the other hand, the bottom-up approach presumes a decentralized organization and involves a reliance on market solutions, and communication between the public and private sector is considered of paramount importance (Vedung, 1996).

As described in Box 9.1, Swedish agricultural policy was revised to a more market-oriented policy in the 1980s. This revision coincided to a considerable

*Table 9.2    Two models for policy implementation*

|                            | Top-down                                         | Bottom-up                              |
| -------------------------- | ------------------------------------------------ | -------------------------------------- |
|                            | Hierarchy                                        | Network orientation                    |
| Administrative structure   | Centralization                                   | Decentralization                       |
|                            | Sectorization; specified division of responsibility | Cross-sectoral and integrated structure |
| Governance                 | Regulated; rights of control and complaint specified | Deregulation Market orientation        |
|                            | Public governance                                | Public and private actors              |
| Problems identified        | Implementation deficit Rigidity                  | Co-ordination deficit                  |

*Source*:   Eckerberg *et al*. (1995).

extent with changes in the policy implementation structure from a traditional top-down approach to a more decentralized bottom-up approach. This tendency of decentralization became increasingly apparent in Sweden during the 1990s when societal tasks and responsibilities were largely delegated to the local level (Petersson, 1998). One of the first steps in this process was the reformation in 1991 of the law that regulates local authorities (municipalities), allowing them more institutional and organizational freedom (Swedish Cabinet Bill 1990/91:117).

The policy implementation for wetland creation has largely been following a traditional top-down model. Since 1989, a number of national grants have been introduced to support wetland creation (Table 9.3). The grant designs differ and involve a varying degree of flexibility. Although the *Landskapsvård* grant system does not have wetland creation as its main goal, it is of interest here as it gives a good example of a more flexible subsidy system, which allows for negotiations and agreements to take place at the level of the individual farmer. *NYLA* and *Omställning* 90 are less flexible in this sense since they involve imposed, fixed and non-negotiable contracts (even though they too are concluded on a voluntary basis).

Also the *Miljöstöd* grant, the main national subsidy system for wetland creation introduced in 1996, is characterized by some degree of flexibility. After signing a 20-year contract with the government, the farmer receives a fixed annual amount of money. Contrary to the NYLA and Conversion 90 contracts, it is to a large extent up to the farmer how he wishes to create the wetland on his land. The NYLA and Conversion 90 are characterized by

*Table 9.3   National grants for wetland creation in Sweden in the 1990s*

| Introduction | Subsidy | Design | Purpose |
|---|---|---|---|
| 1989/90 | NYLA ('New features in the landscape') | No contract, money transferred in a lump-sum after the wetland has been created and approved | To encourage plantation of avenues and groups of broad-leaved trees, wetland creation, and the creation of buffer zones along watercourses |
| 1991 | Omställning 90 ('Conversion 90') | No contract, money transferred in a lump-sum after the wetland has been created and approved | For the permanent conversion of arable land to forestry, land for energy crops and wetlands |
| 1991 | Landskapsvård ('Protection of the agricultural landscape') | 5-year contract, negotiated between the farmer and the government, paid annually | The farmer is obliged to cultivate or graze according to certain requirements |
| 1996 | Miljöstöd ('Environmental support') | 20-year contract, no negotiation, money transferred annually | To promote biodiversity through the creation of wetlands, buffer zones along watercourses and extensive grazing land |

*Source:*   Lindahl (1998: 17–18).

payment after approval. The contract is uniform in the sense that the signing is not preceded by any negotiations. There are no opportunities for contract adjustments based on individual conditions or circumstances.

The national grant systems presented in Table 9.3 are not the only ones available. In some parts of Sweden, complementary, locally based and locally funded policies have been developed. One example of such a local grant system, combining traditional Swedish agri-environmental policy strategies and top-down implementation with non-conventional local (bottom-up) approaches to environmental policies, is an environmental programme for wetland creation in the Kävlinge River drainage basin in south-west Scania. This programme will be discussed and evaluated in more detail in section 4 after the presentation of theoretical background of the analysis in the next section.

## 3   THEORETICAL BACKGROUND

Environmental resources and the services they provide to society, such as water and air quality, often are public goods. Public goods are usually characterized by (1) non-rivalry where one individual's consumption of the good does not reduce the amount available to other individuals; and (2) non-excludability where individuals cannot be excluded from consuming the good once it has been supplied. While pure public goods are rare, there are many environmental goods and services partially exhibiting non-rivalry and/or non-excludability characteristics see, for example, Cornes and Sandler, 1996). Studying the difficulties associated with the supply and management of such goods and services has a long academic history (see Ostrom, 1990 for references going back to Aristoteles, Thomas Hobbes and William Forster Lloyd).

Maintaining or increasing the provision of public goods often requires considerable efforts by several actors in society (collective action). For example, measures like wetland creation, changing agricultural practices or advanced sewage treatment methods are needed to increase water quality in eutrophicated watercourses and seas. According to Mueller (1989), the non-rivalry characteristics of public goods tend to encourage co-operation between these actors since everyone benefits from the goods and services once they are supplied. However, the non-excludability characteristic gives an incentive to strategic behaviour. If individual A succeeds in having individual B pay for the costs of supplying a public good, A becomes a 'free rider' as A is able to consume the good without paying for it. As a result, an awkward 'prisoner's dilemma' may arise. The incentive to behave strategically suggests that public goods are rarely supplied as a result of voluntary co-operation. In particular, this is likely to be true when the number of individuals involved is relatively large. In such a case, an individual's sense of responsibility for maintaining or increasing the provision level (including quality) of the good is less evident (Olson, 1965).

According to Olson (1965), the incentive to free-ride requires selective measures, which affect the individual, not the collective as a whole. In addition, there are special cases where spontaneous individual action resulting in an efficient provision of a public good can be expected (Mueller, 1989). Such cases usually involve small communities and 'weakest-link technology' to maintain or increase the provision of a public good. Such a technology exists when the amount of the public good provided corresponds to the smallest individual contribution to the public good by any member of the community.[3]

There is empirical evidence contradicting Olson's recommendation, which shows that individuals sometimes tend also to contribute to a common good in cases when selective measures, externally imposed by, for example, national or local authorities, are not present (Ostrom, 2000). There are even results indicating that externally imposed measures introduce a risk of crowding out already-existing co-operative behaviour.[4] Ostrom (2000) notes that these empirical findings largely remain to be resolved by a new emerging modern theory of collective action.

There are two types of selective measures available in practice: coercive measures or measures which somehow encourage pro-social behaviour.4 Neglecting coercion here and focusing instead on the promotion of voluntary participation, one option to maintain and increase the provision of public goods and services is to limit the number of individuals involved. This is expected to achieve a closer link between individual behaviour and the result of joint efforts, making it easier to identify free riders. This may include locally designed institutions for the provision of public goods. The design of local institutions and solutions for the management of environmental resources has been emphasized by a large number of scholars (for example Ostrom, 1990 and 1992; Baland and Platteau, 1996; Berkes and Folke, 1998). Interestingly, there seems to be an increasing tendency in Sweden to decentralize the welfare state and lay down responsibilities for societal tasks on a local level.

While regulators increasingly tend to rely on voluntary agreement, this does not mean that they expect spontaneous individual action. On the contrary, instruments encouraging voluntary participation are typically present, either 'carrots', such as possibilities to obtain subsidies, or 'sticks', such as threats of introducing mandatory participation if the voluntary approach turns out to be unsuccessful.

The former approach sometimes involves subsidies intended to cover farmers' extra costs caused by their voluntary participation in an environmental protection and enhancement programme. However, these may not be sufficient if there are also other determinants of participation than purely financial ones. On the other hand, the subsidy may for some farmers be unnecessarily generous in the sense that they would also be willing to participate at a lower subsidy rate. A regulator rarely has information that allows him to differentiate between subsidies according to willingness to participate, but a given rate of participation may be accomplished at a lower subsidy rate if sufficient farmers have other motives than purely financial ones to participate.[5] This suggests that knowledge about non-financial motives, if any, is an important piece of information. Farmers are likely to be interested in an increased probability that authorities also take non-financial motives into account when an environmental programme is designed. Authorities can use this type of information to enhance the probability that the programme will be successful.

## 4   CASE STUDY

### 4.1   The Kävlinge River Programme[6]

The Kävlinge River Programme, a water and nature conservation programme focusing on the creation of wetlands and riparian buffer zones in the Kävlinge River drainage basin in south-west Scania in the southern part of Sweden (Figure 9.2), officially started in 1990. The river basin is located in the heavily cultivated south-western part of the County of Scania. The region has had a considerable loss of wetlands in the agricultural landscape over the past centuries. Nowadays, wetlands make up less than 1 per cent of the whole area (Emanuelsson *et al.*, 1985).

The Kävlinge River Programme was officially initiated by the Water Protection Association of the Kävlinge River, in which nine municipalities and a number of industrial companies are represented. The consultant firm Ekologgruppen i Landskrona AB was chosen to implement the programme, which was constituted as the Kävlinge River Programme by a cooperative agreement between the nine municipalities for 12 years from 1 July 1995 onwards.

The programme's main objective is to reduce the nutrient load to the sea by means of the creation of 300 hectares of ponds and 210 hectares of riparian buffer zones, complementing improved waste water treatment methods and changes in agricultural practices (for example increased winter crop cultivation, smaller livestock farming, lower livestock densities, manure spreading restrictions).

The institutional organization of the programme is based upon the co-operative agreement between the nine municipalities. A Programme Board, whose

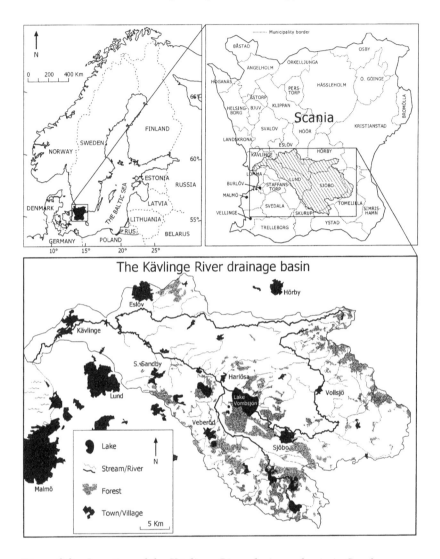

*Figure 9.2    Location of the Kävlinge River drainage basin in Sweden*

members are officials from the nine municipalities, governs the programme. One official from the County Administrative Board of Scania is a co-opted member. The board meetings are chaired by an official from Lund, while two municipality officials from Lund and Eslöv are the Executive Secretary and Secretary respectively. Two representatives from the consultant firm

Ekologgruppen are also always present at the board meetings. The implementation of the programme is managed by the Executive Committee, which consists of officials from all nine municipalities. Also this committee is chaired by a municipality official from Lund. A Consultation Committee has been set up to form a formal link to stakeholder groups and the scientific community.

The nine cooperating municipalities have agreed in principle to cover 60 per cent of the programme's total costs. However, this agreement is open to renegotiation every three years. The municipalities' share of the total costs was somewhat lower (56 per cent) in the first period of the project (1 July 1995–30 June 1998). A grant from EU/Life covers 25 per cent of the total costs, while the remaining 19 per cent is obtained from a national *Miljöstöd* grant, contributions from regional foundations, contributions and donations from the landowners themselves to irrigation pond projects (Ekologgruppen, 1998). The proportion of the total costs paid by each municipality is determined by the area, population size and location of the municipality in the drainage basin. Municipalities situated in the western part of the drainage basin bear a relatively higher cost.

The consultant firm Ekologgruppen is responsible for the implementation of the Kävlinge River Programme. Dissemination of information about the programme plays a crucial part in the implementation since its success largely depends upon the willingness of the drainage basin's more than 1300 landowners to convert some of their land into wetlands. Booklets, meetings, media attention, letters and phone calls have served as important information channels.

The landowners have generally been much more interested in the creation of ponds than riparian buffer zones (Ekologgruppen, 1998:9). The potential locations for wetland creation are evaluated on the basis of, *inter alia*, land use and the size of the drainage basin of the feeder stream to the potential wetland. For each location, a draft design of the wetland is set up and discussed with the landowner and the County Administrative Board. Municipal leasing of the land to be converted is also negotiated with the landowner. The term of the lease is 30 years for ponds and 10 years for riparian buffer zones. The leasing agreement does not change the property rights to the land, which means that the landowner's hunting and fishing rights, if present, are not affected. The Swedish right of public access may however be applicable to the converted land, which would allow the general public to visit the wetland.

Landowners are offered rental payments which equal the wetland construction costs plus the opportunity costs of land, measured as the market value of the land subject to conversion (see Söderqvist, 2002a) for an analysis of the construction costs). If a landowner is believed to benefit financially from the conversion (for example irrigation benefits), the policy is to pay no more than 60 per cent of the construction costs. Negotiations between the landowner and the programme result in a preliminary leasing agreement. The subsequent step is to invite firms to tender for the construction of the wetland. After selection of the most favourable tender, the wetland is constructed in consultation with Ekologgruppen. The latter also inspects the construction work. The official leasing contract is signed when the construction work has been completed.

In summary, the implementation of the programme can be characterized by the following key elements:

1. The programme is a *local* initiative and is largely funded by the municipalities.
2. The co-operative municipal agreement covers the Kävlinge River drainage basin as a whole and therefore is *catchment-based*, corresponding to the requirements set out in the new European Water Framework Directive (see SOU, 1997a, b and 2002). Likewise, the programme includes a strategy for the *dissemination of information* about the drainage basin and wetland creation. This too is consistent with one of the key features of the EU Water Framework Directive.
3. The Programme depends upon landowners' *voluntary participation*. Participation is encouraged by persuasion through the information provided and the economic compensation based on the costs incurred. Negotiations between landowners and the municipality result in contracts which are based upon the specific conditions and circumstances of the individual farmer.
4. The construction of the wetland is carried out by an independent company (Ekologgruppen) and *not* by the landowners. This company also is the *mediating agent* between the authorities and the farmers in the sense that it handles the contacts with the farmers, including the negotiations preceding the signing of the contract.

## 4.2   Objectives, Methodology and Data Collection

The success of environmental programmes such as the Kävlinge River Programme, supplying important environmental goods exhibiting public good characteristics, depends to a large extent upon co-ordinated efforts of individual actors in the area and the provision of the right incentives which motivate and stimulate collective action. In order to assess the socio-economic and institutional conditions for such collective action, stakeholders' opinions and actions associated with the Kävlinge River Programme were examined, in particular the motives of landowners to participate voluntarily. The data collection included the following stages (for more details, see

Söderqvist and Lewan, 1998; Lindahl and Söderqvist, 2001; Lewan and Söderqvist, 2002):

1. *Examination of written documentation and stakeholder mapping* at the end of 1996, beginning of 1997. The documentation and discussions with a few key informants allowed a preliminary listing of stakeholders. This list included 121 persons and organizations, including 68 landowners, and can be regarded as what Grimble and Chan (1995) refer to as 'focal group' and 'reputational' approaches to stakeholder identification.

2. *Meetings with stakeholders.* In March 1997, the listed stakeholders were all invited to participate in two identically designed meetings which lasted about two and a half hours each. In total, 41 stakeholders attended these meetings. The meetings were held in Eslöv on 7 and 8 April 1997, and their main aim was to provide a forum for discussions about the advantages and disadvantages of the Kävlinge River Programme. Additionally, three focus group meetings were organized with the general public living in the drainage basin, in Sjöbo on 28 October 1997 (11 participants), in Kävlinge on 30 October 1997 (4 participants) and in S. Sandby on 27 January 1998 (9 participants).

3. *Mail questionnaire.* Although the meetings provided ample opportunity to exchange information between the invited stakeholders and the researchers who organized the meetings, it was not possible for all invited stakeholders to attend the meetings. Moreover, it was felt that some of those who attended the meetings found it difficult to express their opinion at the meetings, either because of a lack of time or the presence of other participants. Therefore, an open-ended mail questionnaire was also sent out in March 1997 to all of the 121 listed stakeholders who were invited to the meetings. The questionnaire included questions regarding landowners' participation in the programme, important people or organizations behind the implementation of the programme, their motives for participation, and the programme's advantages and disadvantages. The response rate was 51 per cent. Sixty-two stakeholders returned the questionnaire, of which 20 also attended one of the meetings. Hence, information was collected, either through the meetings or the mail survey, from 69 per cent of the 121 listed stakeholders. A separate mail questionnaire was furthermore sent out to a random sample of 200 farmers living in the Kävlinge River drainage basin.

4. *Face-to-face interviews.* The findings of the meetings and the questionnaire were summarized and sent back to the participants of the meetings and the people who replied to the questionnaire. They were then given the opportunity to react on these findings in a final follow-up meeting. The findings were furthermore validated through seven face-to-face interviews in December 1998 with persons who were identified as playing a key role in the design and implementation of the programme.

## 4.3   Results

### 4.3.1   General results

In Sweden, there are about 50 catchment-based water management associations. Catchment areas are, however, not necessarily consistent with current administrative borders, which may jeopardize the necessary coordinated collective effort. A survey of their activities has shown that they are mainly concerned with water quality monitoring, not with strategic water management planning (Gustafsson, 1999). The latter task is instead handled by municipalities and county authorities, which entails a risk of either a too limited or broad perspective in relation to what would be needed for a catchment-based water management strategy.

The case study introduced here shows that putting a co-ordination mechanism into place at a regional level in order to achieve objectives that basically concern an entire river basin, requires first of all the support of local politicians and municipality officials driven by a genuine interest in the environment. The key people identified in this case study take the 50 per cent emission reduction target seriously and show ingenuity in finding ways to realize it. Broadly speaking, they are a good illustration of the Agenda 21 expression 'think globally, act locally'. However, the dependence of the entire programme on just a few key people as the main driving force behind it all is risky should these people for whatever reason disappear from the scene and institutions for preserving their intentions have not been established.

Nevertheless, the 50 per cent emission reduction target, formulated at international and national level, has been highly influential at the local level in this case study. The consultant company Ekologgruppen and the local scientific community at the University of Lund seem to have played an important role in bringing up the idea of choosing wetland creation on agricultural land as a complementary measure to more conventional nutrient abatement methods.

Although the Water Protection Association of the Kävlinge River is an existing catchment-based organization, it was felt that it was not functional and effective in formulating strategic river basin policy plans and implementing these. Therefore, the municipalities of Lund and Eslöv took the initiative to create a new organization, involving all municipalities in the catchment area, despite the facts that agricultural land use is not traditionally considered a municipal policy issue and that financial funds were scarce during a period of time when many municipalities underwent budget cuts.

The implementation of the programme was made possible as a result of co-operative agreement. Politicians and officials not only chose the implementation framework, they always have been and still are very much part of the implementation process through, for example, their responsibilities as members of the Programme Board or the Executive Committee. The framework includes a number of components which have facilitated the implementation of the programme. One key component is the municipalities' willingness to provide and search for financial funding of the programme, resulting in no or just a very small financial burden on the participating farmers themselves.

As often is the case in Swedish agri-environmental policy, the programme adopted a combination of policy instruments, in this case a strong emphasis upon communication and subsidies for its implementation. A combination of voluntary participation, information, negotiations and subsidies covering the costs of implementation are a necessary condition for widespread interest in participation among farmers, but most probably not a sufficient one.

Based on the data collected and analysed, the programme seems to include one other key component: trust. Gaining trust costs time and considerable efforts, and can only be accomplished if the principal (that is the authorities) is willing and capable of engaging in a deliberative and inclusionary communication process with the target group (agents), and there exists mutual respect between both landowners/farmers and principal for their situation, and underlying motivations to participate on a voluntary basis.

Ekologgruppen's role as an independent mediating agent between the authorities and the target group is expected to have been a major contributing factor to this constructive atmosphere. In view of this important facilitating role during the entire process of programme design and implementation, the current mediating agent cannot easily be replaced. Hiring a consultant firm for carrying out the programme does also not necessarily give the principal more flexibility since changing consultant is likely to be very costly owing to the loss of the accumulated trust and knowledge.

### 4.3.2 Motivations to participate in the Kävlinge River Programme

In order to obtain information about landowners' motives whether or not to participate, a mail survey of 200 randomly selected farmers in the Kävlinge River drainage basin was carried out in 1998 (Söderqvist, 2002b). One hundred and nineteen farmers replied and returned the completed questionnaire (response rate of 60 per cent), of which 13 per cent indicated that they were involved in the programme already, 33 per cent reported to have an interest in participating, 35 per cent reported a reluctance to participate and 19 per cent did not know or were unsure whether or not to participate.

In order to find out the motives for landowners' willingness to participate in the programme, the questionnaire included (1) follow-up questions about their own motives whether or not to participate and (2) a question about the motives they believed other landowners might have for participating. Table 9.4 provides an overview of the answers.

The most often stated reasons refer to environmental improvements in general, such as reduced nutrient emissions or a cleaner river and sea ('improved environment'). Biodiversity is another important motive. This

*Table 9.4    Motives for willingness to participate in the Kävlinge River
Programme*

| Motives to participate | | Own motives[1] | Landowners' motives in general[1] |
|---|---|---|---|
| 1. | Private agricultural benefits | | |
| | Grants | 6.6 | 19.2 |
| | Goodwill | 1.6 | 3.3 |
| | Use of marginal land | 0.0 | 4.2 |
| | Irrigation | 3.3 | 9.2 |
| | Moderation of waterflows | 1.6 | 1.7 |
| | Crabfish production | 0.0 | 0.8 |
| | Total | 13.1 | 38.4 |
| 2a. | Private environmental benefits | | |
| | Interest in and responsibility for the environment | 14.8 | 11.7 |
| | Hunting | 1.6 | 3.3 |
| | Fishing | 1.6 | 2.5 |
| | Total | 18.0 | 17.5 |
| 2b. | Public environmental benefits | | |
| | Improved environment | 34.4 | 25.0 |
| | Biodiversity | 14.8 | 7.5 |
| | Aesthetics | 6.6 | 6.7 |
| | Total | 55.8 | 39.2 |
| 3. | Other motives | | |
| | Watercourse nearby | 9.8 | – |
| | Restoration of old wetlands | 1.6 | – |
| | Prevent overgrowing of existing water | 1.6 | – |
| | Restructuring of agriculture | 0.0 | 0.8 |
| | Instructive and educating | 0.0 | 0.8 |
| | Other types of motives | 0.0 | 1.6 |
| | Total | 13.0 | 3.2 |
| No motive | | 0.0 | 1.7 |
| Total | | 99.9 | 100.0 |

*Note*:    1. Percentage of all stated motives.

*Source*:    Söderqvist (2002b).

category includes reasons which refer to advantages for wildlife for the sake of wildlife itself, not because of improved hunting or fishing opportunities for man. Hunting and fishing are two separate and less often stated motives for landowner willingness to participate in the programme.

Based on Weaver (1996), the motives mentioned by landowners have been categorized in Table 9.4 into:

1. Private agricultural motives, that is. motives associated with farm profitability;
2a. Private environmental benefits, that is private benefits derived from environmental improvements;
2b. Public environmental benefits, that is public benefits derived from environmental improvements;
3. Other motives.

The first category contains those motives that are most strongly associated with farmers' financial situation. As shown in Table 9.4, private agricultural benefits are more often perceived by a landowner as the main reason for participation of landowners in general than for his own participation. The opposite is true for public environmental benefits; they are more often stated as the main motive for own participation than for landowners in general.

Interestingly, there was a tendency among respondents who were not willing to participate in the programme to perceive private agricultural benefits as the main reason for farmer participation. In other words, one might say that a farmer who has a cynical view on other farmers tends to be reluctant to participate in the programme. This finding corresponds with previous research results, indicating that individuals tend to be relatively more willing to demonstrate co-operative behaviour if they believe that other individuals are also willing to contribute to the common good (Ostrom, 2000).

This suggests that financial motives may be expected to be a commonly shared concern among the respondents who said they were not willing to participate in the programme. According to Table 9.5, about 20 per cent of all motives stated by these respondents referred to the farmer's limited supply of land or uncertainty about whether the grants are sufficiently high. Other common types of motives are a respondent's high age (10 per cent), uncertainty about whether or not to continue as a farmer (8 per cent) or reasons related to the particular characteristics of the landowner's land such as 'no nearby watercourse' (17 per cent).

The results indicate that public environmental benefits are an important reason for farmers' participation, but there is a significant difference between what farmers say about themselves and what they say about other farmers. On average, respondents seem to rate their own concern for public environmental benefits more highly compared to other farmers.

*Table 9.5    Motives for* not *being willing to participate in the Kävlinge*
*River Programme*

| Motive | % of all stated motives |
| --- | --- |
| No watercourse nearby | 16.7 |
| Marl-pits, ponds or ditches already present | 8.3 |
| There is enough water already | 1.7 |
| Not enough land; no suitable land; can't afford to give up any land | 10.0 |
| The grants may not be sufficiently high | 8.3 |
| Not enough benefits from participation | 1.7 |
| Bureaucracy | 3.3 |
| Obligations | 3.3 |
| Don't want such things on my land | 1.7 |
| May look artificial | 1.7 |
| High age | 10.0 |
| May not continue as a farmer | 8.3 |
| Not enough time | 3.3 |
| Tenant farmer | 3.3 |
| Uncertain about what is suitable for my land | 8.3 |
| Don't know the effects | 5.0 |
| Don't have enough information | 5.0 |
| Total | 99.9 |

*Source*:    Söderqvist (2002b).

However, although respondents tended to judge other farmers to be relatively more concerned about farm profitability, they also believed other farmers do take public and private environmental benefits seriously. Motives
associated with public environmental benefits were mentioned in 40 per cent
of all the cases (Table 9.4).

In a statistical analysis (Söderqvist, 2002b), these tendencies are confirmed
in the sense that attitudes and perceived personal consequences are the most
important determinants of farmers' willingness to participate in the
programme, whereas determinants that are more associated with farm profitability are statistically not significant. Weaver's (1996) analysis indicated that
the latter determinants would have a strong impact if private agricultural bene-

fits were the dominant motive for participation. Evidently, the incentive structure is more complex than that described in this case study.

Hence, it can be concluded that financial considerations (the subsidy level) are not the sole determinant of farmers' willingness to participate in the programme. It is also important that the programme is designed in such a way that (1) farmers gain in terms of increased private environmental benefits (hunting, fishing and so on) and (2) farmers are convinced by the programme's public environmental benefits.

The importance attached to public environmental benefits seems to contradict the need for selective measures with merely individual instead of collective effects in order to stimulate collective action to maintain or improve the common good. However, the answers to the questionnaire indicate that general environmental improvements are to some extent also perceived as a private benefit. It is also possible that the motives are structured in a hierarchical way. However, this could not be detected from the answers to the questions in the questionnaire. Reimbursement of the costs incurred when creating wetlands may constitute a necessary, but not a sufficient condition for participation. However, the analysis shows that it cannot in general be viewed as a sufficient condition. Other types of motives also have to be considered in the design of an environmental programme in order to stimulate participation.

## 5   DISCUSSION AND CONCLUSIONS

The case of the Kävlinge River Programme illustrates how a drainage basin-based environmental programme can be established as a complement to national policy. Local and regional initiatives such as the Kävlinge River Programme possess qualities that national policy often lacks, that is bottom-up agreement and consensus about the concrete implementation of the policy and close contact with the policy's target group and their concerns and interests.

The analysis and evaluation of the Kävlinge River Programme indicated that interactive personal communication with the target group is one of the key elements to the question why it has been possible to implement a national policy for wetland creation in this region. Other key elements can be summarized as follows:

- the existence of a clear overarching policy objective (the 50 per cent target) to which everyone was committed;
- the devotion and endurance among key persons (officials and politicians) in participating municipalities;
- strong commitment among municipalities to finance the implementation of the policy;

- the combination of traditional agri-environmental policy instruments and well streamlined interactive forms of communication in a safe, trustful and constructive atmosphere between principal (authorities) and agents (landowners);
- the presence of an independent mediating agent between authorities and the target group.

Formulation and implementation of the programme required substantial efforts among a number of key people in the municipalities in the river basin. The people behind the authorities in these municipalities were convinced about the social and public benefits for the entire river basin once the programme was implemented. They showed a genuine interest in the environment and believed in the effectiveness of wetlands as an important additional cost-effective measure to reduce the emission of nutrients to the sea and maintain or improve biological diversity in the area at the same time. Their commitment to collective action and the common good was best reflected in their willingness to find funds for the programme.

The fact that the authorities (municipalities) bear most of the costs of implementing the programme, (and in the end the taxpayers in these municipalities), probably contributes to its success (see also Winter, 1994: 32–36), but also shows that the property rights to a clean and healthy environment are not laid down on the target group of landowners, but the community as a whole. The 'polluter pays' principle evidently does not seem to apply to this case study. The use of voluntary agreements also emphasizes this. Voluntary agreements clearly start from the point of view that individual landowners own the property rights regarding the use of the land. They are free to use it as they see fit even if this means a decrease of environmental quality or a loss of biodiversity. If society wishes to prevent this they ought to pay the farmer for maintaining and improving public environmental benefits.

In this case study, two interesting findings are, first of all, that a majority of the farmers showed a willingness to participate in the programme for reasons of public environmental benefits, while less than 20 per cent mentioned private (agricultural or environmental) benefits as the main reason to participate. A large proportion of the nutrient load to the sea results from the runoff of nutrients from agricultural land. Secondly, discussions with groups from the general public indicated that some inhabitants of the Kävlinge River drainage basin believe it is only fair that taxpayers ultimately pay for the costs of wetland creation since they too share in the responsibility, either as consumers of agricultural products or as beneficiaries of a cleaner and healthy environment as a result of the implementation of the programme (Söderqvist and Lewan, 1998).

Farmers' perceptions and attitudes towards the public environmental benefits are evidently of importance. These perceptions obviously depend on farmers' knowledge of how nature works, the type of information they receive and from whom they receive this information (trust). The analysis showed that farmers who were able to form an opinion about the perceived personal consequences when joining the programme tended to show a relatively high willingness to participate. Perceived consequences to society as a whole turned out to be a relatively less important determinant of participation. This suggests that a principal or regulator aiming for a sufficiently high rate of participation in order for an environmental programme to be successful in achieving its objectives, does best to choose a communication strategy which emphasizes the personal consequences of participation rather than merely providing information about the broader consequences to society as a whole (public environmental benefits).

Finally, as mentioned, the success of an environmental enhancement programme in terms of participation rates also depends upon the information source behind the communication strategy. An important finding in this case study was that once it is made public that some farmers started to participate in the programme, this is likely to encourage other farmers to participate as well. Examples of 'good practice' case studies or examples of other local farmers participating in the programme and using them as 'ambassadors' for the programme, allowing or perhaps even stimulating them to speak to other farmers about their own experiences with the programme, is expected to encourage voluntary participation. The advantage of a locally based programme, such as the Kävlinge River Programme, is that it provides relatively good opportunities for informal dissemination of such information.

## NOTES

1. This chapter is based on some of the main findings in the Swedish case study in ECOWET. The case study is more comprehensively described in Söderqvist *et al.* (1999).
2. This section is largely based on a more detailed exposition in Lindahl (1998).
3. Examples of such a technology may appear artificial, but one possible illustration is the following. Consider the protection of a lake against the dumping of used cars. Assume that the lake is surrounded by land patches owned by different individuals. In such a case, the protection of the lake as a public good against the dumping of used cars depends to a large extent upon the protection accomplished by the landowner who is the least effective in protecting the lake against car dumping.
4. Voluntary participation in environmental protection programmes has gained increased attention and is being used as an important tool to achieve environmental objectives (Segerson and Miceli, 1998; Carraro and Lévêque, 1999).
5. Crépin (2002) compares different theoretical contractual designs between a regulator and farmers, taking into account the presence of asymmetric information, that is where farmers do and the regulator does not have information about the net costs of wetland creation.
6. The description of the programme is based on the situation at the time when the case study was carried out, that is between 1996 and 1999.

# REFERENCES

Baland, J.-M. and J.-P. Platteau (1996), *Halting Degradation of Natural Resources: Is there a Role for Rural Communities?*, Oxford: Oxford University Press.

Berkes, F. and C. Folke (eds) (1998), *Linking Social and Ecological Systems: Management Practices and Social Mechanisms for Building Resilience*, New York: Cambridge University Press.

Carraro, C. and F. Lévêque (eds) (1999), *Voluntary Approaches in Environmental Policy*, Dordrecht, The Netherlands: Kluwer Academic Publishers.

Cornes, R. and T. Sandler (1996), *The Theory of Externalities, Public Goods and Club Goods*, Dordrecht, The Netherlands: Kluwer Academic Publishers.

Crépin, A.-S. (2002), 'Incentives for wetland creation', chapter 3, in *Tackling the Economics of Ecosystems,* doctoral thesis, dissertations in Economics 2002:6, Department of Economics, Stockholm University.

Drake, L., K P. Hasund and D. Vail (1997), *The Greening of Agricultural Policies in Industrial Societies,* Brunswick: Cornell University.

Eckerberg, K. and A. Niemi-Iilahti (1997), 'Local implementation of agri-environmental policy: Comparative studies in the Nordic countries', in K. Eckerberg, I-M. Gren and T. Söderqvist (eds), *Politics and Economics of Baltic Sea Environmental Enforcement,* Beijer Occasional Paper Series, Beijer International Institute of Ecological Economics, The Royal Swedish Academy of Sciences, Stockholm, pp. 45–62.

Eckerberg, K., P.-K. Mydske, A. Niemi-Iilahti and K. Hilmer Pedersen (1995), 'The use of environmental policy instruments in Nordic and Baltic countries', in K. Eckerberg, I-M. Gren and T. Söderqvist (eds), *Policy Instruments for Combating Water Pollution to the Baltic Sea: Perspectives from Economics and Political Science*, Beijer Occasional Paper Series, Beijer International Institute of Ecological Economics, The Royal Swedish Academy of Sciences, Stockholm, pp. 22–45.

Ekologgruppen (1998), 'Kävlingeå-projektet. Årsrapport 1997', ['The Kävlinge River Programme. Annual Report 1997'], Ekologgruppen i Landskrona AB.

Emanuelsson, U., C. Bergendorff, B. Carlsson, N. Lewan and O. Nordell (1985), *Det Skånska Kulturlandskapet*, Lund: Bokförlaget Signum.

Ewel, C. (1997), 'Services from wetland ecosystems', in G. Daily (ed.), *Nature's Services: Societal Dependence on Natural Ecosystems*, Washington, DC: Island Press.

Gren, I.-M. (1993), 'Alternative nitrogen policies in the Mälar Region', *Ecological Economics*, **7**, 159–72.

Gren, I.-M., K. Elofsson and P. Jannke (1997a), 'Cost-effective nutrient reductions to the Baltic Sea', *Environmental and Resource Economics*, **10**, 341–62.

Gren, I.-M., T. Söderqvist and F. Wulff (1997b), 'Nutrient loads to the Baltic Sea: ecology, costs and benefits', *Journal of Environmental Management*, **51**, 123–43.

Gren, I.-M., C. Folke, R.K. Turner and I. Bateman (1994), 'Primary and secondary values of wetland ecosystems', *Environmental and Resource Economics*, **4**, 55–74.

Grimble, R. and M.-K. Chan (1995), 'Stakeholder analysis for natural resource management in developing countries', *Natural Resources Forum*, **19**(2), 113–24.

Gustafsson, J.-E. (1999), 'Vattenförvaltning i avrinningsområden – möjligheter och lösningar i olika länder', ['Water management in river basins – possibilities and solutions in different countries], *Vatten*, **55**, 251–7.

Hansson, S. and L.G. Rudstam (1990), 'Eutrophication and Baltic fish communities', *Ambio*, **19**, 123–5.

Holmström, S. (1988), 'Svenskt jordbruk 1930–1987. En koncentrerad översikt om jordbrukspolitik, teknik, produktivitet och lönsamhet', *Kungl. Skogs- och Lantbruksakademiens Tidskrift, Supplement 20*, Stockholm.

Jansson, Å, C. Folke and S. Langaas (1998), 'Quantification of the nitrogen retention capacity in natural wetlands in the Baltic drainage basin', *Landscape Ecology*, **13**, 249–62.

Jansson, Å., C. Folke, J. Rockström and L. Gordon (1999), 'Linking freshwater flows and ecosystem services appropriated by people: the case of the Baltic Sea drainage basin', *Ecosystems*, **2**, 351–66.

Larsson, U., R. Elmgren and F. Wulff (1985), 'Eutrophication and the Baltic Sea: causes and consequences', *Ambio*, **14**, 9–14.

Leonardson, L. (1994), 'Våtmarker som kvävefällor: svenska och internationella erfarenheter', Report 4176, Swedish Environmental Protection Agency, Stockholm.

Lewan, L. and T. Söderqvist (2002), 'Knowledge and recognition of ecosystem services among the general public in a drainage basin in Scania, Southern Sweden', *Ecological Economics*, **42**, 459–67.

Lindahl, T. (1998), 'Wetland creation in Sweden in an agricultural policy context', Beijer Discussion Paper Series No. 113, Beijer International Institute of Ecological Economics, The Royal Swedish Academy of Sciences, Stockholm.

Lindahl, T. and T. Söderqvist (2001), 'Building a catchment-based environmental programme: a stakeholder analysis of wetland creation in Scania, Sweden', accepted for publication in *Regional Environmental Change* subject to revision. Revised version submitted 27 September, 2001.

Löfroth, M. (1991), 'Våtmarkerna och deras betydelse', Report 3824, Swedish Environmental Protection Agency, Stockholm.

Lundberg, J. (1999), 'The functional roles of birds in wetlands', master degree thesis, Department of Systems Ecology, Stockholm University, Stockholm.

Lundberg, J. and F. Moberg (2001), 'The role of mobile link species for ecosystem functions: effects of global environmental change and the implications', manuscript in review, Natural Resources Management, Department of Systems Ecology, Stockholm University.

Mitsch, W.J. and J.G. Gosselink (2000), *Wetlands*, third edition, New York: John Wiley.

Mueller, D.C. (1989), *Public Choice II*, Cambridge: Cambridge University Press.

Olson, M. Jr. (1965), *The Logic of Collective Action: Public Goods and the Theory of Groups*, Cambridge, MA: Harvard University Press.

Ostrom, E. (1990), *Governing the Commons: The Evolution of Institutions for Collective Action*, New York: Cambridge University Press.

Ostrom, E. (1992), *Crafting Institutions: Self-Governing Irrigation Systems*, San Francisco: ICS Press.

Ostrom, E. (2000), 'Collective action and the evolution of social norms', *Journal of Economic Perspectives*, **14**(3), 137–58.

Petersson, O. (1998), *Kommunalpolitik. Tredje upplagan*, Norstedts Juridik, Stockholm.

Rockström, J., L. Gordon, C. Folke, M. Falkenmark and M. Engwall (1999), 'Linkages among water vapour flows, food production, and terrestrial ecosystem services', *Conservation Ecology*, **3**(2), 5, http://www.consecol.org/vol3/iss2/art5.

SCB, Statistiska Centralbyrån (1996a), *Naturmiljön i siffror. Femte utgåvan*, Statistics Sweden, Stockholm.

SCB, Statistiska Centralbyrån (1996b), *Jordbruksstatistisk årsbok 1996*, Statistics Sweden, Stockholm.

Segerson, K. and T.J. Miceli (1998), 'Voluntary environmental agreements: good or bad news for environmental protection?', *Journal of Environmental Economics and Management*, **36**, 109–30.

SEPA, Naturvårdsverket (1997), 'Nitrogen from land to sea: main report', Report 4801, Swedish Environmental Protection Agency, Stockholm.

SEPA, Naturvårdsverket (2002), 'Eutrophication: a management problem', Report 5213, Swedish Environmental Protection Agency, Stockholm.

Söderqvist, T. (2002a), 'Constructed wetlands as nitrogen sinks in Southern Sweden: an empirical analysis of cost determinants', *Ecological Engineering*, **19**, 161–73.

Söderqvist, T. (2002b), 'Are farmers prosocial? Determinants of the willingness to participate in a Swedish catchment-based wetland creation programme', manuscript accepted for publication in *Ecological Economics*.

Söderqvist, T. and L. Lewan (1998), 'Wetland creation in the Kävlinge River catchment, Scania, South Sweden: A pilot study on implementation, perceived benefits, and knowledge of ecosystem services', Beijer Discussion Paper Series No. 115, Beijer International Institute of Ecological Economics, The Royal Swedish Academy of Sciences, Stockholm.

Söderqvist, T., A.-S. Crépin, C. Folke, I.-M. Gren, Å. Jansson, T. Lindahl, J. Lundberg, M. Sandström, H. Scharin, O. Byström and G. Destouni (1999), 'Ecological–economic analysis of wetland creation in Sweden: Final report on the Swedish case study in the research project', *Ecological–Economic Analysis of Wetlands: Functions, Values and Dynamics (ECOWET)*, Beijer Occasional Paper Series, Beijer International Institute of Ecological Economics, The Royal Swedish Academy of Sciences, Stockholm.

SOU (1997a), *En ny vattenadministration: Vatten är livet. [A new water administration: Water is life]*, Intermediate Report, Governmental Committee on Catchment Areas, SOU 1997:99, Ministry of Environment, Stockholm.

SOU (1997b), *Miljösamverkan i vattenvården. [Environmental cooperation in water management]*, Final Report, Governmental Committee on Catchment Areas, SOU 1997:155, Ministry of Environment, Stockholm.

SOU (2002), *En ny svensk vattenadministration. [A New Swedish Water Administration]*, Status Report, Governmental Committee on Swedish Water Administration, SOU, Regeringskansliets utredningsavdelning, Göteborg, Sweden.

Swedborg, E. (1980), *Lantbrukspolitik för 80-talet. Besluten 1977–79. Bakgrund, riktlinjer och tillämpning*, LTs förlag, Stockholm.

Swedish Cabinet Bill 1990/91:90, *Ny miljöpolitik [New environmental policy]*, Stockholm.

Swedish Cabinet Bill 1990/91:117, *Ny kommunallag [New law for municipalities]*, Stockholm.

Swedish Cabinet Bill 2000/01:130, *Svenska miljömål – delmål och åtgärdsstrategier [Swedish Environmental Objectives – Subobjectives and Strategies for Implementation]*, Stockholm.

Turner, R.K., J.C.J.M. van den Bergh, T. Söderqvist, A. Barendregt, J. van der Straaten, E. Maltby and E. van Ierland (2000), 'Ecological–economic analysis of wetlands: scientific integration for management and policy', *Ecological Economics*, **35**, 7–23.

Vedung, E. (1996), 'Policy instruments: Typologies and theories', in M.-L.

Bemelmans-Videc, R.C. Rist and E. Vedung (eds), *Policy Instruments and Evaluation*, New Brunswick, NJ: Transaction Books.

Weaver, R.D. (1996), 'Prosocial behaviour: private contributions to agriculture's impact on the environment', *Land Economics*, **72**, 231–47.

Winter, S. (1994), *Implementering og effektivitet, [Implementation and efficiency]*, Herning, Denmark: Forlaget Systime a/s.

# 10. Management of a multi-purpose, open access wetland: the Norfolk and Suffolk Broads, UK

**R.K. Turner, R. Brouwer, S. Georgiou, I.J. Bateman, I.H. Langford, M. Green and H. Voisey**

## 1 INTRODUCTION: A REGIONAL PERSPECTIVE

The Norfolk and Suffolk Broads, a complex (freshwater, brackish and saline zonal area) wetland of both national and international significance lies at the heart of the East of England (Anglian) region. This region and its catchments represent the driest area of England and Wales. In the face of the growing scarcity of water resources and the need for a more integrated assessment and management strategy, much discussion in the UK has focused on the efficiency of water use and the efficient allocation of water resources among different users. Given the generic goal of sustainable water resource management, the environmental regulator for England and Wales, the Environment Agency, is developing an integrated assessment and management framework in which water is an integral component of a catchment-wide ecosystem. This approach, together with a new perspective on flooding and flood alleviation policy will have significant implications for the Broads wetland.

The Environment Agency strategy has attempted to look 25 years ahead (via scenario analysis) in order to maintain enough water for human uses, together with an improved water environment (EA, 2001). Its analysis has indicated that surface water throughout the region is already fully committed to existing abstractions and the environment during the summer, and that no significant additional quantities of water are available then. This has implications within the Broads where fenland is particularly susceptible to lowered water table conditions. Winter surface water is still available over most of the region, apart from some small chalk catchments and coastal streams. Much of the region's groundwater resources are already in broad balance and, therefore, any new abstractions would be subject to rigorous local assessment before they could be granted. In some areas, abstraction rates are already judged to be excessive. Scenario analysis has been used to consider future demand for water, which is likely to be dominated by public water supply. The rate of growth of this requirement is among the fastest in England and Wales. Finally, the region is probably the most at risk in the UK from climate change and in particular fluvial and coastal flooding risks.

The response strategy, at catchment and above scales, will include improvements to existing public water supply schemes and the development of new resources (for example water transfer schemes). The latter option brings with it a number of ecological uncertainties as river flows are diverted into new catchments. Much emphasis will be placed on increased efficiency in water use; with household metering being debated widely together with the implications for existing and new tourism facilities; other examples of efficiency-enhancing schemes include farmers being encouraged to either switch regimes or invest in on-farm storage of water, or to adopt both options. Broadland will also be the test bed for an innovative flood alleviation scheme which will pioneer 'soft' engineering solutions wherever feasible; and will be financed through a public–private partnership scheme.

## 2   INSTITUTIONAL ARRANGEMENTS

Broadland is managed by an official agency, the Broads Authority (BA), with powers similar to other UK National Park authorities, plus a navigation duty. But the BA is not subject to the Sandford Principle, which mandates primary status for nature conservation in all the other UK National Park areas. The BA's statutory duties are focused around the requirement to balance navigation, nature conservation and recreation/amenity interests.

Its three core purposes can be summarized as:

- conservation of the Broads wildlife
- conservation of the Broads cultural heritage and promotion of understanding as well as enjoyment of the Broads
- protection of the interests of navigation.

This complex political, economic and environmental trade-off process is becoming even more difficult as a result of recent EU Directives (notably The Birds and Habitats Directive). This regulatory approach has at its core a rather 'static' interpretation of nature protection. Such an interpretation does not sit easily with the BA's remit of 'balancing' different interests in order to manage sustainably all the assets within its executive area. The navigation duty sometimes proves to be at odds with the provision of quiet public enjoyment and the conservation of the area's natural beauty. A further recent EU Directive, The Water Framework Directive, has added to the complexity of the BA's management task. This Directive has introduced management duties that extend spatially up to the catchment scale and that also emphasize a co-ordinated approach across different functional activities. The Directive also highlights the need for a more deliberative and inclusionary approach to decision-making. The growing influence of these Directives, together with Sustainable Development principles, will be pinpointed in the following sections.

## 3   ENVIRONMENTAL CONTEXT

The Broads provide a large variety of habitats and landscape types, which are linked to form a lowland wetland ecosystem. The area consists of a network of rivers and shallow lakes surrounded by calcareous fens and drained marshes. The area (approximately 300 km$^2$) has national park status and the Broads Authority (BA) was established in 1989 to co-ordinate its management with duties for conservation, recreation and navigation. The statutory duties of the BA, however, constrain the range of available policy options, because no one interest (that is nature conservation, recreation and tourism promotion or maintenance of navigation rights) can be assigned dominant significance. The Authority has to operate by making sometimes pragmatic trade-offs, subject to EU Directives and national legislation and guidance, including the UK's sustainable development strategy.

The rivers and connected broads are intensively used for recreational boating, involving around 100 boatyard operators in the area. The main threats to the conservation of the wetland ecosystem are water pollution, further growth of water-based tourism, intensification of agricultural and other land use in the wider catchment, neglect of the fens and carr woodland and increased risk of saline intrusion and flooding (Madgwick and Phillips, 1996).

The Broads wetlands provide a buffer against extreme hydrological conditions, providing water storage in times of flood, and water release during drought. Wetlands also have the capacity to change water quality through the removal of chemical pollutants such as nitrogen and phosphate. A third major function is the provision of a nationally and internationally important habitat for flora and fauna (including a number of rare species) which in turn attracts tourists to the area. Most recently it has been recognized that management of the surrounding fenland has to be made more effective and efficient. This will involve a switch from traditional labour intensive cutting methods to a more mechanized approach. The BA has also been pioneering a scheme which aims to utilize the biomass produced by the fen in a variety of ways – animal bedding, feed pellets or as a source of energy (Broads Authority, 2000), see Table 10.1.

The BA is currently trying to achieve a set of high level objectives encompassed within its duty to achieve a sustainable balance between the sometimes competing interests within its executive area. The task is further complicated by the recognition that at least catchment-scale management is required, by the reality of insufficient scientific data, and the mismatch between the administrative boundaries and the environment systems that are to be conserved. Given its nature conservation duty, the objective is to maximize ecosystem function diversity, that is to conserve the ability of the wetland to provide as wide a range of 'valued' goods and services as is practicable. The Broads environment (three overlapping zones containing saline, brackish and freshwater conditions respectively) is coming under increasing pressure from human activity, climate change and sea level rise. Much of the fen and drained marsh areas have become degraded and require substantial restoration investment. Even the areas in a favourable ecological condition require active management and investment to maintain their status. At the project level, a diverse set of objectives are being pursued, ranging from reedbed creation to biomass processing to bring the fen under sustainable management.

Simultaneously, the BA has a duty to enhance the enjoyment of the Broads by visitors, which it fulfils through information centres and access-related facilities. It is also the local planning authority and is therefore responsible for planning applications and enforcement action, while seeking to protect the cultural heritage of the area. Finally, BA provides 125 miles of lock-free navigation, which it has a duty to protect and maintain for the safe enjoyment of the public. The need to dredge this system continuously and safely dispose of the dredged material has become an increasingly costly exercise, funded solely by boating interests' toll revenue. Figure 10.1 summarizes the range of pressures and related use conflicts that have arisen in Broadland.

We now turn to consider some of the research work, utilizing a mixed methodological approach, which has been carried out to address the policy challenges facing the Broads Authority in terms of the interrelated management problems it faces. This includes the funding and valuation of schemes to selectively protect nature conservation, recreation and other economic interests from flooding; stakeholder analysis looking at the management of public access to the Broads; and an analysis of the problem of eutrophication and some related feedback effects on the management of the Broads and related tourism pressures.

*Table 10.1  Wetland functions and associated socio-economic benefits in the Broads*

| Function | Biophysical structure or process maintaining function | Socio-economic use and benefits | Threats |
|---|---|---|---|
| **Hydrological Functions** | | | |
| Flood water retention | Short and long term storage of overbank flood water and retention of surface water runoff from surrounding slopes | Natural flood protection alternative, reduced damage to infrastructure (road network etc.), property and crops | Conversion, drainage, filling and reduction of storage capacity, removal of vegetation |
| Groundwater recharge | Infiltration of flood water in wetland surface followed by percolation to aquifer | Water supply, habitat maintenance | Reduction of recharge rates, overpumping pollution |
| Groundwater discharge | Upward seepage of ground water through wetland surface | Effluent dilution | Drainage, filling |
| Sediment retention and deposition | Net storage of fine sediments carried in suspension by river water during overbank flooding or by surface runoff from other wetland units or contributory area | Improved water quality downstream, soil fertility | Channelization, excess reduction of sediment throughput |
| **Biogeochemical Functions** | | | |
| Nutrient retention | Uptake of nutrients by plants (N and P), storage in soil organic matter, absorption of N as ammonium, absorption of P in soil | Improved water quality | Drainage, water abstraction, removal of vegetation, pollution, dredging |
| Nutrient export | Flushing through water system and gaseous export of N | Improved water quality, waste disposal | Drainage, water abstraction, removal of vegetation, pollution, flow barriers |
| Peat accumulation | In situ retention of C | Fuel, Paleo-environmental data source | Overexploitation, drainage |
| *Ecological functions* | | | |
| Habitat for (migratory) species (biodiversity) | Provision of microsites for macro-invertebrates, fish, reptiles, birds, mammals and landscape structural diversity | Fishing, wildfowl hunting, recreational amenities, tourism | Overexploitation, overcrowding and congestion, wildlife disturbance, pollution, interruption of migration routes, management neglect |
| Nursery for plants, animals, micro-organisms | Provision of microsites for macro-invertebrates, fish, reptiles, birds, mammals | Fishing, reed harvest | Overexploitation, overcrowding and wildlife disturbance, management neglect |
| Food web support | Biomass production, biomass import and export via physical and biological processes | Farming, fen biomass as alternative energy source | Conversion, extensive use of inputs (pollution), market failures |

*Source:*  Modified from Turner *et al.* (2000) and Burbridge (1994).

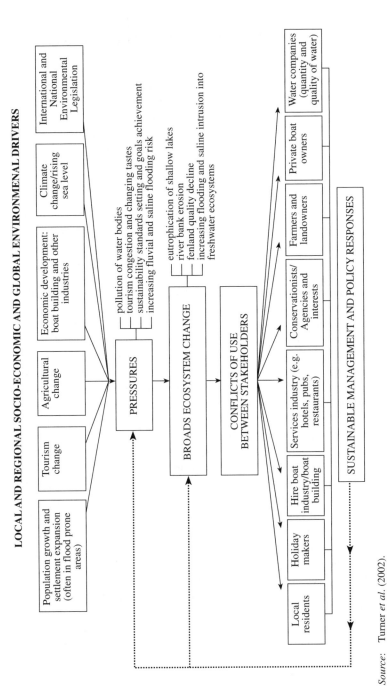

**LOCAL AND REGIONAL SOCIO-ECONOMIC AND GLOBAL ENVIRONMENAL DRIVERS**

Population growth and settlement expansion (often in flood prone areas)

Tourism change

Agricultural change

Economic development: boat building and other industries

Climate change/rising sea level

International and National Environmental Legislation

**PRESSURES**

pollution of water bodies
tourism congestion and changing tastes
sustainability standards setting and goals achievement
increasing fluvial and saline flooding risk

**BROADS ECOSYSTEM CHANGE**

eutrophication of shallow lakes
river bank erosion
fenland quality decline
increasing flooding and saline intrusion into freshwater ecosystems

**CONFLICTS OF USE BETWEEN STAKEHOLDERS**

Local residents

Holiday makers

Hire boat industry/boat building

Services industry (e.g. hotels, pubs, restaurants)

Conservationists/ Agencies and interests

Farmers and landowners

Private boat owners

Water companies (quantity and quality of water)

**SUSTAINABLE MANAGEMENT AND POLICY RESPONSES**

*Source:* Turner *et al.* (2002).

*Figure 10.1 Pressures facing the Broads and consequent conflicts of use*

## 4   THE VALUATION OF NATURE CONSERVATION, RECREATION AND OTHER ECONOMIC INTERESTS AT RISK FROM FLOODING

As a consequence of the ongoing and increasing risk of flooding within Broadland, in 1990 the National Rivers Authority initiated a wide ranging study to develop an 'effective and cost-effective strategy to alleviate flooding in Broadland for the next 50 years' (Bateman *et al.* 1992). Following on from work on the market costs and benefits of flood alleviation schemes (Turner and Brooke, 1988), the principal task of the CBA was to estimate values for the non-market goods concerned. In particular estimation of the nature conservation and informal recreational values were seen as a central objective of this study. In 1991 a contingent valuation (CV) study was commissioned to assess the benefits of preserving the existing landscape, ecology and recreational characteristics of the area relative to their expected values in the absence of a Broadland-wide flood alleviation scheme. The study consisted of two surveys: (i) a postal survey of households across the UK designed to capture the values which non-users might hold for preservation of the present state of Broadland and (ii) an investigation of the values held by users for the same scenario as elicited through an on-site survey. Further theoretical and methodological investigations were undertaken via a second on-site survey conducted in 1996.

The results of the postal survey of non-users are reported elsewhere (Bateman *et al.,* 1992). We focus here on the various on-site CV surveys of visitors to Broadland. Users were asked their willingness to pay, in the form of extra personal taxation, for flood defences in Broadland, in the expectation that this would provide protection for the existing landscape, ecology and recreational characteristics of the area.

The survey questionnaires were designed in accordance with the 'Total Design Method' (Dillman, 1978) and pre-tested through focus group and pilot exercises. The information provided included visual, map and textual materials detailing the nature of Broadland, the flooding problems and flood defence options together with necessary details supporting a willingness to pay question such as payment vehicle, payment time frame, and so on. The studies generally conformed to the CV testing protocol laid down subsequently by the NOAA blue ribbon panel (Arrow *et al.*, 1993).

The 1991 Survey design was extensively pre-tested across a total pilot sample of some 433 respondents. One of the many findings of this process was that a tax-based annual payment vehicle appeared optimal when assessed over a range of criteria (Bateman *et al.*, 1993). In addition to the main objective of benefit estimation, the study also investigated the impact on stated values of various elicitation methods.

The final questionnaire was applied through on-site interviews with visitors at representative sites around Broadland, 2897 questionnaires being completed. This sample was composed of 846 interviewees given an open-ended (OE) elicitation WTP questionnaire and the remaining 2051 facing in turn the single bound dichotomous choice (1DC) and interactive bidding (IB) elicitation questions. The OE elicitation method asks the respondent 'How much are you willing to pay?', to which he or she is free to state any amount. The 1DC elicitation method faces respondents with a single question such as 'are you willing to pay £$x$?' and then the bid level £$x$ is varied across the sample. The IB method supplements the initial question with two further dichotomous choice questions reducing £$x$ or increasing £$x$ according to the answers given. The respondent is then finally given an OE question, the answer to which determines the WTP value used by the analysts. Prior to any WTP question, respondents were presented with a 'payment principle' question. Negative responses to this question reduced sample sizes to 715 (OE) and 1811 (1DC/IB) respectively.

The theoretical validity of responses to the various WTP questions was assessed through the estimation of a series of bid functions. The analysis indicated that a consistent set of predictors explain WTP responses including measures of respondent income, experience of Broadland and participation in related activities and interest in environmental issues. It was also found that there were strong impacts on the stated values of varying the elicitation method, with OE responses providing the most conservative estimates and the IB format yielding intermediate results. Table 10.2 shows the mean and median WTP amounts estimated from the responses given to the dichotomous choice elicitation questions. These are shown for various parametric and non-parametric estimation methods used in the analysis (Brouwer and Bateman, 2000). In addition, the comparable mean and median WTP estimates from the 1996 survey are also shown. The mean and median WTP values found in both the 1991 and 1996 surveys are similar and therefore provide some evidence of temporal stability over the period between the two surveys.

The 1991 CV study fed into a wider cost–benefit analysis that also examined the agricultural, property and infrastructure damage-avoidance benefits of such defences (Turner, Adger and Doktor, 1995). The benefit–cost ratio of the latter items was calculated at 0.98 (NRA, 1992). However, even if only a conservative measure of WTP (using the OE responses) for the recreational and environmental benefits of flood prevention is considered, the benefit–cost ratio increases substantially to 1.94 indicating that the benefits of a flood alleviation strategy are almost twice the associated costs. The results, including findings from the CV study were submitted to the then Ministry of Agriculture, Fisheries and Food as part of an application of central government funding support for the proposed flood alleviation strategy. Following lengthy consideration of this application, the Environment Agency announced

*Table 10.2  Mean and median WTP values based on parametric and non-parametric models[1]*

| | 1991 | | | | 1996 | | | |
| | Parametric | | Non-parametric | | Parametric | | Non-parametric | |
| | Linear-logistic | Log-logistic | Turnbull approach | Ayer et al. approach | Linear-logistic | Log-logistic | Turnbull approach | Ayer et al. approach |
|---|---|---|---|---|---|---|---|---|
| Mean WTP | 248.2 | – | 180.1 | 116.1 | 257.2 | – | 204.3 | 83.5 |
| Standard error | 12.1 | – | 101.6 | – | 17.9 | – | 14.9 | – |
| Median WTP | 248.2 | 144.2 | – | 70.0 | 257.2 | 207.9 | – | 51.5 |
| Standard error | 12.1 | 9.7 | – | – | 17.9 | 29.1 | – | – |
| Min–max | – – + | 0 – 200 | 0 – 200 | 0 – 200 | – – + | 0 – 200 | 0 – 200 | 0 – 200 |
| n | 1747 | 1747 | 1747 | 1747 | 1108 | 1108 | 1108 | 1108 |

*Note:* 1.  In 1991 prices.

258

in 1997 that it had received conditional approval for a programme for 'bank strengthening and erosion protection'. The actual scheme is being taken forward from 2001 on the basis of a long-term private–public partnership scheme (between the EA and relevant government support ministries and a private engineering firm consortium).

While the valuation work indicates that the public does put significant value on the environment that Broadland provides, the costs of flood protection provision are also likely to escalate in the future, in particular if climate change related impacts are experienced. Over the 1990s the Environment Agency has formulated a selective approach to flood alleviation and not a strategy which will provide an area-wide uniform level of protection. A number of communities and business sites are currently at high risk from flooding (so-called 'undefended areas') as levels of protection vary across the area. The Broadland area is the subject of an experiment in terms of flooding alleviation scheme funding. A joint public and private funding initiative (PPP/PFI) has been launched which provides public funding over a 20-year period, to be spent by a private consortium. Regulatory agencies, the Environment Agency and the Broads Authority, will be part of a project board which will oversee the operation of the scheme and will ensure that it is compatible with the range of national area and local management plans (see Figure 10.2). Apart from the long term partnership feature of the PPP/PFI, it is also envisaged that local stakeholder consultations and liaison will be an important component of the arrangements. This is in line with guideline arrangements that have been set out in the EU Water Framework Directive.

## 5 MANAGING PUBLIC ACCESS TO ENVIRONMENTALLY SENSITIVE AREAS: A STAKEHOLDER ANALYSIS

Boats are the best and often only way to access the Norfolk and Suffolk Broads. Sailing on these waterways requires a high level of skill. The alternative for most people is motor boats. For the majority of people who are not able to own their own boat, the hire boat industry is a convenient alternative. However, the number and popularity of motor boats brings with it the problem of overcrowding and affects the very reasons why people appreciate and visit the Broads. Large numbers of motor boats have a negative effect on the natural environment and disturb the peace and quiet that most people appreciate when visiting the area. This is an issue which is central to the Broads Authority's management remit, and has recently been researched (Brouwer, Turner and Voisey, 2002).

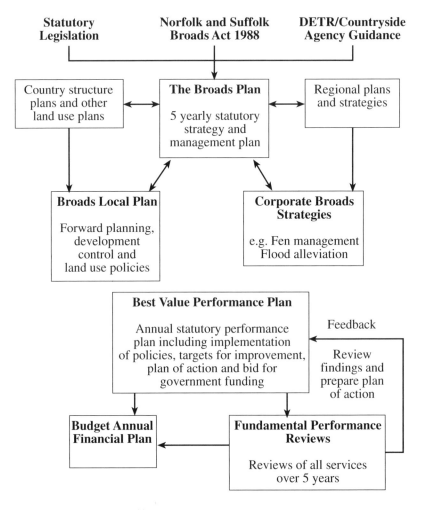

*Source*:   Broads Authority (2002).

*Figure 10.2   The planning regime*

In order to assess boat users' perceptions of the overcrowding issue and to facilitate improved management, between summer 1997 and spring 1998 a mixed methodology stakeholder analysis was undertaken combining a quantitative survey of some 238 respondents and two qualitative focus group sessions. These analyses targeted both those who hire and own boats on the Broads, be they local residents or living elsewhere in the UK.

The main objectives of this research were (i) to assess the perception of overcrowding held by the two main user groups of the Broads waterways, and (ii) to explore their attitudes to and preferences for various ways to manage the perceived and experienced problems, including the use of economic instruments.

The combination of face-to-face interviews and group discussions was expected to provide an interesting and policy-relevant blend of qualitative and quantitative information. The survey generated mostly quantitative data, while the data from the group discussions was mainly qualitative in nature. Both survey formats suffered from a low number of '*statistically valid*' observations, so that results have to be interpreted with the necessary care. However, both survey formats nevertheless produced useful insights into the current situation in the Broads (Brouwer, Turner and Voisey, 2002).

More experienced and frequent users of the Broads such as local residents and private boat owners perceived overcrowding and congestion as more of a problem than less experienced and more infrequent users. Obviously, the former have a better idea of problems that may arise and usually have a long-term interest in the area, whereas the latter perhaps visit once or twice and maybe never again. From the group discussions with local motor boat owners, it became clear that the problems associated with overcrowding are not only an issue of quantity, although this was the main focus of the questionnaire survey. How people spend their holidays or day out in the Broads is equally important. Increasing awareness of the unique characteristics of the Broads, such as the slow pace of the narrow rivers and small shallow lakes, and corresponding behavioural changes in the way the Broads waterways are used were considered major focus points in any strategy to address overcrowding problems.

The way the authority responsible for the Broads addresses or manages the conflicting interests in the area was distrusted by the local boat owners. Although a few boat owners still felt a need to address the quantity of boats as well as the quality side of the problem, half of the boat owners did not trust the responsible authority to take their recreational navigation interests sufficiently into account in managing the area. Some strategic behaviour may have played a role here since some boat owners were concerned that discussing ceilings on the number of boats would limit their own right of access to the Broads waterways. Many were afraid that suggested management options such as voluntary zoning in time and space of different recreational activities to balance recreational and conservation interests would result little by little in a complete shutdown of the area for motorized navigation. Although the majority of boat owners believed that recreational navigation and nature conservation were indeed conflicting interests, most did not think that these conflicts were irreconcilable. However, they felt that they were underrepresented in the Broads Authority and given insufficient opportunity to express their opinions in decisions that affect them as an important stakeholder group in the area. Partly in response to the trust and accountability deficit problem, the BA has enacted a number of institutional changes, which are examined in more detail in the penultimate section of this chapter.

Whereas trust in the authority responsible for managing the area played a major role in the group discussions, public right of access, fairness and possibly some strategic behaviour also significantly influenced the results from the questionnaire survey. Half of the surveyed sample felt that present boat numbers do not cause any problems, even though interviewing took place at the busiest time of the year in the most crowded part of the Broads. The other half felt that boat numbers should be reduced, and were even willing to contribute financially to achieve this goal.

However, the fairness of excluding others from using the Broads waterways significantly influenced whether or not respondents agreed with the principle of reducing public access by increasing the price of access, that is, a market based approach. Visitors who considered the effects of higher hire prices on others while answering this question were less likely to agree with the principle of raising hire prices to reduce overcrowding than visitors who did not.

Some strategic behaviour is suspected to underlie the responses of those respondents who claimed that current boat numbers were not a problem since, in effect, they were asked whether they consider themselves to be part of a problem. Moreover, the proposed changes in the Broads to reduce overcrowding by increasing hire prices may have been perceived as very real or likely, promoting some people to behave strategically by denying that there currently is an overcrowding problem.

An economic, market based approach can be an effective tool for reducing boat numbers in the Broads, and therefore congestion and overcrowding. Visitors were very sensitive to suggested increases in hire prices. However, the general acceptability and hence political feasibility of using a market based approach solely to reduce overcrowding symptoms in the Broads seems rather low, and is expected to be reinforced if the local and regional economic impacts of reduced access to the Broads are also considered. A combination of policy tools is more likely to be successful and this was confirmed by the findings of the group discussions. Overcrowding and congestion is as much about the quality of boat usage as it is about the total number of boats on the Broads. Therefore, policies need to address both these aspects to be successful. Another key element to the management of the Broads waterways and the implementation of policies to tackle problems such as overcrowding is the institutional framework provided by the BA. It appears from the research presented here that there have been missed opportunities to involve stakeholders in decision-making, thereby improving the effectiveness of management strategies. New institutional reforms are meant to address this challenge (see section 7).

# 6   COMBATING EUTROPHICATION AND RELATED FEEDBACK EFFECTS

The trade-off process involved in the management of the Broads is becoming more difficult as a result of recent EU Directives (notably the Birds and Habitats Directive) and this has been highlighted in the case of Hickling Broad. This is a water body that over the last 30 years or so has become a focal point for private and other sail and power boaters. Rights of navigation are restricted to a specified channel, but boating has become possible over a large part of the surface water body. In more recent years as water quality has been improved, aquatic plant growth has accelerated and sections of the water body have become virtually inaccessible to navigation.

Restoration policies promoted by the BA have reduced nutrient flow into the Norfolk Broads and greatly improved water quality. In Hickling Broad these measures have proved to be especially successful insofar as they have encouraged the return of previously threatened aquatic plants. However, the thickness of plant growth served to slow down boat traffic and adversely affected local sailing competitions. As part of its overall commitment to supporting the sustainable development of the Broads, the BA has a statutory duty to maintain the area for the purposes of navigation. It also tries to encourage environmentally friendly boating. But, the increasingly dense beds of aquatic plant (a rare species of stonewort) growth were obstructing non-powered and electrically-powered craft, and local boatyards began to revert to using diesel-powered craft on Hickling Broad, thereby increasing noise and water pollution.

All these factors threaten the economic viability of Hickling Broad as a leisure resource and were perceived to have serious impacts upon the local tourist industry. The BA therefore decided to address the problem, starting with a series of small-scale plant cutting trials in 1994, followed by more extensive cutting in 1995. After a dramatic change in 1998, when the water went from being turbid to clear and macrophytes grew to an unprecedented height of 1m, above the bed of the Broad, the BA sought to introduce a more widespread cutting policy. English Nature (EN), the statutory agency for nature conservation in England and Wales, opposed this on the grounds that the cutting of aquatic plants is likely to have a significant effect on the conservation of the Broads, a candidate Special Area of Conservation (SAC). SACs are further designations created under the EC Habitats Directive, which aim to contribute towards biological diversity by conserving natural habitats and wild fauna and flora of significance to the European Community. Each member country should contribute to the designation of SACs, which together will result in a coherent network of SACs, called Natura 2000. The Directive requires governments to protect natural habitats and their wildlife species, while taking account of economic, social and cultural requirements and regional and local characteristics. Whereas EN cannot prevent the BA's intended programme of cutting, when part IV of the 1994 Regulations is applied to the Authority's harbour functions the approval of the Secretary of State will be required before the Authority can proceed. In addition, if any other body with sufficient interest in the matter considers that the BA are not complying with the obligations imposed on them by the Habitats Directive and/or the 1994 Regulations, they may take injunctive proceedings against the Authority to stop the works.

The BA decided that in line with UK government policy, candidate SACs should be treated as if they were approved SACs and that assessment of the potential impact of the proposed cutting on the conservation features of the Broad would be carried out. The BA established, in early 1999, a team of independent experts to help conduct the assessment in order to determine whether the management actions (plant cutting) represent a significantly adverse effect on the ecological integrity of the site. The panel reported in July 1999 and unanimously agreed that, given the application of the precautionary principle, the extensive cutting programme originally proposed did pose a threat to the integrity of the ecosystem. The panel therefore recommended a reduced cutting programme, covering only 14.8 ha of the water body in blocks around the navigation channel. The total open water area available in the Broad is 130 ha, excluding fringe reed swamp which covers 11 ha. The cutting regime must allow plants to grow up to 40 cm above the bed of the Broad, and was to be completed before August 1999, accompanied by a careful monitoring effort. The panel also highlighted the need for a wider spatial area management plan which encompassed the relevant river system, the Upper Thurne.

The scale of plant cutting approved by the BA was in line with the panel's recommendations and meant that boating activity across the traditional area of 80 ha of the Broad would be severely curtailed. The wider management plan idea was also accepted together with the need to monitor over-wintering birds on Hickling Broad and to quantify more precisely the socio-economic impacts of curtailed sailing activities in Hickling Broad. The monitoring of cutting operations has resulted in the cut height being increased to 60 cm above the bed of the Broad.

The BA reviewed its policy and the environmental condition of Hickling Broad in the spring of 2000. It was found that the clarity of the water in the lake had regressed and that the stonewort plant community had collapsed back towards the lake bottom. The expert panel concluded that neither the water quality deterioration nor the lack of plant biomass was due to the plant cutting programme. They believe that the Broad is still in an unstable condition and that increased winter rain and river flows in the wider catchment have probably flushed more nutrients and sediment into the Broads, causing the increased water turbidity. In the light of these conditions the expert panel advised against any plant cutting if the turbidity conditions do not improve. If the water does clear then a similar plant cutting programme to that undertaken in 1999 will be recommended. During the summer of 2001 plant growth accelerated once again, but this time overall water turbidity conditions did not improve. The expert panel recommended a policy of no plant cutting.

The BA has also been engaging in stakeholder consultations and has agreed with the navigation interests that the area to be potentially cut in the future should be configured in a way as to give sailors and other boaters the maximum feasible 'manoeuvring space', without increasing the total plant cut area. A socio-economic analysis of the implications of reduced or no sailing/boating activities on Hickling Broad was also commissioned. The analysis indicated that the potential financial losses that might be incurred if plant growth was not curtailed in the future would be localized. Much of the possible lost activity at Hickling would transfer to other sites in the Broads and so economic losses at the regional scale would be negligible.

Clearly management of a dynamic and multiple use ecosystem is hindered if an inflexible interpretation of the EC Directives is adopted. A more flexible interpretation is essential to allow, in the Hickling case, experimental plant cutting and monitoring. Other management action to maintain navigation and recreation interests throughout the Broads executive area, will also fall foul of a static interpretation of the provisions of the Habitats Directive. Some room for manoeuvre may be possible in terms of whether all management actions necessarily need to be interpreted as 'projects' and therefore as requiring impact assessments. For an authority like the BA, the cost implications alone would make such a ruling impracticable. From the UK government perspective, there is an element of 'wait and see' in its position, as it monitors how events play out in the Broads context. From the BA's perspective there is a need to achieve a working compromise, or at least to engage stakeholders in an ongoing process of dialogue (O'Riordan and Ward, 1997). Efforts are under way to promote such a deliberative and participatory process in order to achieve a reasonable compromise between navigation and conservation needs. It is also now clear that the management objective can only be the maintenance of relative stability in Broads conditions and that the catchment scale has to be the minimum basis adopted.

The stakeholder dialogue has been constantly widened and now has also to encompass flood risk and policy response issues. The BA has therefore been encouraged to look at its organizational structure and to determine whether it is currently configured in a way that is most appropriate for a transition to a more sustainability orientated agency. The short answer it came up with was no.

## 7   INSTITUTIONAL CHANGE

The combination of the lack of trust/accountability felt by some stakeholders in the BA, the need for a more integrated and catchment-based management plan and strategy and the general trend towards the setting up of more inclusionary and deliberative forms of decision-making, has served to galvanize efforts directed at organizational reform.

The UK government is currently reviewing all National Parks and the BA sees this as an opportune time to set out its case for increased funding, given the particularly complex management tasks it has been set. The BA is required by a 1988 Act to prepare a Broads Plan every five years. A new Plan is due in 2003 and the BA sees the development of this new Plan as a way of taking forward both a more integrated and inclusionary strategy, in line with sustainability thinking. The BA sees an opportunity to construct a new relationship with Government, based on a higher level of funding but also a clearer line of accountability. A five-year costed Action Plan will run in parallel with the Broads Plan and beneath this an annual Business Plan setting out the targets for the year; the full picture is given in Figure 10.2.

As part of the transition to a more sustainability oriented organization, the BA is proposing to change its name, and has changed its committee structure and its internal staff/management structure. Figures 10.3 summarizes the old and new committee structures. The new proposals serve to streamline the bureaucracy, reduce staff and member meetings, other resource costs, and reinforce the integrated management theme. Longer term, the total number of the members of the Authority (currently a mix of local authority elected members and government appointees) would also be reduced. But this change would require legislative reform. In order also to take forward a more inclusionary decision-making process, a range of advisory panels and groups that currently exist has been combined into one body, the Broads Forum, which is independently chaired and represents all the relevant stakeholders. To ensure the necessary support for all these institutional changes the staff structure of the BA was also reformed. The old structure reflected the functions of the Authority: conservation, recreation and tourism, planning and administration. They tended to polarize opinions and to inhibit a co-ordinated management approach. The fragmented management of the practical day-to-day work of the Authority therefore militated against priority setting, coping with regular maintenance work, and responding to particular 'surprises'. The new structure jettisons the vertical tripartite functional division and instead imposes a more horizontal integrated arrangement.

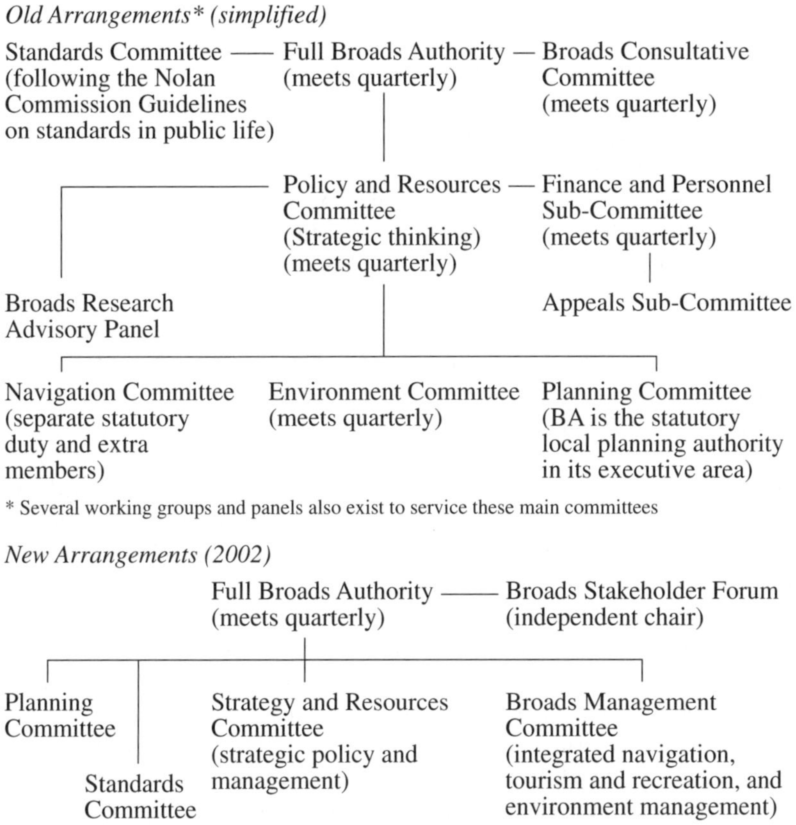

*Old Arrangements\* (simplified)*

Standards Committee —— Full Broads Authority — Broads Consultative
(following the Nolan        (meets quarterly)        Committee
Commission Guidelines                                (meets quarterly)
on standards in public life)

                          Policy and Resources — Finance and Personnel
                          Committee               Sub-Committee
                          (Strategic thinking)    (meets quarterly)
                          (meets quarterly)

Broads Research                                     Appeals Sub-Committee
Advisory Panel

Navigation Committee      Environment Committee   Planning Committee
(separate statutory       (meets quarterly)       (BA is the statutory
duty and extra                                    local planning authority
members)                                          in its executive area)

\* Several working groups and panels also exist to service these main committees

*New Arrangements (2002)*

                  Full Broads Authority —— Broads Stakeholder Forum
                  (meets quarterly)        (independent chair)

Planning          Strategy and Resources   Broads Management
Committee         Committee                Committee
                  (strategic policy and    (integrated navigation,
        Standards management)              tourism and recreation, and
        Committee                          environment management)

*Source*:  BA personal communications, 2001/2002.

*Figure 10.3    Broads Authority committee structures*

# 8   DISCUSSION, CONCLUSIONS AND POLICY IMPLICATIONS

The Broads wetland area is a classic multiple use resource under heavy and sustained environmental pressures and subject to dynamic ecosystem change. The DPSIR organizing framework was successfully used to scope the magnitude and significance of the environmental change problems and consequent sustainable management policy response issues. The saline water inundation/flooding and its alleviation, tourism requirements and preferences and water quality-related conflict problems, have been highlighted.

The co-evolving semi-natural/human system represented by the wetland and surrounding catchment will continue to pose complex scientific and management problems. It is clear from the Hickling Broad experience, for example, that there is still a significant degree of scientific uncertainty surrounding the factors that influence the ecosystem and its ambient quality. Thus the scientific management objective can only, realistically, be the maintenance of relative stability within limits. As our scientific understanding improves, the limits may be more precisely defined.

From a methodological perspective it also becomes clear that a mixed quantitative/qualitative approach is necessary in order to address the various stakeholder conflict situations and their possible mitigation. The use of cost–benefit analysis (CBA) in environmental decision-making and the contingent valuation (CV) technique as input into CBA to elicit monetized environmental values has stimulated an extensive debate. Critics have questioned the appropriateness of both the method and the technique. Some alternative suggestions for the elicitation of environmental values are based on a social process of deliberation. However, just like traditional economic theory, these alternative approaches may be questioned in terms of their implicit value judgements. The view taken in this research was that instead of making a priori assumptions, research efforts should be focused on the processes by which actual public attitudes and preferences towards the environment can best be elicited and fed into the policy process. Our research findings support both the individual WTP based approach and a participatory social deliberation approach. This suggests that a combination of both approaches can be appropriately deployed. More work is, however, required in order to be able to state more confidently which valuation contexts are most appropriate and what exact configuration of the mixed methodology should be used.

In the case of the flood alleviation planning for Broadland, a WTP-based valuation exercise did produce a set of meaningful monetary valuations, confirming *inter alia*, previous survey results in the early 1990s and before. A combination of quantitative and qualitative social research formats, including face-to-face interviewing and focus group discussions were used to reveal user group views. Underlying tensions and actual and potential resource use conflicts were revealed in, for example, the boating and overcrowding research.

The case of Hickling Broad provided a stark example of conflict, between nature conservation and navigation interests. It also highlighted the problems that EC Directives such as the Birds and Habitat Directives can potentially pose for management agencies seeking to control the rate of change in dynamic, complex and multiple use environmental systems. An overly static interpretation of the provisions of such Directives will exacerbate significant cost and stakeholder conflict problems, not just in wetlands but in other areas under environmental change pressure such as coastal zones (Salomons *et al.*, 1999).

A key to resolving present failures thus seems to be behavioural change at the local level. Increased scientific knowledge of wetland ecosystems and their benefits to society has to be gained hand-in-hand with efforts to increase public awareness of these benefits. Such a communication is however only likely to be successful if due account is taken of the potential difference in world views between the scientists and local people. Likewise, special attention should be paid to existing stakeholder structure, and existing local ecological knowledge and local institutional arrangements for maintaining wetlands. Such institutions may constitute a basis for building wetland management institutions that have already gained social acceptability at the local level, in contrast to governmental regulations imposed in top-down fashion.

# REFERENCES

Arrow, K., R. Solow, P.R. Portney, E.E. Learner, R. Radner and H. Schuman (1993), 'Report of the NOAA Panel on contingent valuation', *Federal Register*, 15 January, **58**(10), 4601–14.

Bateman, I.J., I.H. Langford, K.G. Willis, R.K. Turner and G.D. Garrod (1993), 'The impacts of changing willingness to pay question format in contingent valuation studies: an analysis of open-ended, iterative bidding and dichotomous choice formats', CSERGE Working paper, GEC 1993–05, Centre for Social and Economic Research on the Global Environment, University of East Anglia and University College London, UK.

Bateman, I.J., K.G. Willis, G.D. Garrod, P. Doktor, I.H. Langford and R.K. Turner (1992), 'Recreational and environmental preservation value of the Norfolk Broads: A contingent valuation study', unpublished report, Environmental Appraisal Group, University of East Anglia, UK.

Broads Authority (2000), *Life 97 ENV/UK/00511: New Wetlands Harvests Final Technical Report*, Broads Authority, Colegate, Norwich, UK.

Broads Authority (2002), *Best Value Performance Plan*, Broads Authority, Colegate, Norwich, UK.

Brouwer, R. and I.J. Bateman (2000), 'The temporal stability of contingent WTP values', CSERGE Working paper, GEC 2000–14, Centre for Social and Economic Research on the Global Environment, University of East Anglia and University College London, UK.

Brouwer, R., R.K. Turner and H. Voisey (2002), 'Public perception of overcrowding and management alternatives in a multi-purpose open access resource', *Journal of Sustainable Tourism*, **9**(6), 471–90.

Burbridge, P.R. (1994), 'Integrated planning and management of freshwater habitats, including wetlands', *Hydrobiologia*, **285**, 311–22.

Dillman, D.A. (1978), *Mail and Telephone Surveys – The Total Design Method*, New York: John Wiley.

Environment Agency (EA) (2001), *Water Resources for the Future: A Strategy for the Anglian Region*, London: HMSO.

Madgwick, F.J. and G.L. Phillips (1996), 'Restoration of the Norfolk Broads: final report to E.C. Life Programme', BARS14, Broads Authority, Norfolk, UK.

National Rivers Authority (NRA) (1992), 'A flood alleviation strategy for Broadland: final report annex four – Cost Benefit Studies', NRA, Anglian Region, Peterborough, UK.

O'Riordan, T. and R. Ward, (1997), 'Building trust in shoreline management: creating participatory consultation in shoreline management plans', *Land Use Policy*, **14**(4), 257–76.

Salomons, W., R.K. Turner, L.D. de Lacerda and S. Ramachandran (1999), *Perspectives on Integrated Coastal Zone Management*, Berlin: Springer.

Turner, R.K. and J. Brooke (1988), 'Management and valuation of an environmentally sensitive area: Norfolk Broadland, England, case study', *Environmental Management,* **12**(2), 193–207.

Turner, R.K., W.N. Adger and P. Doktor (1995), 'Assessing the economic costs of sea level rise', *Environment and Planning A,* **27**, 1777–96.

Turner, R.K., I.J. Bateman, S. Georgiou, A. Jones, and I.H. Langford (2002), 'An ecological economics approach to the "management" of a multi-purpose coastal wetland', *Regional Environmental Change*, forthcoming.

Turner, R.K., J.C.J.M. van den Bergh, T. Söderqvist, A. Barendregt, J. van der Straaten, E. Maltby and E.C. van Ierland (2000), 'Ecological–economic analysis of wetlands: scientific integration for management and policy', *Ecological Economics*, **35**(1), 7–23.

# 11. Spatial hydro-ecological and economic modelling of land use changes in wetlands[1]

## J.C.J.M. van den Bergh, A. Barendregt, A. Gilbert, M. van Herwijnen, P. van Horssen, P. Kandelaars and C. Lorenz

## 1 INTRODUCTION

Various studies have tried to study wetlands by integrating elements from hydrology and ecology, and from ecology and economics. Different approaches are presented by Barbier *et al.* (1994), Barendregt *et al.* (1992), Gilbert and Janssen (1998), Turner *et al.* (1998) and Brouwer *et al.* (1999). Nevertheless, integrating elements of the three fields in a single study, as reported in this chapter, is less common. General discussions as well as surveys of integrated modelling and evaluation of ecosystem management are offered by van den Bergh (1996), Braat and van Lierop (1987), Costanza *et al.* (1993), and Zuchetto and Jansson (1985).

The present study integrates information, concepts and models from social and natural sciences to analyse and evaluate land-use scenarios for the Vecht area ('De Vechtstreek') in the Netherlands. The groundwater table reaches the surface almost everywhere throughout this region. Typical wetland vegetation is found both in areas under agricultural use and natural areas. The approach followed is based on explicit spatial scenario formulation, modelling and evaluation. A valuation study was, however, considered too difficult, given the size and heterogeneity of the area. Valuation studies seem more suitable for smaller, more homogeneous areas (Gren *et al.*, 1994; Turner *et al.*, 1998).

This chapter is structured as follows. Section 2 provides the context for the study area, including a description of its present situation, its historical development, the problems it faces, prevailing policy and management practice, and development scenarios that will be studied with the integrated model and evaluation procedure. The present study has served to develop a method for examining solutions to these problems that is based on spatially disaggregated scenario analysis. Section 3 describes the construction of a spatial model of the

Vecht river basin, representing economic activities, hydrological processes and ecological responses. Section 4 covers the integrated modelling exercise including the development of performance indicators for the two evaluation objectives, viz. economic efficiency and environmental quality and, an evaluation of the environmental change scenarios with respect to these criteria. Sections 5, 6 and 7 present the main results. A more detailed report of the study can be found in van den Bergh *et al.* (1999).

## 2    THE STUDY AREA: ENVIRONMENTAL PRESSURES, STATE CHANGES AND POLICY RESPONSES

The Vecht area is located between the river Vecht to the west, the sandy hill ridge 't Gooi circa 8 km to the east, the Randmeer (part of a large lake which formerly was connected to the sea) to the north, and the city of Utrecht to the south (see Figure 11.1). The area is a wetland with many shallow lakes and fens interspersed with agricultural fields. Even where a solid soil is present, the water table is close to the surface.

The area overlaps two provinces (North Holland and Utrecht), covers some 262.6 km$^2$ including 10 municipalities, and has a population of 212 839. Large urban centres lie just outside the area. Agriculture and nature are the main land uses in the area; industry is virtually absent. Agricultural activities consist mostly of dairy farming with about half of the area covered by pastures. The majority of these are wet and located on peat soils. Surface water management in the polders is necessary to maintain these pastures with water tables about 40 cm below the surface. A system of ditches and pumps maintains water tables to a precision level of centimetres. The pastures are important for nature as well as agriculture: for example they provide nesting areas for many wading birds, plant species characteristic of wetlands coexist with pasture species, and the ditches and canals provide habitat for a variety of aquatic species.

Most species-rich and heritage landscape areas are owned by nature conservation organizations, both governmental and non-governmental. The variety in natural and artificial lakes, reedbeds, marshes, grasslands and alder forests creates a mixture of different succession phases characteristic of this type of wetland as well as a mixture of landscapes. The value of nature in this area is high. The whole area is part of the Dutch Ecological Network and one of its lakes, Naardermeer, is listed as a Ramsar wetland. This value is also reflected in the intensive outdoor recreation, including sailing, camping, and walking and cycling, that is characteristic of the area. In particular, many people from the nearby cities of Utrecht, Amsterdam and Hilversum are regular visitors to the area.

About a thousand years ago the Vecht area was largely bog (oligotrophic,

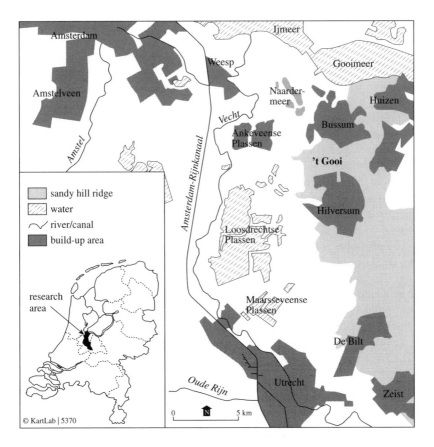

*Figure 11.1    The research area and its environs*

*Sphagnum* species) and uninhabited by humans. Its landscape was very differ-ent from the present one, which is largely a product of human habitation. Human activities meant land reclamation, with small ditches being dug to drain the upper soil. In the 16th and 17th century, the demand for fuel from the growing populations of Amsterdam and Utrecht was met, in part, by mining peat from the bogs, resulting in an enormous change in the landscape. Peat was dredged, leaving behind small ponds interspersed with strips of uncut areas where the peat was deposited to dry. Profit motives kept these strips as small as possible, sometimes so small that wave activity in the ponds eroded them. As a result many large lakes developed during the 18th and 19th centuries. One of these lakes (now polder Bethune) and a natural lake (Horstermeer) were reclaimed in the 19th century to facilitate agricultural exploitation. During the 17th and 18th century the landscape at the edge of this area was also re-shaped. Wealthy merchants from Amsterdam established estates with extensive gardens close to the river. Near the hill ridge at the eastern border, the sandy soil was excavated for use in the construction of canals in Amsterdam. The profits from this venture were used to establish estates in the areas from which the sand originated. These estates are now famous for their contribution to the national landscape and architectural heritage.

Until the middle of this century the competing land usages, agriculture, nature and housing in the Vecht area were roughly in balance. The intensity of agriculture and other human activities was relatively low and therefore biological diversity was high. This situation changed after 1945: intensive forms of recreation developed, notably sailing; the surface water became polluted; groundwater was abstracted for drinking water purposes; and agriculture intensified. All these developments increased the pressure on the area's wetlands.

The pressures and environmental changes that affected the Vecht wetlands area are intimately related to its hydrology, its chemistry and its physical planning. The balance between surface water and groundwater has changed. Groundwater and rainwater are the original sources of water for the wetlands. During the 1970s, 20 million $m^3$ of drinking water were abstracted annually from the hill ridge, reducing the input of groundwater substantially and resulting in lower water tables and less seepage in the wetlands. To compensate for high levels of evapotranspiration in the summer and to minimize soil subsidence as a result of mineralization of peat soils with their exposure to air, surface water from the river Vecht was let into the area. Further, the two reclaimed lakes (Bethune and Horstermeer), with their artificially low water levels, have effectively reversed the direction of local water flows. This was originally east to west, from the hill-ridge to the river, and is now more west to east, from the river to the wetlands.

A second problem, partly related to the changes discussed above, is that of water chemistry. The wetlands are suffering from nutrient enrichment as a result of a number of factors: the penetration of nutrient-rich water from the river Vecht into the wetlands, intensified agriculture, local sewerage treatment plants, mineralization of peat soils, and outflow from illegal waste-dumps. Algal blooms and a deterioration of the quality of nature in the area have been recorded. In particular, certain types of aquatic vegetation have disappeared, including a number of important 'red list' (threatened and protected) species. This problem is exacerbated by the absence of buffered groundwater in the root zone of the vegetation and increased acid deposition from the air.

A third problem is the pressure from the spatial pattern of human activities. Recreation and nature conservation are the main 'activities' in the central parts of the Vecht region. Recreation pressure has, however, been building steadily upwards. New marinas and campgrounds have been created, despite the potential conflict with nature. Attempts to intensify agriculture have met with mixed success due to technical restrictions on water tables and physical planning regulations to protect nature. Agriculture is the dominant economic activity in terms of profits in the north-west and the south of the area.

The post-1945 landscape, comprising extensive agriculture and relatively undisturbed wetlands, has been replaced by a landscape fragmented by human activities, notably housing and infrastructure. The areas available for nature have not only decreased in size, but are no longer interconnected. As a result, many areas have become too small to continue to support viable plant and animal populations.

Policy within the study area focuses either directly on specific activities, such as recreation or water use, or on the combination of different activities in specific areas via land-use regulation or physical planning. Policy drivers originate from three levels: national, regional and local. Municipalities and provinces, together with various special interest groups, undertake the actual management.

The national government preserves the international value of nature in the Vecht area via the imposition of Ramsar status for the wetland reserve 'Naardermeer'. This reserve is also incorporated in the assigned areas in the Habitat Directive (EU). The entire Vecht area is in the list of 'Areas Important for Birds' (Birds Directive, EU), which will be integrated with the Habitat Directive in the European ecological network NATURA 2000. The Vecht area has been assigned the 'green course' label (VROM, 1990), implying that the area is to remain rural or natural in character. In the Dutch Nature Policy Plan (LNV, 1990) it is defined as part of the ecological network of the Netherlands. This requires conservation of its nature reserves, and that farmers actively stimulate the development of nature in agricultural areas between nature reserves.

Physical planning promulgated by the two provincial governments, is consistent with the national policy, but is far more detailed. It defines the nature and agricultural areas, denotes areas for construction of buildings, and controls economic development. Trade and industry in the area are very much restricted by physical planning. The two provinces have, however, different opinions about agricultural development. The province of Utrecht strives as much as possible for physical or spatial separation of economic activities and nature areas, while the province of North Holland aims for an area where nature and agriculture are interwoven. The rationale behind the latter is that both nature and agriculture are part of the cultural landscape.

At the local level, 10 municipalities oversee a policy which generally conforms to provincial policy. Nevertheless, local decisions, especially with regard to housing, often conflict with higher level decisions. Other important local institutions include the Water Boards, which have created a separate set of regulations and taxes to support the management of surface water tables and surface water chemistry. Several local, regional and national nature preservation and nature management organizations, notably 'Natuurmonumenten' (an NGO) and 'Staatsbosbeheer' (the forestry service within the Ministry of Agriculture, Nature and Fisheries) have developed very detailed plans for nature creation, management, protection and restoration. Specific local and regional nature management activities focus on abstraction and storage basins for drinking water, restoration projects and nature development projects.

This section presents development scenarios for the Vecht area that will be tested by the models and then subsequently evaluated. These scenarios reflect choices made in physical planning, nature policy, agricultural policy and regulation of recreation, that is the main political and economic interests in the area. The scenarios are in line with contemporary policy perspectives. In particular the nature and recreation scenarios attempt to improve environmental quality in a corridor that runs north to south through the study area. The scenarios are spatially disaggregated and are formulated at the level of grids and polders. This contributes to both the accuracy and realism of the descriptions. The hydrological parameters are defined at a grid level (500 m × 500 m) and the economic parameters at a polder level (on average 200 ha). This is related to the fact that the hydrological model assumes homogeneity at the level of grids, and the economic model at the level of polders. Any information at a grid level can be easily aggregated to the polder level. Given that the integrated modelling approach is static, the scenarios are also static. They will be used in a comparative static analysis, where changes from a reference (or base) scenario are compared across alternative scenarios. Each scenario specifies land use and water levels at the polder level for the 73 polders which comprise the study area (see Figure 11.2).

## 3   ENVIRONMENTAL CHANGE SCENARIOS

The four development scenarios for the Vecht area are

- Reference (base or business-as-usual)
- Stimulation of agriculture
- Stimulation of nature
- Stimulation of recreation (see Table 11.1 for details).

These scenarios take the present conditions into account. Scenarios II to IV focus on core human activities in the region, and allow comparison of quite

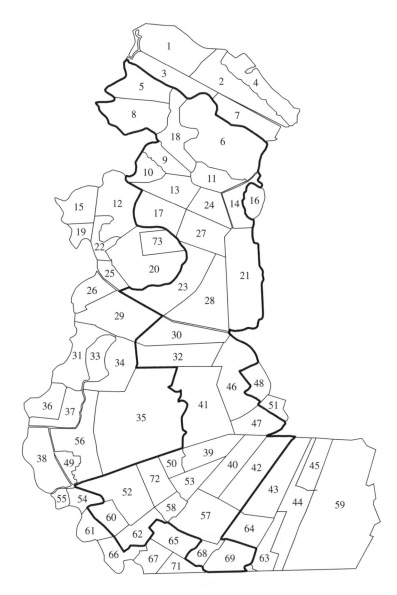

*Figure 11.2   The study area, its polders, and the corridor targeted by the scenarios for improved environmental quality*

*Table 11.1   Development scenarios for the Vecht area*

| Scenarios | Hydrological settings per polder | Economic settings per polder |
|---|---|---|
| I.   Reference | Present situation in all polders | Present situation in all polders |
| II.   Stimulation of agriculture (3 types of polder settings | 0: no change in water table<br>1: no change in water table<br><br>2: –0.2 m | 0: no change in land use<br>1: 50% conversion of present to intensive agriculture<br>2: 100% conversion of present to intensive agriculture |
| III.   Stimulation of nature (3 types of polder settings) | 0: no change in water table<br>1: +0.1 m<br>2: +0.2 m | 0: no change in land use<br>1: 50% of present agriculture converted to nature<br>2: 100% of present agriculture converted to nature |
| IV.   Stimulation of recreation (5 types of polder settings) | 0: no change in water table<br>1: +0.1 m<br>2: +0.2 m<br>3: polder flooded<br>4: no change in water table | 0: no change in land use<br>1: 50% of present agriculture converted to nature, and investments for outdoor recreation<br>2: 100% of present agriculture converted to nature, and investments for outdoor recreation<br>3: polder flooded and opened for recreation<br>4: water based recreation stimulated or intensified on existing open water |

distinct, although still realistic, future states of the Vecht area. Table 11.1 summarizes the scenario settings. Note that the agricultural scenario is very similar to the reference scenario because the present situation is largely the product of actions to improve the productivity of agriculture. Moreover, agriculture is subject to many spatial and hydrological restrictions needed to protect (a minimum level of) existing nature. These seriously limit opportunities for improving existing agricultural conditions and for extending the area used for agricultural purposes.

## 4　THE INTEGRATED SYSTEM OF SPATIAL MODELS

Figure 11.3 illustrates the three basic analytical levels that were encompassed by the study. The first level involves the formulation of development scenarios for the Vecht area that include consistent hydrological and economic parameters connections. The second level entails integration of hydrological quality and quantity modelling, vegetation response modelling, and economic modelling and accounting. The hydrological–ecological part of the modelling and analysis was performed on a grid basis, and subsequently aggregated to the level of polders, to make it consistent with the economic analysis.

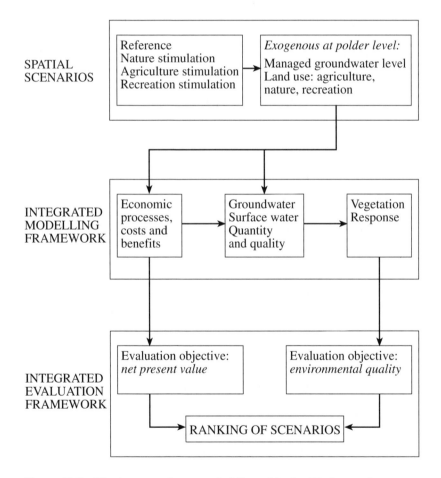

*Figure 11.3　The integrated approach followed in the 'Vecht area' case study*

Integration at this level includes explicit links between the natural science and economic models. This has focused on the inclusion of nutrient surpluses from agriculture in the water quality modelling, and on the influence of water quantity and quality on plant species occurrence.

The third integration level is split into two steps. The first one aggregates output from the models into performance indicators reflecting objectives in the evaluation. While the full study generated three performance indicators (see van den Bergh *et al.*, 1999), this chapter presents only two: net present value and environmental quality. The final and essential step in the integration is the evaluation procedure in which these performance indicators were used to rank scenarios. Two objectives drive this evaluation: economic efficiency and environmental quality. The latter attempts to capture ecological criteria describing how well wetland ecosystems are functioning.

Nature in undisturbed wetlands is in balance with its abiotic conditions. The aquatic and terrestrial vegetation represented by characteristic species is the key ecological element to be predicted. The basic site factors influencing the presence of a certain type of vegetation are local water levels (hydrology) and local concentrations of nutrients and major ions. Water flows result from an interaction between groundwater and surface water. The quality conditions are strongly influenced by the transport of chemicals by sub-regional water flows, and to some extent by atmospheric deposition.

Against this background the natural science modelling has coupled three models:

- a model of water quantity, which describes amounts of groundwater and surface water expected at specified locations in the present hydrological conditions;
- a model of water quality, which describes the chemistry of groundwater and surface water at specified locations; and
- an ecological model, which describes the expected presence of some 250 wetland plant species at specified locations given local environmental conditions.

The quantitative water model creates input for the qualitative water model, while both these models predict the abiotic site conditions that serve as input for the vegetation response model (see Table 11.2). A set of boundary conditions is needed to define the domains of the models. Some of these boundary conditions can be manipulated in scenarios, others, such as soil texture, are static in the time domain adopted here. Each of the models requires spatially differentiated input. For the storage and representation of spatial data, a raster or grid representation has been chosen with a raster cell size of $500 \times 500$ m in ArcInfo and PCRaster GIS. A raster representation is suitable to depict

*Table 11.2    Input and output of the three natural science models*

| Model | Input | Output |
|---|---|---|
| (1) quantitative hydrology | – surface water tables<br>– groundwater tables<br>– boundary conditions in soil | – level of groundwater per cell<br>– water balance per polder |
| (2) qualitative hydrology | – chemistry of local surface water, groundwater and rain;<br>– the water balance from (1)<br>– nutrient input from economic model | – the chemistry of surface water and groundwater |
| (3) ecology/ vegetation | – water tables from (1)<br>– chemistry from (2)<br>– local conditions per polder<br>– some management options | – the probability of encountering 250 plant species per cell |

spatially varying continuous variables such as surface level and groundwater tables. Overlay computations can be done quickly with these raster maps. The most important spatial unit in this study area is the polder, which in all cases is larger than such a raster cell.

The flow of groundwater is modelled with the model code MODFLOW (McDonald and Harbaugh, 1984). This code solves three-dimensional flow problems using a finite difference matrix-solving module, and has been widely applied. The model area is divided into several layers of blocks with the same lateral conductivity; each block is assumed to be homogenous in conductivity. In each block a centred point is defined, for which the flow is calculated. For a three-dimensional set of model nodes, the model code generates a solution for the differences between each node. Apart from the flow term between nodes other sources or sinks of water can be modelled (McDonald *et al.,* 1991; Prudic, 1989). The hydrological model covers an area of approximately 24 × 28 km. Water budget terms are calculated for each cell in the whole area.

In order to model the chemistry in surface and groundwater each cell in the quantitative model of the top layer is considered as a bucket. The chemical conditions of groundwater, surface water and precipitation entering each cell contribute proportionally to its net chemical concentration. For each model cell net in- or out-fluxes of groundwater, surface water and precipitation are known; only the net input fluxes are considered. Precipitation is an input flux (a surplus of 200 mm per year). Changes in boundary conditions of the quantitative model cause fluxes to model cells and result in revised water chemistry conditions.

In the context of the nature and agriculture scenarios, extra conditions are incorporated in the qualitative model. This includes technical removal of phosphate from surface water through a phosphate removal plant. Under the nature and recreation scenarios, several polders with high nature values are provided with such plants. The economic model describes (changes in) the intensity of agricultural practices and subsequently predicts changes in the amount of nutrient runoff at the surface. This, together with the effects of mineralization, is converted to the surface water chemistry.

The ecological model ICHORS (Barendregt *et al.,* 1993) predicts the occurrence of wetland plant species. The model is based on general linear modelling regression techniques (Nelder and Wetherburn, 1974). It describes the statistical relationships between the conditions in the environment (a total of 25 variables) and the presence of 250 plant species. This model was selected because it is non-spatial, can be used on a grid scale with changes in environmental conditions, and has been applied in earlier studies addressing changes in hydrology (see Barendregt *et al.,* 1992; Barendregt and Nieuwenhuis, 1993). The statistical relations in ICHORS originate from data sets with hundreds of samples collected from all types of wetlands throughout the region. The environmental conditions comprise soil type, land-use management, groundwater level, and concentrations of major ions and nutrients in groundwater or in surface water. The model estimates the probability that each wetland plant species will be found at a given site. Since environmental conditions can result from specific management options or external events and trends, the model is suitable to estimate the effect of scenarios.

The economic model was developed with two basic objectives:

- to present economic indicators (that is changes in net present value and employment) for each scenario and polder, to contribute to the multicriteria and;
- to calculate the changes in the runoff of nutrient flows under each scenario, to enter into the ecohydrological model; this covers environmental indicators for the runoff and surplus of nitrogen and phosphate.

The economic model focuses attention on financial cost–benefit analysis and indicators, that is it only considers financial transactions and excludes (social) costs and benefits for which no market price is paid, such as those related to changes in the provision of environmental amenity, aesthetics and so on. The reason is that this study also presents separate ecological indicators that measure improvements in environmental quality. In the evaluation step economic and ecological indicators are combined. This means that if the environmental improvements are incorporated in the economic indicators the evaluation would represent a sort of double counting.

In order to perform the above task a spatial economic model is formulated that describes agriculture, nature conservation and outdoor recreation. The

*Table 11.3    Input and output of the spatial-economic model*

| Input | Output |
| --- | --- |
| Scenarios and settings (per polder and ha) | Economic indicators (per polder) (input in evaluation procedure) |
| Economic and nutrient data (per ha) | Nutrient indicators (per polder) (input in hydrological model) |
| Environmental quality indicators (per polder) (output from hydrological model) | |

inputs to the spatial-economic model consist of the settings under specific scenarios as defined earlier; economic, agriculture, environmental data on a hectare level for the various scenarios and settings; and environmental quality indicators per polder. Table 11.3 lists the inputs and outputs of the spatial-economic model.

Under the agricultural scenario, agriculture is intensified in various polders (see polder settings in Table 11.1). The revenues are calculated per hectare for the current conditions and intensified future situation. The changes in revenues compared with the present situation are the benefits. In addition, employment and environmental indicators are calculated. Under the nature scenario, parts of agricultural land are converted into more natural conditions. The costs of this conversion include those of acquisition, restructuring and maintenance, as well as the costs of forgone benefits of agriculture (that is the opportunity costs). These opportunity costs are the current revenues provided by farming activities. The environmental indicators that change due to a reduction in agricultural land are measured in physical terms. The recreation scenario is similar to the nature scenario, but with some additional changes, that is the land areas that are converted into more natural areas are opened for recreation. Thus some polders that are open water are opened for recreation and some polders are flooded for the purpose of water-recreation.

By converting land from agriculture to nature conservation and to recreation various types of costs arise. The first type are opportunity costs (or forgone benefits) resulting from a reduction in agricultural area. The second type of cost is related to an increase of area for nature conservation. The costs of expanding the naturalized areas are divided into four categories (see Figure 11.4): acquisition costs, restructuring costs, maintenance costs and opportunity costs (forgone agricultural benefits). The costs of acquiring land arise at one point in time, while the costs of restructuring are spread over ten years. Cost can also be distinguished on the basis of land-related and water-related recreation.

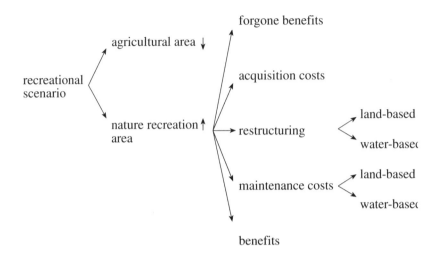

*Figure 11.4   The various costs and benefits related to the nature-recreation
scenario*

## 5   MODEL RESULTS

The natural science modelling gave rise to the following insights.
Environmental conditions for the stimulation of characteristic wetland species
in the Vecht area should be as follows: high water tables; water with low
concentrations of chloride, magnesium, sulphate, sodium, potassium and nutrients (phosphorus, nitrogen, ammonium); and buffered conditions with notably
high pH-values due to high concentrations of calcium and hydrocarbonate. Two
opposing influences affect water quality and subsequently the presence of the
desired plant species. First, drainage attracts fresh groundwater from surrounding areas, which positively affects the wetland species. Second, maintaining
high water tables inevitably requires the inflow of water from the river Vecht,
which is rich in nutrients and has a relatively high salinity level; this has a negative effect on the wetland species. The net effect of these processes is also influenced by: acidification resulting from the infiltration of rainwater; drainage
with subsequent mineralization of peat and release of additional nutrients; and
intensification of agriculture with extra input of manure and fertilizers. As a
result of these – partly conflicting – processes, stimulating nature conservation
will only be possible in specific parts of the region.

The results obtained with the vegetation response model are as follows.

Plant species characteristic of fresh and nutrient-poor locations are predicted at specific locations with a discharge of groundwater. Many species characteristic of polluted water are predicted at locations where river water dominates the water balance. It appears that many species are only stimulated in a restricted number of grid cells, namely those that are much affected by the conditions in the scenarios. This effect may therefore be masked by the aggregation process when a whole area is evaluated.

In order to be used as a spatial model the input of the vegetation response model needs to consist of (an input map of) spatially differentiated data. Therefore, the ICHORS regression equations are imported into a GIS system (van Horssen *et al.*, 1999). This leads to an output map with plant response values for each species per grid cell. Some of the input data for the regression models is static information, for example soil texture and land use. Other data concerns hydrological information on discharge or recharge of groundwater, groundwater table and depth of surface water, and the chemistry in surface water and groundwater. Evaluation of the model output arising under different sets of conditions enables the assessment of whether certain groups of species are stimulated under particular scenarios (Barendregt and Nieuwenhuis, 1993). An example of the results of the vegetation response model is given in Figure 11.5.

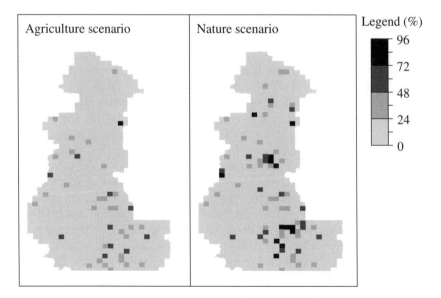

*Figure 11.5    The predicted probability of presence of the aquatic plant species* Utricularia vulgaris *per grid cell in the agricultural scenario (left) and in the nature scenario (right)*

*Table 11.4   The net present value per region under the three scenarios (changes in million € relative to the reference scenario)*

| Region | Agricultural scenario | Nature scenario | Recreation scenario |
|---|---|---|---|
| North | 76.99 | −109.02 | 698.73 |
| Middle | 35.00 | −34.20 | 741.61 |
| South | 63.60 | −83.16 | 542.29 |
| Total | 175.59 | −226.38 | 1982.65 |

Table 11.4 gives a concise overview of the results obtained with the economic model. It shows the net present value (NPV) of changes aggregated per sub-region (North, Middle, South and Total). The NPV of the agricultural scenario is calculated from the increased benefits of intensifying agriculture in various polders. The intensification of agriculture has a positive effect on the NPV, because the benefits per hectare of agricultural land increase.

Under the nature and recreation scenarios, part of the agricultural land is allowed to return to nature. The difference is that, under the recreational scenario, nature areas are open to recreation. A further two polders in the recreation scenario are inundated for water-based recreation. Under the nature scenario the costs of converting agricultural land are the only financial indicators on which the calculation of the NPV is based. Therefore, the NPV is negative, that is there are costs, but no financial benefits. The latter are implicit in the environmental quality indicators. Including them in monetary terms would lead to a sort of double counting in the evaluation phase.

In the recreation scenario some acquired polders are converted into recreational areas: both land recreation and water-based recreation. The NPV of the recreation scenario is based on the costs of converting the land (including maintenance and opportunity costs) and the benefits of spending on recreation. The resulting NPV under the recreation scenario is positive: the increase in recreational benefits (that is the spending on recreation) outweighs the costs of converting to this land use. Note that in the nature and recreation scenario three phosphate removal plants are installed to extract phosphorus from the water in an attempt to improve the quality of the water, and so the quality of nature. The results in Table 11.4 show that the recreation scenario gives rise to much higher benefits than the agricultural scenario, which is partly due to the latter including fewer land-use changes relative to the reference situation.

Two objectives for scenario evaluation were identified: net present value and environmental quality. In the latter context, an index of environmental quality based on the output of the vegetation response model and, to a lesser extent, of the hydrological model was constructed. Output from the former consists of the probability of occurrence of some 250 plant species per 500 m × 500 m grid cell. At a theoretical level indicators of environmental quality attempt to capture three ecosystem characteristics, process, structure and resilience (see Schaeffer *et al.*, 1988; Karr, 1991; Costanza *et al.*, 1992; van Ierland and de Man, 1993; Steedman, 1994; Holling *et al.*, 1995; Ghilarov, 1996; Folke, 1999). These aggregate characteristics were taken to be represented by:

- process: presence of species typical of nutrient-rich conditions and presence of species with the potential to form peat;
- structure: presence of species typical of fen and peatlands;
- resilience: presence of species suggesting that the natural successional series in these wetlands has been diverted.

A selection of plant species per category was made on the basis of expert judgement. Four indicators (eutrophication, peat-formation, diversity and non-resilience) were then calculated per grid cell as the average probability for the selected species per scenario. In the case of the peat-forming indicator, an additional constraint was added – the value of this indicator was set to zero when water level (as estimated by the hydrological model) was lower than 15 cm below ground level. Such water levels would prevent peat formation even if the relevant species were present. Grid cell values for these indicators were then aggregated to derive polder values. Further, the eutrophication and non-resilience indicators were given a negative value as they make negative contributions to environmental quality.

The indicators were then combined to derive an index of environmental quality. In this combination, it was assumed that the three ecosystem characteristics contribute equally to environmental quality, and that the eutrophic and peat-forming indicators contribute equally to ecosystem process. This procedure is summarized in Figure 11.6 and the results are given in Appendix Table 11.1.

The scenarios, particularly nature and recreation, focused on stimulating the return of typical wetland vegetation in a corridor which runs from north to south through the study area. The results show that this was achieved, although the degree of improvement in natural conditions was somewhat limited. There are two likely explanations for this.

First, indicators for environmental quality require aggregation across species and across space. The results obtained from the vegetation response model, when closely examined, show that a scenario only changes the probability of occurrence of a small number of species per grid cell vis-à-vis the reference scenario. This is the product of the heterogeneity of the study area. Aggregation across species could be diluting real improvements to wetland quality. Second, raising water levels does not necessarily mean improving conditions for wetlands, owing to the hydrological balance between nutrient-rich Vecht river

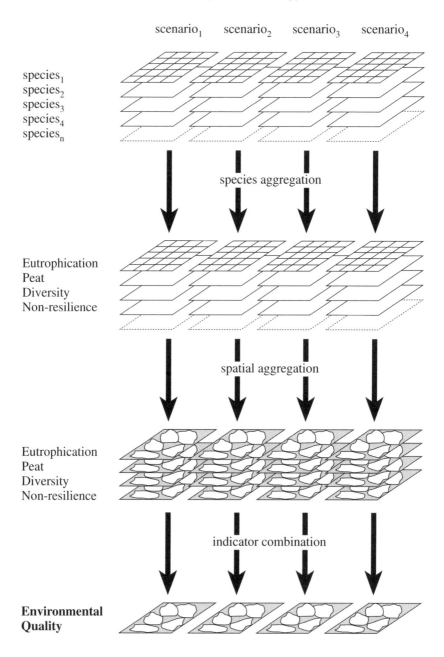

*Figure 11.6    Aggregation of model output to an index for environmental quality*

water and nutrient-poor groundwater. The influence of groundwater can be increased only by further reducing groundwater abstraction in the hill ridge. This factor was not incorporated in the scenarios.

## 6  THE EVALUATION OUTCOMES

The evaluation aimed at ranking the scenarios and assessing any sensitivity in this ranking. A combination of multi-criteria and spatial evaluation (see van Herwijnen, 1999; van Herwijnen and Rietveld, 1999) within the software package DEFINITE (Janssen and van Herwijnen, 1994) was used.[2] The objectives of the evaluation were: economic efficiency (approximated by NPV) and environmental quality (approximated by the index described above). These two performance indicators were calculated for each polder.

The subsequent evaluation of the scenarios on the basis of these indicators can proceed in two ways, as indicated in Figure 11.7. The two paths differ according to the order of the two sub-steps:

* aggregation across space, deriving a single value for each performance indicator per scenario, then standardizing and combining indicators to derive a single value per scenario; or,

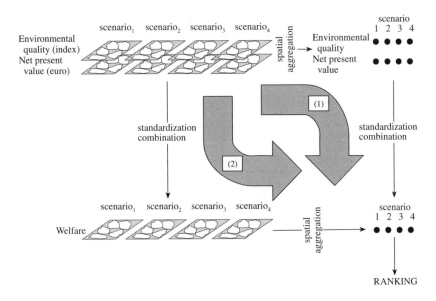

*Figure 11.7   Scenario evaluation and ranking*

- standardizing and combining performance indicators, deriving a single value for each location per alternative (a map per alternative), then aggregating across space to derive a single value per alternative.

Van Herwijnen (1999) has shown that these paths can yield different rankings of scenarios. The first path above would lead to the results presented in Table 11.5. Scores for each indicator have been standardized between 0 and 1, then combined in the last row. The combination rule is the simplest, namely additive with equal weights. The combination of NPV and the index of environmental quality is termed 'welfare'.

The ranking of the scenarios, from most to least preferred, is clearly: Recreation > Nature > Agriculture > Reference.

On path two, using the same procedures for combining the two performance indicators leads to the set of maps presented in Figure 11.8. Two remarks are in order here. First, the difference between the Reference and Agricultural scenarios is very small, which is because the latter includes few land-use changes relative to the reference situation. Second, the corridor up the middle of the region and targeted for nature restoration is also shown in these maps. The darker the map, the more preferred the scenario.

Although a visual ranking from these maps suggests the same result as for path one, there is uncertainty in ranking of the Nature and Recreation scenarios. This is also true for the Agriculture and Reference scenarios, but since they score so poorly, their precise ranking is less relevant. Not only is it difficult to separate these two scenarios, but polders that score highest in the Recreation scenario lie outside the targeted corridor. If only this corridor is considered, Figure 11.8 suggests that Nature might be the more preferred of the two scenarios.

*Table 11.5    Derivation of a single score per scenario according to path 1 in Figure 11.7*

| Performance indicator | Unit | Reference | Agriculture | Nature | Recreation |
|---|---|---|---|---|---|
| Net present value | NPV (million €) | 0 | 175.6 | –226.4 | 1982.6 |
| *Standardized score* | *Index [0, 1]* | *0.10* | *0.18* | *0.00* | *1.00* |
| Environmental quality | Index [0,100] | 0 | 0.24 | 7.24 | 6.22 |
| *Standardized score* | *Index [0, 1]* | *0* | *0.03* | *1.00* | *0.86* |
| **Welfare** | **Index [0, 100]** | **5** | **11** | **50** | **93** |

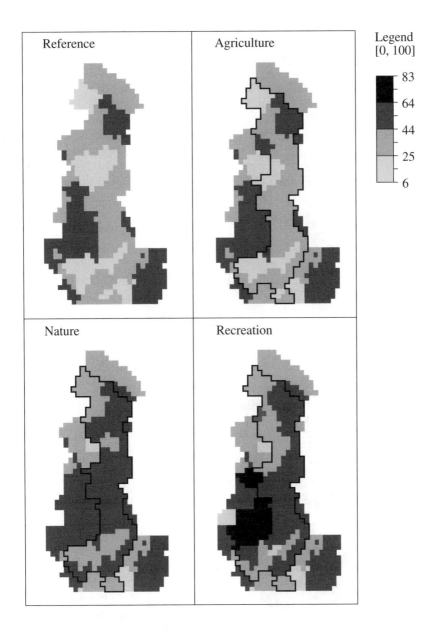

*Figure 11.8    Welfare per polder*

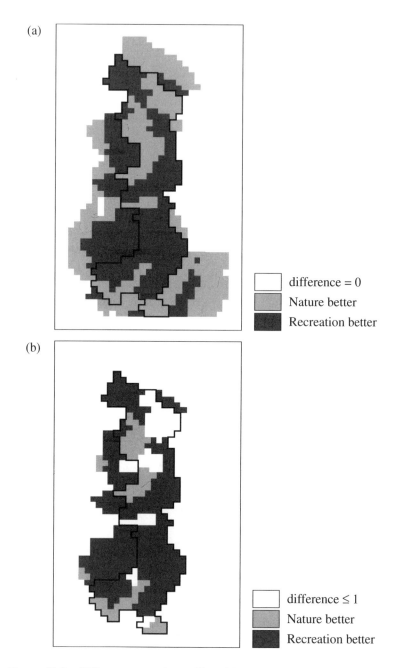

*Figure 11.9    Difference map for welfare (Nature against Recreation)*

Figure 11.9 tests how different the results from the two scenarios are by presenting difference maps for welfare. These maps consider only the Recreation and Nature scenarios, and show which of the two scores best for each polder. White areas denote polders where the two scenarios score equally (Figure 11.9a) or where the difference between the two is less than or equal to one unit of welfare (Figure 11.9b). Many of the polders where Nature is the better scenario are lost in Figure 11.9b, showing that the difference between these scenarios is very small. No polders with Recreation as the better scenario are lost in Figure 11.9b. This suggests that, where Nature is the better scenario, Recreation is often a close second, while the converse does not hold.

The conclusion from the above discussion is the following ranking of scenarios: Recreation > Nature > Agriculture > Reference.

There is, however, a degree of uncertainty associated with the preference for recreation over nature. Maintaining spatial detail in the evaluation has exposed this uncertainty.

## 7  CONCLUSIONS AND FURTHER RESEARCH

The Vecht area is a wetland area with many functions, uses and values. This study has focused on the spatial dimension of interactions among hydrological, ecological and economic processes and clearly shows that spatial differences matter.

Spatial differentiation started with a formulation of scenarios, at the polder level, in which either agriculture, nature or recreation was stimulated. A system of interactive models generated output from which various indicators were calculated for each scenario. The natural science component of this study consisted of water quality and quantity models that generated spatial abiotic conditions for a vegetation response model. The economic component was represented by a spatial-economic model describing agriculture, nature conservation and recreation, generating output which input to the hydrological model. Output from the models was used to generate aggregate performance indicators used to evaluate the scenarios.

This evaluation showed that the recreation scenario was the most preferred scenario with nature the second most preferred. However, care should be taken with this result as no feedback from increased recreational use to environmental quality has been considered. Examples of such adverse impacts include trampling, litter and noise. Species that are not represented in the ecological model, such as birds and mammals, are likely to be sensitive to these adverse effects and to large numbers of visitors. A degree of uncertainty in this ranking appeared when the spatial character of the performance indicators was maintained for as long as possible during the evaluation. The study area is too large to be treated as a hydrologically, ecologically or economically homogeneous area. More research is possible on details of the various elements of the method of integrated research adopted in this study. The different types of intensive and extensive agriculture may require more attention. Further work is also possible on specifying set-up costs of scenarios, which have been only roughly covered here. Finally, it would be interesting to look at other scenarios, in which various technological solutions are examined. These may include water quality improvement technology, or stimulating multifunctionality and capturing nature values via creative integration of infrastructure, housing, recreation and nature. In terms of evaluation, other spatial equity criteria and aggregation functions can be considered.

The results indicate the value of using spatially disaggregated models and indicators, and of maintaining this detail for as long as possible during the evaluation. Aggregation can average out spatial differences within and among scenarios. Moreover, the pattern of aggregation can influence the ranking of alternatives. Space matters especially in studies of wetlands because hydrological processes are inherently spatial. This study has shown that it is possible to match the distinct scales of description of ecological and economic systems, although it requires much time and persistence from the researchers involved. The resulting approach for impact analysis and evaluation of land-use scenarios can support management and policy. Future work should focus on including more details about local management practices and negative feedbacks of recreation on ecosystems. Moreover, incorporating temporal dynamics to spatial analysis would be an interesting, if ambitious undertaking.

# APPENDIX

*Table A11.1  Environmental quality (index, [0, 100]) and Net Present Value (million €) per polder for the four scenarios*

| Polder No. | Reference Environmental quality | NPV | Agriculture Environmental quality | NPV | Nature Environmental quality | NPV | Recreation Environmental quality | NPV |
|---|---|---|---|---|---|---|---|---|
| 1 | 42.7 | 23.9 | 44.3 | 32.4 | 42.7 | 23.9 | 42.7 | 16.3 |
| 2 | 43.4 | 22.1 | 42.6 | 28.2 | 43.4 | 22.1 | 43.3 | 22.1 |
| 3 | 39.6 | 3.6 | 39.6 | 8.5 | 39.6 | 3.6 | 39.6 | -4.9 |
| 4 | 45.2 | 45.2 | 45.2 | 43.9 | 45.2 | 45.2 | 45.2 | 35.9 |
| 5 | 37.6 | 4.5 | 37.8 | 10.6 | 47.6 | -30.4 | 46.8 | 37.8 |
| 6 | 53.3 | 72.0 | 52.9 | 70.2 | 53.6 | 71.3 | 53.6 | 64.9 |
| 7 | 41.8 | 2.7 | 41.6 | 6.4 | 50.3 | -39.2 | 49.7 | 52.6 |
| 8 | 38.2 | 5.9 | 38.2 | 13.8 | 47.1 | -39.5 | 46.7 | 58.2 |
| 9 | 41.8 | 2.3 | 41.8 | 5.3 | 49.1 | -32.7 | 43.1 | 43.2 |
| 10 | 42.5 | 2.3 | 42.6 | 5.3 | 48.6 | -32.7 | 48.9 | 35.3 |
| 11 | 48.5 | 3.2 | 48.5 | 0.0 | 48.5 | 3.2 | 48.5 | 3.2 |
| 12 | 41.6 | 97.9 | 41.6 | 96.5 | 41.4 | 97.9 | 41.5 | 194.4 |
| 13 | 45.4 | 52.8 | 45.2 | 53.4 | 48.1 | 49.3 | 46.1 | 57.0 |
| 14 | 46.7 | 2.7 | 46.0 | 3.2 | 53.8 | -39.2 | 53.1 | 41.2 |
| 15 | 45.4 | 19.8 | 45.6 | 22.9 | 45.5 | 19.8 | 45.5 | 19.8 |
| 16 | 48.8 | 0.0 | 48.8 | 0.0 | 48.8 | 0.0 | 48.8 | -18.5 |
| 17 | 44.9 | 70.2 | 48.6 | 70.2 | 49.4 | 70.2 | 46.5 | 59.4 |
| 18 | 40.1 | 3.6 | 40.4 | 4.3 | 47.1 | -52.3 | 47.1 | 69.4 |
| 19 | 48.6 | 0.9 | 48.7 | 2.1 | 48.4 | 0.9 | 48.4 | -4.1 |
| 20 | 36.1 | 7.7 | 36.1 | 18.1 | 43.7 | -111.2 | 40.4 | 144.8 |
| 21 | 42.7 | 50.2 | 42.3 | 43.4 | 49.6 | -3.4 | 48.5 | 109.7 |

*Table A11.1 (continued)*

| Polder No. | Reference Environmental quality | Reference NPV | Agriculture Environmental quality | Agriculture NPV | Nature Environmental quality | Nature NPV | Recreation Environmental quality | Recreation NPV |
|---|---|---|---|---|---|---|---|---|
| 22 | 41.0 | 0.5 | 41.0 | 0.0 | 44.4 | 0.5 | 42.7 | −0.3 |
| 23 | 36.3 | 81.8 | 37.1 | 82.3 | 47.4 | 56.1 | 45.5 | 105.1 |
| 24 | 40.4 | 11.0 | 39.8 | 14.0 | 50.0 | −6.5 | 49.8 | 26.0 |
| 25 | 41.1 | 1.4 | 40.8 | 3.2 | 51.9 | −10.3 | 51.4 | 11.5 |
| 26 | 47.3 | 2.7 | 47.3 | 6.4 | 47.1 | 1.6 | 47.1 | −3.0 |
| 27 | 36.1 | 21.0 | 39.2 | 25.9 | 45.7 | −8.1 | 44.0 | 52.1 |
| 28 | 41.6 | 38.5 | 41.5 | 39.1 | 51.1 | 10.5 | 50.1 | 70.3 |
| 29 | 47.2 | 140.3 | 47.2 | 140.3 | 52.5 | 140.3 | 51.8 | 271.9 |
| 30 | 45.4 | 63.0 | 45.4 | 61.1 | 52.1 | 35.0 | 52.5 | 96.2 |
| 31 | 46.6 | 71.5 | 46.5 | 73.3 | 53.0 | 61.0 | 52.3 | 76.2 |
| 32 | 43.4 | 53.6 | 45.4 | 53.7 | 51.5 | 46.6 | 49.0 | 61.9 |
| 33 | 48.8 | 26.3 | 48.8 | 26.3 | 48.8 | 26.3 | 48.8 | 26.3 |
| 34 | 49.4 | 96.5 | 49.4 | 96.5 | 49.4 | 96.5 | 49.4 | 96.1 |
| 35 | 45.9 | 429.9 | 45.8 | 429.9 | 45.9 | 429.9 | 45.7 | 846.5 |
| 36 | 38.8 | 2.7 | 38.8 | 6.4 | 38.8 | 2.7 | 38.8 | −8.7 |
| 37 | 38.5 | 2.3 | 38.5 | 5.3 | 38.5 | 2.3 | 38.5 | −7.5 |
| 38 | 50.3 | 22.4 | 50.3 | 29.1 | 50.3 | 22.4 | 50.3 | 14.0 |
| 39 | 40.1 | 4.1 | 39.4 | 4.8 | 49.5 | −59.5 | 49.9 | 78.5 |
| 40 | 35.3 | 21.1 | 34.9 | 21.7 | 46.0 | −35.5 | 45.3 | 87.2 |
| 41 | 42.4 | 67.3 | 42.6 | 68.3 | 50.2 | 21.9 | 48.9 | 121.4 |
| 42 | 45.1 | 31.0 | 44.0 | 37.7 | 52.2 | −8.1 | 50.8 | 68.9 |
| 43 | 47.4 | 6.4 | 47.5 | 14.9 | 47.9 | 5.7 | 47.9 | −3.6 |
| 44 | 51.4 | 12.4 | 51.9 | 17.3 | 51.7 | 11.7 | 51.7 | 12.4 |

| | | | | | | | | |
|---|---|---|---|---|---|---|---|---|
| 45 | 47.9 | 1.8 | 46.8 | 4.3 | 48.1 | 1.1 | 48.1 | 0.7 |
| 46 | 46.0 | 13.7 | 46.1 | 20.4 | 53.7 | -24.8 | 52.3 | 59.4 |
| 47 | 44.8 | 3.2 | 45.0 | 7.4 | 53.7 | -45.8 | 52.3 | 61.4 |
| 48 | 49.7 | 0.0 | 50.2 | 0.0 | 50.2 | 0.0 | 50.2 | -17.6 |
| 49 | 41.5 | 18.0 | 41.5 | 18.6 | 51.6 | 14.5 | 50.1 | 19.3 |
| 50 | 48.8 | 26.3 | 48.7 | 26.3 | 49.0 | 25.6 | 49.0 | 26.3 |
| 51 | 50.2 | 9.6 | 50.2 | 8.7 | 50.2 | 9.6 | 50.2 | 9.6 |
| 52 | 37.1 | 31.8 | 37.1 | 32.7 | 46.2 | -52.1 | 45.8 | 129.0 |
| 53 | 30.2 | 1.8 | 33.6 | 4.3 | 41.9 | -12.9 | 38.8 | 5.1 |
| 54 | 44.7 | 1.4 | 44.5 | 3.2 | 44.7 | 1.4 | 44.7 | 0.6 |
| 55 | 51.6 | 0.5 | 51.6 | 1.1 | 51.6 | 0.5 | 51.6 | 0.0 |
| 56 | 47.8 | 122.8 | 47.7 | 122.8 | 53.0 | 122.8 | 52.9 | 243.5 |
| 57 | 42.6 | 39.2 | 42.7 | 44.7 | 49.7 | -24.4 | 49.2 | 113.6 |
| 58 | 40.7 | 18.0 | 41.7 | 18.6 | 47.8 | 13.8 | 46.5 | 21.7 |
| 59 | 48.9 | 174.4 | 48.9 | 165.3 | 48.9 | 174.4 | 48.9 | 174.0 |
| 60 | 40.6 | 10.1 | 42.4 | 12.0 | 48.8 | -1.0 | 47.2 | 22.1 |
| 61 | 51.1 | 0.0 | 51.1 | 0.0 | 51.1 | 0.0 | 51.1 | 0.0 |
| 62 | 38.1 | 35.1 | 39.3 | 35.1 | 47.7 | 34.4 | 46.5 | 35.1 |
| 63 | 37.0 | 11.5 | 37.3 | 15.2 | 37.2 | 10.8 | 37.2 | 11.1 |
| 64 | 38.2 | 19.4 | 36.5 | 21.8 | 36.8 | 18.7 | 36.8 | 16.0 |
| 65 | 43.4 | 26.3 | 43.6 | 26.3 | 43.2 | 25.6 | 43.1 | 22.0 |
| 66 | 51.9 | 1.4 | 51.7 | 3.2 | 51.9 | 1.4 | 51.9 | 1.4 |
| 67 | 41.5 | 2.7 | 42.3 | 6.4 | 41.4 | 2.7 | 41.2 | 2.7 |
| 68 | 35.3 | 1.8 | 35.5 | 4.3 | 45.6 | -12.9 | 44.9 | 9.9 |
| 69 | 41.0 | 20.1 | 39.8 | 23.7 | 47.2 | -1.6 | 45.4 | 33.3 |
| 71 | 45.7 | 8.8 | 46.3 | 8.8 | 46.4 | 8.8 | 46.4 | 8.8 |
| 72 | 35.7 | 11.5 | 35.8 | 12.0 | 44.8 | -30.5 | 44.5 | 61.4 |
| 73 | 36.4 | 2.7 | 36.5 | 0.0 | 36.1 | 2.7 | 36.1 | 2.7 |

## NOTES

1.  This chapter summarizes a case study done in the context of the EU project 'Ecological–Economic Analysis of Wetlands: Functions, Values and Dynamics' (ECOWET, contract no. ENV4-CT96-0273). This project ran from June 1996 to June 1999. We are grateful to Ernst Bos and Bas Rabeling for research assistance, and to Dita Smit for editorial support.
2.  Earlier studies have focused on cost–benefit analysis of specific scenarios and measures for the Vechtstreek (Barendregt *et al.*, 1992; Bos and van den Bergh, 2000).

## REFERENCES

Anonymous (1994), *Convention on Wetlands of International Importance especially as Waterfowl Habitat*, Ramsar, Iran, 2.2.1971, as amended by the Protocol of 3.12.1982 and the Amendments of 28.5.1987, United Nations Educational, Scientific and Cultural Organization (UNESCO), Paris, 13 July 1994.

Barbier, E.B., J.C. Burgess and C. Folke (1994), *Paradise Lost? The Ecological Economics of Biodiversity*, London: Earthscan.

Barendregt, A., S.M.E. Stam and M.J. Wassen (1992), 'Restoration of fen ecosystems in the Vecht River plain: cost–benefit analysis of hydrological alternatives', *Hydrobiologica*, **233**, 247–58.

Barendregt, A. and J.W. Nieuwenhuis (1993), 'ICHORS, hydro-ecological relations by multi-dimensional modelling of observations', in J.C. Hooghart and C.W.S. Posthumus (eds), *The Use of Hydro-ecological Models in the Netherlands*, Proceedings and Information No. 47, CHO-TNO Delft, pp. 11–30.

Barendregt, A., M.J. Wassen and J.T. de Smidt (1993), 'Hydro-ecological modelling in a polder landscape: a tool for wetland management', in C. Vos and P. Opdam (eds), *Landscape Ecology of a Stressed Environment*, London: Chapman and Hall, pp. 79–99.

Bergh, J.C.J.M. van den (1996), *Ecological Economics and Sustainable Development: Theory, Methods and Applications*, Cheltenham, UK and Brookfield, US: Edward Elgar.

Bergh, J.C.J.M. van den, *et al.* (1999), *Integrated Analysis of Wetlands: The Dutch Vechtstreek Case Study*, Vol. 3 of ECOWET Report to EU, Ecological–Economic Analysis of Wetlands: Functions, Values and Dynamics, Norwich.

Bos, E.J. and J.C.J.M. van den Bergh (2000), 'A cost–benefit analysis of sustainable nature policy in the Dutch Vecht Wetlands area', in R. Florax, P. Nijkamp and K. Willis (eds), *Comparative Environmental Economic Assessment*, Cheltenham, UK and Northampton, MA: Edward Elgar.

Braat, L.C. and W.F.J. van Lierop (eds) (1987), *Economic–Ecological Modelling*, Amsterdam: North-Holland.

Brouwer, R., I.H. Langford, I.J. Bateman and R.K. Turner (1999), 'A meta-analysis of wetland contingent valuation studies', *Regional Environmental Change*, **1**(1), 47–57.

Costanza, R., B.G. Norton and B.D. Haskell (eds) (1992), *Ecosystem Health*, Washington, DC: Island Press.

Costanza, R., L. Wainger, C. Folke and K.-G. Mäler (1993), 'Modelling complex ecological economic systems', *BioScience*, **43**, 545–55.

Folke, C. (1999), 'Ecological principles and environmental economic analysis', in J.C.J.M. van den Bergh (ed.), *Handbook of Environmental and Resource Economics*, Cheltenham, UK and Northampton, MA: Edward Elgar.

Ghilarov, A. (1996), 'What does "biodiversity" mean – scientific problem or convenient myth?', *Trends in Ecology & Evolution*, **11**, 304–6.

Gilbert, A.J. and R. Janssen (1998), 'Use of environmental functions to communicate the values of a mangrove ecosystem under different management regimes', *Ecological Economics*, **25**(3), 323–46.

Gren, I.-G., C. Folke, R.K. Turner and I. Bateman (1994), 'Primary and secondary values of wetland ecosystems', *Environmental and Resource Economics*, **4**, 55–74.

Herwijnen, M. van (1999), *Spatial Decision Support for Environmental Management*, Ph.D. dissertation, Faculty of Economics and Econometrics, Vrije Universiteit, Amsterdam.

Herwijnen, M. van and P. Rietveld (1999), 'Spatial dimensions in multicriteria analysis', in J.C. Thill (ed.), *Spatial Multicriteria Decision Making and Analysis; A Geographic Information Sciences Approach*, Aldershot, UK and Brookfield, USA: Ashgate, pp. 77–102.

Holling, C.S., D.W. Schindler, B.W. Walker and J. Roughgarden (1995), 'Biodiversity in the functioning of ecosystems: an ecological synthesis', in C. Perrings, K.-G. Mäler, C. Folke, C.S. Holling and B-O. Jansson (eds), *Biodiversity Conservation*, Dordrecht: Kluwer Academic Publishers.

Ierland, E.C. van, and N.Y.H. de Man (1993), *Sustainability of Ecosystems: Economic Analysis*, study commissioned by the Dutch Advisory Council for Research on Nature and Environment and the Biological Council of the Royal Netherlands Academy of Arts and Sciences, Department of General Economics, Wageningen Agricultural University.

Janssen, R. and M. van Herwijnen (1994*), DEFINITE: A System to Support Decisions on a Finite Set of Alternatives*, Dordrecht: Kluwer Academic Publishers.

Karr, J.R. (1991), 'Biological integrity: a long-neglected aspect of water resource management', *Ecological Applications*, **1**, 66–84.

LNV (1990), *Natuurbeleidsplan (Nature Policy Plan)*, Ministerie van Landbouw, Natuur en Visserij (Ministry of Agriculture, Nature and Fisheries), The Hague.

McDonald, M.G. and A.W. Harbaugh (1984). *A Modular Three-dimensional Finite-Difference Ggroundwater Flow Model*, Virginia: US Geological Survey, Open-file report 83–875.

McDonald, G., A.W. Harbaugh, R.O. Brennon and D.J. Ackerman (1991), *A Method for Converting No-flow Cells to Variable Head Cells for the US Ecological Survey Modular Finite-difference Groundwater Flow Model*, Virginia: US Geological Survey, Open-file report 91–536.

Nelder, J.A. and R.W.M. Wetherburn (1974), 'Generalized linear models', *Journal of the Royal Statistical Society of London*, A, **135**, 370–84.

Prudic, D.E. (1989), *Documentation of a Computer Program to Simulate Stream Aquifer Relations Using a Modular, Finite-difference Groundwater Flow Model*, Open-file report 88–729, Carson City, Nevada.

Schaeffer, D.J., E.E. Herrinks and H.W. Kerster (1988), 'Ecosystem health: 1. Measuring ecosystem health', *Environmental Management*, **12**, 445–55.

Steedman, R.J. (1994), 'Ecosystem health as management goal', *Journal of the North American Benthological Society*, **13**, 605–10.

Turner, R.K., J.C.J.M. van den Bergh, A. Barendregt and E. Maltby (1998), 'Ecological–economic analysis of wetlands: Science and social science integration', in T. Söderqvist (ed.), *Wetlands: Landscape and Institutional Perspectives*, Beijer Occasional Paper Series, Beijer International Institute of Ecological Economics, Stockholm, Sweden.

Van Horssen, P.W., P.P. Schot and A. Barendregt (1999), 'A GIS-based plant prediction model for wetland ecosystems', *Landscape Ecology*, **14**, 253–65.

VROM (1990), *Vierde Nota over de Ruimtelijke Ordening (Extra)*, Ministerie Volksgezondheid, Ruimtelijk Ordening en Milieu (Ministry of Public Housing, Spatial Planning and Environment), The Hague.

Zuchetto, J. and A.M. Jansson (1985), *Resources and Society: A Systems Ecology Study of the Island of Gotland, Sweden*, New York: Springer-Verlag.

# 12. Conclusions

## R.K. Turner, J.C.J.M. van den Bergh and R. Brouwer

## 1   INTRODUCTION

At the wetland ecosystem level, the work included in this volume has confirmed that a coherent set of links between wetland boundary conditions, structure, processes, functions and consequent outputs of goods and services from which humans derive both use and non-use value can be established. The precise quantification and valuation of multiple wetland functions and outputs is not, however, straightforward. Function overlap (a double counting problem) and the difficulties surrounding the setting of wetland system boundaries are examples of some of the individual problems that have to be overcome. The unravelling of the complexities involved has required an interdisciplinary research effort based on team work and the deployment of a 'mixed' evaluation methodology (see Chapter 2). Coupled natural science models have been augmented by socio-economic analysis in order to investigate a range of wetland management issues in different locations and across different scales. Environmental change scenarios have also been utilized to introduce an element of dynamism to the analysis.

Most wetland management contexts in Europe involve value, user or interest group conflicts of one sort or another. These conflicts are conditioned by prevailing and prospective policy regimes and the related policy networks. Institutional analysis and stakeholder/interest group mapping exercises are therefore important prerequisites for any decision-aiding toolbox and process (see Figure 12.1).

The integrated ecological–economic analysis has made it possible to identify how particular wetland functions might be of use, rather than simply the degree to which the function is being performed. The extent of demand for the products or services provided, or the effective 'market', also needs to be assessed if the full extent of economic value is to be recognized. So who are the relevant users, that is those who assign economic values to wetlands? It is possible to identify at least nine more or less organized groups of stakeholders (Turner *et al.*, 2000):

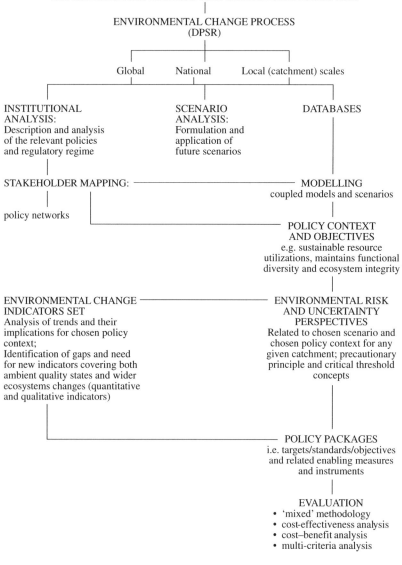

*Figure 12.1    Conceptual framework*

1. Direct extensive users who directly harvest wetland goods in a sustainable way, that is consistent with rapid ecosystem recovery. They thus possess a particular form of ecological knowledge enabled by an institutional setting that may be under increasing environmental change pressure.
2. Direct intensive users who have access to new technology (for example biomass harvesting through mechanical means for subsequent fuel production) that allows more intensive harvesting.
3. Direct exploiters who dredge the sediments in the wetland, or exploit mineral resources, peat, clay and sand without due concern for the 'health' of the wetlands.
4. Agricultural producers who drain and convert wetlands to agricultural land, since, at least in the short to medium run, the soil is fertile, nutrients are plentiful and water is freely available.
5. Water abstractors use wetlands as sources of drinking water, agricultural irrigation, flow augmentation, and so on. These practices may result in a wetland suffering a fall in its water table and consequent quality degradation, or in the diversion of 'polluted' water into the wetland.
6. Human settlements close to wetlands. Many wetlands are located in the transition zone from land to water, and may thus constitute convenient areas for the expansion of human settlements and their infrastructure; a paradox is often evident as the very presence of water is a valuable amenity that needs to be safeguarded.
7. Indirect users benefit from indirect wetland services such as storm abatement, flood mitigation, hydrological stabilization and water purification to individuals and communities across large catchment areas; because of the extensive spatial provision of such services many recipients will be unaware of their origin.
8. Nature conservation and amenity groups combine nature conservation objectives with an enjoyment of the presence of plant and animal species. This aesthetic value of wetlands is often mixed with recreation usage values.
9. Non-users who, geographical distance notwithstanding, attribute non-use value to wetlands, possibly because of their recognition of intrinsic value in wetlands.

Clearly not all stakeholder interests are mutually compatible and the potential for value conflict is high. Policy-makers are therefore required to undertake complex trade-off procedures which can be supported by the decision support system and 'mixed' methodology advocated in this volume (see Chapters 2, 4, 5 and 6).

At the landscape level, the DPSIR scoping and auditing framework has proved to be a very useful device. It has allowed the research to coherently address a range of issues resulting from regional to local environmental pressures and land-use conflicts across Europe; and in the UK case study also to incorporate some of the implications of global climate change. The generic principles underpinning sustainable development objectives have been distilled down into more practical management guidelines via the concept of ecosystem functional diversity, that is that management strategies should seek to maintain as much functional diversity as is feasible in any given wetland context, so that the wetland can retain as much resilience as possible to cope with stress and shock. Maintenance of ecosystem integrity also needs to be monitored over time, and Chapter 3 presents a set of environmental indicators that can assist this process.

A number of approaches to integrated modelling exist, based on generalized input–output models, non-linear dynamic systems models, optimization models, land-use models linked to geographical information systems (GISs), and mixed models. Important elements for integration are connected scenarios, models and indicators, and the arrangement of consistency among units, spatial demarcations, and spatial aggregation of information in various sub-models. An overview of integrated modelling approaches and applications is given in van den Bergh (1996). Considerable effort is required to increase the precision at the natural science description level in order to facilitate the linking to the socio-economic level. The prediction of processes and process changes in a wetland – both short and long term – is of utmost importance in the assessment of wetland functions. Many important functions are directly related to hydrology. Moreover, water is the transport medium for nutrients and other elements, including contaminants. Based on information and models of hydrological processes, nutrient fluxes, sedimentation, erosion, and even flooding can be quantified. The modelling chain can be continued with chemical modelling and the quantification of nutrient balances. Given these data, the likely presence of plant and animal species in the ecosystem may be predicted, as well as the consequent impacts on biodiversity of hydrological changes.

Wetland management can be taken forward via a number of different enabling measures and policy options. These policy packages need to be evaluated in order for 'preferred' options to be identified and implemented. The technical information provided to decision-makers by the decision support toolbox should be seen not as a way of establishing optimal outcomes, but rather as a way of achieving 'better' outcomes as defined by a majority of the stakeholders involved in the wetland situation. It is a satisficing rather than an optimizing process. To assist in this process analysts need to encompass socio-cultural group-based approaches to human behaviour (including valuation) and not rely solely on individual-based approaches (whether they have economic, psychological or sociological foci). Values elicitation and their incorporation into the decision-making process are critically important. So-called deliberative and inclusionary approaches (DIPs) have been championed by some social scientists as the way forward in this context (see Figure 6.1). Supporters of DIPs claim that giving individuals more scope to be included and to participate in real decision-making mechanisms, stimulates a social learning phenomenon. Individuals 'learn', that is. become more informed, about citizenship and collective environmental responsibilities and even obligations. The end result is 'better' decision-making with increased transparency and consequent increases in trust and accountability. There is much that is yet to be learnt about such improved processes, their institutional arrangements and the elicitation and delivery of economic and other forms of information to the various participants in the decision process. However, this pragmatic strategy has much to commend it, without offering false promises, given the inevitable scientific and socio-economic uncertainties that beset the environmental management problematique.

What is not being argued here is that CBA is irrelevant to the wetland management and decision-making process. But in order to make CBAs of wetland policies more reliable, the economic valuation of wetland goods and services has to be as comprehensive as possible. This calls for integrated modelling of the links between wetland ecology (characteristics, structure, processes and functioning) and wetland economics (the demand for the goods and services supplied by wetlands). Secondly, even if improvements in CBAs as a basis for decision-making are desirable, it is clear that the outcome of a CBA is not on its own sufficient. The CBA criterion relies on a particular ethical basis, and it will need to be complemented as policy-makers introduce, or respond to, concerns other than economic efficiency. Moreover, the lack of detailed, quantitative knowledge of wetland functioning (in practice) precludes a full economic valuation of wetlands.

Multi-criteria decision analysis (MCDA) offers one way to illuminate policy trade-offs and aid decision-making in contexts where a range of, often competing, policy criteria are considered to be socially and politically relevant (Nijkamp, 1989; Janssen, 1992). MCDA typically includes multiple criteria, such as economic efficiency, equity within and between generations, environmental quality and various interpretations of sustainability. For example, various versions of 'strong' and 'weak' sustainability have been suggested in the literature, see, for example, Pearce *et al.* (1989), Ayres (1993) and Turner (1993). Weights can reflect the relative importance of each criterion considered in a particular decision context. An MCDA may thus illustrate how a particular policy would impact on and influence the various stakeholder groups. Governments have now formally adopted sustainable development as a policy objective, as well as imposing a range of national conservation measures and designations, complementing the Ramsar Convention, to protect wetlands. Sustainability concerns can be introduced as a series of constraints on an otherwise market-oriented and CBA-based decision-making process.

A strength of an MCDA is that it provides both ecological and economic information as a basis for decision-making. A separate issue is, however, to what extent this information would in fact be taken into account in real policy-making situtations. Ecological information may not adequately influence the final decision in the socio-economic system. For example, short-term commercial interests and related financial gains may appear to be more persuasive than longer-term ecological conservation arguments. The economic information provided by a CBA would perhaps be a more powerful and pragmatic support for conservation interests. But there may be a paradox here. A comprehensive CBA would rely also on a quantification of benefits due to non-market wetlands goods and services, possibly also including non-use value, if the benefit estimation involved the use of contingent valuation techniques. At the first glance, these benefits have the same configuration as 'normal' (market based) economic information; both types of information are measured in monetary terms. On the other hand, non-use value is hypothetical in the sense that it is not revealed by market behaviour. Such information may be a good tool to influence the perception of decision-makers and citizens regarding the high value of wetlands, but its influence in decision-making may be limited by its non-market character, and the opportunities it raises for opponents to challenge its 'subjective' basis in formal proceedings or court cases. This highlights the need for institutional reform and the power of the emerging DIPs, to provide a more appropriate and comprehensive context for wetland evaluation and management.

The analysis in this volume has illustrated that decisions about wetlands are often characterized by inconsistencies in terms of geographical scale; local versus national versus international versus global scale. Three important ways to mitigate these inconsistencies are: (1) to create awareness of wetland values on all levels; (2) to clarify the division of responsibilities between different decision levels in order to arrive at a consistent hierarchy of decision; and (3) to encourage local institutional arrangements that are consistent with sustainable wetland use. While scientific integration and the resulting improved information is a prerequisite for mitigating the fundamental failure of information, more is needed for actually changing policies and stakeholder behaviour. This brings us to the two other forms of mitigation. Firstly, in order to arrive at a consistent hierarchy of decisions, the following levels and responsibilities may be defined:

- global: to define changes and appropriate policy responses at the global scale, such as $CO_2$ fixation in organic soils to prevent global warming and sea level rise (these require international agreements by governments, such as Biodiversity and Climate Change Framework Conventions);

- international regions: to define changes in the sequence of wetlands (landscape ecology scale) such as the range of wetlands profitable for migrating birds, with breeding areas for reproduction, migrating areas with plenty of food and wintering areas to maintain the population (requiring measures such as regulation at the level of the Council of Europe);
- national: to maintain the national biodiversity including the defined national functions of wetland (requiring national instruments and national discussions on the economic and geographical development of designed areas);
- sub-national regions: to maintain the sequence of wetlands in a county or province (requiring regulations available on that regional level such as national park or nature reserve's conservation powers);
- local: to maintain the present biodiversity and local financial returns, available from the local wetlands (requiring local regulations restricting usage, but also mandates given to regional/local authorities to balance the interests of multiple stakeholders in wetland and surrounding catchments areas, for example trade-off navigation, recreation and amenity and nature conservation goals in a wetland area).

International co-operation and agreements within the first three levels would enable an international optimization of the sequence of wetland areas. Relevant sequences of wetlands include those that would facilitate the use by migrating birds of their complete migrating routes, and an international network of wetlands which would maintain all the flora and fauna characteristic to wetlands. As many wetlands are of international significance and in this sense a global heritage, their protection should also be the responsibility of the international community buttressed by a new Global Ecological Framework to strengthen measures such as the Ramsar Convention. An extension of the Global Environment Facility, for example, could be made in order to finance wetland protection schemes. Many important economic decisions are, however, taken at the local or regional levels, both affecting and influenced by the local economy or the functions provided by the wetlands. International and national regulations often fail to address the local subtleties involved in multiple use wetland areas. The EU's Habitats Directive, for example, has at its core a rather static interpretation of conservation. This becomes problematic for local regional agencies which have a mandate to balance a range of stakeholder interests and to manage a rate of change in a dynamic ecological system. Local interest groups are also difficult to influence if the case being made requires an appreciation of the 'wider' benefits of wetland protection, up to the global scale of significance. A key to resolving present failures thus seems to be behavioural change at the local level, and compensatory measures to mitigate local 'losses'. Increased scientific knowledge of wetland ecosystems and their benefits to society has to be gained hand-in-hand with efforts to increase public awareness of these benefits. Such a communication is, however, only likely to be successful if due account is taken of the potential difference in world views between the scientists and local people (Burgess *et al.*, 2000). Likewise, special attention should be paid to existing stakeholder structure, and potentially existing local ecological knowledge and local institutional arrangements for maintaining wetlands (see Berkes and Folke, 1998). Such institutions may constitute a basis for building wetland management institutions that have already gained social acceptance at the local level, in contrast to governmental regulations imposed in a top-down fashion.

# REFERENCES

Ayres, R.U. (1993), 'Cowboys, cornucopians and long-run sustainability', *Ecological Economics*, **8**, 189–207.

Bergh, J.C.J.M. van den (1996), *Ecological Economics and Sustainable Development: Theory, Methods and Applications*, Cheltenham, UK and Brookfield, US: Edward Elgar.

Berkes, F. and C. Folke (eds) (1998), *Linking Social and Ecological Systems: Management Practices and Social Mechanisms for Building Resilience*, Cambridge: Cambridge University Press.

Burgess, J., J. Clark and C. Harrison (2000), 'Knowledges in action: an actor network analysis of a wetland agri-environment scheme', *Ecological Economics*, **35**(1), 119–32.

Janssen, R. (1992), *Multiobjective Decision Support for Environmental Management*, Dordrecht: Kluwer Academic Publishers.

Nijkamp, P. (1989), 'Multi-criteria analysis: a decision support system for sustainable environmental management', in F. Archibuqi and P. Kijkamp (eds), *Economy and Ecology: Towards Sustainable Development*, Dordrecht: Kluwer.

Pearce, D.W., A. Markandya and E.B. Barbier (1989), *Blueprint for a Green Economy*, London: Earthscan.

Turner, R.K. (ed.) (1993), *Sustainable Environmental Economics and Management: Principles and Practice*, London: Belhaven Press.

Turner, R.K. *et al.* (2000), 'Ecological–economic analysis of wetlands: scientific integration for management and policy', *Ecological Economics*, **35**, 7–23.

# Index